Dialogic Education and Technology

COMPUTER-SUPPORTED COLLABORATIVE LEARNING

VOLUME 7

The *Computer-Supported Collaborative Learning Book Series* is for people working in the CSCL field. The scope of the series extends to 'collaborative learning' in its broadest sense; the term is used for situations ranging from two individuals performing a task together, during a short period of time, to groups of 200 students following the same course and interacting via electronic mail. This variety also concerns the computational tools used in learning: elaborated graphical whiteboards support peer interaction, while more rudimentary text-based discussion forums are used for large group interaction. The series will integrate issues related to CSCL such as collaborative problem solving, collaborative learning without computers, negotiation patterns outside collaborative tasks, and many other relevant topics. It will also cover computational issues such as models, algorithms or architectures which support innovative functions relevant to CSCL systems.

The edited volumes and monographs to be published in this series offer authors who have carried out interesting research work the opportunity to integrate various pieces of their recent work into a larger framework.

The titles published in this series are listed at the end of this volume.

Rupert Wegerif

Dialogic Education and Technology

Expanding the Space of Learning

 Springer

Rupert Wegerif
University of Exeter
Devon EX4 4QJ
United Kingdom
R.B.Wegerif@exeter.ac.uk

Series Editor:
Pierre Dillenbourg
Swiss Federal Institute of Technology
Lausanne, CH-1015
Switzerland

Library of Congress Control Number: 2007928579

ISBN 978-0-387-71140-9   e-ISBN 978-0-387-71142-3

Printed on acid-free paper.

© 2007 Springer Science+Business Media, LLC.

9 8 7 6 5 4 3 2 1

springer.com

For Julieta

無　故　當　鑿　當　埏　當　三
之　有　其　戶　其　埴　其　十
以　之　無　牖　無　以　無　幅
為　以　有　以　有　為　有　共
用　為　室　為　器　器　車　一
　　利　之　室　之　　　之　轂
　　用　用　　　用　　　用

Tao Te Ching, verse 11

[Thirty spokes meet at a nave;
Because of the hole we may use the wheel.
Clay is moulded into a vessel;
Because of the hollow we may use the cup.
Walls are built around a hearth;
Because of the doors we may use the house.
Thus tools come from what exists,
But use from what does not.

From: http://www.edepot.com/taoc.html]

CONTENTS

ACKNOWLEDGEMENTS

The research described in this book has been funded by the Economic and Sciences Research Council, The Nuffield Foundation, The Esmée Fairbairn Foundation and the Joint Information Services Council.

I owe a great deal over the years to working with Neil Mercer, Lyn Dawes and Karen Littleton and other members of the 'Thinking Together' research team including Claire Sams, Denise Rowe, Manuel Fernandéz, Silvia Rojas-Drummond and Julieta Pérez Linares. I also thank all the students who lent me their voices and the teachers who supported this work. When it comes to 'thinking skills', I owe a great deal to Steve Williams and Steve Higgins. In the Computer Supported Collaborative Learning community I want to thank, in particular, Maarten De Laat for his comments and help with content, Robin Mason for giving me a great start in the field, Gerry Stahl, Tim Koschmann and Pierre Dillenbourg for their ideas and encouragement, as well as Baruch Schwarz, Reuma de Groot, Andrew Ravenscroft and Simon McAlister for the opportunity to collaborate with them in their interesting projects.

I would also like to thank Granada Media for their support with some of the research described in this book and for copyright permission to use Fig. 9.5. John Raven deserves special thanks for the trouble he took to help me with the special parallel Raven's test pictures used in Chap. 4.

Chapter 1

INTRODUCTION
Challenge of the changing chronotope

> *Capital by its nature drives beyond every spatial barrier. Thus the creation of the physical conditions of exchange – of the means of communication and transport – the annihilation of space by time – becomes an extraordinary necessity for it.*[1]

(Marx, Grundrisse, 1857/2005 p. 538 from: http://www.marxists.org/)

1 THE CHALLENGE

Years ago I sometimes used to phone my bank to get business done and I talked to people I knew, such as the bank manager, in the bank's building on the high street of my local town. Then I found myself talking to people I did not know with pleasant Scottish accents. Recently I had a surprise when I phoned my bank to pay a routine household bill and found myself talking to someone whom I guessed was in India. She seemed a bit uncertain when I asked her about herself, as if she had been warned not to deviate from her script, but nonetheless, with some prompting, I discovered myself in cheerful conversation with a graduate called Alia in busy call centre in Bangalore. As a boy growing up in England, India seemed to me to be a remote and exotic place. Now I was meeting with this same India inserted into the routine activity of paying my bills.

---

[1] I challenge Marx's account of history explicitly in my concluding chapter, but I find the idea of the annihilation of space by time extraordinarily prescient for someone writing in the middle of the Nineteenth Century.

Change often occurs in such small increments that any really big change can be difficult to see. My sense of shock at talking to Alia in India stemmed from the fact that I became personally aware, as if for the first time, of a really big change that had being happening all around me for some time. Since the age of trains new communications technology has always been promising to make the planet smaller. The quotation with which I begin this chapter shows that, even in the nineteenth century Marx claimed that new technology was leading to 'the annihilation of space by time'. In the 1960s Marshall McLuhan referred to the way in which new media such as television were creating a 'global village'. My conversation with Alia brought home to me that, in one small way at least, this once remote sounding promise of technology had finally arrived.

Manuel Castells, a sociologist widely credited with being the best commentator on the Internet revolution that is now happening all around us, argues that new communications technology is leading to a new form of social organisation. There have, of course, been many prophets predicting future revolutions but Castells is more compelling than most because he largely contents himself with documenting actual change. In his trilogy *The Information Age: Economy, Society and Culture* he syntheses a vast range of data in a way that allows the trends to emerge. He argues, sticking closely to the evidence, that there is a convergence towards what he calls 'the Network Society'. He defines this as: 'a society where the key social structures and activities are organized around electronically processed information networks' (Castells, 2002).

In a sense Castell's Network Society is the realisation of Marx's exaggerated claim that time would annihilate space. Of course there have always been networks but the advent of the Internet has transformed the nature of these networks. The difference now is the mediating role played by near instantaneous electronic communication. Castells argues that: 'the economy is not just a world economy but a global economy because it works as a unit in real time on a planetary scale' (Castells, 2005). Whereas in the past the nodes in the economic network were physically located and the links between them were external ones, now physical location is subservient to the network itself and links between nodes are internal ones such that billions of dollars can be transferred from one side of the planet to the other in seconds or, indeed, in as little time as it takes to think about doing it.

One of the interesting conclusions that Castells draws from his analysis is that the social activity that is perhaps most challenged by the shift towards a network society is education. The advent of the Internet, he claims, 'calls into question the entire education system developed during the industrial era', (Castells, 2002, p. 278). This book is offered as a partial response to the challenge he lays down. It begins with the question: what kind of pedagogy do we need to develop for the children of the Internet revolution? The argument of the book, in a nutshell, is that, having posed the challenge to education, new information and communications technology (ICT) may also offer the means to its solution. However, this solution should not be understood in a narrow technological sense as an answer to the question 'how to do it'. The challenge we face is not only a technological challenge it is also a conceptual challenge. Developing a new pedagogy for the Internet age is not only about developing new practices it is also about developing a way to understand our new situation. By claiming, as he does, that current education systems embody a model of education forged in the industrial era, Castells implies that education is still dominated by the industrial metaphor of the production of material goods. This is already an insightful challenge to the proliferation throughout the educational literature, particularly the educational technology literature, of metaphors of education as a process of production and construction with many references to tools, scaffolding and the construction of knowledge, as if knowledge was some kind of object or even some kind of edifice. However, to really understand the issues at stake in education in the twenty-first century, I think that we need to dig a little deeper than the shift from the dominant metaphors appropriate to an industrial economy to those appropriate to a global networked economy. More insight can be generated if we focus on the shift in the dominant metaphors of *space* and *time*, from physical space–time to dialogic space–time.

2 THE 'SPACE' OF LEARNING?

Bakhtin is known for his work on dialogue but he also had interesting things to say about 'space'. In particular he argued that space, as this is presented in novels, is always indivisible from time and he referred to the presentation of space and time together in a text as its 'chronotope' (Bakhtin, 1981, p. 250). He applied this idea to the analysis of genres of Greek novels showing how they could be defined through different configurations of space and time. This idea of a chronotope foregrounds something important to understanding the nature of the impact of new technologies. As both Marx and Castells point out, one of the apparent consequences of the advent and proliferation of faster communications technologies is a different relationship between space and time.

Marx and Castells were analysing at the macro-level of society as a whole. One of the themes in this book is that, even at the micro-level of educational activities, different pedagogies and technologies also produce different 'chronotopes'.

The idea that the micro-genesis of understanding in education can be analysed in terms of space is not a new one. Vygotsky proposed that important learning, the learning of new concepts for example, takes place in a 'zone of proximal development' (ZPD) which he defined as the distance between a child's actual developmental level, shown by independent problem solving, and their potential development shown by their ability to solve problems with an adult (Vygotsky, 1978, p. 86). According to Vygotsky, teachers work in this zone to draw students ahead of themselves. In describing the activity of education in terms of a space of learning Vygotsky's ZPD is a seminal idea. However, this idea of space seems to be thought by Vygotsky and his follows largely on the model of a physical space in a way that is limiting for our understanding of education. His illustrations and description of the ZPD suggest a space of quite circumscribed freedom that opens up within a larger fixed space to serve the function of moving a child from an initial state to a known goal state. Although he did not himself coin the term 'scaffolding' for this process it fits his account very well. The idea of education as scaffolding is that the teacher provides a support to help the learner achieve a goal that they cannot initially achieve unaided and then gradually removes these supports until the learner can achieve the goal.

The concepts of ZPD and scaffolding have proved to be powerful ways of understanding some aspects of education but not all aspects. It does not address easily, for example, the question of how we might teach in a way that promotes creativity, reflection and 'learning to learn'. One way in which we can expand our understanding of the space of learning is to acknowledge that the ZPD is not only a kind of physical space in which co-construction occurs, on the metaphorical model of the mat in front of the child on which bricks are placed, but, more fundamentally, it is also a 'dialogic space' in which learner and teacher engage with each other and, in a sense, learn to see the task through each others eyes. It is not enough for the child to perform the task correctly with the aid of the teacher, this would be training, not education. For there to be education going on, as opposed only to training, the child must understand the meaning of the task. Understanding requires that the child takes on the point of view of the teacher. However, dialogic space, the space of perspectives in a dialogue, is very different from physical space. Most of our ways of thinking about education, including notions such as ZPD and scaffolding, seems to presuppose a way of thinking influenced by the properties of a physical space when in fact education actually takes place in the very different realm of dialogic space.

3 FROM PHYSICAL TO DIALOGIC SPACE

Dialogic space opens up when two or more perspectives are held together in tension. This starting point is already a fundamental challenge to the dominant tradition of western thought, which begins with the assumption of identity. Aristotle points out that two objects cannot inhabit the same space at the same time. It follows, according to Aristotle, that two different things cannot be the same thing or that a thing is what it is and cannot be another thing (Aristotle, 350BCE/2006). In the form of the principle of identity, that $A = A$ and $A \neq A$, this simple insight of Aristotle is the basic assumption behind classical logic and is so embedded in our thinking that it can be found in most theories of education. Aristotle's insight seems to make perfect sense because we are so used to accepting our physical bodily experience as the only way of understanding space. However, new technology has brought in quite different experiences of space, and from these experiences, different metaphors can arise.

In 1992 I was a post-graduate student in a computer science department in Queen Mary and Westfield University College in the East End of London. Everyone was very excited because we had taken delivery of our first decent virtual reality kit. With my fellow students standing around a fairly empty lab I donned cyber-goggles and a cyber-glove and entered bodily into a completely different space. From the point of view of the other students I was staggering drunkenly around the room and their job was to prevent me bumping into the walls and the furniture. However, from my point of view, I was in a strange grid-like world interacting with giant chess figures. All I could see of my body was a ghostly image of my cyber-glove. By lining this up with the controls on the chess figures, such as a huge red chess knight that loomed up in front of me, I could grasp these and control them. If I did it wrong then I walked right through the figures. Somehow I managed to get lost and move away from the chess world that I was supposed to be in. I found myself in a dark space without apparent dimensions or forms. Turning back I saw the world I had left behind glowing in the distance, shaped like a big shoe-box, its three-dimensional grid lines outlined in green light.

This experience was a powerful learning experience for me. It was like leaving normal space behind and looking at it from outside. A sort of 'out of body' experience in a way. In virtual space Aristotle's principle of identity did not appear to apply. I could not only occupy the same space as the red chess knight, but, with the right programming, I could take on the body and position of the red chess knight and experience reality from this perspective. If we ask, with Aristotle, where is the proper location in physical space and time of the Red Chess Knight, there is no easy answer. I guess one could point to programme code or to the behaviour of electrons in a computer chip but that would not be very helpful. My virtual reality experience gave me a new metaphor for physical space, this was the shoe box of three dimensions that I had seen glowing in the distance. On this metaphor physical space is just one perspective on reality, a perspective that is therefore within the larger 'space' of possible perspectives which is 'dialogic space'.

Virtual reality using cyber-goggles and a cyber-glove is still uncommon, but it offers, in an exaggerated form, some of the same features that most people in the developed world now have access to everyday through the Internet. With a few clicks of the mouse it is possible to move from exploring the inside of a hotel in Hong Kong to an overflight of the grand canyon. In the newspapers last week (as I write) it was announced that surveys had found that people in the UK now spend longer using the Internet than watching TV. In this the UK reflects a general trend for the developing world. On average, it is claimed, people are using the Internet for approaching 3 hours a day and watching the TV for just over 2 hours. If we take sleep into account then this means there must be many people who spend longer interacting in 'virtual' spaces than they do in 'real' space. It is frequently noted that time seems different when using the Internet. One comedian joked that an hour of Internet time was equal to 7 hours of normal time, referring to the common feeling that time just seems to disappear when one is on the Internet. The Internet also generates its own sense of space very different from the three dimensions of objective space. Applying Bakhtin's term, the 'chronotope' of the Internet is different from that of physical space–time. Bakhtin also noted that novels can have many chronotopes in dialogic relationships with each other and with the 'outside' chronotope of the reader (Bakhtin, 1981, p. 252). The same is true of the Internet where different interface designs and what are now called 'information architec-tures', produce different experiences of space and time. In a modest way I try, in this book, to bring an awareness of chronotope into discussions of interface designs for education.

Exaggerating the main trend and simplifying for the sake of clarity of exposition, one aspect of the Internet revolution that we are living through is a kind of Copernican revolution in which the world of 'meaning', a world which was previously seen as contained within and based upon the physical world, is expanding and taking over such that the physical world is increasingly experienced as contained within and based upon the world of meaning. This is just another way of expressing something already implied in my description of the experience of getting lost in virtual reality and seeing the simulated 3D world of objective space apparently floating in the distance.

As more and more people get email addresses and Web homes on the net, the capacity for anyone to communicate with anyone else in the world increases. In allowing for multiple relationships and 'local' networks that cross geographical boundaries the Internet has the potential to undermine any attempt to impose any one dominant form of categorising people. Bureaucracies still rely on passports indicating exclusive membership of a geographically bounded single 'nation state', but the increasing number of relationships and activities that cross such geographical boundaries are revealing the fictional and self-fulfilling nature of the assumption that identity is physical and so everyone belongs to one physical location as marbles can be placed within a jar. A new kind of identity is emerging, one that is not simply a 'global' identity in contradistinction to 'local' identities but one that is more multiple, open and flexible than in the past (Poster, 1995: Hermans, 2004: Wenger, 2005).

This is not really a book about space but primarily a book about educational technology. However, the question of space raised here is implicit throughout. One strand of the argument is that many ideas about education are dominated by entrenched metaphors arising from physical space whereas education actually takes place in dialogic 'virtual space' and new communications technology is helping us to see that. The principle of 'identity' is one such deeply entrenched physical metaphor. Most accounts of education seem to assume that it is all about constructing identities of one sort or another, either in the form of the identity of an individual or of 'knowledge objects'. When we switch our perspective from physical space to dialogic space some previously difficult issues in education become clearer, such as how to teach for creativity. Dialogic space is intrinsically creative and the more one enters into it the more creativity one experiences. There is a convergence between the vision of education as induction into dialogue,[2] which I propose, and the 'affordances' or strengths of new ICT. This dialogic approach to education is a challenge to the dominant metaphor of technology in education which is to see technology as a 'cognitive tool' that helps students 'construct'. The dialogic alternative is to see technology as a tool opening up and resourcing the kind of dialogic spaces that enable people to think, learn and play together.

4 REFORMING PEDAGOGY

Although the theoretical framework for education design with technology developed in this book is, I hope, original and challenging, in other ways the kind of argument I am making is a familiar one. It is widely acknowledged that the entrenched idea of the teacher as an authority is no longer easy to sustain if students with access to the Internet can easily 'know' more about any given topic than the teacher does. Many people realise that education, as we have known it, will have to change as more and more of us rely on

---

[2]There is a paradox in this phrase. 'Induction' implies the constraint of socialization into an existing practice whereas 'education into dialogue' is intended as a way to liberate learners beyond mere socialization. This is a version of the central paradox of education, sometimes called the teacher's dilemma, which is that we often need to control learners in order to set them free.

Internet search engines, such as Google, to look things up and find things out. Castells is only following a trend when he describes education in terms of learning to make effective use of the Internet. Real education, he writes, is:

> ... to acquire the intellectual capacity of learning to learn throughout one's whole life, retrieving the information that is digitally stored, recombining it, and using it to produce knowledge for whatever purpose we want. (Castells, 2002, p. 278)

Many educationalists have argued, for similar reasons, that we need to reform pedagogy in the direction of teaching flexible thinking skills, learning to learn and creativity. When they do so they often invoke the real needs of future citizens and workers in the emerging economy variously referred to as an 'information economy' or a 'knowledge economy' (e.g. Paul, 1993; Fisher, 1990). These voices are being listened to by governments and executives because the competitive advantage of countries and of companies is increasingly seen to depend on the creativity of their knowledge workers (e.g. Levin and Rumberger, 1995; Quisumbing, 2005). China, emerging as a leading force in the global economy, recently rewrote its school curriculum to emphasize the development of creativity and general thinking skills. Similar moves are afoot in many countries. With all this support it seems hardly necessary to make the case for teaching creativity and 'learning to learn'.

The real problem, however, is not a lack of a will to change but a lack of any very clear vision of how to change. Education for 'thinking', 'creativity' and 'learning to learn' makes a nice slogan but how do we really do this? For pedagogical designs that work it would help if we first understand what 'thinking', 'creativity' and 'flexible learning skills' really are and where they come from. This is why the first few chapters of this book are dedicated to outlining a coherent theoretical framework linking education for 'thinking skills', 'creativity' and 'learning to learn' with the pedagogical affordances of new communications technology.

It is common to use dialogue in a limited and controlled way as a tool in the construction of knowledge. However, a key part of my argument will be that the dialogic relation of holding two or more perspectives together in tension at the same time always opens up an unbounded space of potential perspectives. If one wants a pedagogy for thinking, creativity and learning to learn it is therefore important to treat dialogue not only as a means to the end of knowledge construction but also as an end in itself.

The idea that dialogic always opens an unbounded potential for meaning might seem like a vague philosophical notion that is hard to give any useful reference to within the everyday world of most human activities. However, this same philosophical notion is embodied in the Internet. The multi-dimensional meaning space of the Internet has been expanding exponentially since its inception in the last decade of the twentieth century. But expanding is a spatial concept, what does it mean in this context? Into what space exactly is the Internet exploding into? Clearly the expansion of the Internet is not only about the extra kilometres of fibre-optic cable or the new servers added every month but is more centrally about the Web sites, blogs, messages and virtual communities through which people interact together. In sum the Internet opens up, exists within, and gives an almost concrete form to, the very real and yet completely intermingled and unbounded space of dialogue.

5 STRUCTURE OF THE BOOK

This book is divided unevenly into two halves. The first and larger half reports some empirical research, but mainly focuses on developing a theoretical framework to serve as a basis for design research into the use of new technology to open up and support the kind of dialogues which take students beyond themselves into learning, thinking and creativity. The research projects reported in the second and smaller half of the book explore a dialogic perspective in the use of technology in education; beginning with the design of software to promote spoken reasoning between young children in primary schools and continuing to studies of computer tools to support the induction of university students into dialogue online. These studies are used to draw out the significance of the dialogic framework proposed and to show how it originated as a response to design challenges in applied research. In the concluding chapter, the two halves of the book are brought together and some suggestions are made as to the kind of design project required to implement and explore this emerging framework further. Through this the book addresses, in a provisional and partial way, some of the conceptual and practical challenges to education posed by the advent of the Internet.

In Chap. 2, *Dialogic: Opening a Space*, I unpack some of the many meanings of the term dialogic and explore how these interpretations relate to education with technology. In this chapter I prepare essential theoretical ground for the development of a perspective linking the use of Computer Supported Collaborative Learning and the teaching of flexible thinking and learning skills by introducing the radical ontological interpretation of dialogic which can be summed up in the phrase: 'dialogue as an end in itself'.

In Chap. 3, *Mediation: From Dialectic to Dialogic:* applies the idea of dialogue as an end in itself to criticize and develop existing accounts of mediation by technology in teaching and learning. This chapter begins by pointing out that Vygotsky, who is often referred to in the same breath as Bakhtin as a 'dialogic' thinker is more correctly referred to as a dialectic thinker. His dialectic account of the mediation of thought and learning by tools, an account developed and applied to the role of educational technology by Wertsch and others, is very different from Bakhtin's dialogic account of the mediation of thought and learning by the perspective of others. Wertsch's version of Vygotsky's account gives technology a direct role in teaching and learning and produces a vision of education as learning to use cultural tools. By contrast applying Bakhtin's account locates learning to use tools within the larger context of learning to engage more deeply in learning relationships and in learning dialogues. The role of technology is redefined in this chapter as an indirectly supportive role, resourcing, expanding and deepening learning dialogues.

In Chap. 4, *Reason: Dialogic as a Direction*, a re-analysis of a series of empirical studies of children talking together around Raven's reasoning tests introduces the idea of dialogue as a direction for education; a direction which issues in general thinking skills. My argument from the evidence is that children learn to think better in groups by learning to listen to each other and to question their own initial ideas. This may sound like common sense but the implication I draw from this goes beyond current established accounts of how children learn to think. This implication is that learning to think effectively requires an orientation of openness towards the other and that the move from a relatively closed orientation to a relatively open orientation can be considered as a direction of development towards the ideal of dialogue as an end in itself. It is interesting that this direction of development corresponds in some of its fruits, e.g. solving reasoning tests, to what would more traditionally be seen as cognitive development or the development of reasoning skills.

In Chap. 5, *Creativity: Playful Dialogue in Schools*, uses a series of transcripts to link playful talk to productive reasoning. Playful talk can be characterised by the use of imaginative analogy which, while creative in the minimal sense, is not, in itself, the kind of creativity valued in the school curriculum. The creativity that teachers and government wish to promote in schools includes the idea of fashioning a 'socially valued product'. I argue, through examples, that teacher guidance and social ground rules can stimulate creativity and direct it towards the construction of metaphors which embody socially valued insights. Creativity, I argue, is opened up by dialogues and is more fundamental to collaborative thinking than explicit reasoning. This leads me to propose replacing the current use of Exploratory Talk as a type of discourse to be promoted within education with the broader concept of Reflective Dialogue. Reflective Dialogue refers to creative shared inquiry using any medium, which may or may not include explicit reasoning depending on the needs of the task.

Chapters 6 and 7 are both entitled *Teaching Thinking*. Chapter 6, sub-titled: *Controversies and Questions*, is a review and discussion of the literature on teaching thinking skills. It develops the argument that ultimately higher order thinking, thinking that is distinctively human, is the responsive, creative and unpredictable thinking that originates in dialogues. Even at its most private, I argue, higher order thinking continues to be essentially dialogic in its structure and its nature. It follows, I claim, that 'higher order thinking' can be taught through induction into reflective dialogue as an end in itself. Chapter 7, sub-titled, *Metaphors and Taxonomies*, explores this argument in relation to the many metaphors and taxonomies that have been offered for describing thinking. This chapter concludes with a map of the aspects and components of reflective dialogue that does at least some of the same useful work for pedagogical design as previous taxonomies of thinking skills such as that of Bloom.

In Chap. 8, *Teaching Thinking with ICT*, reviews the literature linking ICT to teaching thinking skills. The main ways in which ICT has been thought of as supporting thinking within education are linked to three theories of teaching and learning in educational psychology, associationism, constructivism and socio-cultural theory. All three paradigms are said to have things to contribute to a greater understanding of how ICT can promote higher order thinking, however, I argue that research reveals weaknesses in all three paradigms and points a way forward towards dialogic theory. In this chapter I develop a loose dialogic framework for the design of educational activities to teach for higher order thinking skills using Computer Supported Collaborative Learning.

In Chap. 9, *Talk around Computers*, describes an exploratory study of children talking around a range of software which elicited principles for the design of interfaces to support collaborative learning. It continues with an account of how these principles were implemented, as far as possible, in software designs combined with an educational programme to promote effective dialogue. This approach was found to be useful in expanding the amount and quality of dialogue and in improving curriculum learning. A further study teaching maths and science with this approach over one school year, demonstrated that promoting dialogue around computers also had the potential to raise achievement. However, I criticize this research, in the spirit of retrospective self-criticism, as being limited to the neo-Vygotskian framework of using dialogue as a means to the end of knowledge construction.

In Chap. 10, *Computers and Dialogue*, continues the themes of Chap. 9 but takes them further to look at the design of technology enhanced educational activities which induct students into dialogue as an end in itself and no longer only as a means to an end or outcome measure that is conceptualised as being outside of the dialogue. I look particularly at the use of Bubble Dialogue and email exchanges ending with the example of a study of Philosophy for Children dialogues conducted via the Internet.

In Chap. 11, *Supporting Online Dialogues*, moves on to focus on virtual learning environments for adult students. I argue that most of the same pedagogic design principles for expanding dialogic spaces developed in primary schools still emerge clearly from research in this new environment but that they need to be implemented differently. Here I look at how the chronotopes of different interfaces impact on induction into thinking within dialogues and at how aspects of the design of online environments can support the formation of online reflective learning communities.

The concluding chapter, Chap. 12, *Technology and Enlightenment*, begins with a series of dialogues with alternative theoretical frameworks that are influential within research on educational technology in order to bring out what is distinctive about a dialogic framework. The implications of this framework for pedagogical design and the design of research are brought out through illustrations of past projects and also through a programme of possible future projects that could explore and develop this framework further. The theme of history and the impact of the Internet which has been raised in this introductory chapter is returned to in the conclusion in order to frame the message of the book. Two different histories of technology are presented, one driven by the logic of production, the other by the logic of communication and community. I argue that these two histories issue in two very different models of 'enlightenment'. The European enlightenment project has become associated with the application of technical reason to every aspect of social life in order to increase power and control through knowledge and education. An alternative 'dialogic' enlightenment project would see technology and education as a way to support the expansion of dialogue across difference. The aim of this reformed enlightenment project is not expanding 'mastery' so much as expanding global dialogue, deepening mutual understanding and resourcing spaces of creative play.

Chapter 2

DIALOGIC
Opening a space

What is to be done, O Muslims? for I do not recognize myself.
I am neither Christian, nor Jew, nor Magian, nor Muslim.
I am not of the East, nor of the West, nor of the land, nor of the sea;
I am not of Nature's mint, nor of the circling heaven.
I am not of earth, nor of water, nor of air, nor of fire;
I am not of the empyrean, nor of the dust, nor of existence, nor of entity.
I am not of India, nor of China, nor of Bulgaria, nor of Saqsin
I am not of the kingdom of 'Iraqian, nor of the country of Khorasan
I am not of the this world, nor of the next, nor of Paradise, nor of Hell
I am not of Adam, nor of Eve, nor of Eden and Rizwan.
My place is the Placeless, my trace is the Traceless

From Divan-i Shams by Mevlani Rumi (http://www.rumi.org.uk/)

This chapter unpacks some of the many meanings of the term dialogic and explores how different interpretations of dialogic relate to education with technology. In this chapter I prepare some essential theoretical ground for the development of a perspective linking the use of Computer Supported Collaborative Learning and the teaching of flexible thinking and learning skills.

My main aim in this book is to outline the new vision of education with technology that I think we need for the emerging network society. This vision can be distinguished from most other visions through the use of the term *dialogic*. In this first chapter I prepare the ground for the rest of the book by unpacking some of the implications of the term *dialogic*. Most of this chapter is therefore not directly about the use of technology in education but about theory. I hope that readers who are more interested in the application of technology in education will bear with me.

1 SOME VARIETIES OF DIALOGIC

The term dialogic is now widely used in articles and books about education, however, it is being used in a variety of different ways. When a reference is given for the use of the term *dialogic* this is most often to the work of Russian literary theorist and philosopher, Michael Bakhtin (1895–1975). I have found at least five different but interlinked ways of understanding dialogic in the literature, each of which can be traced to, or at least themed with, strands found in the writings of Bakhtin. All of these interpretations of dialogic have implications for research on learning and for visions of education.

1.1 Dialogic as 'pertaining to dialogue'

Dialogic meaning simply 'pertaining to dialogue' is the default dictionary definition that is now proliferating in the literature. Bakhtin wrote that 'if an answer does not give rise to a new question from itself, it falls out of the dialogue' (Bakhtin, 1986, pp. 114, 168). This definition of dialogue, a definition that distinguishes it from social conversations that are not inquiries on the one hand or monologues on the other hand, can be usefully applied in education (e.g. Alexander, 2000, p. 520). However, the idea of dialogue as a shared inquiry, while useful, does not in itself do justice to the full depth of Bakhtin's analysis of dialogic.

Dialogue as shared inquiry has been a method in education since at least the time of Socrates without anyone previously feeling the need to refer to this as 'dialogic'. We are now seeing the use of the term 'dialogic' in contexts where other terms like 'collaborative learning' or 'discussion' or 'social interaction' or 'community of inquiry' were previously used without any new depth of meaning being added. This is unfortunate because it is a waste of a potentially very useful technical term. There are not many accounts of learning that do not include a role for dialogues, including that of Piaget, but if this makes them all 'dialogic' then 'dialogic' is no longer capable of distinguishing between them.

'Pertaining to dialogue' is the default everyday meaning of the term 'dialogic', it is the adjective form of the noun 'dialogue' in much the same way that 'democratic' is the adjective form of the noun 'democracy', but when dialogic is used with a reference to Bakhtin there is an implication that it is a technical term and in this case the reader is entitled to expect something more than a dictionary definition. The dictionary meaning of dialogue, for example, implies a contrast to monologue but Bakhtin developed his account of 'dialogic' out of a reading of Dostoevsky's novels which, as the work of one author, do not qualify as dialogues in the ordinary language meaning of the term (Bakhtin, 1973). Bakhtin has much more to offer than the idea that dialogue is a 'shared inquiry'. 'Dialogic', for Bakhtin, was not a reference to actual dialogues between people as an empirical fact and site of investigation, but it was rather a reference to his distinctive and original way of understanding the meaning of texts.

1.2 Dialogic texts as opposed to monologic texts

For Bakhtin texts, even books, are also 'utterances' which are part of dialogues. Far from being the single voice of a single author, texts, he claimed, contained traces of many voices often engaging in dialogues within the text itself. Bakhtin described several ways in which texts or utterances can be located on a dialogic to monologic continuum, for example he wrote that they can be more or less multi-voiced and they can be more or less 'open to the other'. This account has already been applied to Computer Supported Collaborative Learning and converted into coding schemes to assess the degree of dialogicality of messages in electronic conferencing environments using factors like addressing others, incorporating content of other messages and locating knowledge claims as tentative hypotheses open to correction (e.g. Hui, 2005).

Bakhtin was familiar with the work of Martin Buber who is also a source of dialogic theory in education. Bakhtin's description of texts and utterances relates to a contrast in types of orientation to the other first articulated by Buber who distinguished between an 'I-thou' orientation to the other in dialogue and an 'I-it' orientation (Buber, 1923/1979). He characterized the I-thou orientation as about listening and understanding while the I-it orientation objectifies the other and is ultimately about controlling the other. Buber's contrast is echoed in Bakhtin's account of the difference between the 'authoritative' voice that remains outside of my words and the 'internally persuasive' voice that enters inside them. Bakhtin's account of the impact of what he called 'the persuasive word' is often quoted because it has obvious significance for education:

> Such a word awakens new and independent words, organises masses of our words from within and does not remain in an isolated and static condition: it is not finite but open; in each of the new contents that dialogise it, this discourse is able to reveal ever new ways to mean. (Bakhtin, 1981, p. 343)

Wertsch (1991) refers to Bakhtin's contrast between the 'authoritative' and the 'persuasive' word in his own book, *Voices of the Mind,* and he relates this to a theory of learning as appropriating the voices of others based on Bakhtin's own account of how we appropriate the words of others by taking them into our own store of words, giving them our own accent and our own associations and resonances (Bakhtin, 1986, pp. 293–294). Wertsch's synthesis of Vygotsky and Bakhtin into the idea of learning as the appropriation of social voices and social discourses has been influential in the field of Computer Supported Collaborative Learning. However, the philosophical frameworks of Bakhtin and Vygotsky are so different that this 'synthesis' is problematic (this is an issue which I address in detail in the next chapter, Chap. 3: *Mediation*).

Buber's I-it to I-thou contrast and Bakhtin's contrast between an authoritative voice and a persuasive voice relate to Paulo Freire's contrast between a hierarchic style of educational delivery transmitting a fixed curriculum, which he calls monologic, and a more responsive dialogic method of education which respects the voices of the students (Freire, 1971). Freire associates monologic education with the maintenance of relations of oppression and dialogic education with liberation of the oppressed. Freire's work has been inspirational for many, especially for teachers working with the poor and the underpriveliged. However, critics of Freire point out that his 'dialogic' method occurs within a Marxist framework in which the teacher is acting to raise the consciousness of the students collectively in a way that presupposes in advance what that consciousness will be consciousness of, i.e. their oppression and the need for collective action. It is because he knows in advance what will emerge from dialogic teaching and learning that Freire, like Vygotsky, offers a dialectic rather than a truly dialogic account of education (see Chap. 3 for an elaboration of this contrast).

Influenced by Bakhtin, Hubert Hermans, a psychologist interested in psychotherapy, proposed a model of the dialogical self by which he means the self as a polyphony of competing and cooperating voices (Hermans, 2004). Bakhtin is one of Hermans sources and his account of the coherence of the self is similar in many ways to Bakhtin's account of the coherence of a novel by Doestoevsky, a coherence that emerges through and across the many voices that speak independently within each novel (Bakhtin, 1973). According to Hermans, the voices of a self are triggered by and rooted in different contexts and they can move across the boundary of the self, sometimes being experienced as the voices of others or things physically outside of the self. Hermans' theory has been applied to Computer Supported Collaborative Learning in studies by Beatrice Ligorio and colleagues which suggest that identity issues are important to understanding how people negotiate and reach towards shared understandings in online environments (e.g. Ligorio and Pugliese, 2004).

1.3 Dialogic as an epistemological paradigm

While Bakhtin sometimes contrasts dialogic with monologic, at other times he implies that texts are always really dialogic and that all thought, including thought inside an individual head, is a dialogue between multiple voices. This suggests that one way to overcome the problem of distinguishing the dialogic from the monologic is to universalize dialogic and to understand apparent monologic as a kind of illusion that occurs within dialogic. This is the route that I think is being taken by those who interpret dialogic as an epistemological framework such as the Scandinavian communication theorists Ragnor Rommetveit and Per Linell.

Volosinov, a close collaborator with Bakhtin in the 1920s, wrote:

> meaning is like an electric spark that occurs only when two different terminals are hooked together

and further that:

> In essence meaning belongs to a word in its position between speakers; that is, meaning is realised only in the process of active, responsive, understanding. (Volosinov, 1929554/1986, pp. 102–103)

Similar claims are made by Bakhtin (e.g. 1986, p. 162). This implies that all meaning is really dialogic. Monologic is then presumably an illusion of power, by which I mean that it is not a reality but the impression that authoritative voices try to give that they are speaking a simple unquestionable truth that cannot be challenged. Bakhtin is said to support this universalizing of dialogic when he claims that all utterances are a response to a situation or to somebody else's utterance and are addressed to somebody who is supposed to do something with them (Morson and Emerson, 1990, quoted by Linell, 2003). Rommetveit (1992) and Per Linell (1998, 2003) can therefore claim to be following Bakhtin when they claim that dialogism is 'an epistemological framework'. To make their case they contrast their dialogic paradigm to a monologic paradigm through a number of assumptions, three which I have selected as being of central significance:

1. That any communicative act is interdependent with other acts, it responds to what has gone before and anticipates future responses.
2. That acts are similarly 'in dialogue' with other aspects of context such as cultural traditions and social setting.
3. That meaning does not exist 'ready-made' before dialogues but is constructed within dialogues.

These three points unpack the basic claim of Volosinov that meaning is never simply given but is always created out of the interaction between different voices and different perspectives, and is reinforced by Bakhtin's point that meaning, for us, is always a response to a question (Bakhtin, 1986, p. 168). This implies the further claim that when people understand or 'know' something they do so dynamically in a communicative act that carves out one meaning from a field of competing possible meanings – a field of alternatives that does not exist ready-made but itself is generated by the dialogue. It follows that signs, even a hieroglyph on a temple wall, do not mean anything in themselves, their meaning is a product of an act of reading and that act of reading is always in some way 'dialogic' because the meaning read is an answer to the question or questions that we ask of the text as we read.

Linell and Rommetveit contrast their dialogical paradigm to the monological paradigm that they claim represents the mainstream in social science. The monological paradigm in science is said to seek the universal laws and structures underlying surface phenomena. The ideal motivating this endeavour is to produce a single logically coherent model independent of perspective. The monological paradigm is often accused of overlooking the fact that knowledge is never independent of social, historical and biological contexts that give it meaning. One aspect of the contextual background required to interpret knowledge claims is their position within conversations, including the long-term conversations of a culture. The dialogic claim from Bakhtin, picked up and developed by Linell and Rometveit, is that any utterance, even a scientific theory, is a link in a chain of communication (Bakhtin, 1986, p. 69). The 'facts of nature' for example, only arise as answers to the questions that we ask of nature and if we asked different questions we would 'see' different facts.

Dialogicality means not merely that participants in interactions respond to what other participants do, they respond in a way that takes into account how they think other people are going to respond to them. Rommetveit, quoting Barwise and Perry (1983), calls this circularity 'atunement to the atunement of the other' and points out firstly, that it influences most human behaviour and secondly, that it is impossible to understand the effects of this circularity using monological representations (Rommetveit, 1992). Monological models assume closed systems with regular and therefore discoverable relationships between inputs and outputs. If human behaviour has to be understood in much the same way as we interpret meaning in a continuing dialogue then, Rommetveit claims, monological models are inappropriate.

One of the implications of dialogic as an epistemological paradigm is that there can be no fixed or final meaning for utterances. This is because meanings emerge in the context of a dialogue which is always open so leaving the potential for a reassessment. Bakhtin emphasised this lack of finality, writing:

> There is neither a first nor a last word and there are no limits to the dialogic context (it extends into the boundless past and the boundless future). (Bakhtin, 1986, p. 170)

Bakhtin's point here has obvious implications for research on computer mediated dialogues. It implies that the effort expended by researchers to pin down the exact meaning of utterances and to code them accurately might be misguided. Bakhtin is not arguing here that validity and reliability do not exist but rather that they exist only within dialogues and in those dialogues they are always relative to a perspective. The insight that meaning only exists in dialogue leads him to propose an apparently holistic approach to research in social science, arguing that the meaning of utterances is not to be found in one utterance but only 'in the chain of meaning, which in its totality is the only thing that can be real' (Bakthin, 1986, p. 146). This methodological holism, however, is complicated by the fact that the chain of meaning is said to be open and without boundary, in other words it resists ever being grasped as a totality.

To illustrate this idea that meaning occurs only in an endless and open chain of meaning and to introduce the idea of a dialogic ontology in a seriously playful way, I will use an example taken from biblical scholarship. The opening words of St. John's gospel, some of the most 'authoritative' and 'final' words in the Christian tradition, are 'εν αρχη ηνο λογοσ'. This is traditionally translated into English by the resonant phrase: 'In the beginning was the word'. However, λογοσ (or 'logos') is an enormously resonant word with many more potential translations than 'word'. The interpretation of 'logos' led to a scandal in 1522 when the humanist scholar Erasmus, who had been charged by the church with the task of producing a definitive Latin version of the Bible, translated this opening line as: 'In principio erat sermo'. Sermo could mean 'talk' as in a sermon, but it is also often translated as everyday talk or 'conversation'. Like logos the ancient Greek word αρχη (arch) is also resonant with many possible meanings. One such is 'head' or 'ruler' but another, in the tradition of Platonic philosophy which St. John evokes through his choice of words, could be the 'primary source' or the 'underlying principle'. This suggests yet another possible translation of εν αρχη ηνο λογοσ as 'The underlying principle is conversation'. This was the big problem with Erasmus's translation. While it was possible for the Church authorities to imagine God embodied ('made flesh') in the form of a word, a kind of thing, it was not possible for them to imagine God as a 'conversation'. If Erasmus's translation had been accepted the subsequent history of Christianity might have been quite different. What is particularly interesting to me is that the issues at stake in the theological dispute that Erasmus's translation of the bible caused in 1522 are similar to the issues at stake today in education when we debate the relative merits of monological and dialogical perspectives. Can the ultimate context of meaning be assumed to take the form of an 'identity' such as a 'word' or formula – in the beginning was $E=mc^2$ perhaps? – or is it to be thought of more on the model of an open-ended and multi-perspectival space of dialogue? Erasmus's translation was not accepted but it might have been and it might be again 1 day. This illustrates the point that even the most foundational words in a culture, as well as the most ordinary words, shift their meanings at different points in an ongoing dialogue that has no obvious limits as to what may become relevant, nor any clear stopping conditions.

Some readers might now be thinking that, in a book on educational technology, bringing in Erasmus and St John's gospel is a diversion too far. I understand that concern but would reply that this book is also about how we can promote creativity and flexible thinking skills. An important aspect of Bakhtin's account of dialogicality is the idea developed by Bakhtin of 'intertextuality', or that texts always contain references to other texts and are read as a dialogue between texts. My interpretation of his notion of 'great time' is that, at a certain level, all texts are always in dialogue with all other texts. I am exemplifying this by illustrating that Erasmus's sixteenth century translation of the Bible is still relevant to scientific concerns today. This radical intertextuality is, I will argue in later chapters, at the heart of creativity and flexible thinking and learning skills and so needs to be taken on board by educationalists if we are to be able to design for the development of these general skills.

1.4 Dialogic as a social ontology

Ontology is a word used in philosophy to refer to inquiry into the nature of 'being' or whatever it is that can be said to exist. In referring to dialogic as an epistemological framework, Per Linell is saying that dialogic is not so much about how the world really 'is' as about how we come to know about the world. However, dialogic as epistemology, on this model, often appears to assume an implicit ontology of subjects facing an objective world which these subjects come to know about through talking together. This is problematic since Bakhtin's arguments can also be read as taking us beyond epistemology, or a concern with how we know things, towards ontology, or a claim about what is really there. In the human sphere, which he indicates by referring to the 'world of meaning', he is claiming that what is really there is never a single or fixed meaning but always a dialogue.

In the context of a reading of Dostoevsky, Bakhtin made it clear that he intended to question the philosophical principle of identity, at least as this applies to human beings:

> Man is never coincident with himself. The equation of identity "A is A" is inapplicable to him. (Bakhtin, 1973, p. 48)

Sidorkin relates Bakhtin to Buber in asserting that the basis of being human (or human being) is not some kind of identity such as 'a self' in the face of 'a world' but the opening of dialogue (Sidorkin, 1999). The self, for Bakhtin, is defined through dialogue and is at its most authentic as the opening of a difference between perspectives. Social science, similarly, Bakhtin claims, does not aim at a reduction to identity but at an understanding of the other that preserves that otherness (Bakhtin, 1986, p. 169).

Sidorkin follows Bakhtin in limiting this ontological claim to a claim about the essence of being human. Markova also makes an ontological claim for dialogic, but like Sidorkin she also limits this by calling it a 'social ontology' and 'an ontology of humanity' (Markova, 2003, p. 90). Presumably she is implying that, while culture and language and subjects are dialogically constructed, stars and trees might really exist just as they are independently of any dialogue about them. This echoes a distinction made by Bakhtin in his notes where he writes that:

> Meaning cannot (and does not wish to) change physical, material and other phenomena; it cannot act as a material force (Bakhtin, 1986, p. 165)

Bakhtin continues that he is happy about this because he points out that contextual meaning is more powerful than a material force since it can completely change the way in which material things are interpreted while leaving them, physically, exactly as they are (Bakhtin, 1986, p. 165). However, and perhaps inevitably, Bakhtin speaks with more than one voice on this point. In 'The Problem of the Text', Bakhtin argues that understanding a dialogue as a researcher implies participating in that dialogue as a 'third voice'. The researcher's perspective is a necessary part of the dialogue and the understanding produced is always dialogic. As a passing comment he compares this situation to the experimenter in the experimental system referring in brackets to quantum physics and claiming that the observer is always 'a constituent part' of the world (Bakhtin, 1986, p. 126). The reference to quantum physics is presumably a reference to the conclusions of Heisenberg and Schrodinger that the perspective of the observer does in fact impact on the material reality of what is observed (see Penrose, 1989, for a comprehensive discussion of these positions and the possible role of consciousness in precipitating 'material reality'). Bakhtin gives another tantalizing hint when he introduces his idea of the 'chronotope' in novels which is the idea that different texts produce different configurations of space and time with a reference to Einstein and the claim that this use of 'space' and 'time' is partly metaphoric but not entirely (Bakhtin, 1986, p. 250). Theoretical physics was not Bakhtin's specialist area and it is not my specialist area but he marked the possibility, at various points, that dialogic is not only a 'human ontology' but may be something more fundamental and universal.

2 FROM IDENTITY TO DIFFERENCE

To understand the ontological definition of dialogic, which is the basis of the theory of education with technology that I put forward in this book, it is necessary to first come to terms with the recent shift in some schools of thought from what could be called 'identity thinking' to what could be called 'difference thinking'. This shift is often associated with post-modernism in general and with Jacques Derrida in particular (although the idea of ontological difference really originated with Heidegger). However, beyond philosophy, it could also be that the popularity of this new way of thinking relates to changing human practices associated with the historical shift towards a networked society which I outlined in the introduction. As I mentioned in the introduction, this shift is not only a change of intellectual fashion but reflects a changed experience of space and time brought about by new information and communications technology. The widespread interest in and reference to 'post-modernism' does not stem from many people being influenced by the difficult texts of philosophers such as Derrida but from the widespread feeling that our lived reality is different now from what it was and that we need to understand how and why it is different.

One way of understanding the essential nature of the shift is through the idea of 'identity thinking'. Heidegger claimed that the history of Western philosophy is dominated by the metaphor of 'identity' or the assumption, attributed to Aristotle, that a thing is what it is and not another thing (Aristotle, 350BCE/2006). While this assumption of identity appears to make sense when we are talking about objects in physical space it is unhelpful when we use it to refer to meaning. When things are just what they are – for example these black marks on the page or on the screen in front of you – then they have no meaning. It is only when they are also something else that they take on meaning. This problem leads to various reference theories of meaning that try to preserve identity thinking by describing signs as things that refer to other things, including in this category of the signified 'thought things' or concepts as well as material things or objects.

Derrida claims that reference theories of meaning are fundamentally muddled. He makes fun of the identity metaphor by playing with the letter 'a'. By inserting it into the French word difference to make a new word 'différance' he gives it almost infinite but also indefinite meaning. If the letter 'a' was just what it was and not another thing then this kind of play with the multiple meanings of 'a' would not be possible. Influenced by Saussure, Derrida suggests that a better metaphor for looking at meaning than identity is the metaphor of 'difference'. Signs, on Saussure's theory, mean not by what they are so much as by the difference that they make within the system of differences which is a language. The 'a' inserted into the word 'difference' is able to mean something because it is not 'e' – although physically 'a' and 'e' are very similar: turn them upside down and invert them and they are almost the same.

Fig. 2.1. The 'difference' between 'a' and 'e'

One thing that is being made clear by this play with letters is that 'a' cannot be made to mean anything except in contrast to other letters such as 'e'. I believe that this is a similar claim to the claim from Bakhtin that an utterance in a dialogue does not mean on its own but only in relation to other utterances that it responds to or evokes.

Derrida, however, does not accept Saussure's 'structuralist' account of meaning as a property of relations of differences within a system, he claims that the system of differences has no boundary. This simple step is important and has implications that many find challenging. As with Bakhtin's claim that the dialogue has no 'last word', the claim that language (or the system within which differences mean) has no boundary implies that there can be no fixed meaning of a term (any significant difference) because there is always the possibility of a new interpretation. It also implies that differences that mean cannot be thought of only as the differentiation of a prior field of possibilities but rather must be thought of as precipitating or constructing their own context. Making meaning through an infinite process of differencing that has no limits is not the same as differentiating a limited field. This is what distinguishes the new difference thinking of Derrida and other thinkers often called 'post-modern' from the kind of difference thinking found already in Hegel's dialectic. Differences are also the basis of meaning and thought in Hegel's system but they are a differentiation of an initial simple 'Being' and this process of differentiation of Being from itself leads ultimately to a return to 'Being' but this time as a more complexly internally differentiated whole. For Derrida there is no 'Being' or even being – there is only différance.

3 BACK TO BAKHTIN

Bakhtin points out several times in different texts that the aim of dialogue is not to reach intersubjective agreement in the sense of simple coincidence of perspectives because such coincidence would bring an end the flow meaning (e.g. Bakhtin, 1986, p. 162). Like Volosinov's metaphor of meaning as an electric spark that requires two poles to ignite, this suggests the idea of dialogic as a difference or gap or opening without which there would be no meaning.

The idea that meaning implies an opening of difference connects Bakhtin's dialogic to the theme of 'difference thinking' that I have tried to articulate above. Bakhtin tends to locate this opening in the difference between two voices or texts in a dialogue (e.g. Bakhtin, 1978, p. 162). This is true at the level of experience but Bakhtin also argues that voices and texts are constructed within and through dialogue, which implies that the opening of dialogue is also in some way to be understood as an underlying principle such that a difference between perspectives has 'always already' opened a potentiality for meaning even before we start to talk or to think.

This analysis of dialogic as an opening of a space of meaning connects Bakhtin to Derrida who, in his seminal essay 'La Différance' argues that meaning is a product of an, always prior, act of making a difference that includes the differing of space and the deferring of time (Derrida, 1973, 1968). Derrida presents his understanding of difference through a critical development of ideas from Heidegger. In Heidegger's 1957 lecture on 'Identity and Difference' (Heidegger, 1969) he interrogates what he calls the 'A = A' principle of identity thinking and finds the origin of meaning in an unmediated 'ontological difference', which he refers to as the difference between Being and beings. Heidegger's account of this ontological difference is also an account of how 'mankind' and Being belong together in what he calls 'the event of appropriation' (ereignis) which he describes as a movement of 'overwhelming' and 'arrival' and as the circling (his word is 'ineinander') of the Being of beings and the beings of Being around the invisible unmediated difference between them (Heidegger, 1969, p. 69).

I have to admit that I am not sure that I understand what Heidegger is trying to say by this concept of ereignis. One way that I have found to make

Heidegger's distinction between beings and Being useful for me is through Merleau-Ponty's more visual account of the difference between figure and ground. This is the more simple to grasp idea that, that things or objects always stand-out from and are defined against an implicit background. Merleau-Ponty, whose later work was strongly influenced by Heidegger, offers an account of perception that shares some of the structure of Heidegger's account of 'ereignis'. When a person stands up within a landscape, a horizon instantly forms around them stretching away in every direction as far as the eye can see (perhaps Heidegger's concept of 'arrival') but at the same time as the person's gaze precipitates this horizon they also experience themselves placed as an object within their horizon as if the gaze of the horizon was looking at them and locating them within it (a possible picture of Heidegger's concept of 'overwhelming'). Merleau-Ponty refers to these two sides, the looking out and the looking in, together as a 'chiasm'. 'Chiasm' is a term now increasingly taken up by dialogical theorists in psychology and education (e.g. Shotter, 2001). This word is borrowed from grammar where it refers to the reversability of the subject and the object in a sentence and is used by Merleau-Ponty to refer to the mutual envelopment (a translation of Heidegger's term 'ineinander') and reversibility between two total perspectives on the world around an 'unbridgeable gap' or 'hinge' which is also, he writes, an opening or 'déhiscence' of meaning (Merleau-Ponty, 1964, pp. 194, 201: 1968, pp. 148, 153).

Bakhtin, in his notes on 'Methodology for the Human Sciences' appears to reach towards a similar view to that of Merleau-Ponty's chiasm writing:

> Thought about the world and thought in the world. Thought striving to embrace the world and thought experiencing itself in the world (as part of it). An event in the world and participation in it. The world as an event (and not as existence in ready-made form). (Bakhtin, 1986, p. 162)

By 'event' Bakhtin means something like the act of making a difference. He may be claiming here that the world does not exist until an act of making a difference separates a self (or perspective) from a world. In this passage Bakhtin comes out explicitly against the ontology of subjective selves in objective worlds trying to understand them through dialogues, which may be implicit in the epistemological interpretation of dialogic referred to earlier. Here he is suggesting that our sense of the world and of our own perspective within it are mutually constructed out of a kind of dialogue. This passage reinforces the interpretation that Bakhtin's *dialogic* joins Heidegger's *ereignis*, Derrida's *différance* and Merleau-Ponty's *chiasm* as a variation on the theme of ontological difference. Of course there are many important differences between these accounts and if I was writing a book of academic philosophy I would have to try to unpack these. However, this is a book about the philosophical foundations of Educational Technology in the

Twenty-First Century and for that the main point of these theories lies in two assertions: firstly that meanings are not things, they are not reducible to knowledge objects or 'cognitive artefacts', and they should not be thought of in terms of identity; secondly that meaning arises out of and depends upon an original 'creative difference' or 'opening' that could be thought of as the opening of dialogue.

This discussion of ontology is also relevant to understanding educational technology in the context of the Internet because if we remain with the monologic default assumption of an objective physical world made up of definable separate identities causally related to each other, then the meaning space opened up by the Internet cannot be understood. Only a dialogic ontology of difference, in which an infinite space of potential meaning is opened up by voices in dialogue, can make sense of the virtual space of meaning opened up by the Internet and so can understand how the phenomenon of an Internet is possible in the first place.

4 EDUCATION INTO DIALOGUE

It is common now to write about learning in terms of trajectories of identity (e.g. Wenger, 1999, 2005). These accounts are often intended to replace more rationalist accounts such as that of Piaget which refer to a movement of 'decontextualisation' involving abstraction and generalization. Piaget's metaphors all suggest upward movement. In replacing such accounts, this dimensionality often seems to have been lost. The idea of shifting in identity can seem rather horizontal, like wandering over a flat landscape, without much sense of there being anywhere more worth getting to than anywhere else. Accounts of changes in 'core identity' brought about by education are often fascinating but it is not always clear in what way, if any, the end result, the 'educated' identity, is really different in quality from the starting identity. Basil Bernstein, for example, provides an account of teaching as a 'vertical discourse' as opposed to the 'horizontal discourse' of everyday knowledge but he does so, at least in his later work, in a way which is careful not to value the one over the other but to see both as situated social constructions (Bourne, 2003). The dialogic ontology I introduced earlier implies, however, a real-dimensional change in learning which parallels the idea of the vertical ascent and de-contextualisation of knowledge, but in a new and almost an inverted kind of way. A rationalist view of development has to posit real cognitive structures as the end point of the de-contextualisation of knowledge. The dialogic view I am proposing begins with the idea of the other as ungraspable and suggests a movement of the letting go of identity in order to understand the other and, at the same time, the self.

This implies the paradoxical aim of identifying with non-identity expressed by Merleau-Ponty in the phrase 'what there is to be grasped is a dispossession' (1964, p. 191). I give some very concrete illustrations of what this might mean in educational terms in Chap. 4. This same insight is expressed well by the poet Keat's idea of 'negative capability'. Appropriately enough, in the context of a discussion of dialogic, Keat's proposed this idea in a letter to his brother which described an insight that had emerged in a conversation earlier that same day:

> I had not a dispute but a disquisition, with Dilke on various subjects; several things dove-tailed in my mind, and at once it struck me what quality went to form a Man of Achievement, especially in Literature, and which Shakespeare possessed so enormously – I mean Negative Capability, that is, *when a man is capable of being in uncertainties, mysteries, doubts, without any irritable reaching after fact and reason' (Sunday 21 Dec. 1817 Hampstead. http://englishhistory.net/keats/letters.html)*

The idea expressed by Keats here of an identity built on 'identifying with non-identity' is an oxymoron. While the term oxymoron is often used to indicate a simple contradiction, as in 'an argument that goes nowhere', I prefer the use of oxymoron in literary criticism to refer to a conjunction of words which, at first view, seem to be contradictory or incongruous, but whose surprising juxtaposition may express a deeper truth. In this case the deeper truth is a trajectory of identity development that includes a dimension of depth towards negative capability, not an active grasping at truth but a capacity for dispossession which issues in creativity.

5 DIALOGIC EDUCATION AND TECHNOLOGY

Each of the five ways of understanding dialogic which I outlined above have implications for education and the role of technology in education.

1. Dialogic defined as pertaining to empirical dialogues suggests the promotion of dialogue as chains of questions in classrooms both through teacher–pupil dialogues (Alexander, 2004) and through establishing communities of inquiry (Wells, 1999; Lipman, 2003).
2. Dialogic understood as being about the open and polyphonic properties of texts and utterances brings in the need for intertextuality in classrooms (Maybin, 1999; Kozulin, 1996) and the appropriation of social discourses as a goal in education (Hicks, 1996; Wertsch, 1998; Koschmann, 1999). Diane Hui's work shows how the 'dialogic' property of utterances, dialogic in the sense of being open and responsive to the other, predicts

sustainability and success in online learning communities (Hui, 2005). Beatrice Ligorio applies Herman's account of the dialogic self to explore how dialogic self-formation and play is part of online learning (Ligorio and Pugliese, 2004).

3. Dialogic as an epistemological framework supports an account of education as the discursive construction of shared knowledge (Bereiter and Scardamalia, 1989; Mercer, 1995).

The first three interpretations of dialogic, while perfectly valid, are easily co-opted into an understanding of education as about the construction of an identity of some kind. This is a shame because it fails to make use of the more challenging and radical implications of Bakhtin's version of dialogic. None of these approaches actually require therefore the specialist technical term status for dialogic implied by a reference to Bakhtin.

In contrast to the other understandings of dialogic, dialogic taken to be an ontological principle, whether as the social ontology proposed by Sidorkin and Markova or in the more fundamental ontologies of Heidegger and Merleau-Ponty, has implications for practice that are intrinsically and distinctively 'dialogic' in the Bakhtinian sense. Only this ontological definition of dialogic is radical enough to resist becoming another method or tool in the default 'modernist' understanding of education as producing or constructing an object. The alternative vision offered by an ontological definition of dialogic applied to education is of moving learners into the space of dialogue. This is the direction of 'negative capability' suggested by Keats as the source of increased creativity. Heidegger similarly refers to this movement into the creative gap of difference when he writes that the most important thing to be learnt is learning itself and, to achieve this, teachers need to be even more teachable than their students (Heidegger, 1978, p. 380). In short, on the ontological dialogical model, dialogue is not primarily a means to the end of knowledge construction, or the acquisition of skills and identities, but is to be seen as an end in itself. The dialogic gap is what is most really there in the first place and also what is most to be learnt: this ontological dialogic is therefore the most important aim of education.

This might all sound very philosophical, and indeed it is, but it marks a profound shift in orientation towards teaching and learning with dialogue; a shift which has important implications for practice. So far Computer Supported Collaborative Learning has by and large used dialogue as a means to the end of knowledge construction and often called that use 'dialogic' – so what would it mean to be more truly dialogic? As I bring out in Chap. 4, the slogan 'dialogue as an end in itself' does not mean just talk for talk's sake but indicates a challenging direction of development for individuals and society towards a greater capacity for creative thinking and a greater capacity for learning to learn intimately linked to an ethics of openness to the other.

Summary

This chapter unpacked some of the different interpretations given to the concept of dialogic drawn from the writings of Bakhtin and argued for the value of an ontological interpretation that relates Bakhtin's dialogic to the more general 'post-modern' shift from 'identity thinking' to 'difference thinking'. The main educational implication of this is the importance of promoting dialogue not only as a means to knowledge construction but also as an end in itself. This chapter has done some essential theoretical groundwork necessary to developing a framework that can link educational technology to the teaching of flexible thinking and learning skills such as creativity and learning to learn. In Chap. 3 I apply the understanding of dialogic developed here to a critique of socio-cultural theory in the form developed by Wertsch which is perhaps currently one of the most popular paradigms in design for Computer Supported Collaborative Learning.

Chapter 3

MEDIATION
From dialectic to dialogic

"No," said Kitty, blushing, but looking at him all the more boldly with her truthful eyes; "a girl may be so circumstanced that she cannot live in the family without humiliation, while she herself..."

At the hint he understood her.

"Oh, yes," he said. "Yes, yes, yes – you're right; you're right!"

And he saw all that Pestsov had been maintaining at dinner of the liberty of woman, simply from getting a glimpse of the terror of an old maid's existence and its humiliation in Kitty's heart; and loving her, he felt that terror and humiliation, and at once gave up his arguments.

From Tolstoy, Anna Karenina. *(http://www.gutenberg.org/files/1399/)*

Chapter 2 introduced the idea of an ontological interpretation of dialogic which was summed up in the phrase: 'dialogue as an end in itself'. In this chapter that idea is applied to criticize and develop one of the most influential accounts of mediation by technology in teaching and learning. I begin by pointing out that Vygotsky, who is often referred to in the same sentence as Bakhtin as a 'dialogic' thinker was, in fact, a dialectic thinker. His dialectic account of the mediation of thought and learning by tools, an account developed and applied to the role of educational technology by Wertsch and others, is very different from Bakhtin's dialogic account of the mediation of thought and learning by the voices of others. Wertsch's version of Vygotsky's account gives technology a direct role in cognition and in teaching and learning and producing a vision of education as learning to use cultural tools. By contrast my version of Bakhtin's account locates this kind of learning within the larger context of learning to engage more deeply in learning relationships and in learning dialogues. The 'mediating' role of technology is redefined as an indirectly supportive role, resourcing, expanding and deepening learning dialogues between people and between different perspectives.

Studies of computer supported learning often refer to Vygotsky's notion of the mediation of cognition by technology when they need a theoretical grounding. Bakthin and 'dialogic' are frequently referred to in the same sentence or paragraph as references to Vygotsky as if they were quite compatible thinkers. The implication is that Bakhtin's account of thinking 'mediated' by the perspectives of others in a dialogue is compatible with Vygotsky's account of thinking mediated by tools, including language considered as a tool. I find this strange because, apart from the fact that they were both Soviet Russian males of the same age, Bakhtin and Vygotsky seem to have very little in common.

The concern to distinguish Bakhtin from Vygotsky might sound like a concern more appropriate to the study of the history of ideas rather than to educational technology. This is not the case, however, because how we understand the 'mediating' role of technology in cognition is central to debates about design frameworks for CSCL. Bakhtin's account of mediation by the perspective of others is radically different from Vygotsky's account of mediation by tool use. The application of Vygotsky's perspective tends to a view of technology in education as supporting the social construction of knowledge considered as some kind of artefact (e.g. as a 'knowledge object'), the dialogic perspective that I outlined in Chap. 1 focuses on the role of technology in deepening and expanding the space of dialogue as an end in itself. This is important because, from this perspective, knowledge is not an object but an event: 'spark of insight' is the metaphor that Bakhtin prefers. My argument is that the main question for CSCL, and education more generally, should not be, how do we build more objects but, how do we generate more insight.

1 WERTSCH'S NEO-VYGOTSKIAN THEORY OF EDUCATION

Jim Wertsch has emerged as a key theorist for educational technology. More than anyone else he is responsible for the synthesis of Vygotsky and Bakhtin often referred to as socio-cultural theory (Wertsch, 1991). His neo-Vygotskian account of how mind is mediated by cultural tools is both a theory of education and a theory of the role of technology in education (Wertsch, 1998). In this chapter, I focus particularly on a paper by Wertsch and Kazak first written in 2005 because it offers the clearest account yet of how Vygotsky's view of mediation can be generalized into a theory of education as a whole. However, the argument is more general than simply a critique of this paper since every claim which I take up can also be found in other writings by Wertsch or in which Wertsch is the lead author (there is a list in the references).

Wertsch often repeats that 'cultural tools have constraints as well as affordances' so he may well agree with me that, while his theory of learning as being taught how to use cultural tools illuminates some aspects of education, there are other aspects which it obscures. I have been influenced by Wertsch's work in the past and have found it useful in understanding and improving the way in which children are taught to think together through being drawn into particular ways of using language (see Chap. 9). However, I have become increasingly concerned that this version of socio-cultural theory does not provide an adequate account of how children learn to think creatively. I suspect that this is because creativity originates in the dialogic relation, rather than in the use of pre-existing cultural tools. Wertsch and Kazak's paper (In press) is the position paper in the section of a book on Theorizing Learning Practice that is headed 'dialogic theory of learning' yet in their paper they do not seriously discuss the issue of dialogic, pointing out that, since their theory is about mediation it is, therefore, about dialogue. I want to challenge the idea that the dialogic relation can be addressed through a focus on mediation by tools and I would also like to challenge the possible implication here that Vygotsky was a dialogic thinker. I will argue that accounts of learning dialogues in terms of what Wertsch calls their 'mediating means' presuppose the prior achievement of a dialogic relation between people through which signs can be interpreted as meaning something. While Vygotsky could reasonably be called a dialectical thinker, he is not a dialogical thinker. Wertsch is right to suggest that a focus on cultural tools is compatible with a dialogic account of learning but a dialogic account goes further and so leads to a different overall understanding of the nature and purpose of education.

2 VYGOTSKY AS A DIALECTICAL THINKER

I am always surprised when I read references in educational literature to Vygotsky as a 'dialogical' thinker (e.g. Wells, 1999; Kozulin, 1986; Shotter, 1993; and many more). I can only imagine that the passages which leap out at me when I read Vygotsky's main work, *Thinking and Speech* (also translated as *Thought and Language*), do not appear so significant to others. In Chap 6 of Thinking and Speech, Vygotsky affirms his commitment to a monologic philosophical position several times in terms which are so clear they could hardly be misunderstood. For example he uses the model of classical mathematics to suggest that ultimately concepts are all subsumed into a logical system which he refers to as a system of equivalences:

> The higher levels in the development of word meaning are governed by *the law of equivalence of concepts*, according to which any concept can be formulated in terms of other concepts in a countless number of ways. (Vygotsky, 1986, p. 199 emphasis in original)

He then uses an image of a global grid to affirm that this grid of concepts is a totalising system with an image rather similar to the current global positioning satellite network:

> If we imagine the totality of concepts as distributed over the surface of a globe, the location of every concept may be defined by means of a system of coordinates, corresponding to latitude and longitude in geography. One of these will indicate the location of a concept between the extremes of maximally generalised abstract conceptualisation and the immediate sensory grasp of an object – i.e. its degree of concreteness and abstraction. The second coordinate will represent the object reference of the concept. (Vygotsky, 1986, p. 199)

Many of those who quote Vygotsky as if he was a dialogic thinker compatible with Bakhtin are most influenced by the edited collection of translations of his work which appeared in 1978 under the title: *Mind in Society*. This collection is suspect as a representation of Vygotsky. The editors of this collection themselves point out in the preface that:

> In putting separate essays together we have taken significant liberties. The reader will encounter here not a literal translation of Vygotsky but rather our edited version from which we have omitted material that seemed redundant and to which we have added material that seemed to make his points clearer. (Cole et al., 1978, Preface, p. x)

Jim Wertsch acknowledges the possibility of a monological reading of Vygotsky in one article where he refers to Vygotsky as 'an enlightenment rationalist' (Wertsch, 1996). However, Wertsch claims, there is ambivalence in Vygotsky's texts and the implication of his theory of signs as psychological tools often led him beyond a simple one-way street view of development. One theme running through Vygotsky's work is dialectical method and his use of dialectical thinking might also explain this apparent ambivalence. A key feature of dialectic in Hegel and Marx is that it attempts to integrate real dialogues and struggles into a logical story of development leading to unity either in the 'Absolute Notion' of Hegel or the rational society under global communism of Marx. It is possible that Vygotsky engaged more with Hegel than with Marx (Van der Veer and Valsiner, 1991) and the influence of Hegelian dialectic is certainly very evident in many of his theoretical formulations. At one point Vygotsky implies that his whole approach to psychology can be described as the application of the Hegelian dialectic to the issue of individual cognitive development:

> Thus we may say that we become ourselves through others and that this rule applies not only to the personality as a whole, but also to the history of every individual function. This is the essence of the progress of cultural development expressed in a purely logical form. The personality becomes for itself what it is in itself through what it is for others (Vygotsky, 1991, p. 39).

The account he gives here of development from 'being-in-itself' to a more complex, self-related, 'being-for-itself' through the passage of 'being-for-others' is borrowed directly from Hegel (see, for example, Hegel, 1975, p. 139).

Dialectic and dialogic sound similar and often look similar. However, making a distinction between them is important for some versions of dialogic theory. For those postmodernists influenced by Levinas's ethical critique of monological reason, including Derrida and Lyotard, dialectic was often seen as the worst kind of monologic precisely because it was monologic dressed up to look like dialogic (Descombes, 1980). The argument is that the 'other' which often appears in the dialectic algorithm, is not genuinely other at all but merely a prop for the development and expansion of the 'self', in the form of a totalising system of explanation and control. 'Difference', Lévinas claims, is posited by dialectical thinking only to be appropriated and reduced to 'equivalence' in systems of 'representation' (Lévinas, 1989, p. 77). Like Buber, Lévinas was a Jewish theologian as well as a philosopher and he contrasted the 'egology' of western rationalism to the 'wisdom' of responding to the 'infinite' call of 'the Other', an infinite call that, he claimed, disrupts all totalising systems of thought.

Bakhtin was similarly clear about the significance of the important distinction to be made between dialectic and dialogic:

> Take a dialogue and remove the voices (the partitioning of voices), remove the intonations (emotional and individualizing ones), carve out abstract concepts and judgments from living words and responses, cram everything into one abstract consciousness – and that's how you get dialectics. (Bakhtin, 1986, p. 147)

To paraphrase and repeat Bakhtin's main point here: dialectic is a dynamic form of logic leading all apparent differences to be subsumed into identity in the form of a more complexly integrated synthesis, it is not dialogic since dialogic refers to the interanimation of real voices where there is no necessary 'overcoming' or 'synthesis'. I interpret the Vygotsky of Thinking and Speech as a dialectical thinker who gave dialogue a role in his theory of development. While he offers insights which have been read by some in a dialogic way, it is misleading to refer to him as a dialogic thinker or to refer to his theory of education and development as a dialogic theory.

3 LEARNING TO USE CULTURAL TOOLS AS A THEORY OF EDUCATION

Wertsch and Kazak (In press) ground their theory of teaching and learning on what they call the Vygotsky-Shpet perspective which they claim can be found in the last chapter of Thinking and Speech, Chap. 7, where Vygotsky writes about the development of word meaning. Although this sounds very specific to linguistics it is a restatement of arguments Wertsch made about the role of cultural tools in earlier works (e.g. Wertsch, 1998). It is interesting, Wertsch and Kazak write, that Vygotsky gives such importance in the last chapter of Thinking and Speech to his 'discovery' that word meanings change. This points us, they continue, to the way in which using signs often leads us to say more than we know that we are saying. So novices in a discourse may take up words that have complex meanings and use them with very limited understanding, but in a way that is sufficient for communication with teachers, who can thereby draw them up to more advanced levels of understanding. From this Wertsch and Kazak develop a more general theoretical position which is that all education is about 'know how' rather than 'know that' – specifically knowing how to use cultural tools appropriately and skillfully. The outcome of education, they say, is not individual cognition so much as distributed cognition between people and their cultural tools. The methodological challenge posed by this theory is the need to assess 'how well students have mastered words and other semiotic means'. Wertsch and Kazak illustrate how their theory helps us to understand the role of graph paper and key concept words in the Lehrer classroom data provided for the Allerton symposium within which the paper was first presented (see Koschmann, In press). In their analysis, cultural tools, such as words and graph paper, serve as a robust, yet flexible, mediating means, which enable inter-mental relations to be established even between people with very different levels of understanding.

Although Wertsch and Kazak base their theory on Vygotsky I am sure that they would agree that their reading is necessarily a selective one due to the ambivalence in Vygotsky referred to often by Wertsch (1985: 1996). It is therefore worth saying more about what Vygotsky himself might have meant by the idea, that is perhaps implicit in his work, that we say more than we know when we use words. In Chap. 7 of *Thinking and Speech*, Vygotsky makes a distinction between a word's proper meaning and the contingent 'sense' of words that stems from the associations that they form from the ways in which they are used. The 'meaning' of words for Vygoksky is, he repeats several times, a 'generalisation or a concept'. In earlier chapters of *Thinking and Speech*, Vygotsky outlines the development of the meaning of words from contextualised and concrete uses (syncretism) through fuzzy generalisations (complexes) to proper concepts (Vygotsky, 1987: also see commentary by Van der Veer and Valsiner, 1991, p. 263). The higher stages of concepts are characterised by more abstraction and generalisation (Wertsch, 1996, p. 25) while the lower are characterised as based upon more contingent, concrete and fuzzy criteria. Vygotsky described the initial stage of children's thinking as 'participatory', a style of thinking which Vygotsky claims that children share with primitive people and with schizophrenics, (Vygotsky, 1986, p. 236) while the highest stage of thinking is characterised as abstract rationality exemplified by the 'law of equivalence', which I quoted above.

From this account of the development of concepts, it would make sense if Vygotsky were to suggest that we mean more than we know that we mean when we begin using potential concept-words, because, simply by using them, we are taking the first step on a one-way journey that will lead us all the way up into pure reason and scientific thought. 'Sign-vehicles', on this theory, act like a kind of ski-lift for development; children can latch on to them while still in the valleys of concrete thought (which is, he thinks, 'schizophrenic', 'primitive' and 'participatory' thought) and be lifted by them to the high-altitude universal abstractions of reason and science. According to Vygotsky, the mechanism that drives this ski-lift is formal education. In the 'zone of proximal development' (see Chap. 1) teachers engage with children in order to train their spontaneous concepts into the already laid down routes of scientific concepts.

Wertsch and Kazak sum up their theory with the formula:

> the act of speaking often (perhaps always) involves employing a sign system that forces us to say more (as well as perhaps less) than what we understand or intend.

The addition here, of the small escape clause 'as well as perhaps less' in brackets, shows their caution in relation to Vygotsky's ski-lift theory of development. But can Vygotsky's theory survive transplantation if the intrinsic telos of concepts towards abstraction, generalisation and Truth is removed? What is the value of a ski-lift that does not carry us up a mountain? As Wertsch and Kazak themselves point out, words can be taken to mean more than we know because of the way that others interpret them and so they can also sometimes be taken to mean less than we know or they could be taken to mean something completely different. Certainly words like 'histogram', which figure in the account of the classroom data of Lehrer and Snabel which they analyse and which I re-analyse below, have a dictionary meaning, which the teacher leads the students towards, however, the *proper* meaning of such terms is presumably defined by the curriculum. If so then the same approach could be applied to teaching any content whatsoever, including, for example, scholastic doctrine about the numbers and the powers of the Cherubim and Seraphim in medieval Byzantium or Nazi accounts of the physiological differences between Aryans and Jews. This theory accounts for how we teach defined meanings in the existing curriculum, but it does not appear to offer a place for the development of new meanings through critical thinking and through creativity.

4 REVISITING VYGOTSKY'S EXAMPLES

Wertsch and Kazak ask the question: 'how is it that we can know more than we say?' This is, they imply, a version of the bigger question 'how is learning possible?' Their answer appears to involve the claim that engagement with signs and cultural tools has some sort of intrinsic force that carries people beyond themselves into the pre-established culture. This may be because of the cultural uses that have shaped the signs and tools in the past but it is also because 'robust' sign-vehicle can be engaged with at varying levels of understanding thus serving as a focus for inter-subjectivity between teachers and students. Wertsch and Kazak attribute this claim to Vygotsky, especially to Chap. 7 of *Thinking and Speech*. While not challenging this interpretation of Vygotsky's intentions, I think it is interesting that in Chap. 7 of *Thinking and Speech*, Vygotsky offers an example from Tolstoy that, if attended to closely, suggests a different view. This alternative view is that it is *other people* who lead us to greater understanding in dialogues and not the signs that we use.

Vygtosky quotes an incident from Anna Karenina (Vygotsky, 1986, p. 237), which he writes, was based upon Tolstoy's own experience, in which Kitty and Levin declare their love for each other in a written dialogue using the first letters of words in place of full words. For example:

She wrote: I c n a o t.

His face brightened suddenly: he had understood. It meant: 'I could not answer otherwise then.'

Somehow, despite the almost impossibly minimal nature of the signs involved, they manage to understand each other perfectly. Cheyne and Tarulli (1999) point out that Vygotsky's expressed intention in this passage is to illustrate how language use becomes abbreviated as it approaches the unity and silence of inner speech. This incident, when isolated by Vygotsky, seems, as Cheyne and Tarulli comment, 'far-fetched' but in the novel 'Anna Karenina' itself Tolstoy sets up this scene with a previous dialogue that helps us to understand it. The setting is a gathering in a grand house. At dinner the role of women had been discussed. When Kitty and Levin meet up later in the drawing room Levin continues this topic. Tolstoy writes:

Levin was of the opinion of Darya Alexandrovna that a girl who did not marry should find a woman's duties in a family. He supported this view by the fact that no family can get on without women to help; that in every family, poor or rich, there are and must be nurses, either relations or hired.

"No," said Kitty, blushing, but looking at him all the more boldly with her truthful eyes; "a girl may be so circumstanced that she cannot live in the family without humiliation, while she herself..."

At the hint he understood her.

"Oh, yes," he said. "Yes, yes, yes – you're right; you're right!"

And he saw all that Pestsov had been maintaining at dinner of the liberty of woman, simply from getting a glimpse of the terror of an old maid's existence and its humiliation in Kitty's heart; and loving her, he felt that terror and humiliation, and at once gave up his arguments.

It is just after this dialogue that Kitty sits at a card table and taking up the chalk, starts doodling leading to the exchange of cryptic sentences reported by Vygotsky. However, with this prior exchange, Tolstoy has introduced us to the 'mechanism', through which they are able to achieve the extraordinarily close understanding described. Theirs is not some sort of static silent unanimity of coinciding souls but an active dialogue between two people with different backgrounds and different views. Tolstoy makes it clear that Levin does not discover the case for the emancipation of women through arguments of any kind but through a single look in Kitty's eyes that enables him, suddenly and immediately, to experience the world from her point-of-view. Tolstoy makes it very clear that the most important 'mediating means' of their later understanding is not the chalk, the card table, the letters of the alphabet or the implicit words behind the letters – but their love for each other and the 'mutual envelopment' that results, allowing each to reverse their roles and think what the other might be trying to say even before they say it.

If signs play a small role in the understanding achieved by Kitty and Levin they play an even smaller role in the next extract from literature that Vygotsky offers. This is a description by Dostoevsky of what he calls a whole conversation carried out by a group of drunk workmen using only a single expletive. Each time this expletive is spoken it carries with it an attitude which leads to a response repeating the same word but with a different emotional tone. The word here has no positive content at all, it is a shared focusing device, a vehicle for the expression of feelings and a kind of 'hinge' around which the conversation can revolve.

5 TWO TRIANGLES FOR THINKING ABOUT DIALOGUE AND DEVELOPMENT

Anne Edwards argues convincingly that Vygotsky's most significant contribution to educational studies is the idea of tool mediated action (Edwards, 2005). She illustrates the significance of this with examples of how the way in which young children solve arithmetic problems reveals the tools that they are using, which may be external tools such as pencil and paper or mental strategies. Following Vygotsky, she presents this in diagrammatic form as a mediation triangle (see Fig. 3.1).

Vygotsky does not claim to have originated this triangle but attributes the basic idea that 'mind is mediated' to Hegel. He quote's Hegel's account of 'the cunning of Reason' or how Reason achieves its intended ends indirectly 'by causing objects to act and react on each other in accordance with their own nature' (Vygotsky, 1978, p. 54). Vygotsky continues with a quote from 'Das Capital' where Marx applies this Hegelian concept of mediation to understand human tool use, describing how the physical properties of objects are used by 'man' as 'forces that affect other objects in order to fulfil his personal goals' (Marx, Capital, p. 199, quoted by Vygotsky, 1978, p. 54). According to Vygotsky, signs can be subsumed under the category of tools because they mediate our actions in a similar way. Marx explicitly included language and consciousness as 'tools', in this sense, referring to language as 'practical consciousness' implying that it is first a tool for the coordination of productive activity and then becomes internalised (Marx, 1977, p. 167).

Vygotsky's originality, therefore, lies not in the idea that cognition is mediated by signs and tools, an idea already central to Hegelian and Marxist dialectic, but in applying this dialectic to individual psychology in order to sketch an account of the development of the 'higher mental faculties'. To illustrate this Vygotsky gives the simple example of how tying a knot in a handkerchief can be used as a tool to aide memory (Vygotsky, 1978, p. 51). The knot-sign then becomes a cognitive tool whose aim is not to change objects in the world but to control internal mental processes. In a similar way he claims that rational thought results from the 'internalisation' of 'scientific' language mediated by formal schooling (e.g. Vygotsky, 1986: p. 206; Daniels, 2001, p. 53–55).

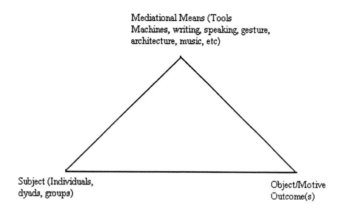

Fig. 3.1. Vygotsky's mediational triangle (version from Edwards, 2005)

Bakhtin's dialogic perspective, described in detail in the previous chapter, Chap. 2, was developed as a contrast to the dialectic assumed by Vygotsky. That this dialogic perspective is not easily compatible with Vygotsky's account of education, can be brought out through reconsidering Vygotsky's analysis of the how children first learn to use signs by learning how to point. Vygotsky writes that infants grasp towards an object that they want but cannot reach and then their mother, interpreting their reaching action as a desire for the object, gives them the object. Eventually, Vygotsky claims, infants learn sign-mediated action, that is they learn that they can achieve their desires through others by using signs (Vygotsky, 1981, pp. 160–161 quoted by Wertsch, 1985, p. 64). Wertsch takes this account of learning how to point to be paradigmatic of the teaching and learning of cultural tools in general. It sums up Vygotsky's account of mediated action in the zone of proximal development whereby teachers interpret children's spontaneous sign use ahead of the children's conscious understanding in order to draw them, at first unconsciously, into a more culturally mediated use of signs (Wertsch, 1998, p. 133).

However, Vygotsky's account of how children learn to point through trying first to act directly on the external world has been questioned by more recent work in developmental psychology. Baron-Cohen provides convincing experimental evidence that autistic children have no trouble mastering 'proto-imperative' use of pointing to show that they want something but fail to master more communicative 'proto-declarative' use of pointing as a sign intended to direct another's interest (Baron-Cohen, 1994, quoted by Vila, 1996, p. 194). Peter Hobson argues from this, and other evidence, that the establishment of an initial dialogic relationship with the mother (or other primary caregiver) is an essential precursor to the development of decalrative pointing and all other forms of symbolising. Those infants who, for whatever reason, fail to establish a dialogic relationship with their mothers, fail to follow the mother's gaze and so fail to understanding 'pointing' as a sign (Hobson, 2002, 1998).

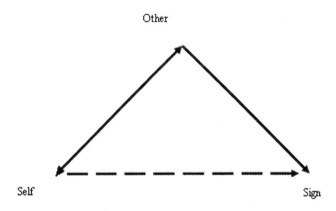

Fig. 3.2. Self-other-sign adapted from Hobson and Moscovici

Hobson's straightforward claim is that infants learn to read and to use signs in the context of a dialogic relationship which first gives those signs a meaning. He illustrates this with a self-other-sign mediation triangle (a similar 'dialogic' triangle is offered by Moscovici (1984) reproduced in Markova, 2003, p. 152).

As with infants learning to point, a dialogic perspective argues that education more generally takes place within dialogic human relationships in which students learn to see things from at least two perspectives at once, their own point of view and that of their teacher.

The self-other-sign triangle makes mediation by others look similar to, and therefore perhaps compatible with, mediation by tools. However, as Bakhtin points out, relationships between things are very different from relationships between voices (Bakhtin, 1986, pp. 138 and 162). For each participant in a dialogue the voice of the other is an outside perspective that includes them within it. The boundary between subjects is not therefore a demarcation line, or an external link between self and other, but an inclusive 'space' within which self and other mutually construct and reconstruct each other. Any sign taken to be a mediation between self and other, a word or a facial expression, must pre-suppose the prior opening of a space of dialogue within which such a sign can be taken to mean something.

The argument here about a modest difference between two triangular representations of 'mediation' has implications for theories of development and of education. Wertsch and Kazak's theory is that the use of cultural tools carries us beyond ourselves. This seems to follow from Fig. 3.1, the subject-tool-object triangle, as does their idea that the aim of education is to draw learners into the effective use of cultural tools. An alternative approach is that we are carried beyond ourselves by learning to take the perspective of other people. This is represented in Fig. 3.2, the self-other-sign triangle. On this, more dialogic account, language and culture are seen as an inexhaustible field of perspectives that open up in the space between people in dialogue. While the first triangle suggests the aim of education as the mastery of tools, the second suggests the aim of being drawn our beyond the self towards understanding of the other and, through the specific other, out to otherness in general.

6 UNPICKING THE 'SYNTHESIS' OF VYGOTSKY AND BAKHTIN

As was mentioned in Chap. 2 Wertsch refers to Bakhtin's contrast between the 'authoritative' and the 'persuasive' word in his book *Voices of the Mind* and elaborates from this a theory of learning as appropriating the voices of others based on Bakhtin's own account of how we appropriate the words of others:

The word in language is half someone else's. It becomes "one's own" only when the speaker populates it with his intention, with his own accent, when he appropriates the word, adapting it to his own semantic and expressive intention. (Bakhtin, 1986, pp. 293–294)

Wertsch used another idea from Bakhtin to describe the process of appropriating the voices of others as involving stages of 'ventriloquation' whereby learners begin by speaking the voices of others without integrating them and then gradually, the initially foreign voices become indistinguishable from their own voice (Wertsch, 1991). This account replaces Vygotsky's concept of the internalization of tools with Bakhtin's account of the appropriation of cultural voices but remains within Vygotsky's developmental framework to argue that learning involves the appropriation of cultural voices.

However, a 'voice' is not a tool but an answer to the question 'who is speaking'. This raises a conceptual problem for Wertsch's synthesis of Bakhtin and Vygotsky: are we appropriating cultural voices or are they appropriating us? The problem of 'ventriloquation' as an educational 'tool' can be dramatized through an example from ethnography. When a Tibetan oracle priest invokes a protective deity and allows that deity to speak through his voice he loses consciousness and can remember nothing at all of what the spirit said and did when in possession of his body (Govinda, 1988, pp. 178–192). From the modernist perspective embodied in Vygotsky's subject-tool-object triangle, it is clear that the 'deity' here is a cultural tool used by the priest, but from inside the local cultural context it is equally clear that the deity is the agent and the priest is the tool. In a similar way in education it is not obvious that students appropriate an 'educated voice', for example, as a tool or whether this voice appropriates and makes use of students. The idea that, in education, discourses acquire subjects is a recognized 'post-modern' theme often sourced to Foucault (e.g. Walkerdine, 1988).

Bakhtin points out that all words are voiced and have traces of multiple voices. He writes, in a comment on structuralism: 'But I hear *voices* in everything and dialogic relations between them' (Bakhtin, 1978, p. 169). One implication of this is brought out by Merleau-Ponty when he writes that signs 'possess us' as much as we possess them (Merleau-Ponty, 1968, pp. 151, 190). Vygotsky also, possibly, referred to this in an indirect way when he quoted Levy-Bruhl to describe the pre-conceptual thought of children and 'primitive' people as 'participatory' and similar to the thinking of schizophrenics (Vygotsky, 1986, p. 236). Vygotsky's account of development involved the dialectical overcoming of participatory thought in the direction of a rational adult self. A dialogic perspective, on the other hand, assumes such 'participation' as the ineluctable context of thought.

7 AN EMPIRICAL ILLUSTRATION OF THE ARGUMENT

To illustrate the implication of their focus on cultural tools for education Wertsch and Kazak offer an analysis of data from a science classroom provided by Rick Lehrer and colleagues (Koschmann, In press; Lehrer and Snhauble, 2004). In the data the children are being helped to learn about histograms by graphing the heights of plants that they were previously growing in such a way that they can discover the average height. Wertsch and Kazak's theory of learning as learning how to use cultural tools leads them to offer an account of how teachers draw children into the desired use of graph paper. The focus on the dialogic relationships between people within which learning occurs, which I propose in this chapter as a corrective to Wertsch and Kazak's focus on tools, does not aspire to replace this account but to augment it. To show how this might work in practice I will revisit in turn each of Wertsch and Kazak's illustrations of their theory from the data.

7.1 Illustration 1: Teacher–student interaction

This illustration demonstrates the practical value of Wertsch's synthesis of Vygotsky's zone of proximal development idea and Bakthin's idea of the appropriation. If the pedagogical objective is to teach how to use histograms, as it seems to be here, then there is little point just modelling how to make histograms because this will not be taken in by the learners. The best way to teach this is to engage students in the problem for which histograms are a solution, that is the problem of representing a spread of data in a way which makes finding typical values possible, and then, once they have struggled with this problem, to offer them histograms as a solution to what has now become 'their' problem. This is exactly what we see happening in this extract. The students engage with the problem and eventually the teacher (in fact the researcher Leona Snhauble acting as a teacher) uses the group's shared focus on the graph paper as a way of guiding them to the solution – histograms. When the solution is offered the whole group appear to understand how it solves their problem and they seem pleased with it and even grateful to the teacher for giving it to them.

The teacher here sits as part of the group, seeming to hunch down so that she does not tower over the children, often with her hand over her mouth. When, 23 min into the activity, she moves to propose a way forward, she does so in a very tentative and hypothetical way, her hand hovering over the graph paper as if very unsure and working out the solution as she goes along.

Transcript Extract 1: Teacher showing group how to make a histogram.

(Day 27: 24.14 to 26.19)
Notes: The teacher is LS; {indicates overlapping speech; (.) indicates a pause and figures give the length of the pause, / indicates a chunk

LS	Well what if we had a column, (0.5) say (0.5) let me think about this for a minute (.) 200 and 30, 225 250 (.) what if we did something and we had one square and we said lets put all the ones in there that go from this to this and then every number that was in that value we'd put a little X (0.5) you know like the frequency checks we did before?
Elena	ohh!
LS	So you could make, kind of, a way of seeing more X's when there are more (3.0) I'm not making myself very clear, am I?
Jane	I don't know what you're talking about actually (laughs)
Elena	But we could, we…
LS	Do you get a sense of what I'm talking about, Jane?
Elena	Yeah but
Jane	That's Elan (laughter about LS's mistake over the name)
Tod	Say it again (.) maybe they'd follow (.) because if you know, they don't listen. (pointing to girls) Say it again.
LS	No, I wasn't very clear (.) I was thinking (.) we certainly don't have 225 numbers across here so if we said let us a square and put al the once that go from say 30 to 50 or 60 and then every time we see a number you could put an x above it? … You understand what I'm saying?
Elena	Yeah
LS	So It would give {a line of xs for all the numbers between 30 and 60
Elena	{and then could like put
LS	And then {we'd have another square between 60 and 90
Elena	{and then we do like 90
LS	LS: Or maybe we could do it with 20 I don't know lets count/20 40 60 80 1–20 40 60 80 1/I don't know (.) maybe we could even do it by tens/10 20 30 40 80 1 – 20 30 40 50 60 80 90 1/If we did every ten (.) every group of 10
Elena	OK, yeh we could do that
LS	Well that's one way of doing it but I don't know if it makes sense to you guys?
Jane	That's a good idea
Elena	It makes sense to me
Tod	Oh, I get it, so yeah – yeah – so there'd be… (He seems to lose his sense of what he is saying and starts laughing and they all laugh with him)
Elena	Ok, we {have 10…
Tod	{So the ones … you'd write one through ten?

The teacher's tentativeness in this transcript with frequent use of 'I don't know' and 'Let's think' and 'maybe' and the many hesitant pauses, contrasts markedly with the certainty she expresses in her notes when she writes:

```
These kids seemed incredibly clumsy with
organizing this rather large data set
(larger than we've seen before). Even
putting the numbers in serial order was
difficult and time consuming for these kids.
```

This contrast in the texts here suggests that her tentativeness, either consciously or intuitively, was intended to open up the text of her speech to the others. Her pauses here were not empty; they were filled with the facial expressions of the children in the group, showing their comprehension or lack of it. The teacher constantly searched their faces to check their response and everything she said was tailored to that response. At first she sees, from their faces, that they don't understand so she apologises and tries again. This time she succeeds in drawing them into her perspective partly by pretending that she does not know what she is doing and modelling the process of working it out from scratch. The children join her in doing this, following her gaze and her gestures as she approaches the graph paper. When she counts the lines on the graph they were all counting together (at least those whose mouths were visible on the film), moving their lips in unison with her words. After this she says:

Well that's one way of doing it, but I don't know if it makes
sense to you guys?

And this time they all seem to get it and the children start talking now, making explicit how they are going to set about doing the graph.

The teacher is not the only one contributing to the construction of the dialogic space in the group. Clancey has also analysed this same data and he brings out how the humour in this group, mainly originating with one boy, implies holding more than one perspective at once and so loosens the grip of identity thinking and facilitates the flow of new meanings (Clancey, In press, see also my account of 'playful talk' as a source of creativity in Chap. 4). Elena also contributes actively, supporting the teacher and sustaining her with her smiling gaze and her agreements. Twice Elena starts talking at the same time as the teacher and carries on in parallel to the teacher for a while. Just looking at the transcript it might appear as if she is trying to take the floor and is being drowned out by the dominant voice of the teacher but on the video it looks more like the teacher's voice comes in as a supporting voice, making audible Bakhtin's 'answering words' that run parallel to the words of the other as we appropriate the voice of the other into our voice.

The central role played by the graph paper in this episode might be related to the fact that a particular use of this graph paper is the teaching objective of the activity. Wertsch and Kazak claim that the graph paper, as a 'sign-vehicle' and robust cultural tool, is facilitating the creation of intersubjectivity between teacher and children. However, in her notes on the day the teacher (in fact researcher Leona Snhauble) seems to think that the graph paper might have been a problem.

> Maybe passing out graph paper was the source
> of some of the confusion, for example, kids
> looking for ways to make coordinate systems.
> The graph paper, coming in close conjunction
> with the recent graphs of the wicking, may
> have pushed some of the kids in that
> direction.

It seems that the children might have been misled by what they saw as the 'affordance' of the graph paper for plotting co-ordinates. This reminds me of the similar issue that often arises with key words in teaching science. Everyday words, like 'force' are given a special meaning in science which leads to confusions. Teachers often complain that it is much easier to teach a new concept with a new word that is untainted with everyday associations. While, clearly, the children are being taught how to use a cultural tool, it is not obvious that it helps to maintain intersubjectivity at different levels of understanding, this is the job done by the dialogic relationship established between teacher and the learners. The teacher has to lead the children to lift their attention from the graph, which seems to speak to them of co-ordinates, in order to carry them along a different path with her voice, her gaze and her gestures.

It is not obvious to me that all learning is learning how to use cultural tools, as Wertsch and Kazak claim. What if the pedagogical objective was something quite different such as learning that 'the Battle of Hastings took place in 1066' or, 'learning how to love'? From a more dialogical perspective, what is general to many types of learning is the importance of establishing a 'robust' dialogic relationship between teachers and learners, or between groups of co-learners: relationships between people that are capable of sustaining within them different levels of intersubjective understanding about the pedagogical aim, *whatever that happens to be.*

7.2 Illustration II: Student-student interaction

In Wertsch and Kazak's second illustration they seem to argue that a group of children do not really know what they are doing until a teacher comes along and, using the graph paper to support intermental engagement, steers them in the right direction. This account does not do full justice to the efforts that the group make to sort out their different perspectives and to find a shared way forward before the teacher arrives. They seem very engaged with the task, challenging freely, responding to challenges with reasons and struggling hard to find ways to understand each other. At one point there is a dramatic transition when Alice suddenly sees a point that Janice and Watt have been making, which is, if I have understood it correctly, about how the structure of the graph can indicate information so that each datapoint on the graph does not need to be fully labelled. At this transition there is an evident release of tension from their faces and bodies and a 'marking and celebration' of their achievement (Packer, In press).

Changing one's mind in an argument is a very interesting phenomenon and could perhaps serve as a focus in any analysis of the micro-genesis of understanding in dialogue. Alice precedes her change of mind by listening intently to Janice then turning her head away from Janice a little, as if for a moment of private thought, then she lifts her head slowly with a long drawn out 'Ohhh!' her eyes widen as her mouth opens into the 'O' shape which is at the same time a kind of smile. I assume that this dramatic enactment of a new understanding is cultural in origin but I don't really know that and the physiological basis of opening ones eyes wider in this way to indicate new insight would be interesting to explore. Is it the argument that Julia has just given that enables her to see things so differently? Before Alice's conversion, Watt had just said:

"That's what you're telling them with the graph – that's why we're making the graph!"

And then Janice had added:

"We're saying: 'it's day nineteen, – how is it going?'"

making an exaggerated welcoming gesture with her hand drawing in an imaginary viewer to look at the graph.

It seems that Alice's change of mind here does not stem from the force of any abstract logic so much as from a shift in perspective to see the graph from a projected future point of view – the point of view of the addressee of the graph as a vehicle for communication. The signs that lead to this change of mind are not 'tools' but 'epiphanic' signs (Leimann, 2002) on the model of the invocation of a voice, for example the gesture of drawing in the alternative perspective.

There was also some loss of face involved in this change of mind. Janice immediately sits down and says 'Finally!' smiling smugly up to the camera.

Alice then feels obliged to dispute Janice's implicit claim to have caused her change of mind, saying:

'You weren't making that point though!' wagging her finger at Janice.

Clearly there was something at stake for her in not changing her mind and yet she found herself forced, almost despite herself, to see their point. In the act of changing her mind she is divided within herself. A dialogical account of the self from Hermans et al. (1992) or Valsiner (2004) would suggest that there are multiple I-positions at play and that the change of mind itself is a bit like a political 'coup' as one group take over control of the means of expression. However, the leverage that enables this does not come from the graph paper here but from the idea of the addressee of the finished graph considered as an outside and future perspective projected forward from the dialogue and yet influencing it from within.

The quality of the relationships in the group is crucial to this achievement of unforced agreement. Although there is an element of what Mercer calls 'disputational' talk in this group, which is conversation as a kind of competition which participants try to win and lose (Mercer, 2000) it is primarily 'exploratory talk' illustrated by the fact that reasons are given and minds can change. Types of dialogue can be characterised through intersubjective orientations and shared ground rules (Wegerif and Mercer, 1997). The ground rules operating in this group mean that challenges are responded to with reasons, not with breakdown of communication, and that changes of mind are possible, although, as we have seen, quite difficult.

This group work constructively together and do seem to be learning about perspective taking and about the affordances of graphs. However, they are perhaps not learning fast enough, from the point of view of the teachers, about how to use histograms. Eventually a researcher acting as a teacher (Richard Lehrer) intervenes to point them in the right direction. He is not part of the group but stands to one side. Although the learners do take on board his suggestions they do so in a very different spirit from the way in which Alice changed her mind in the face of arguments from Watt and Janice. In the first 'change of mind' incident Janice is excited and fully engaged with the task, as are the others. After the teacher intervention, however, she sits back looking disengaged and says:

'Who is gonna to erase all this cos I don't wanna'

The exaggerated slurring together of syllables in her speech matches her body posture and facial expression. The impression is that, for Janice at this moment at least, the teacher's guidance here leads to resistance rather than to appropriation.

Anyone comparing the video sequence transcribed in illustration I above, when the teacher successfully draws the children into her way of seeing, with that in illustration II would see immediately that the teacher in the second example is not positioned as part of the group because he is standing to one side and towering over them. Of course this is only one incident in a continuing relationship. When the same teacher returns to the group it is noticeable that he squats down to be at their height. However, small incidents can be revealing of how dialogic relations support or hinder understanding. If we compare these two incidents we can see something of the different effects on learners of what Bakhtin calls the internal, 'persuasive' voice as opposed to the outside, 'authoritative' voice.

8 DISCUSSION AND CONCLUSION

Wertsch and Kazak are persuasive that, in the Lehrer data, children are being led to use a cultural tool appropriately. However, my re-analysis of the same data, suggests that this kind of learning takes place through dialogic relations within which people can interpret each others signs and take each others perspectives. It is the quality of these relationships, more than the robust nature of the cultural tool, that determine whether or not the teacher's words are successfully appropriated. Clearly the focus on the role of cultural tools in Wertsch and Kazak's analysis, and my focus on the dialogic relation, can be combined. However, as a general account of education, Wertsch and Kazak's focus on the role of tools seems to be limited in a way that a focus on dialogic relations is not.

Dialogic teaching should not aim only at the appropriation of particular voices in a debate but also the 'appropriation' of the dialogical space of the debate. Such teaching combines the construction of knowledge with what could reasonably be called the 'de-construction' of knowledge. By this I mean only that it is possible to promote awareness of the field of possibilities at the same time as teaching a particular use. It would be interesting, adopting a community of inquiry approach, to explore with the class exactly what is gained and what is lost when a piece of white paper is divided up by a grid and so turned into 'graph paper'. The aim of a dialogic approach to teaching is to maintain a relation between the foreground figures that are being taught and the background open potential for meaning from which these figures emerge and to which they return.

Wertsch and Kazak's account of education as domestication of the imaginations of children may well reflect aspects of the current reality of education but it should not be used to define the limits of education. Dialogic theory suggests that a different approach to education is possible, an approach through which the taking of multiple perspectives can be encouraged and valued. All representations can be taught as moments in an ongoing dialogue or as provisional possibilities in a boundaryless field of potential meanings. In Chap. 4, I will argue that this induction into a space of possibility is the basis of education for creativity. Through this kind of teaching dialogue emerges as, not only a means to achieving shared knowledge, but, more importantly, as an end in itself.

The Vygotskian account of mediation by tools, including words, that is advocated and applied by Wertsch and Kazak, leads to a description of how learners are drawn beyond themselves by cultural tools. A dialogic account of mediation by the perspective of others leads to a focus on the quality and nature of teaching and learning relationships and shows how learners are drawn beyond themselves by learning to see through other's eyes. It is interesting that, in the example, the others in question were not just the specific others addressed, nor the teachers, but 'a third' or 'superaddressee' (Bakhtin, 1986, p. 125). In this case this third perspective was a projected future audience for the work being constructed. They were pulled beyond themselves, not by the communicative tools they were using but by entering into a kind of dialogue with the future addressee of their communication. The Vygotskian perspective gives technology a direct role in teaching and learning which is understood as learning how to use cultural tools. A dialogic perspective gives technology a more indirect role, as serving to open, maintain, resource, expand and deepen the space of dialogue between people and within people, a space of dialogue which allows for creativity and learning. This role of technology is described in more depth and detail in Chap. 8.

Summary

I began this chapter by rejecting the common idea that Bakhtin and Vygotsky are compatible and can be combined in a single 'socio-cultural' research tradition. Vygotsky, I argued, was a dialectical thinker and not a dialogic thinker. In fact Bakhtin's dialogic was expressly developed in contrast to the kind of Hegelian dialectic that Vygotsky adopts and applies to education. I presented various arguments to show that dialectic mediation by tools and dialogic mediation by taking the perspective of the other in a dialogue are very different ideas with different implications for teaching and learning. The empirical study included in this paper argued that applying dialogic leads to a different focus in studies of learning. Whereas the Vygotskian focus on tools, including words, advocated by Wertsch and Kazak, leads to an account of how learners are drawn beyond themselves by cultural tools, a dialogic perspective focuses on relationships and shows how learners are drawn beyond themselves by taking the perspective of others and otherness in general. This dialogic perspective on mediation suggests a different role for educational technology. Rather than mediating learning directly technology can be used to open, maintain, resource, expand and deepen learning dialogues between people. Against the metaphor of knowledge as some kind of object with the corollary that the aim of education should be inducting people into the skills that they need for construction, I have argued in favour of the metaphor of understanding as a spark, or arc light, of illumination with the corollary that education needs to create and support the conditions that produce more sparks and more illumination.

Chapter 4

REASON
Dialogic as a direction

In this chapter I apply the dialogic account of education developed Chaps. 2 and 3 to the issue of teaching thinking. I use evidence from empirical studies of talk in classrooms to argue that thinking can be taught by improving the quality of dialogues. What groups and individuals appear to be learning as they learn to think better on tasks such as reasoning test problems, is not simply specific skills and strategies but also a more general capacity to engage in dialogue. I describe this as a shift in identity towards identifying with the space of dialogue and I argue that this direction is the primary thinking skill from which other skills such as creativity and reasoning develop.

1 BACKGROUND AND INTRODUCTION

In the mid-1990s I worked with Neil Mercer and Lyn Dawes on ways of improving the educational quality of the talk of small groups of primary school children working together around computers. We developed an intervention that promoted ground rules that we thought would improve the quality of collaborative learning and thinking. Initially we assessed the effectiveness of this intervention in improving the quality of the talk of groups of children by video recording and transcribing children working together in groups of three around computer software before and after the intervention promoting ground-rules for talk. This enabled me to compare the kind of talk that they used both qualitatively and quantitatively (Wegerif, 1996a).

I was not totally happy with this method because, while I could show that the talk of some of the groups we selected changed between the pre- and the post-test in ways that we wanted and that teachers found desirable, I could not show, to my own satisfaction at least, that the post-test talk was really 'better' talk. My unresolved questions were: did the way of talking we were promoting really help the children to 'learn' or to 'solve problems' or to 'think'? And if so how exactly did it do this? I therefore proposed an off-computer experimental assessment of the quality of talk using non-verbal reasoning tests. The fact that these tests had right or wrong answers and that, for individuals, solving them correlated with educational achievement helped provide a clearer measure of the 'success' of the talk that the children were using (for examples see Figs. 4.1–4.3). As well as providing quantitative results that could be statistically analysed, the other great benefit of this experimental design for me was that, by analysing the video recordings of groups of children talking together on these test problems, we could see what kind of talk helped them to solve the problem and get a correct answer and what kind of talk actually hindered them from solving the problem together.

We used versions of Raven's Progressive Matrices, a test that has been widely used since the 1920s and that has the advantage, already mentioned, of correlating well with academic achievement and also with 'g', a statistical construct from various tests that some associate with the idea of general intelligence (Carpenter et al., 1990, p. 428, see Perkins, 1995, for a good discussion of 'g' and intelligence tests). As well as 'testing' children working collaboratively in groups we also gave children commensurable tests working as individuals. The results of the initial study suggested that the intervention programme we devised of teaching children how to talk more effectively did indeed improve their ability to solve these reasoning test problems both when working together and also, interestingly, when working as individuals. These results have since been supported by various follow-up studies on the same model in the UK and Mexico (there is a summary of all studies in Wegerif et al., 2005).

At the time, writing with my collaborators, I presented the results of this study as evidence in support of Vygotsky's thesis that 'all that is internal in the higher mental functions was at one time external' (Vygotsky, 1991, p. 36). This seemed to make sense. 'Reasoning' is often referred to as a higher mental function, perhaps the highest, and we had taught children how to engage in reasoning externally and the statistical evidence suggested that they had, to some extent, 'internalised' the way of thinking that they had first learnt talking together with others. The fact that ways of talking together should have a measurable impact on tests of thinking ability, both when used to measure group thinking and when used to measure individual thinking, was presented in terms of Vygotsky's claim that language can serve as a cultural tool 'mediating' cognition such that learning to use language in appropriate ways is the same as learning to think. However, even as I argued for this conclusion I felt uncomfortable with it. It was not that this was not true but it seemed to leave out the most important thing which was the mystery of how people actually solved the problems together. I knew that the evidence was more ambiguous and complex than the Vygotskian story of using words as tools seemed to suggest.

Following Douglas Barnes, Neil Mercer had labelled the 'productive' way of talking together that we were promoting 'exploratory talk' and defined this by saying that 'reasoning is visible in the talk' (Mercer, 1995, p. 102). This definition, plus the use of reasoning tests to assess the impact of the teaching of exploratory talk, as well as an analysis of transcripts that included counting the incidence of logical connectors such as 'because' (Wegerif and Mercer, 2000) produced the impression that our focus was teaching explicit reasoning. However, actual practice in classrooms where we worked with teachers to promote more 'exploratory talk' was much more than modelling and rewarding explicit reasoning. The requirement to 'give reasons' was just one of the list of ten or so 'ground rules' which we suggested could be used to help define exploratory talk; other 'ground rules' included respecting the opinions of others, allowing them time to speak, encouraging them to give a view, asking open 'why' questions, exploring alternatives before converging on agreement, and many more (Wegerif and Mercer, 1997). In practice there was a focus on establishing an atmosphere of mutual trust in which all children were included as respected participants in a process of shared thinking.

In this chapter, I will re-evaluate some of the evidence presented by earlier publications as an argument for the claim that ways of using language can serve as a tool for thinking. I do not argue that this was or is a false account, but rather that it is a misleading account. The evidence suggests that the main way in which ways of using language can serve as a tool that supports thinking is not directly, as Vygotsky, Wertsch, Mercer, Wells and others (such as Wegerif as well of course) appear to imply, but indirectly, through opening up a dialogic space between people in which creative thought and reflection can occur. This and other evidence leads me to re-evaluate the current definitions of 'exploratory talk' arguing that explicit reasoning is not an essential element but defines a particular specialisation of a more general kind of exploratory dialogue which I label 'reflective dialogue'. For me the effectiveness of exploratory dialogue is not found in the words that are used so much as in the quality of the dialogic space that is opened up and maintained between people and perspectives in the dialogue. This approach offers a way of including in our understanding of educationally useful dialogue, not only the critical thinking supported by the mechanisms of explicit reasoning but also the less visible but possibly more fundamental processes of reflection and creative emergence.

2 DIALOGUE AND LEARNING TO THINK

As I mentioned above, the experimental design used in a number of studies enabled us to compare successful talk in solving reasoning test problems with unsuccessful talk. Comparative analysis of the successful and the unsuccessful talk of the same group of children about the same problems helped to reveal what aspect of the dialogue really made a difference. Various illustrations and extracts of this analysis have been published in different articles and book chapters with the general argument that they show that language can be used more effectively as a tool for thinking. Here I will revisit three of these already published examples in order to argue that, on closer analysis, they do not make the case for language being used directly as a tool for thinking use so much as for the way in which language can be used indirectly to facilitate shifts in relationship and identity which open up a space for thinking.

In the first extract of talk, Elaine, John and Liam are talking about a Raven's problem before our intervention promoting exploratory talk. They did not get it right. In the second extract, from the test given 3 months later after they had completed all of the lessons, they succeed in solving the same problem. The focus of my analysis is on why they succeed in solving the problem in the post-test condition when they failed in the pre-test condition.

3 EXAMPLE 1: LEAPFROG

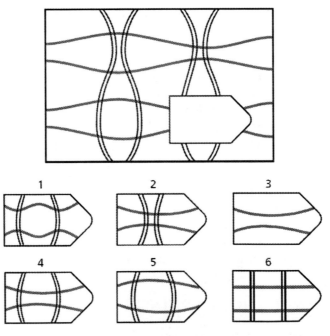

Fig. 4.1. Problem A[3]

---

[3]Problem A, B and C are not the original Raven's problems but very similar parallel problems specially produced for publication purposes with the help of John Raven, the copyright holder, who has been supportive of this line of research.

Transcript extract 1: John, Elaine and Danny: Before talk lessons: Problem A.

Elaine: No, because it will come along like that (*Elaine circles answer 5*)

Transcript extract 2: John, Elaine and Danny: After talk lessons: Problem A.

John: Number 5

Danny: I think it's number 2

John: No, it's out, that goes out look

Danny: Yeh but as it comes in it goes this

Elaine: Now we're talking about this bit so it can't be number 2 it's that one

Elaine: It's that one it's that one

Danny: Yeh 'cos look

Elaine: 4

Danny: I agree with 4

(John nods his assent and Elaine circles answer 4)

3.1 Commentary

This is one of the earlier problems in the Raven's series and one that most groups got right the first time. If you look just at the darker lines running vertically you might think that the answer is number five because that continues the pattern for these lines. This (false) conclusion is that which the children reached in their initial 'pre-test' attempt. Elaine did not pause to consider alternatives or to reach agreement with her group, but circled answer five. That she used the word 'because' reflects the fact that she was responding to someone else's suggestion, made through silent pointing at one of the pictures. In this pre-test condition there was little discussion. The children rushed through all the problems given without much talk.

After the intervention programme consisting of a series of ten Talk Lessons (see Dawes et al., 2004), the three children took more time over the problem. As before, it seems that the pattern of the dark lines is noticed and John offers number five as the answer. But this answer is only made as a suggestion. Danny puts forward number two as the answer, apparently because he is looking at the horizontal pattern of the lighter lines. John explains (through a combination of words and pointing) that the vertical black lines have to 'go out'. Danny in turn explains that it cannot be number five because the light lines have to 'go in'. Each of the two boys has adopted a different perspective; John takes the side of the dark lines, Danny that of the light lines. Each can see enough to refute the position of the other but this does not produce the solution. Elaine then comes up with the answer which combines the dark lines going out with the light lines going in, that is number four. Once she has expressed this both Danny and John can see that she is right.

3.2 Analysis

These children followed the ground rules of exploratory talk which had been taught to them. They explored different alternatives, responding to challenges with reasons and tried to reach agreement before moving on. There are some claims and refutations offered with reasons but most of the 'reasoning' is implicit in pointing at feature of the pattern perhaps accompanied by the phrase ''cos look'. The most obvious difference between the pre- and post-test situations is the amount of time given to the problem. Instead of a focus on a finding an answer, almost any answer, as quickly as possible so that they can complete the task, they pause and consider the problem engaging with it and with each others suggestions. The way of working together that they have developed, a relationship in which they expect challenges and alternatives, helps to open up sufficient space and time for reflection allowing the whole pattern to emerge. The words used here are little more than extensions of pointing, markers noting and sharing a perspective which they can then collectively consider and either reject or build upon. The perspectives pointed to by John and Danny, almost certainly help Elaine to leapfrog to a synthetic vision that takes their two points of view into account in offering a third. 'Tools' such as pointing and using words are important here but the actual act of solving the puzzle is not verbal but a direct vision that occurs out of the tension created by the two different suggestions. This is not a mechanical solution but a creative leap. The words prepare a space for this by articulating perspectives which can then be more easily considered and rejected as stages on a path to the solution.

4 EXAMPLE 2: LEARNING TO PAUSE

The children in Example 1 relied on non-verbal communication – pointing – to argue their positions. In this second example explicit verbalisation plays a bigger role. The following group, Keira, Perry and Tara, were particularly interesting because before our special lessons they had scored lower working together than the highest of their individual scores whereas after the lessons they scored higher working together than the highest individual score. This result suggests that they were doing better together than any of them could have done working alone. Before the talk lessons this group scored 39 out of a possible total of 60. After their lessons they achieved 47. There were eight questions that they had failed to solve in the pre-test which they managed to solve in the post-test. Focusing on the talk around these questions enabled me to compare successful talk with unsuccessful talk about the same problems and with the same children.

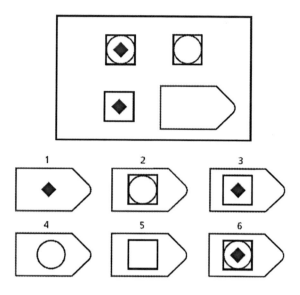

Fig. 4.2. Problem B

Here is an example of the group's pre-intervention talk (Transcript extract 1, which failed to produce the correct answer) and also of their post-intervention talk (Transcript extract 2, which led to them finding the correct answer). On both occasions, they are dealing with the same problem (a version of which is shown in Fig. 4.2 below).

Transcript extract 3: Keira, Perry and Tara: Before talk lessons: Problem B

Perry:	B12.
Keira:	We haven't done that.
Tara:	(giggles) this is where your Mum can see what you're really like at school Perry.
Tara:	Square and diamond, it's 2.

Perry:	No it's not.
Tara:	It is 2.
Perry:	No it's not.
Tara:	It is.
Perry:	No it's not.
Keira:	It's that one 6.
Tara:	It is.
Perry:	No it's not it's got to be a square and a circle.
Tara:	Its that, it has to be that, it has to be that, it has to be 6 because look they've only got that (pointing to the pictures).
Keira:	Look first they are starting with one of them things over (pointing) and then it has to be black.
Perry:	Right, 6.
Keira:	No it isn't Perry.
Tara:	That's number 2 because it goes bigger and bigger and bigger (Tara is looking at the next question).
Keira:	It isn't Perry, look at that one, no it isn't Perry.
	(Perry is writing '6', which is the wrong answer. Keira pushes him).
Perry:	Keira! All right someone else be the writer then.
Keira:	Me (forcibly takes paper).
Tara:	No, Keira you have to sit in this chair to be the writer (Tara takes pen).
Tara:	Give it to Perry because he's quicker at it.
Keira:	Give me the pen (takes the pen)
Keira:	Are we finished on that one, are we on that one now.
Tara:	You're not allowed to do it.
Perry:	Let Tara have a go when we get up to E.
	(Turn to next exercise)
Keira:	Well what do you think it is you dur brain? (addressed to Perry)

Transcript extract 4: Keira, Perry and Tara: After talk lessons: Problem B

Perry:	I think it's number...
Tara:	I think it's number 4 to be honest.
Perry:	I don't, I think it's number 6.
Tara:	I don't, I think it's number 3 look because that one (pointing) has that in the middle and it's got a half one in the middle.
Perry:	Complicated ain't it?
Keira:	No, because that one is that, I think it's that one
Perry:	No, because look at that and look at that (pointing) they are the same, you can't have two the same and it's got that one on, look Sue, it's got that one on and it's got that one on so its out of them three.
Keira:	That one, one, 'cause that's a...
Perry:	Yes, but it's got to be that.
Tara:	That has got to be a diamond, a square with a diamond with a circle in that one, number 6, do you agree?
Perry:	No, what do you mean?
Tara:	OK no it's got to be square.
Keira:	I think it's number 6, that's the one.
Perry:	No it ain't.
Keira:	I think it's number 6.
Tara:	No 'cause it's got to swing round every time, so there is a circle in it.
Keira:	Yes but it hasn't got a circle in there has it and that one has (indicating).
	(3 s pause. Concentrated faces)
Keira:	It's that because look that's got a square so it's just got to be empty.
Perry:	With no circle in so it's just got to be an empty square.
Keira:	No they are just normal boxes.

| Tara: | Look, that's got a triangle, that's got a square. Look. That's got a square with a diamond with a circle in, that's got a square with a diamond in and that's got a square with a circle in so that's got to be a square. |

Tara: Look, that's got a triangle, that's got a square. Look. That's got a square with a diamond with a circle in, that's got a square with a diamond in and that's got a square with a circle in so that's got to be a square.

Perry: I don't understand this at all.

Tara: Because, look, on that they've taken the circle out yes? So on that you are going to take the circle out because they have taken the circle out of that one.

Perry: On this they have taken the circle out and on this they have taken the diamond out and on this they have put them both in, so it should be a blank square because look it goes circle square.

Keira: It's got to be a blank square. Yeh it is.

Perry: Do you agree on number 5, do you agree on 5?

(Perry writes '5', which is the correct answer)

4.1 Commentary

In the pre-intervention talk of Transcript extract 3, Perry challenges Tara's first suggestion ('It is 2') without giving a reason. Tara offers no further justification for her suggestion. This leads into a series of exchanges typical of 'disputational' talk, in which participants simply assert their opposing views without reasoning. Keira then suggests 'It is that one 6' and this is taken up by Tara, and both she and Keira offer reasons. '6' is apparently agreed upon, and Perry writes it down. However, Keira then appears to change her mind without saying what her new opinion is (or she may be objecting to him writing the answer down before checking properly with her and Tara; we do not know as no reason is made explicit). There is then a dispute about who should be writing the answers on the answer sheet.

Transcript extract 4 illustrates some ways that the talk of the same children changed after the intervention programme. Compared with their pre-intervention talk, there are more long turns at talk, as more elaborate explanations are given. Again, Tara is the first to propose an answer, but this time she does this not as a statement ('it is 2') but as an elaborated hypothesis with a question encouraging debate ('That has got to be a diamond, a square with a diamond with a circle in that one, number 6, do you agree?'). Perry asks for more explanation. This time his challenge prompts Tara not into a conflict but into an attempt to be more explicit. Through this effort Tara appears to see that she is wrong and changes her claim. Perry and Keira again engage in a 'disputational' exchange but this is short-lived. After a pause (for individual thought?) the children return to using language to think explicitly together about the problem. They come to agree that it is a kind of subtraction problem which they express in the form 'taking the x out of y'. They find and agree upon the correct answer.

4.2 Analysis A: Original Vygotskian mode

Many features of the talk are different in the second transcript section. Explicit reasons for claims are given, challenges are offered with reasons, several alternatives are considered before a decision is reached, and the children can be seen seeking to reach agreement together. Explicit reasoning may be represented in talk by the incidence of some specific ways of using language, and we can see here some 'key features': the hypothetical nature of claims is indicated by a preceding 'I think', reasons are linked to claims by the use of 'because' or 'cause' and agreement is sought through the question 'do you agree?' Explicit reasoning requires the linking of clauses and leads here to longer utterances.

When analysing the transcripts, I found that in less successful 'pre-test' talk episodes 'because' commonly was used in the context of a speaker simply pointing at a physical item without making any reasoning explicit. In the more successful 'post-test' talk sequences, 'because' was more often used to introduce an explicit, verbalized, reason. These different ways of using 'because' are illustrated in the transcript extracts already given:

(a) (Unsuccessful talk. Pre-intervention)

Tara: Its that, it has to be that, it has to be that, it has to be 6 because look they've only got that (pointing to the pictures).

(b) (Successful talk. Post-intervention)

Tara: Because look on that they've taken the circle out yes? So on that you are going to take the circle out because they have taken the circle out of that one.

In comparing these two ways of using *because* we see a shift in the talk from pointing to the physical context towards pointing to a verbal context which the children construct together. This shift is also reflected in a far greater number of long turns at talk being taken in the more successful talk. This construction of a shared verbal context can be seen in Perry's response to Tara's reasoning in example (b):

(c) Perry: On this they have taken the circle out and on this they have taken the diamond out and on this they have put them both in, so it should be a blank square because look it goes circle square.

In referring to the process of 'taking the circle out' Tara is verbalising something that cannot be pointed to directly in the picture. She is referring to a hypothetical change, one that exists only in language. Turning back to Fig. 4.2 we can see that it provides a solution to the problem. Once Tara has made this relationship verbally explicit Perry is able to see it and he echoes Tara's construction. This use of language to 'model' relationships and processes was often found in the more successful talk of all the groups. Expressions such as 'the same', 'getting fatter', 'that and that make that' or 'add that to that and you get that' were all used.

4.3 Analysis B: Ontologic dialogic mode

I have used this example frequently in publications because it appears to offer a strong case for the verbal co-construction of shared knowledge (Wegerif and Mercer, 2000; Wegerif and Dawes, 2004). 'Taking the circle out' is a metaphor for something that can not be seen directly by pointing at the picture. It seems reasonable to claim that one aspect of what is happening here is the use of language as a 'cognitive tool'. However, there is also much more going on that is missed in any analysis that focuses on language use alone. On the video, for example, we can see long pauses in the which all members of the group lean in to the picture with furrowed brows. Eventually, and not motivated by any obvious utterance, the light of understanding dawns on Tanya's face. She struggles to share what she has seen with the others but fails to find adequate words at first, this strongly suggests that her insight was not initially a verbal construction. Now something very important happens, Perry admits that he does not understand the problem at all in a way that invites Tanya to try again at explaining it for him. In the pre-test condition this could not have happened. In the pre-test he was competing with Tanya over who was cleverest whereas now they are both focused on solving the problem. The way in which the children in the post-test are able to change their minds, criticise their own claims and admit that they do not understand and ask for help indicates a major shift in attitude. This shift in attitude or 'identity in the dialogue' can be summed up as a shift from identifying with their self-position as something that needs to be asserted or defended towards identifying more with the dialogue itself. Motivated by Perry's appeal Tanya manages to find an expression, 'taking the circle out', that communicates her vision to Perry. Perry now gets excited and, in a much more animated tone, he repeats what she has said almost word for word but in a way that shows that he is now communicating his own understanding. The words here have helped Perry to see the problem as Tanya first saw it, they have served as a conduit for a new perspective on the problem that first emerged in the silence of shared concentration. This has become possible because their centres of identification have shifted from competing self-images to an identification with the shared space of the dialogue between them. As with the first example this way of relating and working appears to have opened up a space and time of reflection in which a new way of seeing the problem and solving the problem has spontaneously emerged. Of course, as with the first example, that emergence could be said to have been scaffolded by talk together. Scaffolding in this sense does not imply construction. It is more like the bamboo stick one might use in a garden to help a new tomato plant grow tall enough to bear fruit. The bamboo support stick does not explain the almost magical growth of the plant, it merely indirectly supports and directs it. More important than the expressed words to solving the problem was the quality of the dialogic silence as a space for reflection and creative emergence.

5 EXAMPLE 3: INCLUDING THE OTHER

Example 2 illustrated the importance of changes in the way group members relate to each other. The ability to listen to others and to learn from them appeared more important to solving reasoning test problems than any mechanisms of explicit reasoning. This was a common theme in the groups we followed and is illustrated also by the next two sequences in which Natalie, Jane and Liam are trying to solve Ravens problem E1.

Transcript extract 5: Jane, Liam and Natalie: Before talk lessons: Problem E1

Jane: E1.

Liam: We've only got three more to do.

Jane: I know what it is.

Natalie: That, that (rings number 3, a wrong answer, on the answer sheet).

(sound of page turning)

Transcript extract 6: Jane, Liam and Natalie: After talk lessons: Problem E1

Natalie: E1.

(pause)

Natalie: Right I know. Wait a minute – look, that and that and that and that and that and that together – put it all together and what do you get you get that.

Liam: Yeh, cos' they've all got a dot in the middle.

Natalie: Wait a minute.

Jane: I actually think it's…

Natalie: I think it's number 6.

Liam: Or number 7?

Natalie: Who agrees with me?

Liam: No it's number 7 cos' that and that makes that. Number 7 yeh.

Natalie: Yeh.

Jane: Number 7. E1 (rings number 7, the right answer, on the answer sheet).

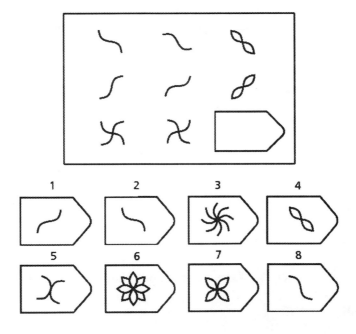

Fig. 4.3. Problem C

5.1 Commentary

In the first pre-test sequence these children hardly talk about the problem at all whereas in the second post-test sequence they spend slightly longer discussing it. Liam gives a reason for his view. On the video Jane and Natalie can be seen pausing when they hear his reasoning, apparently reflecting, before agreeing with him.

5.2 Analysis

The analysis is based on more information that the transcript extract alone. (This is given in full in Wegerif, 1995 and also appears in Wegerif and Mercer, 1997). In the class girls had not wanted to work with boys and when the teacher arranged them in mixed gender groups there were many complaints. In the pre-test condition Natalie and Jane co-operated well but agreed with each other so quickly that they did little sustained thinking. Jane offered few suggestions. Liam occasionally protested but was ignored. His disagreements were treated as disruptive and indeed at times they were. After the intervention programme the whole group are seen working well together. The combination of all of the children's ideas provides the critical element that the group needed to solve some of the more difficult problems. This appears to be achieved by Natalie and Jane taking Liam's disagreements seriously as intellectual challenges and not just social challenges. While in the pre-test his challenges sometimes took the form of hitting the table in the post-test they are constructive, using reasons to help take the group understanding forward.

As with Tara, Perry and Keira, this greater success was associated with a change in the way the group used language, especially questions. When I extracted all the questions asked in this group there were many more in the post-test, mostly in the form of Jane asking: 'What do you think Liam?' This is a change in language but not as a tool directly supporting cognition but as a tool indirectly supporting cognition by supporting inclusion which creates a space in which better cognition can occur. Liam's inclusion in the discussion was important not because he knew the answers; individual test results show that he was not better at solving these kind of test problems than the two girls. But his tendency to challenge meant that important alternatives were now considered before conclusions were reached. Jane and Natalie no longer accepted each other's first suggestions. Again, to reiterate the main point of all three of these 're-analyses': the ground rules of Exploratory Talk were working here to support shared thinking but they were not working directly as a 'cognitive tool' but indirectly through opening and maintaining a productive dialogic space out of which creative solutions to problems emerged.

6 EXPLORATORY TALK AND TEACHING CRITICAL REASONING

Raven's Standard Progressive Reasoning tests were designed to measure a type of thinking in general referred to as non-verbal reasoning. We set out to improve the educational quality of talk around computers in classrooms. Our success in improving the solving of reasoning test problems by groups of children and by children working individually indicates that we ended up teaching an aspect of thinking in general. Factor analysis reveals that a range of tests designed to assess different kinds of 'intelligence' have a common element often referred to as 'g' which is taken by many to be a measure of general intelligence. If it was only possible to use one test to assess 'g' the statistical evidence suggests that that test should be the Raven's test as the results on this test come closest to 'g' (Carpenter et al., 1990). Our demonstration that by improving the quality of dialogue we can improve the results on 'non-verbal' reasoning tests therefore questions many of the traditions of intelligence testing. Our results suggest that, to some extent at least, intelligence is a property of dialogues and not therefore not entirely a product of the way in which the brains of individuals are wired.

The fact that results on Raven's tests are a reasonably good predictor of academic achievement, combined with the fact that individuals scored higher marks on reasoning tests after our intervention and our group testing, makes it plausible to claim that by promoting such reflective dialogues in class-rooms we were teaching an aspect of better thinking in general (at least in the context of education). The generality of the impact of Exploratory Talk is born out by studies which showed improved results in the curriculum areas of Maths and Science in classrooms (Mercer et al., 2004).

The definition of Exploratory Talk which we implemented included an emphasis on the importance of explicit reasoning which I want to question with a new focus on reflective space. While my re-analysis of the three examples above suggests that part of the way, perhaps the main way, in which the ground rules of Exploratory Talk were effective was in opening a reflective space it remains true that the explicit use of language to formulate hypotheses and to challenge these was an important part of success in solving the Reasoning test problems. Explicit reasoning can be formalized into algorithms that can be applied to help some problem solving tasks independently of the dialogic relation. It would therefore not be unreasonable to describe explicit reasoning, rather like logic, or the rules of long-division, as a tool that can directly support a certain kind of thinking. This kind of thinking could be called 'critical', as opposed to 'creative' thinking.

Lipman distinguishes critical thinking from creative thinking through the emphasis in critical thinking on judgement which applies criteria to ideas in order to select the good from the bad. Robert Ennis, more broadly, defines critical thinking as: 'reasonable reflective thinking that is focused on deciding what to believe or do'. Critical thinking for Ennis includes such acts as 'formulating hypotheses, alternative ways of viewing a problem, questions, possible solutions, and plans for investigating something'. The examples of successful 'post-test' talk around reasoning tests that I have given above all exhibit critical thinking in the sense of both Lipman and Ennis. While some of the ground rules of Exploratory Talk served to open a creative space of dialogue I think it is also clear, in the case of the reasoning tests, that promoting the use of Exploratory Talk, which included an emphasis on making reasoning explicit and accountable, proved to be a way of teaching critical thinking. In the next chapter, I will look at the relationship between dialogue and creativity and I will argue that we need a broader concept than Exploratory Talk to take into account creative thinking as well as critical thinking. I call this 'Reflective Dialogue' to distinguish it from Exploratory Talk. In the typology of higher order thinking skills I develop in Chap. 5 I argue that Reflective Dialogue can be specialised to develop critical thinking, through a focus on explicit tools of thinking; creative thinking, through a focus on the dialogic space itself, or empathetic thinking, through a focus on understanding the other.

7 THE DIRECTION OF DIALOGUE AS AN END IN ITSELF

These three examples given above illustrate some of the ways in which group dialogues change as they become more effective at solving reasoning test problems together. Observation and video analysis suggests that, as seen in Example 2, before difficult puzzles are solved there are often long pauses during which the children stare together at the problem with slightly furrowed foreheads. When a solution is seen this is evident in the body language and the eyes of the child who 'sees it first' they then tries to communicate it to the others, often failing initially and forging new 'tools' together in the form of phrases such as 'taking the circle out' or 'the lines are getting bigger'. It seems plausible that expressing the features of puzzles clearly and exploring and rejecting a range of alternative possible solutions helps to prepare the ground for such breakthroughs, but it is clear that the use of explicit language as a shared tool for thinking does not mechanically cause the emergence of the productive new metaphor or way of seeing the puzzle. This would probably not surprise the originator of the test, John Raven (senior), since he affirmed that the test measures what he called 'educive' thinking which is inherently creative and cannot be modelled through the application of an algorithm or other mechanical tools (see Raven et al., 1995).

The empirical finding that group solutions to the more difficult reasoning test puzzles emerged, apparently uncaused, out of a particular kind of silence, perhaps raises a question mark about the centrality given to explicit reasoning in definitions of Exploratory Talk. The role of explicit reasoning is further questioned by the findings of a study conducted by researchers in Mexico comparing the impact of teaching Exploratory Talk on a divergent shared writing task as well as on a convergent reasoning test task. This study found that the talk around the shared writing task improved significantly in many ways, as did the quality of the creative product, but that this improvement was not associated with any increase in explicit reasoning (Mazón et al., 2005; Rojas-Drummond et al., 2006). While all studies confirm that promoting more use of Exploratory Talk in classrooms produces educationally desired outcomes it is not completely clear that the key mechanism is, as has been claimed, 'the use of language as a tool for reasoning' (Wegerif and Mercer, 2000). It is possible that this provisional conclusion may have been influenced by assumptions built into the methodology such as the choice of reasoning tests as a task for the assessment of the quality of talk and also the methodological choice to focus analysis on transcripts of talk. An alternative possibility is that the ground rules of Exploratory Talk, ground rules such as asking each other open questions and listening with respect, serve to open and maintain a dialogic 'space of reflection' which facilitates the emergence of creative solutions to problems (Wegerif, 2005).

As well as changes in the quality of the talk between children the intervention programme promoting Exploratory Talk also led to changes in the identity of the children, at least as this was exhibited in dialogue. In the pre-test 'disputational' talk of the children in Example 2, above, there is clear evidence of a fairly narrow sense of 'self in dialogue' – a self-image defined against the others such that the advantage of one self is to the detriment of the other. In Example 3 this initial narrow identity commitment was gender-based with 'cumulative' sharing but uncritical talk between the two girls in the group and 'disputational' talk between the girls and the boy. A similar pattern emerges in some of the Mexican data collected by Sylvia Rojas-Drummond and Manuel Fernandez with the children competing in the pre-test not only as individuals but sometimes also as 'boys' being dismissive of 'girls' or vice versa (Wegerif et al., 2005). 'Cumulative' talk does not then imply an openness to the other but an identification with a group image. In groups which adopted a cumulative style of talk challenges were avoided or ignored because they were found disruptive of the feeling of group solidarity. In contrast to the fairly narrow identity commitments seen being defined in the pre-test talk, the more successful post-test dialogue exhibited many examples of children apparently arguing against their own positions, admitting their ignorance, asking for help and changing their minds. This suggests a different kind of identity-in-dialogue crucial to reflection and creativity, an identification not with any bounded image, an image of self, or group, gender, ethnicity, etc., but an identification with the space of dialogue itself as a vantage point from which one can evaluate and criticize even one's own position.

If this analysis is correct the key change to observe therefore, in the direction of more effective problem solving dialogue, is not so much the use of longer utterances and more logical connectors such as 'because', but the ability of Perry in the post-test to humbly admit that he did not understand, to invite Tara to explain her solution to him and then to adopt her words as his own with pride. In general across many examples the various teams of people involved in this research have seen that improvements in the quality of shared thinking are accompanied by children being able to listen to others, change their minds, and argue against their own initial positions. This observation leads me to propose a general direction in the development of more effective reflective thinking dialogues away from self-identification and towards an identification with the dialogue itself.

I think that a focus on the changing identity commitments implicit and explicit in the relationships of children as they learn to think together helps to balance or correct an analytic focus on changes in patterns of word use. When engaging more effectively in dialogue the children do not only change the way that they use words, they also change the way in which they relate to each other. This focus on identity should not be taken to imply a return to the individual focus of traditional psychology. Identity in dialogue is a part of relationship. For example, in dialogue within a group which has a disputational style whatever is said will be interpreted in terms of self-assertion and self-defence making a more exploratory style difficult. Habermas refers to this issue when he distinguishes between a communicative orientation, which involves at least trying to understand the other, and a strategic orientation, which seeks to manipulate or coerce the other. Habermas refers to these orientations not as individual attitudes so much as structural properties of intersubjectivity (Habermas, 1991, p. 286). This idea is useful in that it suggests the possibility of a unit of analysis which is the dialogue itself which can be characterized through the kind of intersubjective relations it embodies, perhaps critical, empathetic or playful. From the dialogic perspective which I proposed in Chaps. 1 and 2 individual identity is always forged in dialogic relation to other voices (which in a sense are then part of the identity) so types of individual are analytically and ontogenetically secondary to types of dialogue.

There is increasing interest in learning as a 'trajectory of identity' (e.g. Wenger, 2005). Most who write about identity distinguish, in some way or other, between peripheral short-term task-related identities and more central or 'core' identities that becomes a kind of default identity or baseline that individuals carry with them between dialogues and between situations. I hope that the shift in identity we can observe in groups working around tasks in classrooms where Exploratory Talk is promoted lasts longer than the task and that a more exploratory and a 'dialogic' – in the sense of open to the other – sense of identity transfers from the situation to the core identity of the children involved. Working with several schools in Milton Keynes the research team collected some evidence of this in the changed atmosphere in the class, in reported changes in ways of handling disputes in the playground and also in changes in the way individuals approached examinations, however, we failed to do any research on the long-term far transfer effect of the impact of our intervention programme on identity.

This idea of a core identity that develops over time is important for education and was also important for Bakhtin. Unlike some literary critics who made the move from identity thinking to difference thinking which I described in Chap. 2, Bakhtin did not argue for the 'death of the author' or the end of the 'self'. What he did argue though is that some authors are more dialogic than others and he implied that this is a good thing for the depth of insight in their work. In particular he argued that Dostoevsky was a highly dialogic writer allowing his characters to develop their own independent voices and engage in real dialogues within his unified and distinctively Dostoevskian text (Bakhtin, 1973). This suggests a direction for self-development from being relatively closed to being relatively open, from being uncomfortable with other perspectives and seeking to incorporate them into an expanded self (the more Hegelian approach) to becoming able to feel comfortable in a space of dialogue characterized by multiple perspectives. In my view the classroom studies of children talking together around Raven's reasoning tests showed that Bakhtin's account of dialogic authorship is not only relevant to literary criticism but also to education. What they point to very clearly is a direction of identity development through education in the direction of becoming more dialogic. More than that they also show that development in this direction leads to what have been called general thinking skills, in this case reasoning. To reiterate the main finding of the research programme that I described: the most important indicator of groups of children learning to think better together, in a way that was measurable and that transferred to individual performance on reasoning tests, was not their use of logic or strategy but their ability to listen to each and to change their minds.

In this chapter, I used a re-analysis of a series of empirical studies of children talking together around Raven's reasoning tests to introduce the idea of dialogue as a direction for education: a direction which issues in general thinking and learning skills. My argument from the evidence is that children learnt to think better in groups by learning to listen to each other and to question their own initial ideas. This makes sense but it also implies that we need to challenge and overturn most established accounts of how children learn to think. The implication of this finding is that learning to think effectively requires a move from a relatively closed orientation to a relatively open orientation. This is what I am calling a direction of development into dialogue as an end in itself. In this chapter I have looked at empirical evidence of the development of a kind of thinking, including explicit reasoning, which is best called critical thinking. In the next chapter, Chap. 5, I look at the relationship between dialogue and creative thinking.

Chapter 5

CREATIVITY
Playful reflective dialogue in classrooms

O O O O that Shakespeherian Rag –
It's so elegant
So intelligent
T.S. Eliot, From 'The Wasteland'
(http://www.everypoet.com/Archive/poetry/t_s_eliot/t_s_eliot_the_waste_la
nd.htm)

In the last chapter, Chap. 4, I developed the idea of dialogue as a direction for education through exploring the impact of teaching Exploratory Talk on the solving of reasoning test problems. However, the emphasis on explicit reason in definitions of Exploratory Talk is questionable. While explicit reasoning is good for developing critical thinking but is not always the best way of encouraging creative thinking. In this chapter I use transcript evidence to argue that creativity is more fundamental to productive dialogues, a category which includes the solving of reasoning test problems, than explicit reasoning and that creativity can be promoted through and educational design. This chapter is in two parts, in the first part I present a research programme based on teaching explicit reasoning, in the second I 'deconstruct' this programme, revealing the importance of the neglected 'other' of explicit reasoning: playful talk.

In practice in classrooms effective dialogues are complex, multi-faceted and task-related with many aspects that a teacher, as educational designer, might wish to pull out and promote. It is interesting then that definitions of Exploratory Talk, that kind of talk which it is argued should be taught in classrooms as a tool for improving thinking and learning, focus on the idea that 'reasoning is visible in the talk' (e.g. Mercer, 2000, p. 98 and Wegerif and Mercer, 1997). This reference to the importance of teaching explicit reasoning relates Exploratory Talk to a long tradition in education. Both Aristotle and Plato argued that the promotion of reason should be a central aim of education. The movement for universal education that began in eighteenth century France, was part of the larger Enlightenment project and was at least in part inspired by the belief that education for all would expand the influence of reason in society and therefore fuel social progress. Recently this Enlightenment project has come in for heavy criticism but in many ways education today continues the Enlightenment project (Biesta, 2006). Is explicit reasoning really central to dialogues that help children think and learn or is that just an unchallenged assumption of the Enlightenment?

In this chapter I explore that question using evidence from four transcript extracts. I argue that while explicit reasoning might help improve collaborative thinking for some kinds of task and some kinds of thinking it is not universally useful. Instead I suggest that close observation of dialogues in classroom highlights the fundamental importance of creativity, rather than explicit reasoning, to the success of Exploratory Talk, even when the task set is something as narrow and 'rational' as the solution of reasoning test problems. This analysis also suggests that, as with explicit reasoning, the extent and quality of creativity found in classroom dialogues is influenced by shared ground rules. In the conclusion I argue that this implies the need to expand our understanding of effective educational dialogue to incorporate creativity.

However, before I criticise Exploratory Talk I want to bring out its practical value as a guide for teaching. The evidence I provided in the last chapter demonstrated that teaching Exploratory Talk really worked in improving the quality of the collaborative thinking in the context of solving reasoning test problems. It worked not through teaching reasoning in the abstract but through inducting children into a form of dialogue. The concept of Exploratory Talk represents a useful kind of model in educational design which it is reasonable to call a dialogic model. The success of Exploratory Talk in teaching some general reasoning skills supports the more general case that useful dialogic models of higher order thinking skills can be constructed and applied to good effect within education. If, as I will argue, creativity is more fundamental to higher order thinking skills than explicit reasoning and, as I also suggest, explicit reasoning can sometimes limit or prevent creativity, then it is important to develop an educationally useful model of a kind of dialogue that supports creativity. I end by proposing a more inclusive and flexible concept of reflective dialogue that can support both critical reasoning and creative reasoning.

1 COMPLEXITY AND DIALOGIC MODELS

The dialogic perspective which I outlined in Chap. 2 is a challenge to the predominantly monological tradition of model-making in social science. Dialogicality means not merely that participants in interactions respond to what other participants do, they respond in a way that takes into account how they think other people are going to respond to them. Rommetveit, quoting Barwise and Perry, calls this circularity 'atunement to the atunement of the other' (Rommetveit, 1992). This mutual atunement means, as Rommetveit brings out, that we cannot understand utterances or communicative actions outside of their context in a dialogue and also that the context is indeterminate being an infinite or unbounded chain of possible interpretations.

One way that may be helpful for thinking about the problem of modelling dialogues in education is to consider a dialogue as an open complex adaptive system and consider the problem of simulating this as a computer programme. According to Casti, computer modelling of systems used to rely on the 'monological' assumption that inputs to a system lead to outputs in a determined and therefore predictable way. This worked well for relatively closed and simple systems, like billiard balls on a table or planetary bodies in space. However, research on complexity has demonstrated that these assumptions do not apply for the majority of systems that we are involved in, from evolution to the fluctuations of the economy, because these systems, like dialogues, are open complex adaptive systems. A complex adaptive system is any system in which several agents reciprocally adapt to each other. Once agents reciprocally adapt to each other the circular feedback loops involved produce a level of complexity that makes monological modelling unproductive. Where agents in a system have a limited or perspectival view of the system as a whole and have to use this to make decisions as to how to respond to other agents taking into account how those agents, using their limited perspectival view, will react to this response then it is no longer possible to predict the outcome using a mathematical model. One solution adopted to studying complex adaptive systems is to simulate them with programmes in which multiple agents are each given a set of rules of behaviour and possibly also rules on how to adapt those rules and then set loose to interact. Casti argues that such simulations represent a new scientific method distinct from methods of experiment and linear mathematical modelling that were developed in the study of closed and relatively non-complex systems (Casti, 1997). Such studies have found that the interaction of many agents each following simple rules can result in the 'emergence' of new self-organising systems that can not be predicted or explained by the rules that the agents are following. One striking possible example of this is the simulation of flocking behaviour which was achieved by giving virtual birds three simple rules to guide their flight, keep a minimum distance from neighbours, fly at about the same speed as neighbours and always fly towards the perceived centre of the mass of birds. Understanding flocking had been seen as a hard problem until this simulation clarified how it might work in practice as a property emerging from quite simple ground rules for responding to the behaviour of other agents in the system (Waldrop, 1992, pp. 241–243). An illustration of 'emergence' in complex adaptive systems closer to dialogues is provided by Robert Axelrod's various demonstrations of the emergence of co-operation and what look like ethical principles of loyalty and honour in the behaviour of agents in simulations of social interaction over time (Axelrod, 1984).

Historically reason has been codified in various ways that have not taken dialogical circularity into account. This is obviously true of accounts of argument found in formal logic but it is equally true of the various lists of 'critical thinking skills' that underpin many educational programmes (e.g. Ennis, 1987). In the monological paradigm it is normal to see models as a way of getting a handle on reality which we can use to inform interventions that change things. Models of reason have served precisely this purpose in education. For those who adopt the assumptions of the dialogical paradigm, on the other hand, the role of models is not so straightforward. In the next section I will discuss what it means to create a pragmatically effective dialogical model of reason.

2 THE CONCEPT OF A 'DIALOGICAL MODEL' OF THINKING

What would a dialogic model of higher order thinking that could be an effective support for pedagogy look like? I argue that any such model would need to specify at least two aspects of dialogue, intersubjective orientations and shared ground rules. The example of Exploratory Talk shows that such a model can be a useful support to pedagogy.

2.1 Intersubjective orientations

Habermas begins his account of communicative rationality by drawing a distinction between 'a success-oriented attitude' and 'an attitude oriented to reaching understanding' (Habermas, 1991, p. 286). While he does not dismiss the strategic or profit-maximising rationality that issues from a success-oriented attitude he argues that this kind of rationality is parasitic on a more fundamental communicative rationality issuing from an attitude oriented to reaching understanding. Use of the word 'attitude' carries with it the danger of being interpreted as only referring to individual states whereas Habermas makes it clear that he is referring to ways in which participants in a dialogue can orient themselves to each other. He refers to this as the 'structural properties' of intersubjectivity. To emphasise this I will use the term 'intersubjective orientation' in place of attitude.

Habermas is not generally seen as a dialogic thinker but his claim about the centrality of intersubjective orientations connects his later work to the very different tradition of Jewish writer and theologian, Martin Buber. As was mentioned in Chap. 1 Buber draws a distinction between the 'I-thou' type of relationship, characterised by mutual responsiveness, and 'I-it' relationships in which an active subject confronts and dominates a passive object (Buber, 1970). Bakhtin was familiar with Buber and he makes a similar distinction when he contrasts the 'authoritative' voice, that demands that we either accept or reject it to the 'persuasive' voice (Bakhtin, 1981, p. 343) that enters into us and stimulates our own answering words.

As I mentioned in Chap. 3 evidence confirming the significance of intersubjective orientations for the development of human reason has been offered by Peter Hobson (2002). A developmental psychopathologist, Hobson studied the difference between the development of thinking in autistic children and in normal children. He claims to demonstrate, using experimental evidence as well as case studies, that the normal development of thinking crucially depends on the quality of the relationships formed in the first 18 months of life. In one experimental study the quality of dialogic relationships between mother and 3-year-old child was shown to predict IQ scores.

These varied sources all suggest that some notion of 'intersubjective orientation' is important to any dialogical model of reason.

2.2 Shared ground rules

Buber's 'I-thou' relationship might be a pre-condition for the emergence of reason, as Hobson claims, but it is not, in itself, reasoning. In Habermas's account of communicative rationality a second level of description of reason is often referred to as the social rules governing what he calls an 'ideal speech situation'. Habermas takes up rules first proposed by Robert Alexy as 'the Rules of Reason' (1990, pp. 165–167). In Habermas's formulation in 'Discourse Ethics,' these are:

1. Every subject with the competence to speak and act is allowed to take part in a discourse.
2a. Everyone is allowed to question any assertion whatever.
2b. Everyone is allowed to introduce any assertion whatever into the discourse.
2c. Everyone is allowed to express his attitudes, desires, and needs.
3. No speaker may be prevented, by internal or external coercion, from exercising his rights as laid down in (1) and (2).

These particular rules have been criticised by Seyla BenHabib and others as being too formal. Benhabib's claim is that reasonableness stems not from the abstract rights of *a universal other* but from recognising the needs of *a concrete other* (BenHabib, 1992) which presupposes an attitude of care not mentioned by Habermas. But while Habermas can be challenged on the details his important insight here is that we need shared social rules to open up a space for thinking between, what he refers to as, the Scylla of coercion on the one side and the Charybdis of unreflective consensus on the other.

The conclusion of this brief discussion of approaches to dialogical modelling is that a dialogical model of reason has to take some account of the possibility of different intersubjective orientations and could consist of a description of the social ground rules followed by agents in an interaction.

3 'EXPLORATORY TALK' AS A DIALOGICAL MODEL

So far I have argued from a discussion of the literature that dialogical models of reason require at least two levels of analysis: an account of fundamental intersubjective orientations and an account of social ground rules followed in an interaction. This can be illustrated more concretely in the idea of 'Exploratory Talk' that has been influential in education in the United Kingdom since the 1970s (Barnes and Todd, 1978). The concept of Exploratory Talk was first put forward by Douglas Barnes and has more recently been developed and championed by Neil Mercer. Exploratory Talk is presented by Mercer (1995) as emerging in the context of a characterisation of three 'types of talk' found empirically in a study of collaborative learning in classrooms. The three 'types of talk' described by Mercer can also, as a later article made clear (Wegerif and Mercer, 1997) be seen as reflecting orientations of the kind that Habermas referred to as 'structural properties of intersubjectivity'. The three 'types of talk' Mercer refers to are:

- *Disputational talk*, which is characterised by disagreement and individualised decision making. There are few attempts to pool resources, or to offer constructive criticism of suggestions. Disputational talk also has some characteristic discourse features – short exchanges consisting of assertions and challenges or counter assertions.
- *Cumulative talk*, in which speakers build positively but uncritically on what the other has said. Partners use talk to construct a 'common knowledge' by accumulation. Cumulative discourse is characterised by repetitions, confirmations and elaborations.
- *Exploratory talk*, in which partners engage critically but constructively with each other's ideas. Statements and suggestions are offered for joint consideration. These may be challenged and counter-challenged, but

challenges are justified and alternative hypotheses are offered (cf. Barnes and Todd, 1978). Compared with the other two types, in Exploratory Talk *knowledge is made more publicly accountable* and *reasoning is more visible in the talk.*
(Wegerif and Mercer, 1997)

Despite our best efforts at the time and since, this analytic framework has sometimes been interpreted as a coding scheme which all utterances or other chunks of talk can be made to fit. It was intended rather differently as a loose analytic framework arising from the intuitions of practitioners and of use as a heuristic by practitioners. When teachers look at a group in their class and listen briefly they have to judge quickly and roughly how they are getting along. In order to do this they do not have the time and resources to code all the utterances but they can assess, as experienced participants in dialogues, the kind of relationship that is embodied in the talk, whether that is cumulative, disputational or exploratory. In other words the types of talk schema is not a classification at the level of words, utterances or even, ground rules, but at the level of intersubjective orientations intuited by participant observers.

To understand the nature of the distinctions being made in the classification of 'types of talk' it is worth briefly considering what happens when there is a transition in the type of talk. We are probably all intuitively familiar, as participants, with the possibility of abrupt transitions in dialogues: for example, a shift from a cooperative enquiry into personal competition when something said suddenly pulls us back from open participation into an acute awareness of our own separate identity and separate interests and the need for these to be defended.

The next sequence illustrates an abrupt transition of this kind, three 9-year-old pupils were working on the Ravens reasoning test puzzles described and illustrated in the last chapter, Chap. 4. As a group they have been given only one answer sheet for these puzzles and asked to co-operate to reach agreement on each answer.

Transcript extract 4.1: A transition

Jane:	Yeah but there's three of them and there's 3 of them and that and that makes that.
Natalie:	No look you get three and 1 and 3 and 1 and
Jane:	Mr Wegerif does that and that make that?
	(*Jane appeals to the researcher who comes over but doesn't intervene*).
Natalie:	I just disagree.
Researcher:	You must give a reason. You must explain why Natalie.

Natalie:	No, because look. (*Points to the page with the graphical puzzle but does not explain.*)
George:	You have to have a reason Natalie.
	(*Natalie leaves the group table and goes over to another group.*)
George:	Natalie you're supposed to be working with us not with Raja.
Natalie:	I'm thinking. (*Shouted from the other table.*)
Natalie:	All right number 3. (*Natalie has come back to the table. She speaks aggressively.*)
Jane:	Don't get in a strop I want to explain something.
Natalie:	I agree, I agree.

Up to this point the children have apparently reached an unforced consensual agreement on the answer to each puzzle. Towards the end of the task, however, Natalie begins to propose answers more strongly than before, and shows exasperation with her partners through her raised voice and sharp manner. She makes it quite clear that she is simply bowing to group pressure in finally saying that she agrees. She gives no reason for agreeing with the others that the answer is number 3 and refuses to listen to Jane's offered explanation. This sequence shows a fairly abrupt breakdown of the cooperative framework, as the talk moves from exploratory towards a more disputational style.

The fact that such transitions occur and are recognised by participants suggests that types of dialogue defined through intersubjective relation have a certain reality within dialogues. Although such 'types of talk' have measurable externally observable effects on features of the dialogue such as the words spoken (the number of 'because's' or other logical connectors for example), the tone of voice, the length of pauses or perhaps even the eyebrows raised and the use of gaze, they are not reducible to these surface features.

Of the three intersubjective orientations referred to above the one closest to traditional ideas of rationality, is exploratory talk. This combines features of cumulative talk, being a kind of cooperation, with features of disputational talk, because it includes challenges and competition. However, the competition in exploratory talk is between ideas not between people. Through an analysis of three exemplars in the previous chapter, Chap. 4, I demonstrated that a key indicator of an exploratory orientation is that participants are able to change their minds in response to good arguments. In the light of the previous discussion of intersubjective orientations it seems that an exploratory orientation is a development from what Habermas would call a 'communicative' orientation with social ground rules which establish a relationship of trust and co-operation within which participants seek to understand each other rather than to manipulate each other.

As I mentioned in the last chapter, the application of Exploratory Talk involved elaborating the research team's idea of an Exploratory type of talk (or intersubjective orientation) into 'social ground rules' appropriate for the specific social context of classrooms. The list of these rules presented in an article by Neil Mercer and myself in 1997 is not fixed or final but gives a fairly good idea of what we meant by a 'social ground rule' and what we meant by 'Exploratory Talk':

1. All relevant information is shared
2. The group seeks to reach agreement
3. The group takes responsibility for decisions
4. Reasons are expected
5. Challenges are accepted
6. Alternatives are discussed before a decision is taken
7. All in the group are encouraged to speak by other group members

The first three rules in the list are ground rules that are shared with cumulative talk; rules that serve to bind the group, share information together and construct knowledge together through seeking agreement. Rules four and five focus on the explicit reasoning that characterises exploratory talk as opposed to other types of talk. The role of challenges was seen as important in distinguishing between cumulative, disputational and exploratory orientations. In Exploratory Talk challenges stimulate joint reasoning, while in cumulative talk they are experienced as disruptive and often lead to a loss of cooperation and a switch into disputational talk. In disputational talk participants may still offer arguments but are in fact focusing on 'winning' rather than on understanding or solving a problem together.

In practice a unique set of ground rules was produced for every class emerging out of dialogue between teacher and pupils. In this way they were always appropriate to their situation. With younger children, for example, we found that the rules that emerged focused more on issues of social inclusion and less on the cognitive (Wegerif et al., 2005). We also found that it was a useful exercise to regularly revisit the ground rules to see if some are no longer useful and if new ones are needed. In this way the shared guiding ground rules of dialogue developed together with the class or group.

In the last chapter, Chap. 4, I mentioned that this model has now been applied in several research studies and found to work well in achieving educationally desired ends including better test results in curriculum areas (e.g. Mercer et al., 1999, 2004; Wegerif et al., 1999; Littleton et al., 2005). Encouraging children to take an exploratory orientation and to use these ground rules has meant working with teachers to 'teach' these ground rules and to turn the classroom into a social and physical environment that supported and rewarded their use. Teacher–researcher Lyn Dawes took the lead in developing teaching programmes for Exploratory Talk (e.g. Dawes et al., 2004). Having the ground rules displayed on the wall, or in yellow sticky notes around the computer screen, is important for this as is the seating arrangement and the frequent reminders from the teacher that the way groups talked together is as important and valued as the answers that they came to. Equally important is the way that the teacher talked with the class modelling the kind of reasoning required (see Sams et al., 2005, for a teacher training pack for using this approach with ICT to promote effective computer-supported collaborative learning).

4 A NEGLECTED FOURTH TYPE OF TALK: PLAYFUL TALK

Having set up the idea of Exploratory Talk as a dialogic model of reason in the first half of this chapter I am now going to 'deconstruct' it in the second half. Deconstruction refers to a 'method' of sorts that is peculiarly dialogic in that it is based upon listening to the voices that have been excluded by a point of view, paradigm or way of understanding. In order to question dominant metaphors and ideas in the history of philosophy Derrida focussed on ideas and metaphors that had been dismissed as marginal to this tradition. Although it sounds rather negative, this method of 'deconstruction' is in some ways expansive because by focusing on the forgotten margins which the thoughts of history defined themselves against, Derrida, whether he intends to or not, revalues these marginal thoughts and thereby makes a larger field of possibilities available to us.

Researchers observing and recording children's talk in classrooms are always aware that there is a great deal of apparently off-task nonsense talk or banter. When the team began thinking about the three types of talk in terms of 'intersubjective orientations' they realised that this off-task banter was itself a type of talk that could be characterised in terms of a fundamental intersubjective orientation, one of playfulness, with a concomitant set of ground rules. At one time Sylvia Rojas-Drummond and I ran a workshop in Mexico which produced a convincing set of ground rudes for playful talk including 'do not take anything said seriously' and 'make images as strange and apparently inconsequential as possible'. However, although this idea was discussed by research teams in the UK and in Mexico, it was not included in presentations of the types of talk idea. The reason for this was that it mostly concerned off-task talk and did not seem very useful to educators. Whenever a member of the research team introduced the three types of talk we did so with the qualification that these were not all types of talk but only some types of talk, those types of talk that were most 'relevant to education'.

It is interesting that the research team, of which I was a part, acknow-ledged the existence of 'playful talk' but dismissed it as marginal to educational objectives whereas we saw exploratory talk, defined through the presence of explicit reasoning, as central to educational objectives. In so far as this 'deconstruction' of the importance we gave to explicit reasoning in classroom talk is a criticism it is a self-criticism. At the time that Exploratory Talk was first applied in experimental studies in classrooms I saw it as an application of Habermas's account of communicative rationality and so I often found myself advocating the importance of explicit reasoning to any definition of Exploratory Talk. However, I came to believe that this focus on explicit reasoning obscured the fundamental importance of creativity to productive talk. Creativity is something found in the 'playful talk' which we had been aware of as a team but had not seen as of educational value. By revisiting and revaluing 'playful talk' now I wish to make the argument that incorporating the understanding of creativity in talk can help to expand the original notion of exploratory talk into a broader dialogical model of higher order thinking for use in education, that includes all dialogue that can lead to new sparks of insight.

To help make this argument I will attempt to trace the connection between playful talk and cognition through four examples taken from transcript extracts of classroom talk.

4.1 Off-task playful talk

It is actually very hard to get children to perform any kind of task at school without their being creative with language. In the following example three 9-year-old children: Karen, Anna and Nick were asked to work together around a piece of software called 'Bubble Dialogue'. This software shows cartoon characters in a difficult situation and the users have to fill in the thought bubbles and speech bubbles of the characters. In this case the cartoon characters were called Jane and Robert. Jane knew that Robert had stolen some chocolates from the sweet shop. Now her money was missing and she thought Robert might have stolen that too. Karen, Anna and Nick were asked to talk together about the issues and think about how the characters would feel. They did not really do that but they did produce some interesting word play. We join them as they construct together what they will type.

Transcript extract 4.2: Funny money

Sharon: I think

Gail: I think Robert stole the stuff

Sharon: That

Nick: That Robert stole my bunny

(Sharon and Gail laugh)

Sharon: My money

Gail: Funny

Nick: It's not money I said bunny

Sharon: It's his money

Gail: I've said bunny

A few lines later they are typing in together the word 'chocolates' and Gail says: 'lovely, *yummy*, chocolates' echoing the earlier use of money, bunny, funny. She then continues in a different voice to indicate that she is quoting:

'life is in a box of chocolates'

Nobody picks up this reference to the film: 'Forest Gump' Three lines later Gail tries another reference to a different context, singing:

'Choc-o-lets. Tasty. Cadbury's Quake'

in the tune of an advertisement for Cadbury's Flake. This time Nick picks this up responding to use of Quake with the word:

'Quavers'

Which is a popular snack also advertised on TV. Sharon, who is typing this whole time, brings them back to the task, as she sees it, by saying:

'Chocolates'

and then beginning to spell it out.

'C, H, O, C'.

For now the others join her in spelling out chocolate, but it is not long before the word-play breaks out again, 'chocolate' being turned by Sharon into 'choc, then it's late'.

Despite the teacher's best efforts these children interpreted the task as more about typing words into the boxes than thinking about issues. This task-interpretation is a common one and probably reflects their educational history. What is interesting though, is that they cannot do this task straight; they rhyme and break into little songs, use silly voices and puns and generally play around with language. In this they are not exceptional. Ron Carter (1999, 2002) argues that this creative 'poetic' use of language is so common in everyday talk amongst equals that it should be considered the norm. This has only become apparent recently because it has only recently been possible to collect large amounts of data of ordinary spoken language. Before the existence of large corpora of recorded talk research tended to focus more on available written texts and word play was believed to be a deviant and specifically literary form found in poems, for example.

4.2 On-task playful talk

I am not going to claim that rhyming 'money, bunny, funny and yummy' is in itself something we should call higher order thinking. However, it is creative in the sense in which we normally use the term creative. Ronald Carter defines creativity in language as 'imaginative analogy' and this is very much what we see here. I will call this creativity type 1. More specialist definitions of the term creativity for use in education also often bring in the idea of 'resulting in a valued product' (e.g. NACCCE, 1999). I will call this creativity type 2. For creativity 1 to lead to creativity 2, shared ground rules are important. This is brought out in a transcript extract given originally by Neil Mercer (1995: p. 101) to illustrate 'cumulative talk'.

This example is from a session in which two 10-year-old girls, Katie and Anne, were working on the production of their own class newspaper, using some desktop publishing software for schools called *Front Page Extra*. At the point the sequence begins, they have been engaged in the task for about an hour and a quarter and are trying to compose some text for their front page.

Transcript extract 2: Fantabuloso (Mercer, 1995, p. 101)

Katie: Okay, so right then. What shall we write?

Anne: We can have something like those autograph columns and things like that and items, messages

Katie: Inside these covers (*pause 3+secs*) Our fun filled

Anne: That's it!

Katie: Something

Anne: Something like that!

Katie: Yeah

Anne: Inside this fabulous fun filled covers are – how can we have a fun filled cover? Let me try

Katie: Inside these (*pause 3+secs*)

Anne: Hah huh (*laughs*)

Anne: You sound happy on this. Fantabuloso (*laughs*)

Katie: Inside these inside these fant, inside these fun-filled, no inside
these covers these fantastic these brilliant

Anne: Brilliant

Katie: Is it brilliant?

Anne: No

Katie: No. Fantast fantabuloso shall we put that?

Anne: Yeah (*inaudible*) fantabluloso

Katie: Fan - tab -u- lo-so

Anne: Loso. Fantabuloso.Katie: Fantabuloso oso

The importance of this example, and why I am returning to it again, is
that here the children, Katie and Anna, apply word play to the task they had
been given. Here creative word-play moves over from just being a bit of fun
to being useful in an educational context. Katie and Anne are taking their
work seriously. They could almost be a couple of creative marketing executives trying to find a new name for a product. Products with very similar
names: Fab, Fanta, Brillo, etc. already exist and were presumably thought up
through a similar kind of shared creative process. The difference between
this and the 'money' transcript is that here the talk is oriented to finding the
best possible solution to the problem set. Sharon, Gail and Nick do not link
their verbal play to the task in hand, it is just a bit of fun, if anything it is
subverting the task. Their play is creative in that it generates lots of new
links and potential ideas – is life really like a box of chocolates? – but they
do not build on any of them. Katie and Anne do build on each others
suggestions. Their creative play becomes something that relates to reasoning
because they apply implicit shared criteria to select the preferred response.
Katie asks 'Is it *brilliant*?', i.e. does this word fit and she agrees with Anna
that it is not quite right. Both then converge on 'fantabuloso'.

4.3 Thinking by resonance

To consider how to produce a dialogic understanding of higher order
thinking that goes beyond a reduction to the potentially mechanical process
of explicit verbal reasoning I will use the analysis of an example of thinking
in the talk of 7- and 8-year-old children engaged in a 'philosophy for
children' session.

As we join them the children are thinking together with a teacher about
issues raised by a picture book that they all have in front of them. The book is

'Where the Wild Things Are' by Maurice Sendak (1963). When we join them they have just read aloud about how the hero of the story's bedroom turns into a forest and the bedroom walls 'become the whole world'. The teacher, Mark Prentice, then encourages them to think about imagination and the meaning of the word 'world'. Below is a lightly edited version of the talk that follows:

Transcript extract 3: Creating and dissolving worlds

Helen:	[You can just start] staring at things and make it into your picture.
Helen:	It can be about 20 things in one place.
Teacher:	Say that again Helen because it's interesting.
Helen:	There's about 20 things in one place.
Teacher:	That you can just look at and stare?
Helen:	Yeh there are also lines on the curtains they could turn into loads of green leaves.
Emma:	Yeh or bamboo stalks.
Teacher:	So you can stare at something and get a different picture?
Emma:	Yeh you could change it into a leopard or something.
Teacher:	Have you ever done that? Stared at something and looked at all the shapes that are inside it?
Alex:	Yeh you could turn that into a big bone or something.
Teacher:	This radiator here – so we have power to change things don't we. How do we do that?
Emma:	I was in my room the other day and I closed my eyes nearly shut and my rocking horse I thought it was this kind of a pot – a shaking pot.
[...]	
Teacher:	Can you create your own world?
Several:	Yes
Teacher:	How can you create your own world?
Several:	Imagining, dreaming
Teacher:	That's interesting so you can create your own world by imagining – did Helen create a world when she started to talk about the curtains up there?

Helen: There's about a thousand worlds all in one person's head, all
             in one place

[...]

Teacher: What do you think – Alex?

Alex: Well one time I invented my own country which I called
             Alexland cos I became my bedroom a whole country and I
             pretend all my toys are alive

Teacher: So you created a world

Alex: Yes

Teacher: Now is that a real world?

Alex: Well sometimes I feel like its really real but then when I've
             found something like a catalogue, which I pretend you couldn't
             get catalogues and stuff like that, then the world just disappears

Teacher: So it disappears when you look at something else

Alex: Yeh when I look at something – when I go downstairs it just
             disappears, because my bedroom's the best place – because
             my toys are up there.

The teacher's role is very interesting. He is not giving them ideas but
facilitating the group thinking by repeating key points and asking prompting
questions.

Here there are few challenges or explicit reasons. Instead the children
seem to build on each other's comments with similar memories and ideas.
Helen's idea that things can seem to be different as if 'there were about 20
things in one place' is picked up by Emma and Alex who share examples of
this. This is what has been called cumulative talk because there is a sharing
of experience and ideas without challenges or critical grounding. But it is
nonetheless apparent that some serious thinking is going on. This leads to the
realisation, articulated by Alex, that there can be two different worlds, his
own world and the adult world, and that objects from the adult world, found
in his world, can make his world dissolve. It could be argued that this is not
reasoning but just a description of his experience. However, reasoning is
implicit in the description. This way of describing experience is a way of
seeking to understand it and these descriptions reveal the world in a new
way. This is perhaps what Wittgenstein calls a 'perspicuous representation'
(Wittgenstein, 1967). Alex describes his experience but with insight into its
general structure.

This description of how his world can dissolve in the face of anomalous
objects is given in response to a prompt by the teacher that could be taken as

a challenge. 'Is it really real?' But Alex does not reply to this with any explicit reasoning of the kind 'yes it is, because' or 'no it isn't, because' – he replies with a description that is also an anecdote:

> Well sometimes I feel like its really real but then when I've found something like a catalogue, which I pretend you couldn't get catalogues and stuff like that, then the world just disappears.

We could say of this that Alex offers a reason why Alexland is not really real. However, the whole utterance here is much more than just a piece of explicit reasoning, it is also a sharing of his experience in a way that invites us inside that experience.

For me, Alex's understanding that one world can be dissolved by the presence of an artefact from another world is a powerful piece of thinking. However, I understand this through the similar ideas that it evokes for me but probably not for Alex. I am thinking of the role of catalysts in chemistry turning one kind of substance almost instantly into a very different kind of substance. I am also led to the idea of a paradigm shift in the development of science that has been described by Thomas Kuhn as a radical shift to a different world view sometimes sparked by anomalies within the original paradigm.

My response to what Alex says takes me beyond what is given, not through explicit reasoning but through a kind of internal resonance in which the perspective he articulates opens onto other inside perspectives that I have read about or experienced. This is thinking as a dance of positions in the dialogic space of possible positions that I first mentioned in the introduction to the book. It is precisely through this kind of resonance that the children seem to be building on each others ideas. One child sees a forest of green leaves emerging from the shapes in the curtain, another sees the radiator on the wall as the spinal bone of an animal a third sees her rocking chair as a 'shaking pot' and so they share their perspectives and build together the idea of different worlds and the factors that influence how these different worlds form and dissolve. Alex's very clear statement of a powerful idea does not come on its own but emerges within the context of this dialogue. It is probably as new for him as for the others in the group.

Creative play with words and ideas assumes an orientation of mutual trust and support where each participant knows that what he or she says will be accepted. In studies of exploratory talk around reasoning test problems referred to in the previous chapter, Chap. 4, children frequently rejected the suggestions of others saying something like: 'No, I don't agree because of x, y, z'. They were taught to use language in this way. In the example above it would be unlikely that anyone would reply to Alex's claim that you can see the radiator as a big bone by saying 'No, I don't agree, because...'. It is unlikely that such an explicit challenge would be productive. Instead the participants try to make the best sense they can of a different perspective, and this effort to listen and understand opens up a space of reflection in which ideas can resonate together and new ideas can emerge.

4.4 Metaphors to solve a reasoning test problems

In the last chapter, Chap 4, I re-analysed episodes of talk around ravens reasoning tests to argue that the promotion of Exploratory Talk led to development in the direction of dialogue as an end in itself. I exemplified this by showing that members of post-test groups which solved more problems together than in the pre-test condition were more able to admit that they were wrong, listen to others and change their minds. I also mentioned that, even in the context of solving reasoning tests, the explicit reasoning in the talk seemed less significant to their success than the way in which the ground rules of the talk facilitated a creative space in which new metaphors emerged. To make this case, in continuity with the use of extracts in the three previous examples in this chapter, I will reproduce here a few lines from the transcript of talk around problem B which was presented in full in the previous chapter.

Transcript extract 4.4: 'Taking the circle out'

> Tara: Look, that's got a triangle, that's got a square. Look. That's got a square with a diamond with a circle in, that's got a square with a diamond in and that's got a square with a circle in so that's got to be a square.
>
> Perry: I don't understand this at all.
>
> Tara: Because, look, on that they've taken the circle out yes? So on that you are going to take the circle out because they have taken the circle out of that one.
>
> Perry: On this they have taken the circle out and on this they have taken the diamond out and on this they have put them both in, so it should be a blank square because look it goes circle square.

The key phrase here is: 'taking the circle out'. This phrase, which appears to solve the puzzle, is, of course, a metaphor. No-one is really taking anything out of anywhere, but by thinking about the puzzle in this way, as if they were manipulating shapes on a table, they are able to see relationships within it that are not otherwise apparent. As I mentioned in the last chapter this use of language to model relationships and processes through physical metaphors was often found in the talk of children solving reasoning problems. Expressions such as 'getting fatter', 'that and that make that' or 'that turns around' or 'add that to that and you get that' were common.

The talk of Trisha and Perry is clearly Exploratory Talk. It contains explicit reasoning. But it is interesting that, in order to see the problem together, they need to creatively construct a new shared metaphor. This act of creation links this talk to the talk of Transcript extract 2 above: *fantabuloso*. In one case a new word is created to complete a newspaper headline and in the other a new phrase is created to sum up the solution to a problem. In both cases the new word or phrase emerges out of an extended dialogue in which the participants are struggling to create shared understanding and find a solution to a shared problem.

4.5 Discussion

The first example given, that of Sharon, Gail and Nick, illustrates an almost random playful kind of creative wordplay as an end in itself with no obvious external motivation. In the second example, that of Anne and Katie, a similar kind of poetic resonance between words is put to use to help complete a written assignment. In the third example, from a 'Philosophy with Children' session, resonance between images, perspectives and ideas helps children articulate and understand their experience of the construction and dissolution of different worlds of experience. The final example, with Perry and Trisha, illustrates how the creative generation of a new metaphor was essential to a group finding a shared solution to a reasoning test problem. The argument I wish to make through these examples is that verbal creativity (creativity type 1 as mentioned earlier) is an underlying and essential ingredient of the co-construction of new meaning in dialogues (creativity type 2) and that this includes the case of explicit verbal reasoning.

The creativity we can see in these extracts is not produced by any mechanism. We cannot reduce it to a chain of cause and effects. Derrida argues, by implication, that creativity in language does not need to be explained (Derrida, 1976), it is the absence of creativity that needs to be explained. This position is supported by the empirical findings of corpus linguistics (Carter, 1999, 2002). On the other hand this uncaused creativity appears in a context. This is the context of dialogues between two or more people characterised by intersubjective orientations and shared ground rules. The exploratory orientation that is evident in the last three extracts is found in the context of ground rules that serve to keep people together around a shared focus while also keeping them apart, questioning and evaluating each others utterances. This orientation towards shared inquiry appears not only to allow for creativity 1, creativity as 'imaginative analogy', but also to funnel it into creativity type 2, creativity 'resulting in a valued product'. In this way such dialogues serve to open up a space between people in which creativity spontaneously occurs and also to channel that creativity towards a shared purpose.

Dialogues can be more or less creative. Repeating established conventions in language, for example, is not creative. Transcript extract 3 above, suggests that a creative space can be opened up by turning language back upon itself in the form of open questions. Open questions asking 'what?' or 'why?', in the right social context, trigger a shift to an exploratory attitude. Reflection here means not assuming that we know the answer or that we know what things are, but stepping back from certainty to allow things to present themselves in new ways (something Heidegger perhaps referred to in the phrase 'the step back', 1971).

The talk in the last three transcript extracts given above, illustrates something that could reasonably be called higher order thinking embodied in dialogue. The higher order thinking involved is not the potentially mechanisable thinking of explicit reasoning. In relation to the contrast made in Verse 11 of the Tao Te Ching (the Exergue to this book) it is not so much tool-based thinking as space-based thinking, thinking that leaps and dances in the space of multiple possible perspectives opened up by dialogue.

The empirical finding that group solutions to the more difficult reasoning test puzzles emerged, apparently uncaused, out of a particular kind of silence, questions the centrality given to explicit reasoning in definitions of Exploratory Talk. The role of explicit reasoning is further questioned by the findings of a study conducted by researchers in Mexico comparing the impact of teaching Exploratory Talk on a divergent shared writing task that could have many equally valid outcomes as well as on a convergent reasoning test task that has only one 'correct' answer. This study found that the talk around the shared writing task improved significantly in many ways, as did the quality of the creative product, but that this improvement was not associated with any increase in explicit reasoning (Mazón et al., 2005; Rojas-Drummond et al., 2006). While all studies confirm that Exploratory Talk produces educationally desired outcomes it is not completely clear that the key mechanism is, as has been claimed, 'the use of language as a tool for reasoning' (Mercer et al., 2004). It seems plausible that this provisional conclusion may have been influenced by assumptions built into the methodology, for example the choice of reasoning tests as a task for the assessment of the quality of talk and also the methodological choice to focus analysis on transcripts of talk. The alternative interpretation that emerges from re-analysing this data from a more dialogic theoretical perspective is that the ground rules of Exploratory Talk, ground rules such as asking each other open questions and listening with respect, serve to open and maintain a dialogic 'space of reflection' which facilitates the emergence of creative solutions to problems (Wegerif, 2005).

6 CONCLUSION

Thinking about reason from a dialogical perspective shifts the focus of attention away from abstract cognitive structures and towards the way that people respond to each other in dialogues. Exploratory Talk is a model of higher order thinking embodied in a type of dialogue consisting of an intersubjective orientation and a set of ground rules specifically designed to support collaboration in the classroom. This model has proved an effective support for teachers. Its implementation resulted in a significant improvement in the quality of collaborative learning and reasoning according to a range of measures. However, while Exploratory Talk is a dialogical model of a kind of reason, the focus on explicit reasoning in its definition makes it a limited model. It is clearly a useful pedagogical device or 'scaffolding' but it should not be taken to limit the possibilities of higher order thinking. Through the analysis of transcripts of young children thinking together, I have argued instead that dialogical reason is characterised by the creation of a space of reflection between participants in which resonance between interior perspectives, words and images can occur leading to co-construction when participants build creatively on each other's proposals and creative emergence when new ways of seeing problems appear as if spontaneously after the exploration of a range of alternatives.

The example of 'Exploratory Talk' shows that specific dialogical models of reason can be a valuable tool in education. However, analysis of transcripts presented here suggests that the focus in the definition of Exploratory Talk on explicit reasoning limits its usefulness to particular types of task. Different sets of ground rules could be produced to generate and support other valuable types of dialogue within education. While these would not all exhibit explicit reasoning they would all exhibit what I am calling here dialogical higher order thinking. The understanding of dialogical higher order thinking that I am proposing includes all dialogues, internal or external, where creativity is opened up by the reflective use of language and the inter-animation of different perspectives. An exploratory orientation appears to be important to this larger model of dialogic reason but not necessarily explicit reasoning. Since explicit reasoning and accountability has already been claimed for the definition of Exploratory Talk I propose instead the phrase 'reflective dialogue'. The use of the term 'dialogue' here, rather than 'talk' is intended to bring out that not only the words but also the listening silences are important and that shared exploration is not only mediated by speech but also, potentially, by electronic writing, pictures, dance or music.

In this chapter I used a series of transcripts to link playful talk to effective reasoning. Playful talk can be characterised by the use of imaginative analogy which, while creative in the minimal sense, which I called 'creativity 1', is not, in itself, the kind of creativity valued in the school curriculum. The creativity that teachers and government wish to be promoted in schools includes the idea of a 'socially valued product'. I called this creativity 2. I argued through examples, that teacher guidance and social ground rules could both stimulate creativity 1 and direct it towards the construction of metaphors which embody shared insight thus turning playful talk into creativity 2. Creativity, I argued, was opened up by dialogues and is more fundamental to collaborative thinking than explicit reasoning. This led me to propose replacing the current use of Exploratory Talk as a goal for education with the broader concept of reflective dialogue referring to creative shared inquiry mediated in various ways, i.e. not only 'talk', and which may or may not include explicit reasoning depending on the needs of the task.

Chapter 6

TEACHING THINKING
Controversies and questions

We can learn thinking only if we radically unlearn what thinking has been traditionally

From Heidegger, What is Thinking? 1978, p. 374

[This text is not yet on the Web but much of Heidegger's work is on

http://webcom.com/paf/ereignis.html]

There is a widespread view that we need to teach for general thinking and learning skills but little consensus as to what these skills are and where they come from. This chapter explores some of the key debates about the teaching of higher order thinking skills in order to argue that these dilemmas point towards the need for a dialogic approach. This dialogic direction is not a rejection of the ideal of teaching general thinking skills but a reconceptualization of what teaching thinking means in terms of opening, deepening and broadening dialogic spaces.

One practical impact of new technologies on education can be dramatized by imagining a well equipped student instantly finding out more information and points of view on any given topic than their teacher can possibly know simply by 'googling' that topic accessing the Internet through a mobile device while in class. This sort of scenario makes it apparent why many commentators such as Manuel Castells, quoted in the introduction to this book, argue that education has to shift from a focus on content towards a focus on the flexible learning and thinking skills required for effective participation in global citizenship and a global economy.

The challenge to education posed by globalization and the proliferation of new information and communications technology has been apparent to commentators on education for some time but real change in education in the direction of teaching general skills remains slow. One reason for this may be that, while the challenge is clear, the way forward is not. Calling for more 'flexible thinking and learning skills' is a handy phrase but when teachers and policy makers ask: 'what are these skills exactly, how do we teach them and how do we assess them to show that the teaching has worked?' The response from the educational research community can seem unclear because the project of teaching higher order thinking remains controversial. It is worth considering some of the questions raised about teaching thinking in more detail because answering those questions leads to greater clarity as to the nature of the 'thinking skills' and what it means to teach them. This chapter will consider in turn the following commonly asked questions, showing, in each case, what a dialogic perspective has to offer in taking the debate forward.

1. Do general thinking skills exist?
2. Is there one 'intelligence' or many?
3. What is the relation between teaching general thinking skills and teaching content areas?
4. What is creativity and can it be taught?
5. Are general thinking skills individual or collective?
6. Are general thinking skills culturally situated? (i.e. are they white, male and middle class?)
7. Are general thinking skills historically situated?

1 DO GENERAL THINKING SKILLS EXIST?

1.1 The argument against thinking skills in philosophy

John McPeck argued that thinking is always thinking about something and therefore it does not make sense to talk about thinking in general (McPeck, 1990). For McPeck the different academic subject areas are different 'forms of life' with their own unique logics. Teaching general critical thinking skills is therefore a serious mistake which will lead to superficial learning. In Britain something like this position appears to have strong support amongst some philosophers of education (e.g. Johnston, 2000)

1.2 The argument against thinking skills in psychology

In educational psychology the argument against thinking skills is much the same as that in philosophy but presented differently. Some proponents of the view that learning is 'situated in contexts' and/or is always about 'participation in communities of practice' oppose their 'Specific Learning Model' (Rogoff et al., 1991, p. 315) to the more traditional 'Central Processor Model' of the brain. This Specific Learning Model follows from claiming 'thinking skills' are embedded in 'cultural tool systems', especially local ways of using language to get things done ('language' here is considered to be a tool-system). On this model what is learnt in the context of one cultural task can only be assumed to relate to that task. This position has gained supported from research by Newell and others seeking to create a general problem-solving expert system. Eventually it was concluded that all problem solving, even that in strategy games like chess, requires so much specific domain relevant information that it is not useful to separate the thinking process from the content knowledge (Simon, 1980). The implication is that teaching transferable skills may be just a myth. This position is often supported by the claim that there is no real evidence for transfer (e.g. Hennessy et al., 1993).

1.3 Responses to these arguments

The most balanced rebuttals of arguments against the possibility of teaching thinking skills point out that they fail to engage with the reality of contemporary approaches to practice (Weinstein, 1993; Higgins and Baumfield, 1998). The argument that all thinking is thinking about something is a reasonable objection to some attempts to teach a pure and abstract logic of good thinking. There is little evidence for the automatic transfer of general thinking skills that a 'central processor model' of the mind would predict (Perkins and Salomon, 1989). Apparently, against the claims of Piaget (1947), the brain learns things embedded in a rich context and does not automatically extract general logical rules that could be applied to other contexts (Claxton, 1999, p. 203).

The value of this debate is to expose the misleading metaphors that are applied to Thinking skills. The evidence suggests that higher order thinking is not a product of abstract logical 'cognitive structures' that can be replicated across contexts and people. But it is not sensible to move from this insight to the claim that one cannot therefore teach thinking in general.

Marzano (1998) did a meta-analysis of 4,000 intervention studies in education involving over 1,237,000 subjects. He found that nearly all interventions worked to some extent but that interventions that focussed on the level of meta-cognition, (i.e. teaching thinking and learning strategies), and the level he called 'the self-system' (i.e. how students feel about themselves as learners) were most effective in improving scores on measures of learning.

Marzano's findings strongly support the success of teaching thinking skills if we translate this to mean the teaching of meta-cognitive strategies. Marzano writes that:

Specifically, instructional techniques that employed the metacognitive system had strong effects whether they were intended to enhance the knowledge domains, the mental process within the cognitive system, the beliefs and processes within the self-system, or the processes within the metacognitive system itself.

Similarly teaching that specifically focused on emotions and sense of identity (what Marzano called 'the self system') had a powerful effect on 'learning gains' at every level. Implicit in this finding is a transfer effect from teaching focussing on attitudes and feelings to gains in learning measures.

Hattie et al. (1996) conducted a smaller meta-analysis of 51 study skills interventions. They found that 'Despite, perhaps, the conventional wisdom, most intervention *does* work most of the time' (1996, p. 128). However, separate general study skills programmes were found to be much less effective than teaching meta-cognitive strategies as part of the teaching of content within courses.

The empirical research evidence now seems convincing that something interesting is happening through thinking skills programmes and approaches (Moseley et al., 2005). But another kind of evidence that should not be ignored is the evidence of experience. We all have experience as both teachers and learners, if only in an informal way. We all know intuitively that it is possible for learning to change people and to become part of who they are, wherever they are. We also know that it is possible to learn skills that are used outside the context in which they were originally learnt. That is how we can think at all when faced with a new challenge. The fact that these truths of experience sometimes prove hard to evaluate in a rigorous way should not lead us to deny them, but rather, if there is a problem, to reconceptualise what we might mean by the phrase 'general thinking skills'.

Marzano's results on the importance of addressing self-image as a learner confirms that wide-spread view amongst those who teach thinking that the kind of intellectual confidence and trust in others that enables people to take risks is a general thinking skill relevant to many contexts (Williams and Wegerif, 2006). This provides us with a new metaphor for 'thinking skills': not abstract logic but an embodied and emotional as well as cognitive way of responding and relating to others and to new situations. Successful evaluations of Philosophy for Children, a method for teaching thinking that consists entirely of inducting children into dialogues, suggest that a capacity to engage effectively in dialogue appears to lie behind many of the techniques, habits and dispositions referred to in the literature on thinking skills (Trickey and Topping, 2004). If so this capacity appears to be a holistic and embodied skill that is learnt in one context and applied in many other contexts. Some difficulties that arise when thinking skills are thought of on the model of a mechanism dissolve when thinking skills are thought of on the model of engagement in dialogue. The significance of the methaphor for thinking that we apply will be discussed in more detail in Chap. 7.

2 IS THERE ONE 'INTELLIGENCE' OR MANY?

Intelligence is another terms often used for the sort of successful, productive and valued thinking that I am referring to here, following Resnick (1987), as Higher Order Thinking. The influence of IQ tests in education has led many to see intelligence as a single scale with the cognitively challenged at the bottom end and geniuses at the top end. Against this unitary view of intelligence, Howard Gardner has proposed that there are multiple intelligences which are distinct from each other. He includes interpersonal intelligence, kinetic intelligence, musical intelligence, mathematical intelligence, linguistic intelligence and so on (Gardner, 1999). Gardner's position is important in emphasizing that people have different talents and that there are different ways of thinking that are successful in different contexts. It has been influential in education in promoting educational design that addresses a range of styles of thinking.

Against the multiple view of intelligence, psychologists in the psychometric tradition tend to a consensus that while the measurement of the sort of skills Gardner refers to as intelligences does confirm multiplicity there remains some overlap in these different measures which they refer to as 'g'. What this means is that while some people who are good at 'intelligent' thinking in the context of maths are bad at 'intelligent' thinking in the context of literature or football, enough people who display intelligence in one context also display intelligence in other contexts to indicate that there is probably a common underlying factor.

One problem here is what we mean by the word 'intelligence'. IQ tests were originally devised as a pragmatic tool for predicting success at formal schooling and they still do quite well at that task. This is a measure of potential success in a context which does not necessarily imply any underlying single mental faculty or ability. Sternberg is in this same pragmatic tradition of intelligence research when he offers the broad definition of 'successful intelligence' as 'the ability to achieve success in life, given one's personal standards, within one's socio-cultural context' (Sternberg and Grigorenko, 2000, p. 93). Gardner also focuses on success in contexts when he defines 'an intelligence' as:

A biopsychological potential to process information that can be activated in a cultural setting to solve problems or create products that are of value in a culture. (Gardner, 1999, p. 33)

Perkins, in a magisterial survey of debates about intelligence, teases out some of the components of successful performance in any context, not all of which are easily taught or learnt. Perkins distinguishes between three aspects of intelligence: *neural intelligence*, which varies between individuals but about which educators can do very little except perhaps offering proper access to water and good nutrition: *experiential intelligence*, based on acquired knowledge and relevant to performance on structured and predict-table tasks; and finally *reflective intelligence*, which is required when facing new and unstructured problems or challenges. It is this reflective intelligence that can be addressed by teaching thinking in a way that helps people to become more aware of their own thinking and offers them strategies that might improve this (Perkins, 1995).

Perkins' distinctions here are useful in revealing that a great deal of what has been called 'intelligence' consists either of mechanical brain processing or the product of experience in an area over time such that familiar patterns are recognized and responded to appropriately. Because of this experiential component it is not surprising that intelligence is often seen as culture and context specific. However, there is a component of intelligence required when we face new problems or cross the boundaries of familiar cultures and contexts. Perkins' understanding of 'reflective intelligence' relates closely to Flavell's concept of 'metacognition' (Flavell, 1976). Although meta-cognition is sometimes described in the machine language of computer programming it is essentially about becoming more self-reflectively aware of the processes of ones own thinking which include becoming aware of limiting assumptions and implicit strategies. Inevitably awareness of the limitations of the strategies that they are applying leads people to change their strategies and to try to improve their thinking. That meta-cognition in the form of 'reflective intelligence' can be improved seems plausible since once we become aware of where we are going wrong in our thinking it is possible to apply strategies to address that. To give a simple example from my own research, when I found that some young children were doing very badly on reasoning tests because they were applying the 'strategy' of selecting multiple choice responses at random I was able to address this by getting them to work in groups where they were questioned by peers as to 'why' they thought an answer was correct and why they thought it was better than each of the other possible answers in turn. Unsurprisingly this strategy worked and their scores on the tests went up dramatically (Wegerif et al., 1999). Since these tests were standard Ravens reasoning tests said to be the best single indicator of 'g', this experimental study can count as evidence that, yes indeed, intelligence can be taught.

Some psychometricians such as Caroll (1993) argue that it is probably the speed of neural processing or the size of memory buffers that make some people smarter than others in a range of contexts. Perkins would not necessarily disagree with this but would argue that it is also their capacity for reflection on their own thinking and that this is something that can be increased through education. Reflection is interesting because reflection always implies stepping outside of oneself in order to take the perspective of the other. The perspective of the other may be a specific other as in 'what would Sherlock Holmes do if faced by this same problem' or it may be the perspective of a general other such as Bakhtin's 'superaddressee', the projection of a perspective that is able to see more clearly because it is outside of the process of thinking. In other words, reflective intelligence, which is general to many areas independent of content knowledge and which can be taught, is essentially dialogic. In Chap. 6, I will provide some of the evidence for thinking that this kind of general intelligence is learnt first in the context of real dialogues with real people like parents, teachers and peers.

3 WHAT IS THE RELATIONSHIP BETWEEN TEACHING GENERAL THINKING SKILLS AND TEACHING CONTENT AREAS?

Different positions in the debate about the nature of thinking skills suggest different responses to the question of how to teach thinking skills. Belief in what has been called 'the central processor model' of the mind tends to suggest that teaching thinking skills directly in a separate programme will automatically have a general impact. There are many such separate programmes: Feuerstein's instrumental enrichment (Blagg, 1991) Lake and Needham's top ten thinking tactics (Lake and Needham, 1993), de Bono's CORT (1976) and Lipman's own philosophy for children are examples (Lipman, 2003).

The argument that thinking skills are specific to subject areas, however, suggests developing thinking skills within each subject area separately. McGuiness makes a good argument for a third approach, which, following Swartz and Parks (1994) she calls the 'infusion' approach. The idea is that teaching curriculum content is 'infused' with the teaching of thinking skills. Some examples of infusion programmes are McGuinness' ACTs (McGuinness et al., 1997) and Sharon Bailin's approach to teaching critical and creative thinking in Canada (Bailin, 1994). In the UK this approach is exemplified by Thinking Together (Mercer, 2000; Dawes et al., 2000), Robert Fisher's UK approach to Philosophy for Children (Fisher, 1990) and thinking through primary teaching (Higgins, 2001; Leat and Higgins, 2002).

The consensus seems to be that hard independent evidence for the success of separate thinking skills programmes is limited (Resnick, 1987;

Craft, 1991; Greeno et al., 1996). This consensus, in combination with the shift in educational theory towards the situated and the social, mean that there is a direction towards thinking skills programmes being embedded more in content area teaching. This has implications for the design of educational software to support thinking skills.

While I have argued, following Castells and others, that the advent of the Internet should shift the focus of education from teaching content to teaching general thinking and learning it is ultimately misleading to separate content from more general skills. On the one hand, as McPeck correctly claimed, thinking is always thinking about something (or more accurately, successful thinking implies the application of social criteria of success which in turn implies that the thinking has some sort of goal or product). To understand other people in dialogues and to be able to create and defend new positions in maths or history or computer science, it is necessary to learn and be able to articulate a great deal of what could be called the specific 'content knowledge' relevant to maths or history or computer science. However, this content is not separate from the dialogues which bring it alive and make it relevant. On the other hand good teachers have never simply taught content. Through teaching maths or history or computer science they have also been teaching general thinking and learning skills including those which are hard to separate from the idea of forming character through engaging in a relationship. This is obvious when we acknowledge that general thinking and learning skills are not narrowly cognitive but include attitudes and emotions. As Dewey puts it:

> Perhaps the greatest of all pedagogical fallacies is the notion that a person learns only the particular thing he is studying. Collateral learning in the way of formation of enduring attitudes, of likes and dislikes may be and often is much more important than the spelling lesson or lesson in geography or history that is learned. The most important attitude that can be formed is the desire to go on learning. (Dewey, 1938, p. 29)

4 WHAT IS 'CREATIVITY' AND CAN IT BE TAUGHT?

Creativity is a disputed concept within education. In Chap. 5, I introduced definitions of creativity in everyday use: creativity 1 for the simple generation of new analogies or ways of looking at things and creativity 2 for fashioning a socially valued product. Some of the problems with the word creativity in education result from a perceived tension between these two different ways of using the word creativity. On the one hand many people see creativity as being about individuality and freedom from rules and judgements. This definition lay behind some approaches to education for creativity in the seventies in the UK including ideas like not teaching 'correct grammar' because this might constrain creative writing (Phillips, 1996). On the other hand we often reserve the term creative for products that we value. Role models of creativity tend to be celebrated high achievers, Einstein and Beethoven for example, whose work was not only original but also of excellent quality. This definition of creativity underlies a new focus on creativity in the UK curriculum where it is hoped that education can instil skill at fashioning valued products that can earn tax revenue for Britain in the global networked economy, products like pop-songs and computer games (NACCCE, 1999). Einstein and Beethoven, like video game designers and at least some pop singers, had to become masters of the techniques in their respective fields before they could be creative within them. This insight has led some educators to the view that, for creativity, it is better to teach a subject rigorously until students master it. One problem with this of course is that not everyone who masters a field becomes creative within it. Howard Gardner claims, in a study of highly creative people, that individuals who are destined to be creative in their field are found to be different from others in the earliest stages of their careers in that they are 'explorers, innovators, tinkerers' (Gardner, 1993, p. 32). If so then one thing that education might be able to do is to encourage the character traits that lead people to enjoy exploring and to provide environments that enable them to explore.

It may be that the apparent contradiction between these two views of creativity – creativity as a kind of freedom and creativity as a route to socially recognized success – reflects the double nature of creativity as a phenomenon itself. Albert Ehrenzweig, for example, adopting and developing a psychoanalytic paradigm, proposed a theory of creativity on the basis of his work with artists which involved combining two different mental levels, the conscious differentiated level and what he called the 'undifferentiated unconscious' (Ehrenzweig, 1967). The big insight behind split level or two process models of creativity is that being creative sometimes seems to involve suspending all prior judgements, just playing aimlessly, and waiting for connections to emerge. It is as if one part of the mind, the conscious and controlling part, sometimes needs to be quiet in order for the artist to listen to ideas that emerge from another part of the mind. Something like Ehrenzweig's distinction between two levels of mind does seem useful in explaining the often reported role of dreams and hypnagogic states in creativity. Einstein, for example, wrote that his best ideas came to him in dreamlike states. He claimed he thought up the theory of relativity when sickness forced him to stop working and go to bed for few days. Beethoven similarly claimed that his best work often came to him in dreams. This account also fits everyday creativity or what Craft calls creativity with a little 'c' as opposed to creativity with a big 'C' (Craft, 2005). Anyone who does any kind of creative work, from writing research reports to arranging flowers, knows that it sometimes helps to stop consciously worrying at the problem and to do something else to allow hidden or 'unconscious' processes to produce a solution for us. If stated baldly the two-level model of creativity might be criticized as ignoring the importance of actually 'fashioning' a product, which is an idea as central to the everyday meaning of creativity as simply coming up with a new idea. This is not necessarily the case however, as the idea is that fashioning a product involves many cycles between the structured surface level and the unstructured or chaotically structured depth level.

While some two-level theories of creativity, like Ehrenzweig's, locate the two levels as levels of the individual mind, others suggest that they might be a fixed surface reality contrasted to a background realm of possibilities. Anna Craft, for example, proposes, after a review of the area, that teaching for creativity be conceptualised in terms of encouraging 'possibility thinking', a concept which includes fashioning new products as well as coming up with new ideas and finding new problems as well as solving encountered problems (Craft, 2005). Possibility thinking, she argues, is exemplified through the posing, in multiple ways, of the question 'what if?' This relates to Guy Claxton's suggestion that instead of teaching things as if they were simply true teachers should always raise the possibility that things could be different by saying 'might be' in place of 'is' (Claxton et al., 2006). In practice aspects of teaching for possibility thinking in classrooms include:

—   Posing questions
—   Play
—   Immersion and making connections
—   Being imaginative1
—   Innovation
—   Risk taking
—   Self determination (Burnard et al., 2006)

The effectiveness of this possibility thinking approach has been evaluated in a number of studies in primary classrooms using interviews and ethno-graphic observation (e.g. Cremin et al., 2006). These evaluations suggest that teaching can promote more of what I have called, creativity 1, or simply coming up with a new idea, and also more creativity 2, fashioning of socially valued products. In this context socially valued products are the sort of art-works, ideas and essays that are desired within the school curriculum.

The shift from a 'what is' attitude to a 'what if' attitude involved in teaching for possibility thinking has a resonance with the philosophical method of phenomenology developed by Husserl. This is to 'step back' from the apparent obvious surface reality of things, bracket out all assumptions about them and explore what is essential to them through techniques such as imaginative variation and systematic comparison. So, for instance, to find what is essential to the idea 'triangle' as this arises when one sees a triangle one could imagine all the possible kinds of triangle and compare triangles to ideas that are not triangles. In this way Husserl claimed not to explore experience directly but to explore the 'transcendental' preconditions of experience or its underlying conditions of possibility. This is, in a sense, a way of exploring the underlying 'design space' of objects. To put this very simply, children initially think of a triangle as whatever concrete instant-tiation of a triangle they are first shown, usually an equilateral triangle. Through possibility thinking they might be led to think of the concept triangle not as a single triangle but as a field of possible triangles, including long thin ones and short fat ones as well as the equilateral ones. Here one is moving from the surface of actual things to the underlying depth structure of possible things in a way that increases the degrees of freedom.

Creativity has been described in terms of navigating a design space (Boden, 2004; Sharples, 1999). If possibility thinking makes us step back from the obvious surface of things to the conditions of the possibility of things, this could reasonably be described as a step back into design spaces or 'what if?' spaces. A classic creativity exercise in schools, for example, is to take an everyday object like a teacup and to ask students to design a new one. Working with design spaces can help to simulate aspects of creativity. If one were to model the design space of a teacup on a computer one of the obvious parameters would be 'material'. Normally this is china but if we switch the parameter label 'china' to 'fur' we would create a fur teacup just like the one by Merit Oppenheim featured in the Museum of Modern Art (MoMA) in New York. To be exhibited in MoMA implies that an object exemplifies social criteria of creativity, yet the idea of a fur teacup, along with say crocodile skin teacups, wooden teacups and sackcloth teacups, could easily have been generated by computer programme exploring possible combinations of features in an underlying design space.

That is a good point, but then what about the texts and pictures that are often printed onto teacups? A word or picture on a cup makes all the difference as to how it 'feels', yet the 'space' of all such designs is clearly very large indeed and hard to predict or draw a neat boundary around. This illustration of the complexity of design does not invalidate the idea that navigating a 'design space' plays a part in creativity, it just means that in practice this is not something that could be implemented easily on a computer. The problem is that the number of dimensions needed to define a position within a creative design space are impossible to limit in advance.

While a design space with infinite dimensions cannot be implemented on a computer it may still be a valuable way of thinking about the infinite (in the sense of unlimited) space of possibilities that seems to be implicit behind human creativity. One important weakness with the contemporary idea of a design space, at least as this appears in computer science literature, is a failure to take into account the subjectivity of the designer. Creative design is not only an exploration of an objective space of possible objects but also, more importantly, an exploration of the more subjective space of possible ways of seeing objects. Designers and artists agree that it is by seeing things in new ways that unexpected but fruitful connections are made between contexts of experience. While Margaret Boden is probably right to argue that there must be a space of possibilities implicit behind the working of human creativity, it is not necessary to think of this as an objective 'design space' so much as a space of possible perspectives. The space of all possible perspectives relates to the idea of a 'dialogic space'. While 'design space' is mapped in terms of the features of objects, 'dialogic space' is mapped in terms of the positions of voices or positions in a dialogue (Baker, 2003, suggests a similar kind of space).

The searching a design-space model of creativity might work to produce new 'discoveries' in a tightly constrained field, just as the rules of the periodic table of atoms enabled researchers to predict new elements before they were actually discovered. However, this kind of discovery is not what is normally meant by creativity. Exploring creativity in the context of science concepts, Chi argues that the essence of creativity is to re-represent ideas from one ontological category or set of categories in terms of another ontological category or set of categories (Chi, 1997). Major breakthroughs in science, she argues, involve shifts between ontologies in this way (Chi and Housmann, 2003). She gives contemporary examples of shifting perspective such as the current move to see heart disease as caused by a process, inflammation of the bloodstream, rather than a substance, cholesterol and older examples such as shifting from seeing evolution as a causal process to seeing it as an emergent process. Chi's main point is that creativity is a matter of shifting perspective and can be facilitated if people are more flexible in shifting perspective, especially the deeply embedded perspectives of underlying ontologies such as those that distinguish substances from mental states and those that distinguish causal processes from emergent processes. This account of creativity, from a researcher widely cited in the learning sciences, is very interesting but not very self-reflective. Chi fails to provide an ontological perspective that could explain how creative leaps between ontologies are possible. This is something that a dialogic perspective can offer.

Chi quotes Koestler to define the essence of creativity as being able to view an object from two difference frames of reference (Koestler, 1964 in Chi, 1997). This is close to the minimal definition of dialogic given in Chap. 2 which is holding together two perspectives at once. Holding together two incommensurable perspectives at once opens up a dialogic space which is a space of possible perspectives. This is because being able to see things from another's point of view, like a child following its mothers gaze, is always a creative act and implies the potential to see things from multiple points of view. Dialogic then is creative from the beginning, it is always about 're-representing' things from alternative points of view. Dialogic space, however, is neither Boden's design space nor Chi's ontological category space. Dialogic space is hard to grasp precisely for the reason Chi argues that concepts in science are often hard to understand, this is because it requires a radical shift in ontology. Perspectives in dialogic space are not substances or positions on a map nor are they processes or mental states, they are differences in an unbounded field of possible differences that they themselves bring into being. This new kind of ontology, ontological difference, originating with Heidegger was outlined at length in Chap. 2. Merleau-Ponty put it well when he pointed out that an utterance in a real dialogue is a divergence that structures a field of possible meaning even as it catalyses that field into being (Merleau-Ponty, 1964, p116). However, the metaphor of a field is misleading if it implies that dialogic space has boundaries. Because, as we speak or think or gesture, we are always already within dialogic space and, viewed from within, dialogic space has no boundaries and so is infinite (in the strict sense of not being finite). This makes it sound big but really it is better to think of it not as big or small but simply as a limit to conceptual thought. The space within which thought carves out significant differences by definition has no meaning itself except, perhaps, as a potential for meaning. The idea of a 'space' of dialogue and the idea of a difference between perspectives, that is the smallest possible unit of 'meaning' in a dialogue, are therefore just two ways of approaching the same limit idea which is the idea of the context of thought. Both are negative or limit concepts pointing towards the same underlying context of thought which, because it is the context of thought, cannot itself be thought.

It might reasonably be replied that a limit to thought concept like dialogic space cannot be much use for doing practical things such as pedagogical design. In a sense it is quite right to argue, as Derrida does, that ontological difference is not so much a new ontology as an anti-ontology, not so much a new ground to build on as an undermining of the possibility of there being any ground. If we insist, with Vygotsky, that ideas are all concepts and all concepts are tools like hammers and screwdrivers with which we can build new conceptual structures, then it is true that the idea of dialogic space is not much use. However, some ideas are useful not because of the positive functionality that they offer but, more negatively, they serve by clearing away misunderstanding. Derrida's différance, for example, is not useful as a positive new tool but it is useful as a kind of disruptive joke challenging and dismissing common assumptions about the nature of meaning and the nature of Being. If, as we tend to, we think of everything and ourselves on the model of substance or identity then we produce a stable world of defined things and defined relationships between things within which it is hard to explain creativity. If with Heidegger, Merleau-Ponty and Derrida we 'step back' from the apparently fixed and stable surface of the world and explore how it is constructed and maintained, we discover that creativity is the default rather than the exception. Words, signs, events, gestures are bursting with possible meanings until they are constrained by their contexts to mean specific things. If we switch ontological perspective in this way we discover that creativity as imaginative analogy and creativity as 're-representation' are not constructions that need to be explained but the human baseline, what needs to be explained are the processes that impose uncreativity in the form of stable bounded identities. Design for creativity then becomes not only a matter of positive construction but also has to include the element of opening up a dialogic space. For Derrida this is not a space of possibility so much as a space of impossibility (Biesta, 2001). His point is perhaps that once we remove any ideas of boundaries around this space then it is no longer a space of possibilities, since this implies the design space idea of a mapable space of things that we know we do not know, whereas in fact we also have to deal with things that we do not yet know that we do not know and that seem to us now quite impossible.

The practical value of this ontological account of dialogic space to education for creativity is apparent if we insert it into the two level model of creativity implied in the idea of promoting 'possibility thinking'. If we accept Chi's claim that creativity involves moving from one way of structuring cognition to another then this suggests the need to posit an unstructured background or context into which the first structure can dissolve and from which the second structure can emerge. This suggests that actual creativity involves weaving between a structured level of reality, with goals and criteria of success in reaching those goals, with an unstructured dialogic space in which everything resonates with everything else and in which anything is possible. To become more creative an individual or group has to learn facility in moving between these levels, the levels of identity and dialogue, or the 'what is' level and the 'what if' level.

Education and training have always focussed on developing positive capabilities that help people do things in the world. What is needed for promoting more creativity in education then is to combine education into the positive skills that enable the fashioning of good products with promoting what Keats called the 'negative capability', the ability to remain in uncertainty and multiplicity without reaching prematurely for an answer. This negative skill is precisely what can be learnt by entering into dialogue and learning to live more in dialogic space as well as in identity space.

I have perhaps made the idea of design for opening a dialogic space sound rather more complicated than it really is. In practice this can be very simple. Most of the time we follow implicit rules or 'scripts' that enable us to do things without needing to think about them. This is true in classrooms as well. Young children observed supposedly collaborating at science simulations on a computer, for example, will talk maybe about who should have the mouse or who should sit in which chair but often click happily away at the screen and observe the effects of their clicking in silence without feeling the need to question what they are doing or why they are doing it. Design for opening a dialogic space in this activity could be as simple as putting up a prompt on the screen, when they try to click a 'run simulation' button, asking them to talk about what they expect to observe and why. In the context of a pedagogy that has prepared them for talking together, such a prompt may lead them to turn away from the screen towards each other and generate together a range of possible perspectives some of which they can test out when they return to running the simulation (see e.g. Wegerif, 1996). In this way the possibility thinking in the task has increased and the potential for generating insight has increased.

Csikszentmihalyi (1996) and his team interviewed about a hundred people who could be called creative because they had transformed their field in a publicly acknowledged way, scientists who had won the Nobel prize, artists who were leaders of new movements and so on. He found that when they really engaged with their field and with producing new ideas or products, all reported a sense of joy and of inner reward. Some reported that the quality of time itself changed from being the external context found in the phrases 'killing time' or 'passing time' to becoming an internal flow in which awareness of the passage of time disappeared. This is what it feels like, apparently, when we take up our past experience and make it our own by transforming it in acts of creative expression. This empirical finding can be explained by the idea that creativity involves dissolving the boundaries of identity thinking. In strong identity thinking time is clock time, an objective reality independent of the self. The shift into dialogic space involves a loosening of identity boundaries such that one becomes the field in order to speak and listen with many voices and perspectives at once. In Bakhtin's terminology the structured surface of identity or 'what is' has a very different 'chronotope' or configuration of space and time than the unstructured space of dialogue. Dialogic space, is, according to one interpretation of Bakhtin, ultimately characterized through the chronotope of 'great time' in which all times and places converge together as one single time–space that is not internal or external. Creativity, in the sense of fashioning a socially valued product, weaves these two chronotopes together often rhythmically moving in and out between clock time and great time. It is not surprising, therefore, that the experience of time changes in the process of creativity. The change in the experience of time associated with creativity indicates that the creativity that flowed through Einstein and Beethoven, and that flows through any and all of us when we respond creatively to our experience, is real enough, and not only a culturally and historically situated badge given out to acknowledge the production of valued products. In dissolving space–time boundaries and self-other boundaries to project people into a play of perspectives and ideas, this real creative process is always essentially dialogic.

5 ARE THINKING SKILLS INDIVIDUAL OR SOCIAL?

Thinking skills programmes have traditionally assumed that thinking is an individual faculty. However, the roots of teaching critical thinking are not necessarily individualist. John Dewey, an advocate of teaching thinking, saw thinking as inseparable from social interaction and teaching thinking as a way of contributing to the creation of a better society (Dewey, 1933). Jurgen Habermas (1991) has argued in a similar way that rationality implies the ideal of a more genuinely democratic society in which all relevant voices are really listened to and decisions are taken on the basis of the quality of arguments rather than on the basis of coercive power. One educational impli-cation of Habermas's argument is that teaching thinking skills involves changing the social context to create conditions that at least approximate to what he calls an 'ideal speech situation'. The experimental evidence I referred to in Chap. 4 supports the common sense view that the quality of individual thinking reflects the quality of collective thinking and vice versa (Wegerif et al., 1999). Growing acceptance of the idea that thinking is social as well as individual, because it is embodied in dialogues, can be seen reflected in the language used to discuss thinking skills. There is an increasing use of collective terms such as 'thinking classrooms' (McGuinness, 1998), 'thinking schools' (Wilson, 2000) and 'communities of inquiry' (Lipman, 2003). These terms are quite empty if they are some loose way of suggesting that 'systems' think but they gain credibility if they are linked to establishment of times and spaces for real dialogue within classrooms, schools and communities.

A dialogic perspective is compatible with an understanding of higher order thinking as individual reflection. The accounts of the ontogenesis of individual reflection in the internalization of dialogic space that I have already quoted from Hobson and will offer more evidence for in Chap. 6, suggest that individual reflection is always essentially dialogic. Of course this is conceptually problematic because dialogue is never really just individual or social but always both (and always more than both). The idea of dialogic undermines the division between individual and social since this line is a division drawn within dialogic space (see discussion of this position in Chap. 2). This does not mean, as some have apparently argued, that we can do without the distinction between inner and outer, self and world (Lave and Wenger, 1991, p. 47 seem to suggest this). An individual's inner reflections are clearly not crudely determined by their environment, physical, social or historical. What this means is that human individuals are predisposed, at some point in the first 18 months, to learn to reproduce internally the dialogic opening between perspectives held together in tension that they first encounter outside themselves in relationships with others. From that point on individual creative reflection does not always need to be driven by interaction with others or with the environment. That individual creative reflection is spontaneous and not always driven by contradictions or conflicts with the environment is argued for convincingly by Anette Karmiloff-Smith (1999) who describes this inner process as the creative process of 'representational redescription'. Karmiloff-Smith acknowledges the possibility that the first capacity to represent originates in dialogic relations in the early months when children are very open to others but she argues strongly that all representations afterwards are inside an individual mind (Karmiloff-Smith, 1999, p. 123). However, against this, the ontological dialogic perspective outlined in Chap. 2 argues with Merleau-Ponty that in every dialogue the boundary between self and other, my 'representation' and 'your representation' is transgressed and indeed dissolved. In a real dialogue it is no longer possible to know who is thinking. A dialogic perspective on education and thinking therefore shares with the neo-Vygotskian sociocultural perspective a sense that while, for some everyday purposes, there clearly is a boundary between self and environment, that boundary is permeable and often crossed (Edwards, 2005: Valsiner, 2001).

In the literature on distributed cognition it is common to argue that thinking is always a combination of agents and tools and so the quality of thinking is partly dependent on the quality of the tools (e.g. Perkins, 1993). The argument of Wertsch that the unit of analysis in education should be an agent and their mediating means is a variation on this claim. In Chap. 3 I took on this focus on mediating means in order to argue that the quality of thinking in a dialogue depends above all on the quality of the relationship or the creative dialogic space established between people. Tools might be helpful in establishing that space but they do not do the creative thinking. Here it helps to make a distinction between higher order thinking and automatable thinking. Clearly using a calculator can improve the quality of someone's calculations but it cannot improve the quality of their reflection on the significance of those calculations. When I refer to teaching 'thinking' I am not referring to rules of calculation of the kind embedded in a calculator but to 'higher order thinking' defined by Resnick (1987) as creative thinking that is precisely not the algorithmic or formal reasoning of computers.

The dialogic approach I am proposing is different from distributed cognition because it claims that thinking occurs in dialogues, not in systems. Dialogues require relationships between people: systems require only relations between things. Machines cannot fully participate in dialogues, anymore than most animals can, because they are not capable of the dialogic intersubjectivity required to see things from another's point of view. However, technology can resource and support dialogues to make them more effective and to expand their scope in various ways. This is the topic of Chap. 8.

The idea of 'dialogic' bridges the divide assumed by the question of whether or not thinking is individual or social. If dialogues are accepted as the primary thinking mode then the individual and the social are already indissolubly fused. Individuals can only discover and define themselves through dialogues and in the context of dialogues and exactly the same is true of collective identities such as 'communities of practice'. Not only is reflective dialogue always situated in individuals, as Karmilloff-Smith implies and in social contexts as Lave, Wenger and Engestrom claim but also individuals and social contexts are always 'situated' within dialogues. This is why dialogues can transcend their situation. Thinking is not primarily a property of individuals or of systems but it is primarily an aspect of dialogues. Whether or not dialogues are seen from the outside as dialogues internal to an individual physical body or as 'socially situated' dialogues between physical bodies internal to a bounded social community, when they are seen from the inside then dialogues always occur primarily in dialogic space and dialogic space has no boundary.

6 ARE CRITICAL THINKING SKILLS SOCIALLY SITUATED? (I.E. ARE THEY WHITE, MALE AND MIDDLE-CLASS?)

Some argue that critical thinking skills are not really of general value but are a product of the experience of a particular social group usually described as white, male and professional or managerial. Ruqaya Hasan for example, in a study that shows that there is more language of explicit problem solving and reasoning in the homes of managers and professionals than in blue collar homes, claims that the value given to this way of using language reflects Marx's claim that 'in every age the ideas of the rulers are the ruling ideas' (Marx, 1977, quoted in Hasan, 1992).

Harvey Siegel (1987) and Sharon Bailin (1998) respond to this kind of challenge with the argument that criticisms of critical thinking already imply critical thinking and can only be assessed through the giving and evaluating of reasons. However, this focus on explicit reasoning fails to fully address some of the concerns expressed. Feminist philosopher, Seyla Benhabid (1992) seems to be have more insight into why certain groups feel excluded by the ideal of critical thinking and offers what I think is a constructive way forward. Her argument, based upon Habermas, is that, if we are to bring up children in peace we actually do need some sort of ideal of reason or at least an ideal of 'being reasonable'. This ideal is about how real people solve their problems without resorting to violence through engaging in dialogues informed by an attitude of care and respect.

For Richard Paul, as was noted earlier, critical thinking in the strong sense has to be 'dialogical'. What he means by this is that the critical thinker has an obligation to question his or her own assumptions in order to try to understand the perspective of others (Paul, 1987, 1991). If, as Seyla Benhabid suggests, reason is situated in real dialogues then, in the course of such dialogues, assumptions about what constitutes good reasoning will themselves have to be questioned and allowed to evolve. If there are different ways of thinking with something to offer – and claims have been made for the value of more intuitive and holistic feminine and non-western ways of thinking – then this should emerge in such genuine 'strong' critical thinking dialogues. But any such evolution of our understanding of higher order thinking would only serve to strengthen the process of higher order thinking itself, if this is understood as essentially and originally 'dialogue across difference'. Biesta argues, applying Derrida's 'method' of deconstruction, that democratic dialogue is seen in the response when the established ground rules are challenged by a group who feel excluded by them (Biesta, 2006). This suggests that we need to resist any substantial definition of higher order thinking skills in favour of the idea that higher order thinking is embodied in open self-reflective dialogue that is responsive and evolving. One of the leaders in the field of dialogue within education, Nicholas Burbules, has recently voiced strong criticisms of the ideal of dialogue within education as potentially a way of silencing distruptive voices and imposing a culturally specific value (Burbules, 2006). These criticisms appear to rely on what Bakhtin calls a narrow understanding of dialogue as a form of speech opposed to monologue (Bakhtin, 1986, p. 117). Burbules advocates, 'beyond dialogue', what he calls, following the post-colonial theorist Homi Bhaba, a 'third space' defining this as:

> a zone in which semantic frames meet, conflict, and get attached with meanings neither original party intended, or could have intended

Interestingly Burbules points out that the Internet can operate as a global 'third space' of this kind. Bhaba's concept of a 'third space' owes much to Bakhtin and is a version of what I have been calling 'dialogic space', a space in which different perspectives are held in tension together without any necessary resolution but which produces sparks of insight, learning and creativity.

Bakhtin is often appropriated for situated views of learning and cognition because he located thought within dialogues between real embodied voices by which he meant voices with personalities speaking words that have a social history. However, as I brought out in Chap. 2, he also argued that there is something universal in the nature of dialogues that can take us beyond the limits of our situation. He referred dismissively to 'the narrow space of small time' that so commonly is the context of analysis (Bakhtin, 1986, p. 167). As I mentioned in Chap.2, he apparently rejected the idea of situated cognition when he wrote that:

> In order to understand it is immensely important for the person who understands to be located outside the object of his or her creative understanding – in time, in space, in culture. (Bakhtin, 1986, p. 7)

One can get this outside point of view on oneself only through taking the perspective of the other, the perspective of a far off culture, for example, but this capacity for taking an outside perspective implies a certain generality to the otherness involved or what is sometimes referred to as a Martian point of view. The Martian eye view is invoked as a move in dialogues to question things that are commonly taken for granted as in: 'A visitor from Mars could easily pick out the civilized nations. They have the best implements of war' (Herbert V. Prochnow, via Google). Because the visitor from Mars sees without prejudice this ideal relates to the perspective of the superaddressee proposed by Bakhtin. Utterances in a dialogue, Bakhtin pointed out, are never only directed at a specific addressee but also at a superaddressee, the ideal of a third party to the dialogue who has a capacity to understand what is really meant by the utterance even when the specific addressee cannot understand it due perhaps to his or her limitations (Bakhtin, 1986, p. 126). This ideal of an unsituated perspective is understood by Bakhtin as a projection of situated dialogues and not as a real location hence, he claims, it varies in form from being the perspective of 'God' to being 'the judgement of science'. However, this ideal perspective seems to enter into dialogues such that every dialogue is not only a dialogue with specific others but also, and often this is more significant for education, it is a dialogue with the superaddressee. This is important because it indicates how dialogues can help to lever us out of our situation to see things from a new perspective.

The extent that one thinks that one can accurately specify the key features of a situation is the extent that one thinks that one has a comprehensive overview or map. The claim that cognition is situated in communities of practice for example implies that we know where the boundaries of the community can be drawn. This implies that a map has been sneaked into the dialogue when really establishing the boundaries of any community requires dialogues with the participants in which it will be found that such boundaries are always open to interpretation.

To illustrate the boundary problem one has only to reflect upon one's situation as one thinks. For example: I am thinking now and it feels dialogic to me so I am happy to concede that my thinking here, aided by the technology of my computer, is a dialogue situated within a community but I would not want to exclude anyone in advance from that community. While I am primarily perhaps writing for a small audience of researchers in a similar field of research to my own, many of whom I may know, I am also inescapably, in dialogue with more distant cultural voices like Bakhtin and Marx, not to mention Lao-Tze and Protogoras, as well as all whose voices have entered and shaped me from my grandmother to a man I met briefly in a train station in Ankara whose name I never knew. And we none of us can be sure that our thoughts, however 'situated' they may seem to us, will not one day be translated into Martian and puzzled over for their meaning by aliens. Bakhtin's point is that, while thought may be situated in dialogues, those dialogues have no fixed limit. Paradoxially then, the claim that 'higher order thinking', is embedded in a situation that it cannot transcend implies assuming an unsituated point of view since the only way to limit a dialogue in advance would be to step outside of dialogue in order to be able to draw a boundary around it.

It may well be that defining thinking skills in a narrow way often reflects the experience and self-interest of a particular social group. In the promotion of dialogue across difference shared frameworks and values cannot be assumed. The opening of a dialogic space does not imply the successful achievement of constructive dialogue converging on a shared understanding, but only a willingness to listen, to question ones own assumptions and submit oneself to the tension of conflicting viewpoints. Sometime, even without good will, listening occurs and creative new 'hybrid' ways of thinking emerge. The debate with those critics of the ideal of dialogue who claim it is always socially situated is helpful in expanding and deepening our understanding of dialogue and dialogic thought. It exposes the limits of a superficial understanding of dialogic as simply anything 'pertaining to dialogue' and shows why it is important to go behind actual dialogues to the principle of dialogic that makes them possible. The aim of education implied by this critique is that we should not only promote dialogues that are pre-understood in terms of particular cultural values but that we should also try to open dialogic spaces in which nothing is pre-supposed or excluded in advance.

7 ARE THINKING SKILLS HISTORICALLY SITUATED?

Thinking skills are not some sort of neutral objective mechanism but those ways of thinking that are socially valued. It is not true that educators simply want to teach thinking since everyone somehow learns how to think. The problem is that some people learn how to think badly and educators want to teach them how to think better. Perhaps all discourse of thinking skills and higher order thinking can be reduced to a simple phrase often used by Sternberg: 'good thinking'. But what is and what is not considered to be 'good thinking' is subject to debate and to social and historical context. Resnick's definition of 'higher order thinking' that I have adopted is a definition of a kind of thinking that is socially valued at the moment but has not always been valued and may not always continue to be valued.

It seems plausible that the kinds of thinking that people value most is influenced by the kind of technology that people have at their disposal to help them think. The Ancient Greeks had simple technologies and they valued that kind of thinking that distinguished them most from the animals around them. Aristotle defined man as a rational animal meaning that only man could measure, judge and decide on the basis of reasons (Aristotle, -350/1987). Before the arrival of computers in human history it seemed natural to many to describe 'higher order thinking', or rationality, in terms of abstract reason on the model of formal logic or mathematics. This kind of thinking was really hard, potentially very useful and only a few people could do it well. Computers, however, find formal reasoning easy. What they find hard is the sort of things most people take for granted like coming up creatively with new ways forward in complex, fast-changing and open-ended contexts where there is no certainty of being right. Holding an ordinary conversation, for example, is typical of what it is that humans find natural but computers find extremely hard.

It is not surprising therefore that, as the use of computer-based technology has become more ubiquitous, the focus of thinking skills research has shifted away from the sort of things that computers can do for us, such as formal reasoning or algorithmic problem solving, towards the sort of things that computers cannot yet do. Instead of contrasting human thinking to the thinking of animals, human thinking is beginning to be contrasted to the thinking of machines (e.g. Penrose, 1994; Hobson, 2002). The focus of published thinking skills research is shifting away from teaching logic and towards a greater interest in supporting complex unpredictable thinking (Resnick, 1987), engagement in dialogues (Paul, 1987), intuition (Claxton, 1999) and creativity (Bailin, 1994).

Another aspect of the relationship between history and thinking skills is the changing nature of the economy and of social life. Changes in what Marx would call 'the dominant mode of production' are connected to changes in the kinds of skills required to adapt and thrive. Thinking skills are often said to be the kind of skills that people need to make good decisions (e.g. Ennis, 1996). I think it is plausible to claim that there used to be many fewer difficult decisions for most people to make. Plato, for example, advocated teaching reasoning skills only to the small elite who would have to take all the major decisions, the rulers (and even then, only when they were over 30, see Plato's Republic, 1970). The majority of the population of his ideal 'Republic' would be given a more vocational education fitted to their station. Plato saw little purpose in equipping them with skills that they would not have an opportunity to use. Plato's point, while not very democratic, makes some obvious economic sense in the circumstances of Ancient Greece but not in a society where technology can take on almost every job other than those that require creativity and human relationship.

Reasoning test measures have been taken in a consistent and comparable way since the 1920s. These measures indicate that changes in styles of thinking are not only a matter of changing social fashions but are also sometimes measurable. The Flynn effect is the name given to the discovery by a man called Flynn, that average 'IQ' test scores in developed countries have been rising since testing began (Flynn, 1987 quoted in Neisser et al., 1996). The average increase is three points per decade. This is dramatic. Apparently there were 20 times as many people with IQ's over 140 (9.12%) in Holland in 1982 than in 1952 (0.38%). An IQ over 140 was once described as 'genius' level. This does not necessarily mean that we are much more intelligent than our grandparents, such a claim would depend on one's definition of 'intelligent', but it does suggest that we are thinking differently. One plausible explanation for this is the increasing complexity of life driven by technological change (Neisser et al., 1996). The amount of information that children learn to deal with from the television and other media is much greater now than in previous generations. It should not be surprising if this change in the environment is having a measurable impact on the way that people think. Alternatively, this change may be down to the increase in the quantity and intensity of formal schooling in the period. Since IQ tests were designed to measure an ability to succeed in education it would not be surprising if more training in 'educated' ways of thinking led to increases in IQ tests. This suggestion would fit well with a Vygotsky's claims as to the importance of formal schooling to the development of more logical reasoning which is support by Cole and Scribner's seminal studies of the impact of different kinds of education on ways of thinking (Vygotsky, 1986; Scribner and Cole, 1978).

One point of agreement running through almost every article on teaching thinking skills is that the need to teach thinking skills now is rooted in our particular socio-historical situation. Thinking skills are widely qualified with some phrase such as 'skills for the new century', 'skills for the workers of the future' or 'skills for the knowledge society'. The common argument is that changes in the economy require more people to be actively involved in higher order thinking than was ever the case before. It is usually also claimed that these changes in the economy are driven by the development of new information and communication technologies. The thinking skills literature is full of references to the need to produce new knowledge workers for the new knowledge economies (e.g. Swartz, 2001). One idea behind this is that new technologies have led to increasing automation of the kinds of work that computers can do thereby forcing people into jobs where they have to take more subtle decisions and solve more complex problems (Rassool, 1999, p. 153). A second key idea is that new technology in the work place has led to rapid and accelerating changes in practices and that this puts a premium on 'learning how to learn' since anything more specific that children are taught in school is seen as likely to be out of date by the time they leave. Castells, whom I quoted in the introduction to this book, takes a variation on this approach arguing that, in what he calls the 'Network Society', education will need to be radically re-structured as education for learning to learn so that workers and citizens of the future can adapt flexibly to the rapid pace of change. A third idea now gaining prominence is that a globalised world requires the promotion of openness towards difference and a capacity for questioning ones own position which are not only ethical values but also thinking skills in that they are orientations that lead to increased reflection, insight, creativity and learning (Tomlinson, 1999).

It seems then that it may not be an accident that I am thinking these thoughts and writing this book about dialogic now. I am taking thoughts 'out of the air', thoughts that are around because they belong to the new spirit of the times or the 'zeitgeist'. However, as I mentioned earlier and argue for more in the last chapter of this book, if dialogic thinking is always situated in history and culture there is also a sense in which history and culture are always situated within dialogues. Ultimately dialogues take place not in physical time and space so much as in their own 'dialogic space'. Bakhtin calls the dialogic space which enables every period of history and every culture to engage in dialogue together, 'great time' and refers to this as a mystery (Bakhtin, 1986, p. 167). Something like 'great time' is required to explain how it is in fact possible to learn from dialogues with Plato, Lao Dze, Dewey as well as strangers met in the pub. Although the kinds of thinking we value, promote and practice might change over time, the potential scope of reflective dialogue is ultimately unbounded. I hope that change in history and in the practice of education is not simply moving around aimlessly from position to position within dialogic space but is also moving in a direction beyond fixation in particular positions towards increased awareness of and acceptance of the unbounded depths of dialogic space itself. If so, although this more dialogic perspective may seem new and perhaps even 'timely' to some, it is building on insights that have been present in every culture and historical period because they are implicit in the nature of human thought.

Summary

In this chapter, the first of two chapters on higher order thinking skills, I took on various questions and dilemmas in the field of teaching thinking: Do general thinking skills exist? Is there one 'intelligence' or many? What is the relation between teaching general thinking skills and teaching content areas? What is creativity and can it be taught? Are general thinking skills individual or collective? Are general thinking skills culturally situated? And finally, are general thinking skills historically situated? In tackling each of these I tried to show how taking a dialogic perspective helps to clarify the issues at stake and even sometimes provide useful answers. Through this discussion I generated an account of higher order thinking as essentially dialogic in nature which I will further develop in the next chapter where I look at evidence for the value of this new perspective in teaching thinking.

Chapter 7

TEACHING THINKING
Metaphors and taxonomies

Denken lernen: man hat auf unsren Schulen keinen Begriff mehr davon. Selbst auf den Universitäten, sogar unter den eigentlichen Gelehrten der Philosophie beginnt Logik als Theorie, als Praktik, als *Handwerk*, auszusterben. Man lese deutsche Bücher: nicht mehr die entfernteste Erinnerung daran, dass es zum Denken einer Technik, eines Lehrplans, eines Willens zur Meisterschaft bedarf, – dass Denken gelernt sein will, wie Tanzen gelernt sein will, *als* eine Art Tanzen ... Wer kennt unter Deutschen jenen feinen Schauder aus Erfahrung noch, den die *leichten Füsse* im Geistigen in alle Muskeln überströmen!

[Learning *to think*: in our schools one no longer has any idea of this. Even in the universities, even among the real scholars of philosophy, logic as a theory, as a practice, as a *craft*, is beginning to die out. One need only read German books: there is no longer the remotest recollection that thinking requires a technique, a teaching curriculum, a will to mastery – that thinking wants to be learned like dancing, *as* a kind of dancing... Who among Germans still knows from experience the delicate shudder which *light feet* in spiritual matters send into every muscle!]

From Nietzsche, Twilight of the Idols, 1888, from:
http://www.geocities.com/thenietzschechannel/twig.htm and translation from
http://www.geocities.com/thenietzschechannel/twi.htm]

    This chapter continues the discussion of teaching thinking began in the last chapter, Chap. 6. In the first part I explore some metaphors and conceptualisations of higher order thinking in order to argue that higher order thinking is essentially dialogic. This is not a rejection of the ideal of teaching general thinking skills but a reconceptualisation of what this might mean in terms of opening, deepening and broadening dialogic spaces. In the second part I revisit the popular idea of a taxonomy of thinking skills in education and propose a dialogic taxonomy based on the claim that a capacity for dialogue as an end in itself is the primary thinking skill from which other higher order thinking skills are derivative.

In the light of the widely perceived shift towards a knowledge economy and a network society it is not hard to persuade governments that education should promote higher order thinking and creativity. However, the changes that are required in education are not simply practical ones but also conceptual ones. Of course many teachers and educationalists resist the call to teach differently but another, perhaps even more dangerous response, is to agree with the analysis but then to assimilate the idea of teaching for flexible thinking and learning skills into models of teaching and learning forged in the industrial age to meet the needs of the industrial age. There are 'teaching thinking' programmes that begin by defining the skills required, then further analysing these down into their components or stages, 'teaching' components and stages of thinking much as one would teach any other content on the industrial teaching model and then assessing the result through a multiple choice 'SATs' type pencil and paper test. I go to conferences on teaching thinking and find it surprising and worrying that some practitioners and educationalists appear happy to talk about teaching thinking without more than the most superficial interest in understanding what thinking is or indeed much indication that they feel the need to try out higher order thinking for themselves before teaching it to others. The theory of education as induction into dialogue that I have prepared in the earlier chapters of this book is a perspective from which the teaching of general flexible thinking and learning skills can be understood in a way that is cogent and coherent. In this chapter I turn this philosophical perspective into a framework that can be applied in practice.

In this chapter I begin by exposing and questioning some of the commonly assumed metaphors for thinking. I then present evidence and arguments for the claim that 'higher order thinking', is dialogic all the way through. Finally I bring out the implications of this for education by revisiting some taxonomies of thinking skills and suggesting how these taxonomies could be refocused around the embodied reality of reflective dialogue.

1 PART 1: METAPHORS OF MIND

1.1 Do minds hum or tick?

Metaphors for mind are deeply ingrained and often hard to question or to uproot. I once observed the first 'philosophy' lesson with a group of 5-year-old children. The teacher began by informing the children that the aim of the lesson was 'thinking'. As he said this he pointed at his head. At first, when hard questions were asked some children shouted out answers as if the teacher was looking for a 'right' answer and he reminded them that this lesson was not about 'right' and 'wrong' answers but about 'thinking', again pointing to his head. 'Don't shout out', he said 'Think!'. Eventually the children settled down, put on concentrating expressions, rocked back and forwards slightly and produced a low vibrating noise. This humming grew louder and louder until one of the children spoke out with an idea in response to the teacher's last question. With the next pause for thought the humming began again, faint at first but slowly growing until again someone had an idea to share.

Why were these 5-year-old children humming when they were asked to think? It took me some time to realise that, for these children, the humming noise, as well as the concentrated look on their faces, expressed the fact that they were thinking, which would otherwise have been invisible and inaudible. They knew that there was supposed to be something going on inside them when they were thinking, the teacher had told them so by pointing at his head, and they were expressing the noise that they thought this process of 'thinking' must make.

This reminded me of a friend of mine, an educational psychologist, who sometimes says 'tick, tick, tick, tick' and draws circles in the air with her finger to indicate that she is thinking. Her tick, tick, tick and moving finger signal to observers that the machinery of her brain is working in much the same way as the humming of the children. I asked her when she had started this habit and she remembered that as a child in her home town in Mexico all the children made these ticking noises when they were thinking. Perhaps the difference between her ticking and the philosophical humming is to do with the development of technology. The modern English home does not have much clockwork in it any more but there are many electrical machines and toys that, like computers, tend to hum when they are working rather than to tick.

Of course if you ask them most psychologists will agree that thinking does not require ticking or humming but many of them do nonetheless use more elaborated models of thinking that imply the involvement of some kind of machinery. Perhaps the most famous psychologist of children's thinking,

Jean Piaget, developed a model like this that is still widely used and highly regarded. One of Piaget's students, now a distinguished professor, Anne Nelly Perret-Clermont, amused everyone at a seminar I attended with a photo that she had taken in the town where Piaget was born. It showed a large block-like factory with the name PIAGET painted on it in big bold letters. This was not a psychology factory of course but a watch-making factory still run by some of psychologist Jean Piaget's relatives. Piaget's influential account of thinking as a product of complexly interrelated underlying cognitive structures may not have been explicitly linked to Swiss watch making but it certainly suggests to me a view of the human mind as some kind of finely tooled machine. Some of his key concepts sound as if they could easily be taken from a watch-makers manual. For example the idea of 'decollage' or slippage is used by Piaget to account for why there is sometimes a mismatch between the underlying structure in the mind and children's behaviour in reality due to disturbing environmental factors. There must surely be a very similar term that his cousins the watch-makers use to explain, for example, why the second hand does not move as expected, despite perfectly precise underlying clockwork, due perhaps to excess humidity or some other environmental factor.

The metaphor of clockwork for thinking became widespread across Europe in the eighteenth century. The much more recent advent of electronic computers brought in its train a whole new branch of psychology called 'cognitive psychology' which modelled thinking explicitly on computers. The basic idea is that the brain is like the hardware, meaning the physical computer, and the mind is like the software or the programmes that the hardware of the computer runs. Many models of good thinking use this computer metaphor with talk of 'buffers' and 'modules' and the general assumption that thinking is a type of data processing (e.g. Sternberg, 1977). On this data processing model of thinking there are no mechanical cogs ticking away but only electronic signals flying around. Computers, of course, tend to hum rather than to tick. Is it possible that the humming I heard in the philosophy for children session indicated that an electronic image of thinking has now taken over the place once held by clockwork in the popular imagination?

1.2 Is the mind like a computer?

Metaphors for the mind implicit behind 'scientific' theories have an impact on educational practice. At a recent teaching thinking conference one presenter, a practitioner, quoted Stephen Pinker, Director of the Centre for Cognitive Neuro-Science MIT, as an authority for saying that people do not think in ordinary language but in 'mentalese'. This claim has serious implications for the teaching thinking skills programmes yet is based upon no more than a working hypothesis. Pinker's claim that the mind thinks in 'mentalese' is not a discovery from research but simply an initial assumption of what he affirms as his 'computational theory of mind'. Pinker assumes that the brain is a computer and the mind is made up of the programmes that this computers runs. All thinking is therefore to be seen as data-processing or number crunching of one sort or another. Just as computers operate with a machine code so the brain, on this theory, must have its own machine code or what he calls 'mentalese'.

Although he claims that his bestselling book, *How the Mind Works*, is about the brain the main argument he appears to offer that this model fits the way that the brain actually works is that of 'reverse engineering' (Pinker, 1997). This is the idea that if we can get a computer to simulate something that the brain does then that can tell us something about how the brain actually does it. For example if we can use machine code to programme a computer to apparently hold a conversation then that tells us about what our brains must be doing behind the scenes when we hold a real conversation. This argument from reverse engineering seems curiously circular. First we posit that the mind is like a computer, then we look at how a computer would do something that the mind already does and finally we conclude from this that the mind must really be like a computer. Many counter-examples could be given to show the weakness of this argument. My computer screen for example displays the time on a circular clock face with a little hand and big hand. The time shown is much the same as the time shown on an old-fashioned spring-wound alarm clock but I know that behind the computer display there are no wheels but a purely digital process. This digital 'reverse engineering' of a clock is done with numbers and computer code and so it tells me nothing about how a real old-fashioned clock works with its coiled steel spring and escapement mechanism that regulate the turning of cog-wheels. To find out about how a clock works it is not enough to simulate its outputs on a computer – you have to open it up and look inside. Many would say that the same is probably true of the human brain (e.g. Penrose, 1989).

To his credit Pinker admits that his computational model of mind cannot offer any plausible account of the nature of 'sentience' or 'consciousness' which, he agrees, appears to be unique to organic brains. He writes that:

> There is something peculiarly holistic and everywhere-at-once and nowhere-at-all and all-at-the-same-time about the problems of philosophy. (Pinker, 1998, p. 564)

And argues that this shows that we have not been adapted by evolution to deal with such deep problems and should leave them alone. However, the important element of thinking for many people is not the sort of mechanical computations that machines can potentially do much better than humans ever could, but precisely the sort of reflection in which consciousness seems to play an essential part. If Pinker can say nothing about consciousness then his claim in the title of his book to explain 'how the mind works' is an empty boast. While, as a professor of 'cognitive neuro-scientist' Pinker obviously feels justified in side-stepping around what for many is the central feature of our experience of mind, *consciousness*, to focus on more solvable technical problems, I do not believe that educationalists have this option. The questions of philosophy, although difficult, need to be addressed if we are going to teach thinking.

Pinker's claim that we should avoid consciousness because we do not have the intellectual tools to tackle it reminds me of the story of the drunk man found by a friend one evening crawling on the pavement near a lamp-post. The friend asked him what he was doing and he said: 'Looking for my car key, I dropped it'. 'Let me help', said his friend, 'where exactly did you lose it?' 'Over there by the car', came the reply. 'So why are looking here by the lamp post?' his friend asked reasonably. 'Well there is no point in looking by the car is there? – it's too dark to see anything over there!' the drunk man replied with what seemed to him to be irrefutable logic.

1.3 Is thinking channelling 'spirit voices'?

Mechanical metaphors of mind can help us understand functions that we share with animals or that we can off-load onto computers but they do not yet hold out the prospect of helping us understand the distinctively human thinking involved in becoming more self-aware, more reflective and more creative. One approach to address this lack may be to revive and revalue a much earlier more 'spiritual' metaphor of mind of which there are still traces in many languages. This is to treat valued thinking as a product of dialogue with the gods and the ancestors. Poets were traditionally inspired by 'muses'; voices which spoke to them in dreams. The word 'inspiration' originally referred to the idea of 'spirit' entering into us from without in order to speak through us. "Inspired" thinking or talking originated not with the individual but with the gods. The word 'genius', similarly, originally referred to a god, the god of the household, who could offer good advice. Socrates, who is often referred to as a founding father of "Western rationality" received inspiration of this sort from his 'Daemon' or, in Latin, his 'genius'. He was described by contemporaries as entering into a trance in order to commune with spirit beings. Heidegger makes reference to this tradition when he describes thinking in dialogic terms as always a response to a call, the call of that which is worth thinking about (Heidegger, 1978, p. 381).

Bakhtin, a classical scholar, justifies this more ancient tradition of thinking about thinking when he writes there is no transparent information but the ideas or words we encounter always come from voices which reflect positions within a culture. Dialogues, for Bakhtin, are not only dialogues with physically defined and located 'others' because the words of others are never neutral but always carry with them an ideological charge depending on their provenance. In other words we do not talk only with physical individuals but with the cultural voices that individuals carry. In the USA today, for instance, if someone speaks of being 'pro-life' or 'pro-choice' the innocent little words 'life' and 'choice' locate the speaker within a political movement and lend a particular spin or colour to their words. Beyond the repertoire of cultural and historical voices there is always also, for Bakhtin, the voice of the 'superaddressee', the projection of an ideal addressee which might be paraphrased, in different times and places, as 'God' or 'the scientific community' or 'the judgement of history' but is always a point of view that transcends the immediately given physical, social and historical context of a dialogue. The superaddressee is a real voice or perspective in all dialogues. However, Bakhtin, distances himself from a 'spiritual' account of higher order thinking, or thinking which transcends its context, when he writes of the superaddressee:

> The aforementioned third party is not any mystical or metaphysical being (although, given a certain understanding of the world, he can be expressed as such) – he is a constitutive aspect of the whole utterance, who, under deeper analysis, can be revealed in it. This follows from the nature of the word, which always wants to be *heard*, always seeks responsive understanding, and does not stop at *immediate* understanding but presses further and further (indefinitely). (Bakhtin, 1986, pp. 126–127).

1.4 Towards a dialogic account of higher order thinking

In the introduction to this book I asked the question: if we accept Castells' analysis of the shift towards a networked society then what kind of pedagogy do we need? In educational psychology the sort of skills that commentators such as Castells are claiming will be required to thrive in the knowledge age have usually been referred to as 'Higher Order Thinking Skills' (e.g. Resnick, 1987) or meta-cognitive skills (e.g. Flavell, 1976). However, these skills have traditionally been conceptualised primarily from the perspective of individualistic psychology as mechanisms or processes within individual minds. From this perspective engagement with computers, particularly programming languages and simulations, has been seen as a way of promoting higher order skills and strategies, something I say more about in Chap. 8. Increasingly, however, thinking and learning have been conceptualised in more socially situated ways, as the properties of communities of practice for example (Lave and Wenger, 1991), or embedded in concrete activity systems (Engestrom, 1987) or as a matter of learning to use tools in contexts (Wertsch and Kazak, In press). From these more situated learning perspectives it is easy to conceptualise learning to think as learning specific skills in specific contexts but it becomes harder to conceptualise learning general thinking and learning skills (a point by Greeno et al., 1996). Often this shift in perspective, from a focus on the individual mind to a focus on socially situated practice, has meant that the pedagogical goal of teaching for higher order thinking has been overlooked or rejected as no longer appropriate (Rogoff et al., 1991). This overlooking of teaching general thinking and learning skills is serious problem for educational theory if, as Castells and others claim, the teaching and learning of general thinking and learning skills is precisely what is now required from education in our increasingly networked world.

I argue that even if we accept the shift away from individualistic cognitive psychology towards understanding socially situated practices, it is still possible, if not crucial, to preserve the pedagogic aim of teaching for higher order thinking and learning skills. This can be done if we re-conceptualise higher order thinking and learning skills as primarily a property of dialogues within networks with 'creative dialogic reflection' understood as the highest of higher order thinking skills.

As was noted in Chaps. 2 and 3, Bakhtin's dialogic perspective is often presented within a socio-cultural tradition which emphasises the social situatedness of cognition. Bakhtin is sometimes referred to in support of the claim that cognition occurs within dialogues in which all utterances are spoken by someone and have a specific addressee, an idea which carries the implication that if cognition is a product of dialogues then there is no general cognition but only specific cognition. Bakhtin was certainly concerned to bring cognition back from the abstract heights of dialectic argument down to the concreteness of dialogues between personalities, but is interesting that for Bakhtin, dialogic was also about escaping from situation, or what he referred to dismissively 'the narrow space of small time' (Bakhtin, 1986, p. 167). He wrote that:

> In order to understand it is immensely important for the person who understands to be located outside the object of his or her creative understanding – in time, in space, in culture. (Bakhtin, 1986, p. 7)

He also claimed, as noted above, that utterances in a dialogue, where dialogue is understand as a shared enquiry or chain of questions, are never only directed at a specific addressee but also at a 'superaddressee', the ideal of a third party to the dialogue who has a capacity to understand what is really meant by the utterance even when the actually present addressee may not understand it (Bakhtin, 1986, p. 126). The superaddressee is similar to the ideal of an unsituated universal perspective aspired to by science often referred to as a 'God's eye point of view on the world. This ideal of an unsituated perspective is understood by Bakhtin as a product of dialogues and not as a real possibility since there is in fact no unsituated point of view (if there were it would reveal nothing since meaning is a product of interaction between perspectives). However, if the ideal of unsituatedness is a product of dialogue then so is the equal and opposite ideal of situatedness. In fact these two ideals construct each other and depend on each other. The extent that one thinks that one can accurately specify the key features of ones situation is the extent that one thinks that one has a comprehensive overview. One cannot know ones own situation except through taking the perspective of another in a dialogue and since that dialogue is always open-ended ones situation is always open to interpretation. For Bakhtin dialogic did not imply that cognition was always situated or that it was unsituated – he articulated a third and far more radical position which is that dialogue is the opening of a space out of which and within which we construct both our situation and an 'unsituated' perspective from which we can see that situation most clearly. As was argued in Chap. 2, dialogic implies the irruption of an unbounded potential for meaning wherever two or more perspectives are brought together in the tension of a dialogue (Bakthin, 1986, p. 162). This way of understanding dialogic offers a new way of understanding that which is really universal behind human cognition, dialogic. The empirical examples offered in Chaps. 4 and 5 show that dialogues can be more or less dialogic in the sense of being more or less open to the possibility of something new emerging.

1.5 Cognitive development and dialogic

A link between the idea of an unbounded dialogic space and the develop-ment of creative thought has been brought out by developmental psychology where much recent empirical work suggests that 'ontogenetically' children learn to think creatively through the 'internalisation' of dialogic space. As mentioned in Chap. 2, Peter Hobson argues that the initial dialogic couple between mother and child enables a child to see things from two perspectives at once, its own and its mothers, which opens up what he calls 'mental space' which is the foundation of learning to use symbols and to think symbolically. For Hobson thinking is essentially perspective taking. Hobson's work suggests that what is first internalised is not, as Vygotsky and his followers imply, the content of dialogue, words and gestures and so on, but the space of possible perspectives opened up by dialogue. This initial dialogic space is then presupposed by later 'internalisations' of specific signs and technologies of communication. Hobson, directly related his account of the importance of the relationship with the mother (or other primary care giver) in the early years to the development of general thinking skills when, with colleagues, he conducted an experiment demonstrating a correlation between the quality of the dialogic relation between toddlers and their mothers at 3 years and their IQ scores (Hobson, 2002; Crandell and Hobson, 1999).

Hobson contrasts the normal development of creative human thought to the development of thought in strong autism which occurs when initial intersubjectivity with the mother is not established. Tomasello and colleagues accept this contrast but also contrast normal human development to that of the great apes (Tomasello et al., 2005). Apes, they claim can learn to see others as agents with intentionality but cannot develop a truly dialogic relation with others. Human children, by contrast to apes, have, they claim: 'a species-unique motivation to share emotions, experience, and activities with other persons'. The result of this is, they argue, the development of the ability to engage in shared intentionality, which, following Hobson, I interpret as the ability to see things through other peoples eyes as well as through their own. This skill enables them to participate in culture and shared thinking. Tomasello et al. specifically take on and reject the Vygotskian argument that it is the internalisation of language use that develops human thinking, writing:

> What could it mean to say that language is responsible for understanding and sharing intentions, when in fact the idea of linguistic communication without these underlying skills is incoherent. And so, while it is true that language represents a major difference between humans and other primates, we believe that it actually derives from the uniquely human abilities to read and share intentions with other people.

Hobson and Tomasello are not alone in their account of the importance of dialogic engagement to the development of thinking. Tomosello et al. (2005) offer a review of the literature suggesting that the discovery of the importance of dialogic in cognitive development has the force of an emerging consensus.

1.6 Summary of the argument so far

In the cognitive psychology tradition cognition is generally understood to be a kind of computation (symbolic processing) and so it is easy to conceptualise teaching general higher order thinking skills in terms of programming the mind (or central processor) with more efficient meta-cognitive strategies (e.g. Pinker, 1998). In the very different neo-Vygotskian socio-cultural tradition, cognition is understood in terms of learning to use cultural tools and since these tools are always specific to social and historical contexts it is hard to conceptualise teaching for general thinking apart from teaching the use of cultural tools that span several contexts such as schooled genres of language use (e.g. Scribner and Cole, 1978; Wertsch, 1998). What is offered by the dialogic paradigm I have outlined is a way to understand how education can promote general thinking and learning beyond specific cultural tools but without returning to the questionable abstractions of cognitive psychology. The idea is that development in the direction of dialogue, considered as an *end in itself,* lies behind the teaching and learning of higher order thinking. This is both an individual and a social direction of development since it is about opening, expanding and deepening dialogic spaces wherever they occur. Development in the direction of unbounded creative thinking can be promoted by removing constraining factors, questioning assumptions for example, and also by promoting the taking of the perspective of the other and of otherness in general. Whereas, in the socio-cultural tradition, technology is conceptualised as a mediating means for cognition, from this more dialogic perspective, technology is seen as a facilitator for opening, deepening and expanding dialogic spaces.

2 PART 2: TAXONOMIES OF THINKING SKILLS

There is a big leap to be made from dialogic accounts of the development of human symbolic thinking in the early years to the teaching of thinking to older children and adults. There is perhaps an even bigger gap between philosophical accounts of the context and essential nature of human thought as dialogic and the practical business of teaching thinking. Before exploring new ways to think about teaching thinking it is necessary to consider what is currently meant when people write about teaching general higher order thinking skills.

The introduction to the thinking skills section of the National Curriculum for England (Department for Education and Skills, 2006) succinctly sums up a common view of thinking skills from a classroom practitioners point of view:

> By using thinking skills pupils can focus on 'knowing how' as well as 'knowing what' – learning how to learn.

The National Curriculum then goes on to list five skills:
1. Information-processing skills
2. Reasoning skills
3. Enquiry skills
4. Creative thinking skills
5. Evaluation skills

This definition is similar to many that inform educational practice. It has the strength of simplicity but raises many questions. Are these skills separable or are they more holistically intertwined, for instance can we really evaluate without also reasoning and information processing? Is creativity really a 'thinking skill'? Some insist that it is necessary to 'stop thinking' in order to be creative (Claxton, 1997). Are these skills distributed with machines or exercised alone, can one really 'process information' without the help of technology of some sort, perhaps just pen, paper and files, but then doesn't the skill itself become simply a skill in using the technology? Before exploring these questions further it will be useful to look at selection of different ways of defining thinking skills.

Perhaps the most authoritative definition of 'critical thinking', the term most commonly used in teaching thinking in North America, is that of 'The Delphi Report on Critical Thinking' (Facione, 1990) which represented a consensus from 46 leading experts in the field. The executive summary runs to 20 pages and offers 14 useful recommendations. This report avoids reducing critical thinking to discrete skills but instead emphasises the importance of cultivating dispositions and the social context of critical thinking.

> The ideal critical thinker is habitually inquisitive, well-informed, trustful of reason, open-minded, flexible, fair-minded in evaluation, honest in facing personal biases, prudent in making judgments, willing to reconsider, clear about issues, orderly in complex matters, diligent in seeking relevant information, reasonable in the selection of criteria, focused in inquiry, and persistent in seeking results which are as precise as the subject and the circumstances of inquiry permit. Thus, educating good critical thinkers means working toward this ideal. It combines developing critical thinking skills with nurturing those dispositions which consistently yield useful insights and which are the basis of a rational and democratic society. (Facione, 1990)

Philosopher Richard Paul is sometimes described as the leading proponent of teaching critical thinking (e.g. Weinstein, 1993). Paul would probably accept the definition above but he also goes further in wanting to add a focus on fostering dialogue. Paul argues that, for 'strong' critical thinking, it is important to question one's own assumptions through thinking from the perspectives of others (Paul, 1993).

Sharon Bailin (1998) opposes the use of the term 'skills' on the grounds that its use in psychology leads to it being taken to imply a property of the brain. She argues that critical thinking is essentially a normative and not a descriptive term. She means by this that critical thinking is not merely a description of how we think but is concerned with how we think well. More precisely, she claims, it is about the quality of reasoned judgements, and this can be assessed by shared criteria. Building a bridge that collapses will involve most of the same cognitive and meta-cognitive strategies, and activate the same regions of the brain in the engineers, as building a bridge that stands. But we only want to promote the skills that went into building the bridge that stands. Thinking skills are therefore not just about descriptions of cognitive processes: They involve judgments as to what is good thinking in a particular context and such judgments depend on shared criteria which are socially constructed.

However, in a review for the UK Government's Department for Education and Skills, Carol McGuinness argues in favour of retaining the term 'thinking skills':

> ...the idea of thinking-as-a-skill continues to have both theoretical and instructional force. Firstly it places thinking firmly on the side of "knowing how" rather than "knowing that" in the long standing philosophical debate about the nature of knowing. And secondly much of what we know about skill learning can be usefully applied to developing thinking... (McGuinness, 1998, p. 4/5)

McGuinness goes on to mention how well the 'skills' terminology fits with the increasing importance of ideas of apprenticeship to teaching and learning. In support of Bailin it seems clear that understanding and promoting 'good thinking' requires working with shared criteria for the evaluation of arguments or the assessment of quality. On the other hand McGuinness has a valid point in stating that the idea of thinking-as-a-skill is a useful one for practitioners. In everyday language to describe someone as skilled at something – say at ballet dancing or wood-carving – implies a public performance to which shared criteria can be applied. There is therefore no need to assume a more specialist psychological meaning for the word 'skills'.

Use of the term 'thinking skills' might also be challenged by those who see high quality thinking as a more holistic or unitary phenomenon which combines many specific skills but is more than any of them. In attempting to answer the question what are thinking skills Lauren Resnick's report is often quoted (1987). Resnick chaired a government commission into the teaching of thinking skills which took evidence from many practitioners and other experts. Her main conclusion was that:

> Thinking skills resist the precise forms of definition we have come to associate with the setting of specified objectives for schooling. Nevertheless, it is relatively easy to list some key features of higher order thinking. When we do this, we become aware that, although we cannot define it exactly, we can recognise higher order thinking when it occurs. Consider the following:

- Higher order thinking is non-algorithmic. That is, the path of action is not fully specified in advance. Higher order thinking tends to be complex. The total path is not "visible" (mentally speaking) from any single vantage point.
- Higher order thinking often yields multiple solutions, each with costs and benefits, rather than unique solutions.
- Higher order thinking involves nuanced judgment and interpretation.
- Higher order thinking involves the application of multiple criteria, which sometimes conflict with one another.
- Higher order thinking often involves uncertainty. Not everything that bears on the task at hand is known.
- Higher order thinking involves self-regulation of the thinking process. We do not recognise higher order thinking in an individual when someone else "calls the plays" at every step.
- Higher order thinking involves imposing meaning, finding structure in apparent disorder.
- Higher order thinking is effortful. There is considerable mental work involved in the kinds of elaborations and judgments required.

(Resnick, 1987)

In Bloom's taxonomy of the types of thinking found in education, higher order thinking is said to build upon lower order thinking, or basic skills. However, the term 'higher order thinking' is often used, as by Resnick referred to above, in a non-technical way to indicate the kind of thinking that is to be particularly valued and that educators wish to promote (Resnick, 1987). In this book I follow Resnick to use the term higher order thinking in this sense. Essentially higher order thinking is that kind of thinking which, unlike the cognition claimed for animals and for computers, involves and implies dialogic reflection.

A review of approaches to teaching thinking suggests that teaching thinking is an idea rooted in practice more than in theory and that the practice of teaching thinking skills is broader than some critical commentators realise (Wegerif, 2003). Most approaches to teaching thinking do not focus narrowly on procedural skills. In fact thinking skills programmes promote a variety of apparently quite different kinds of things including, strategies, habits, attitudes, emotions, motivations, aspects of character or self-identity and also engagement in dialogue and in a community of enquiry. Ultimately teaching thinking skills programmes consist of educational activities that practitioners think will improve the perceived quality of their students thinking.

However, while the intuitions of practitioners as to what is and what is not 'good thinking' can sometimes be ahead of theory they can also sometimes be misleading. This is why we do need theory even if theory remains somewhat underdeveloped or, at least, lacking in consensus in this area. Research on the effectiveness of different teaching thinking approaches sheds some light on those aspects of teaching thinking that really work and therefore could contribute to the development of a better theory of thinking for use in education.

2.1 Research on teaching thinking

In Chaps. 4 and 5, I argued from my own empirical research for a link between promoting engagement in dialogues for children aged 8 and 9 and increased critical and creative thinking ability. Research on Philosophy for Children similarly offers evidence for a link between engagement in dialogue and the development of general thinking skills (Trickey and Topping, 2004).

Philosophy for Children, sometimes abbreviated to 'P4C', was first developed by Matthew Lipman, a professor of philosophy, and his associates at Montclair State College, New Jersey in the United States of America (Lipman, 2003). Lipman claimed to develop, influenced by Dewey, a new model of learning – 'Communities of Inquiry', in which teacher and children collaborate with each other to grow in understanding, not only of the material world, but also of the personal and ethical world around them. Philosophy for Children was originally envisaged as a separate subject taught in parallel to the other subjects of the curriculum. However, 'Community of Inquiry' is also a kind of teaching strategy which can be used in any curriculum area.

Lipman wrote his own materials to support philosophical enquiry in classrooms but the essential method is very flexible. In the UK it is common to use picture books a stimulus for enquiry or news stories. Despite this flexibility all P4C sessions follow certain principles and procedures. Some key guiding principles include:

– Proper valuing of each person's interests and questions
– Acknowledgement that each person's experience/story is unique
– Proper valuing of knowledge, along with the recognition that no one is all-knowing or all-wise
– Appreciation of different ways of interpreting and thinking

Such principles are sometimes translated into negotiated ground rules, such as 'not putting each other down', or 'giving each speaker time to finish', etc. which, as with the Thinking Together programme which I referred to in Chap. 5, are then given prominence as the 'ground rules for talk' owned by a class.

Philosophy for Children includes some of the tools and dispositions which have always been characteristic of philosophy, including:

- The skills of argumentation (such as forming conclusions, identifying premises, deductive and non-deductive thinking, exposing poor reasoning and striving for consistency)
- A propensity to question and search for reasons, rather than simply accept what is given
- Identifying, applying and modifying the criteria by which we form judgements (including value judgements) and make decisions
- Making distinctions that allow us to see the complexity of things (focussing on the nuanced "grey" areas that always lie between the black and the white)
- Identifying relationships that help us make sense of things (including relations of cause and effect, means and ends, parts and wholes, centre and periphery, etc.)
- Exercising empathy and imagination by contemplating different ways of proceeding, and representing alternative moral positions and world views (the "What if...?" strategy). (Adapted from Sutcliffe and Williams, 2000).

Philosophy is sometimes seen as primarily a form of critical reasoning. That is certainly one style of doing philosophy, but Lipman's approach is to promote discussions which combine the dimensions of criticality, caring and creativity in equal parts. To come up with analogies or ways of seeing that unpack the meaning of an issue is highly creative. Lipman claims that in a discussion it is important to care about issues and to care for each other in order to seek to understand each others perspective. Community of inquiry can be a warm and supportive social space where children can feel able to risk displaying their ideas (Lipman, 2003).

It is notoriously difficult to evaluate the success of thinking skills programmes partly because they aim at teaching skills that 'transfer' from the context in which they are taught to new contexts (Nickerson et al., 1985). However, a serious evaluation undertaken for Clackmannanshire Council in Scotland indicates that Philosophy for Children can deliver measurable gains (Trickey and Topping, 2004). Interviewed about this report Professor Keith Topping of the University of Dundee explained his method and outlined his findings:

> Some educators argue that improvement in thinking is impossible to measure. However, this review identified 10 rigorous controlled experimental studies of P4C. These studies measured outcomes by norm-referenced tests of reading, reasoning, cognitive ability and other curriculum-related abilities, by measures of self-esteem and child behaviour, and by child and teacher questionnaires. All studies showed some positive outcomes and a consistent moderate positive effect size for P4C on a wide range of

outcome measures. This suggests a gain in IQ of 6.5 points for an average child. (Times Educational Supplement, 19 September 2003).

Trickey and Topping's report provides quantitative evidence for the success of Philosophy for Children. I have myself conducted qualitative studies of Philosophy for Children which led me to argue, initially, that, as opposed to the student centred ideology of some of the teachers, it involved actively teaching a genre with clear rules for shared reasoning (Wegerif, 2004b). However, the student-centred claims of the teachers are not wrong in that, as was apparent in the example I gave in Chap. 4, the rules of philosophical enquiry as a genre in schools, serve to open up a space of reflection in which the experience of the children can enter into the dialogue in a way that allows them to forge their own voice. I interviewed teachers implementing this approach in Northumberland and they claimed that one of the key successful elements of Philosophy for Children is a focus on the constructing of good questions. Philosophy for Children sessions all begin with the elicitation from the participants of the questions they are going to choose to discuss in response to an initial stimulus such as a film or book. Possible questions are proposed, discussed, developed collaboratively and then voted upon. This focus on asking good questions has an effect. Records kept by teachers in the Northumberland project (NRAIS, see Williams and Wegerif, 2006) revealed that children would often begin a series of philosophy lessons asking very superficial questions about stories, questions of the kind 'What did the Dinosaur have for dinner' and end up asking profound questions such as 'What is happiness' that could easily support an hours discussion. Anecdotal evidence from the teachers in Northumberland suggested that they carried this skill in questioning over to their other lessons, to the home environment and also to addressing issues of meaning in their own lives.

The question of how Philosophy for Children might work to promote general thinking skills raises again the question of 'internalisation'. How is it that experience working collaboratively in a community of inquiry can translate into individual improvements on a range of measures of individual general thinking skills? To account for the internalisation of dialogue in early development Tomasello proposes a species specific adaption of the brain triggered by dialogic engagement. Hobson presents evidence that suggests that the better the quality of the dialogic engagement the greater the development of general thinking skills as measured by 'IQ' tests (Crandell and Hobson, 1999). The brain is not only flexible in early childhood but also throughout life such that regular engagement in a practice such as philosophical enquiry would doubtless alter what Guy Claxton refers to as 'the brainscape' of individuals (Claxton, 1999). However, changes in the brain are not enough to explain what is meant by internalisation in the case of a thinking skills programme such as Philosophy for Children.

One way of approaching this issue might be through the simple idea of 'implication' (Wegerif, 2002). This is the idea, similar to internalisation, that what is first made explicit by the teacher, for example the asking of open questions in Philosophy for Children, can then become an implicit assumption within a genre of language use in a group over time. This is loosely based on the idea of implicature developed by Grice who argued that successful conversation implied certain necessary assumptions such as the relevance of information offered (Grice, 1975). Whereas accounts of internalisation focus on individual brains, accounts of implication focus on genres of communicative activity within cultures. In philosophy sessions with 5 and 6-year-olds I observed, for instance, the introduction of the idea that they were expressing a hypothetical opinion rather than the simple truth through using language forms such as 'I think that...'. I then observed this become the implicit assumption of the genre such that the explicit use of 'I think' faded away. The questioning of any and every claim can similarly become an automatic 'implicit' assumption behind every utterance and every thought in philosophy sessions. Dewey's idea of teaching thinking as developing good intellectual habits is useful in understanding how implicit assumptions within cultures can transfer from group practice to individual thinking. Dewey argues that one very important aim of education should be:

> the formation of careful, alert, and thorough habits of thinking. (Dewey, 1933, p. 56).

By engaging children in good habits of thinking, supported by a community of inquiry, it is possible that we can encourage habits that they will carry with them into the rest of their lives. However, whether or not these 'habits' become part of a core identity is probably influenced by factors of self-identity in relation to peer-groups and cultural contexts in a way that is not easy to predict or control (Wenger, 2005).

Resnick, quoted above, provides an excellent list of higher order thinking skills. In working communities of inquiry all of these 'skills' can also be found as the characteristics of a way of working collaboratively. Taking a dialogic approach it becomes unnecessary to distinguish skills exhibited at the level of a dialogue and those at the level of an 'individual'. Dialogues are always both individual and collective and, as I have argued, the dialogic space opened up in a dialogue is not reducible to being located within an 'individual' or a 'group' since how we understand such entities is always a matter for dialogue. In a similar way dialogues always combine many higher order thinking skills all jumbled up and intermingled in such a way that it is not evident that it is useful to untangle them. There has been an assumption in some branches of instructional design (e.g. Suppes, 1979) that lower order skills should be taught first as a basis for the higher skills. This is not the point of view taken by Mathew Lipman. The philosophy method is to induct children directly into the highest possible form of thinking in the belief that all the necessary individual skills will follow from this. If it turns out that lack of some specific skills are preventing a student from participating fully in dialogue, for example, lack of language skills, then that student can be given some extra coaching in those skills separately before returning to the 'higher order thinking' of the central practice of reflective dialogue.

3 PART 3: REFOCUSSING TAXONOMIES OF THINKING

In 1956, Benjamin Bloom wrote *Taxonomy of Educational Objectives: Cognitive Domain*. His hierarchical taxonomy of thinking skills in education has been widely adapted and used in countless contexts ever since. In his taxonomy a list of cognitive processes is organised from the most simple, 'the recall of knowledge', to the most complex, 'making judgments about the value and worth of an idea' (Table 7.1).

Table 7.1. Bloom's taxonomy of educational objectives

Skill	Definition	Keywords
Knowledge	Recall information	Identify, describe, name, label, recognise, reproduce, follow
Comprehension	Understand the meaning, paraphrase a concept	Summarise, convert, defend, paraphrase, interpret, give examples
Application	Use the information or concept in a new situation	Build, make, construct, model, predict, prepare
Analysis	Break information or concepts into parts to understand it more fully	Compare/contrast, break down, distinguish, select, separate
Synthesis	Put ideas together to form something new	Categorise, generalise, reconstruct
Evaluation	Make judgments about value	Appraise, critique, judge, justify, argue, support

Bloom's taxonomy is modest, carefully worked out and firmly rooted in the enduring needs of education rather than in psychological theories. It was designed to meet the needs of educational designers and it has survived because it has proved a useful guide to the kind of thinking skills that educationalists are incorporating in lessons and in the curriculum.

In developing his own alternative taxonomy of educational objectives, Marzano (2000) points out one common criticism of Bloom's Taxonomy.

The hierarchical structure of the Taxonomy, moving from the simplest level of knowledge to the most difficult level of evaluation, is not supported by research. A hierarchical taxonomy of this kind implies that each higher skill is composed of the skills beneath it; comprehension requires knowledge; application requires comprehension and knowledge, and so on. This is simply not true of the cognitive processes in Bloom's Taxonomy. Even the skill of 'recall' is already complex, incorporating supposedly 'higher' skills like 'evaluation' and 'synthesis'.

Anderson and Krathwohl (2001) argue of Bloom's taxonomy that:

> Its greatest strength is that it has taken the very important topic of thinking and placed a structure around it that is usable by practitioners. Those teachers who keep a list of question prompts relating to the various levels of Bloom's Taxonomy undoubtedly do a better job of encouraging higher-order thinking in their students than those who have no such tool.

At the same time even those who use this taxonomy see limitations. Not only, as Marzano points out, are cognitive skills more holistic and intermingled than the hierarchy suggests but also there is little consensus as to what is meant by Bloom's key terms like "analysis," or "evaluation". Increasingly Bloom's taxonomy is not felt to fit. It is notable, for example, given the enormous interest in teaching for creativity in schools all around the world today, that creativity does not figure in Bloom's list. This probably reflects some of the historical changes in how we value different thinking skills which I referred to in Chap. 6, in a section on thinking skills in history. In a recent attempt to revise Bloom's taxonomy by two of Bloom's students, creativity was not only installed, it was given pride of place as the 'highest' of higher order thinking skills in the taxonomy (Anderson and Krathwohl, 2001).

There have been many taxonomies for teaching thinking proposed since Bloom's seminal work (Moseley et al., 2005). Some fit the claims I am making for the centrality to higher order thinking of dialogic reflection rather better than Bloom's taxonomy does (e.g. King and Kitchener, 1994, quoted in Moseley et al., 2005, pp. 231–234). However, all these taxonomies locate thinking skills within individuals whereas the arguments about thinking skills in this chapter all point to the idea that reflective dialogue is the original higher order thinking skill and remains the primary thinking skill upon which other skills are derivative and dialogue is never simply the property or skill of an individual (although, through internalised dialogic space, it is the basis of individual higher order thinking). If something like Bloom's taxonomy is useful for educational designers then it might be useful to produce a similar taxonomy focused around the more embodied practice of reflective dialogue.

3.1 Classifying thinking dialogues

The teaching of thinking as dialogue has a long tradition in western Philosophy going back to the taxonomies of types of argument offered by Aristotle. This tradition of the study of argumentation has been very influential in CSCL and so is worth reviewing in some detail.

3.2 Argument theory

Argument theory has been influential in studies of Computer Supported Collaborative Learning (e.g. Andriessen et al., 2003; Ravenscroft and McAllister, 2006). The roots of argument theory lie in philosophy and conceptual analysis rather than in empirical educational research. Following this tradition argument theory has focussed on the structure and syntax of arguments.

3.2.1 Toulmin's argument schema

Toulmin, whose account of informal argument has been very influential in education, offers a good illustration of this approach to argument which treats it as if it was a kind of 'grammar' (Toulmin, 1958). Criticising over formal and over abstract accounts of good and bad arguments in terms of logical syllogisms rather than ordinary language, Toulmin introduced a description of what he called 'informal logic'. His terminology such as 'warrant' suggests that his perspective was influenced by the kind of argumentation used by lawyers to persuade the judge or jury in courtrooms. His account broke argumentation down into the following moves:

- A *claim* states the standpoint or conclusion, for example: "The Kyoto protocol to reduce global warming is necessary."
- The *data* are the facts or opinions that the claim is based on, for example: "Over the last century, the earth's temperature has been rising as a result of greenhouse gas emissions."
- The *warrant* provides the justification for using the data as support for the claim, for example: "Scientists agree that there is no other explanation for this rise in temperature."
- Optionally, the *backing* provides specific information supporting the warrant, for example: "Scientists have identified the atmospheric mechanisms whereby greenhouse gases cause a warming of the earth's surface."
- A *qualifier* adds a degree of certainty to the conclusion, indicating the degree of force, which the arguers attribute to a claim, for example: "However, the earth's temperature has been found to

fluctuate over geological time, in some cases without any obvious cause."
- Exceptions to the claim are expressed by a *rebuttal, for example*: "The Kyoto protocol would not be necessary if the world's countries voluntarily reduced their output of greenhouse gases." (Examples taken from Andriessen, 2006)

3.2.2 Van Eemeren and Grootendorst's 'pragma-dialectics'

Van Eemeren and Grootendorst (1999, 2004) criticise Toulmin for failing to take into account the fact that an argument always has, or so they claim, two sides, that of a proponent and that of an opponent. Toulmin, they write, gives the perspective of the proponent of an argument ignoring the contribution of the opponent. They build on the work of Toulmin, and the speech act theory of Searle and Austin, which concerns itself with 'pragmatics', or how utterances do things such as persuading people, but they make this kind of analysis more 'dialectical' by locating it in a conversation between two people. The ideal conversation, according to Van Eemeren and Grootendorst, proceeds in four stages:

1. Confrontation, in which the two people verbalise a difference of opinion
2. Opening, in which they agree on procedural and substantive starting points for resolving this difference of opinion
3. Argumentation, in which argumentation is advanced and responded to
4. Conclusion, in which the parties decide jointly whether and how their difference of opinion has been resolved

In the simplest case, for example, one person may express doubt about an assertion. It is then the task of the other in the dialogue, the "protagonist", to justify the assertion to the satisfaction of that person, the "antagonist", using the starting points agreed to at the opening stage.

Following in the tradition of Grice's work on the implicit rules of conversation in general, Van Eemeren and Grootendorst (1992) propose ten rules for the conduct of argumentation as a type of conversation, a type which they call a "critical discussion". These ten rules are of the kind:

- Rule 3: A party's attack on a standpoint must relate to the standpoint that has indeed been advanced by the other party.
- Rule 4: A party may defend his standpoint only by advanding argumentation relating to that standpoint.

According to Van Eermeren, a fallacy is a violation of one of the ten rules. Generically, such fallacies are moves which disrupt or "derail" the process of rationally resolving an expressed difference of opinion.

3.2.3 Walton's dialogue theory

Walton locates argument within the broader concept of dialogue. A dialogue, he writes, is 'a verbal exchange between two parties, according to some kind of rules, conventions or expectations' (Walton, 2000). He continues in the Aristotelian tradition of 'formal studies' of dialogue based on conceptual analysis rather than empirical study. Walton quotes Hamblin to the effect that the formal study of dialogue "consists in the setting up of simple systems of precise but not necessarily realistic rules, and the plotting out of the properties of the dialogues that might be played out in accordance with them." (Hamblin, 1970, p. 256, in Walton, 2000). Whilst in actual dialogues, Walton writes, it is not always clear what the rules are, in formal dialogues the rules are laid down precisely. The idea is that this formal analysis of types of dialogue can be a useful framework for analysing actual dialogues.

He presents his classification of formal types of dialogue in *The New Dialectic* (Walton, 2000). Six basic types of dialogue are described. The properties of these six types of dialogue are summarised in Table 7.2.

Table 7.2. Types of dialogue according to Walton (2000)

Type of dialogue	Initial situation	Participant's goal	Goal of dialogue
Persuasion	Conflict of opinions	Persuade other party	Resolve or clarify issue
Inquiry	Need to have proof	Find and verify evidence	Prove (disprove) hypothesis
Negotiation	Conflict of interests	Get what you most want	Reasonable settlement that both can live with
Information-seeking	Need information	Acquire or give information	Exchange information
Deliberation	Dilemma or practical choice	Co-ordinate goals and actions	Decide best available course of action
Eristic	Personal conflict	Verbally hit out at opponent	Reveal deeper basis of conflict

Argumentation, for Walton, rather as for Socrates in the Meno, consists in that the one party takes the commitments of the other as premises, and then by a series of steps of inference, uses these premises in arguments that aim towards proving an ultimate conclusion to the other party. Although he describes several types of argumentative dialogue they are all then really variations on persuasion.

Walton thinks that the results of a formal analysis of dialogues can be applied to real dialogues in order to assess their quality. He writes: 'Each type of dialogue is used as a normative model that provides the standards for judging how a given argument should be correctly used in a given case'.

3.2.4 Baker's learning mechanisms

All of these traditions arise in conceptual analysis or formal analysis of argument rather than as the findings of empirical studies. Baker (2004) builds upon the tradition of argument theory but in the context of empirical studies of online dialogues. This enables him to identify four benefits or 'learning mechanisms' that may result from engaging in explicit argumentation:

1. Making knowledge explicit (L'explicitation des connaisances): Learners that provide explanations, or make explicit the reasoning underlying their problem solving behaviour, show the most learning benefits. Argumentation provides many opportunities for explanation, and preparing a justification or argumentative defence fosters reflection that often leads to deeper learning.
2. Conceptual change (Les changements d'attitudes épistémiques): Debating a question may raise doubt about initial misconceptions. Conceptual transformation is supported by argumentation.
3. Co-elaboration of new knowledge (La co-élaboration de nouvelles connaissances): In argumentation, learners work together to develop new knowledge. The interactive interpersonal nature of verbal interaction helps to scaffold individual learning.
4. Increasing articulation and clarification of implicit concepts (le changement conceptual): Argumentation obliges learners to precisely formulate question and statements, and articulation transforms and deepens during the argument. (Baker, 2004, pp. 100–101)

3.2.5 Knowledge building and progressive inquiry

Baker's learning mechanisms for online dialogue are similar to Scardamalia and Bereiter's framework for learning and knowledge construction through online social dialogues called knowledge building (1992). Knowledge building, they write, takes place in social settings or communities which are similar to scientific research communities and use constructivist principles (knowledge is a human construction and not something that is to be revealed or transmitted), sociocultural activity (as the medium through which knowledge construction takes place) and apprenticeship (skills of young scientists are acquired by working with a more mature scientist). Scardamalia and Bereiter developed a networked learning environment called CSILE (computer-supported intentional learning environments, now 'Knowledge Forum') that embedded the following knowledge building principles to support online dialogue (Scardamalia and Bereiter, 1994, pp. 44–46):

1. Objectification. Treat knowledge as objects that can be criticised, modified, compared and related, and regarded from different viewpoints, in different contexts.
2. Progress. Knowledge building should lead somewhere and progress should be perceptible to students.
3. Synthesis. Encourage higher order representations and integrations of knowledge rather than the proliferation of loosely connected items.
4. Consequence. Something nice should happen to students as a result of knowledge building operations.
5. Contribution. Contributions to the communal database should be visible, not solely in terms of their independent merits, but also to their contribution to advancement of the group's knowledge.
6. Cross-fertilisation. Maximise changes for students to come into contact with related ideas, kindred spirits and useful information, unrestricted by boundaries of space and category.
7. Social. There should be no discontinuities between work in CSILE and other curricular activities.

The central activity of this 'knowledge building' is progressive discourse related to advancement of knowledge. Hakkarainen (1998) developed a pedagogical model called 'progressive inquiry' to facilitate this process. Progressive Inquiry engages members of a knowledge building community in a step-by-step process of question and explanation-driven inquiry and consists of the following elements (Muukonen et al., 1999):

1. Context: A context is first created in order to clarify why the issues in question are relevant and worthwhile to investigate.
2. Questions: Initial questions guide and direct the search for information.
3. 'Thought shower': In this phase the participants are stimulated to use their background knowledge to offer a first explanation for the problem.
4. Critical evaluation: Through an evaluation of whether, and how well, the working theories explain the chosen problems, the community can assess the strengths and weaknesses of different explanations and identify contradictory explanations and gaps of knowledge.
5. Deepening: By re-examining prior problem statements or working theories, with the help of new information, the community may become aware of their inadequate pre-suppositions.
6. Structuring: At first the community has a broad conception of the problem that leads to general questions. After making an inventory of prior knowledge, and searching for new information, more specific

questions may emerge. The inquiry advances through developing a chain
of (deepening) questions.
7. Concluding: In the last phase the community, by finding answers to
    subordinate questions, approaches step-by-step toward a fuller answering
    of the initial question or problem statement.
8. Shared understanding: By explicitly working towards a shared under-
    standing of the problem at each stage during their dialogue the members
    are able to construct knowledge collaboratively and in doing so advance
    the knowledge of the individual as well the entire community.

3.3 The even more dialogic alternative

Andriessen (2006) and Scardamalia and Bereiter (1994) present developments in argumentation theory as moving from abstract and formal
studies towards taking the empirical reality of human dialogues into account.
However, it is clear that Van Eermeren and Grootendorst's 'Pragma-
Dialectics' and Walton's 'dialogue theory' remain highly idealised and
formalised accounts that are imposed on real situated dialogues rather than
emerging from them. As opposed to 'dialectics', which always begins as a
theory of argument, Bakhtin's 'dialogic' approach begins with embodied,
situated 'living' dialogues.

Dialogicality means not merely that participants in interactions respond
to what other participants do, they respond in a way that takes into account
how they think other people are going to respond to them. Rommetveit,
quoting Barwise and Perry, calls this circularity 'atunement to the
atunement of the other' (Rommetveit, 1992). This mutual atunement means,
as Rommetveit brings out, that we cannot understand utterances or
communicative actions outside of their context in a dialogue and also that the
context is indeterminate, being an infinite or unbounded chain of possible
interpretations.

Historically, reason has been codified in various ways that have not taken
dialogical circularity into account. This is obviously true of accounts of
argument found in formal logic but it is equally true of the various formal
accounts of argumentation described above. In the monological paradigm it
is normal to see models as a way of getting a handle on reality which we can
use to inform interventions that change things. Models of reason have served
precisely this purpose in education. Walton, for example, quoted above, is
happy that his formal models of argumentation, dreamt up in his study, are
applied to real, holistic and situated dialogues in order to serve as a measure
of their quality. For those who adopt the assumptions of the dialogical
paradigm, on the other hand, the role of models is not so straightforward.

Nicholas Burbules took a more embodied and dialogic approach when he distinguished four types of dialogue in education: inquiry, instruction, conversation, and debate (Burbules, 1993). These were defined through norms of communicative engagement according to two main dimensions, criticality versus inclusivity and convergence (headed toward a "correct" or consensual answer) versus divergence (in which the profusion of ideas and perspectives is itself a value).

Burbules taxonomy of classroom dialogue, while useful, is descriptive rather than intended as a guide to teaching dialogue and it does not relate dialogue to the aim of teaching thinking. In Chap. 5 I described the development of a model of dialogue as a form of higher order thinking that emerged from empirical research on the quality of dialogues in primary classrooms. The model proposed breaks down the idea of shared norms into two aspects of dialogue which were partly borrowed from Habermas, intersubjective orientations and shared social ground rules. The cognitive significance of intersubjective orientations were first brought out by Buber's distinction between the 'I-thou' type of relationship, characterised by mutual responsiveness, and 'I-it' relationships in which an active subject confronts and dominates a passive object (Buber, 1923/1970). But there are other orientations influencing the educational impact of dialogue in classrooms, Mercer referred to Exploratory, Cumulative and Disputational 'types of talk' (Mercer, 1995). In Chap. 5 I added 'playful talk' to this list. This taxonomy of 'types of talk' distinguished by their intersubjective orientations has sometimes been interpreted as a coding scheme which all utterances or other chunks of talk can be made to fit but it was meant more as a heuristic for teachers evaluating and promoting dialogue in their class. Exploratory Talk was used as a basis for a teaching thinking programme as described in Chap. 5. In keeping with the dialogic basis of this approach the ground rules of exploratory talk were not imposed but used as a guide for teacher training, actual ground rules then being negotiated within each class and renegotiated frequently, at least each term. The evaluation of the presence and extent of types of talk in classrooms involved four levels of analysis:

1. Intersubjective orientations such as cumulative, disputation or exploratory intuited by researcher each orientation was realised in different social contexts by different sets of
2. Social ground rules such as responding to challenges with reasons and seeking agreement, which in turn are realised by typical
3. Communicative acts and exchanges such as 'why' questions and 'because...' answers and these acts are realised in
4. Measurable surface features of the dialogue such as number and length of utterances and the use of key words

3.3.1 Creativity and reflection

Thinking about reason from a dialogical perspective shifts the focus of attention away from abstract cognitive structures and towards the way that people respond to each other in dialogues. Exploratory Talk is a model of higher order thinking embodied in a type of dialogue consisting of an intersubjective orientation and a set of ground rules specifically designed to support collaboration in the classroom. This model has proved an effective support for teachers. Its implementation resulted in a significant improvement in the quality of collaborative learning and reasoning according to a range of measures (Wegerif et al., 2005; Mercer, 2000). However, while Exploratory Talk is a dialogical model of a kind of reason, the focus in its definition on explicit reasoning links it to the tradition of argumentation discussed above. This is a limitation because many accounts of higher order thinking in education such as that of Resnick (1987) give a more central role to creative thinking. Empirical evidence suggests that in practice creativity is important to the quality even those dialogues seeking to solve reasoning test problems, and this creativity is not necessarily supported by the learning mechanisms of explicit reasoning mentioned earlier but can be supported by certain kinds of dialogue that open up a 'reflective space' which supports the open exploration of possibilities (Rojas-Drummond et al. 2006; Wegerif, 2005). In reasoning creativity is required to think up good alternative positions (anti-logos or devil's advocate positions) in such a way that creative thinking and critical thinking overlap considerably as has been shown in several studies (e.g. Glassner and Schwarz, 2007).

The increasing centrality of creativity in accounts of quality in educational dialogues challenges the three types of talk schema outlined originally by Mercer. This remains true even if we include, as I proposed, a fourth type of talk: playful talk (Wegerif, 2005). We need to understand higher order thinking in embodied terms as a kind of dialogue (even when this is internalised, dialogue is 'embodied' in the sense that it is always a dialogue between voices with personalities) but in broader terms than the explicit reasoning of Exploratory Talk in order to include the creativity found in more playful dialogue. Bakhtin characterised dialogues as shared enquiry such that 'If an answer does not give rise to a new question from itself, it falls out of the dialogue'. What is outside of dialogue is, he suggests, meaningless impersonal 'systemic cognition' (Bakhtin, 1986, p. 168). This definition of dialogue then, corresponds in one respect to higher order thinking as defined by Resnick: it is not algorithmic and in so far as something is a matter of purely formal reasoning that can be programmed and applied then, by definition, it is not 'higher order thinking'.

This focus on a questioning attitude relates Bakhtin's account of dialogue to Dewey's account of reflection as:

> An active persistent and careful consideration of any belief or supposed form of knowledge in the light of the grounds that support it and the further conclusion to which it tends. (Dewey, 1933)

Interestingly Dewey also seems to have developed the idea of dialogic which he referred to as 'transactive' as opposed to merely 'interactive'. The definition of a transactive discussion is, "reasoning that operates on the reasoning of another" (Berkowitz and Gibbs, 1983 citing Dewey and Bentley, 1949).

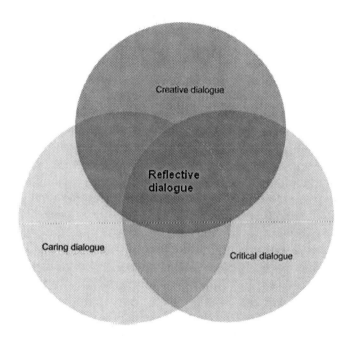

Fig. 7.1. Three dimensions of dialogue (adapted from Lipman, 2003)

Reflective 'transactive' dialogue as shared enquiry, offers a holistic image of embodied higher order thinking. However, within the complex and changing whole of dialogue there are many regions, levels and dimensions. Burbules brings out the importance of the dimension of criticality or how sceptically or supportively participants respond to suggestions (Burbules,

1993). This dimension can be seen in the distinction between the more critical 'exploratory talk' and more supportive 'cumulative talk'. Group creativity, however, does not thrive on explicit critical challenges since participants need to be encouraged to develop their insights in an atmosphere of empathy and trust. This distinction between critical and creative orientations maps a division made by Lipman, the founder of Philosophy for Children. He claims that all dimensions overlap and contribute to the ideal type of thinking which he refers to as 'multi-dimensional thinking' by which presumably he means the kind of 'philosophical enquiry' his method promotes. These three dimensions, which he presents in a Venn diagram, are 'creative thinking, critical thinking and caring thinking'.

The caring dimension, Lipman argues, is not just about having empathy for the perspectives of the others in the discussion so that one cares what they think, although that is important, but is also about caring for the subject matter under discussion.

These three dimensions can be translated into dialogues with different characteristic ground rules as well as some basic ground rules overlapping. Three 'dialogue games' corresponding to these three dimensions have been implemented in an online environment in ongoing research (see Chap. 11). All dialogues share some ground rules, these shared ground rules are located in the central part of the Venn diagram. Critical dialogue is embodied in dialogues with an emphasis on explicit challenges and explicit reasoning. Creative dialogue is embodied in dialogues which open up a reflective space in which issues can be explored with encouragement and trust rather than challenges and explicit reasons. 'Thought shower' (used to be called brainstorming) is a useful technique within creative dialogue, for example, during which even implicit judgment is meant to be suspended. Caring or empathetic dialogue also suspends critical judgment about others in order to work harder to draw out the distinctive otherness of the other. The focus in caring dialogue is not on creating or on judging but on listening and understanding. This is very similar to the claims made for client centred psychotherapy dialogues (Rogers, 1961). Lipman wanted his category of caring to be as much about topics as about other people in the dialogue but this does not make it undialogic. Although the argument has not been made in this book, it is nonetheless worth pointing out that this 'caring' about a topic of discussion stems from and is rooted in dialogic relations in which topics come to take on the status of cultural 'voices' which one can 'relate to' or not. For example if one 'relates to' science and can think of oneself as a scientist one might be excited by discussion of a science problem but if not then the problem may seem meaningless and the discussion is likely to be poor.

These three types of dialogue, creative, critical and caring, are embodied thinking skills. Caring or empathetic dialogue is needed for understanding the other and is required most in the humanities and social science topics. Creative dialogue is important for open-ended design tasks but is also crucial to argument. Critical dialogue is necessary for solving defined problems and making judgments where the key alternatives and variables are already known. However, all three can also be seen as aspects of every dialogue.

While it is a complex whole, dialogue can also be analysed into component 'moments' which, although they should never be abstracted too far from the real dialogues that give them meaning, nonetheless can sometimes usefully be made the focus of teaching. One of the great strengths of Philosophy for Children, for example, has been to abstract out the skill of asking intellectually fruitful questions, a component skill of dialogue in general, and focus extra attention on this skill with time spent constructing good questions collaboratively and considering what makes a good question. Other moments in dialogues that can be identified as dialogic thinking skills are listening to and understanding the point of view of the other (comprehension), expressing a perspective persuasively and coherently as a resource for others (construction) and synthesising or 'weaving' the sense of the dialogue as a whole, not only after the event but also in the act of thinking and learning (synthesising). These are dialogic versions of some of Bloom's general skills of analysis, synthesis and evaluation.

More specific skills are required for dialogues with more specific tasks. These more specific skills might often take the form suggested by Wertsch (see Chap. 2) of skill in using particular terms as tools for thinking (This is also, incidentally, a line of thinking developed somewhat earlier by I.A. Richards who wrote about the 100 key concept words that success in thinking required, see Williams and Wegerif, 2006, p. 82). Thinking about the use of these 'tools' in the context of dialogues and major types of dialogue, such as the creative, the critical and the empathetic (or caring), helps us to understand why some thinking skills (i.e. dialogue skills) such as being able to suspend identity commitments and enter a creative space of dialogue with others, are general across many contexts and others, such as knowing how to use the term 'pedagogic' appropriately, are highly specific to tasks.

Different modes of dialogue transform the moments of dialogue. For example when oral dialogues move into written dialogues in the form of email, then the dialogic thinking skill of listening to the other can be transformed into the skill of textual comprehension, a skill usefully supported by the exercise of producing summaries of texts (e.g. Palincsar et al. 1993). When traditional curriculum activities such as summarising texts to show comprehension, are reinvented from a dialogic perspective they do not remain the same but are now embedded in real contexts of dialogue, for example email exchanges, which have the potential to give them more meaning for students because they are communicating with real others.

I propose refocussing Bloom's hierarchical taxonomy of thinking skills around the more holistic ideal of reflective dialogue. The Venn diagram of Fig. 7.1 illustrates nicely how the main types of thinking are not separate 'thinking skills' nor skills in a hierarchical taxonomy but rather dimensions of reflective dialogue on the analogy of the primary colours as dimensions of light. Indeed the relationship between reflective dialogue and different types of dialogue can be thought of quite fruitfully on the model of the relationship between white light and the different colours that go to make it up. Light is always seen in a context which give it a colour. In many languages such as Maori, it is not easy to decontextualise colour words from objects in such a way that colours can only be thought of as the colour of this or that object much as in English we do not clearly distinguish between the object orange and the colour orange. In a similar way higher order thinking always occurs in a context as apparently thinking about this or that. Situated theories of cognition sometime appear like the equivalent of the Maori language in refusing to separate the thinking from the context in which the thinking occurs. In the past dialogic theory has been appropriated to this situated paradigm but the arguments in this chapter suggest that in fact dialogic can support a new way of understanding that which is general to reflective thought in whatever context. Just as there is an underlying unity to light in the ideal of white light, an ideal never normally seen directly since pure white light underlies the coloured and mixed up light that we normally see, so there is an underlying unity to higher order thought in the opening of dialogic space wherever two or more perspectives are held together in tension. The primary colours of thought, which Lipman proposes as critical, creative and caring, are given by the quality of the relationships within which the opening of dialogic space occurs and the infinite array of secondary colours by the many objects to which reflective thought is applied.

This is a big vision of the nature of higher order thinking and the teaching of higher order thinking which it is hard to test directly. However, this dialogic reconceptualisation of what it means to teach thinking is supported by the findings of the empirical studies I summarised in Chaps. 4 and 5 and by the evidence of the success of thinking skills programmes based around induction into dialogue that I summarised in this chapter. The best way to test and develop this theoretical perspective is to use it to derive principles for the design of environments and activities to promote the teaching and learning of higher order thinking, then evaluate the impact of these pedagogical designs in order to explore the cogency of the theory behind them. The next chapter will look at principles for design studies within the field of educational technology that could test this dialogic perspective. The next few chapters explore how this perspective relates to observations of educational designs in action.

In this chapter I reviewed and discussed the literature on teaching thinking skills. I offered arguments and evidence for the claim that ultimately higher order thinking, the kind of thinking that some argue is distinctively human, is the responsive, creative and unpredictable thinking of reflective dialogues. It follows that 'higher order thinking' can be taught through induction into dialogue as an end in itself. The success of the philosophical inquiry method in schools testifies to this. I concluded that Bloom's famous taxonomy of educational thinking skills should be refocused around the idea of reflective dialogue with different thinking skills understood as embodied in different dimensions of reflective dialogue and in the moments of dialogue such as asking questions. This is not a rejection of the idea of teaching general thinking skills but a reconceptualisation of it in dialogic terms. In the next chapter I apply this analysis of higher order thinking skills to the case of teaching thinking with information and communications technology in order to provide a useful framework for educational research through design studies.

Chapter 8

TEACHING THINKING WITH INFORMATION AND COMMUNICATIONS TECHNOLOGY

This chapter begins with a short review of the literature linking information and communications technology (ICT) to teaching thinking skills. The main ways in which ICT has been thought of as supporting thinking within education are linked to three theories of teaching and learning, associationism, constructivism and socio-cultural theory. Socio-cultural theory is claimed to be the dominant paradigm behind the rise of the CSCL movement. However, all three paradigms are said to have things to contribute to a greater understanding of how ICT can promote higher order thinking. I argue that research findings have revealed problems with all three paradigms which indicate a need for a more dialogic theory. At the end of this Chapter I outline a dialogic framework for research on teaching higher order thinking skills with CSCL.

From its inception the use of computers in education has been linked to the teaching of thinking skills. However, the relationship between computers and teaching thinking has been conceptualised in a range of different ways. Initially computers were seen as teaching machines programmed to directly instruct students in content and skills. Papert and others responded to this with a constructivist learning theory and software that could serve as tools and environments for actively learning thinking skills and thinking habits. Both these movements tended to focus on individual learners. In the last two decades there has been a development of research on computer supported collaborative learning (CSCL) drawing on various theoretical sources including socio-cultural theory and situated learning theory. In the CSCL movement there is considerable interest in teaching group thinking skills in the form of computer mediated collaborative problem-solving and argumentation (e.g. Andreissen et al., 2003). In this chapter I make the case that a truly 'dialogic' perspective could clarify the relationship between information and communications technology (ICT) and teaching thinking in a way that can guide research and practice within the field of CSCL. I apply the dialogic view of teaching thinking elaborated in Chap. 7, which shares with socio-cultural theory the idea that thinking skills originate in mediated dialogues but goes further in claiming that it is not the appropriation of tools but induction into dialogue which is the primary way of learning thinking, with all other thinking skills following from this induction.

1 LEARNING THEORY AND CONCEPTUALISATIONS OF THE ROLE OF ICT IN EDUCATION

Surveys of the use of computers to promote thinking skills by both Hughes (1990) and Underwood and Underwood (1990) draw a sharp distinction between the use of computers as a tutor to teach thinking skills and the use of computers as a tool in order to develop skills indirectly (this distinction originates with Taylor, 1980). Crook (1994), in a similar survey, argues that both these ways of conceptualising the role of the computer in relation to thinking skills are inadequate. He develops a third approach which, following Wertsch, he refers to as the use of computers as a 'mediational means' to 'resource collaborative encounters' (Crook, 1994, p. 227). These three conceptualisations, computer as tutor, computer as tool and computer as 'mediational means', are possibly reflections of three traditions in educational psychology outlined by Greeno, Collins and Resnick in their influential chapter on 'Cognition and Learning' in the 1996 Handbook of Educational Psychology:

- Behaviourist/empiricist: learning as acquiring and applying associations
- Cognitivist/rationalist: learning as acquiring and using conceptual and cognitive structures
- Situative/pragmatist-sociohistoric: learning as becoming attuned to constraints and affordances through participation

Greeno et al. do not mention the dialogic paradigm, perhaps assuming, as so many do, that it is included within what they refer to as 'participatory' models of learning and the socio-cultural tradition. As I argued in Chap. 1, while a dialogic approach can be seen as a development of the socio-cultural tradition, there are ways in which it also offers a distinctive break and demands to be considered as a new paradigm in its own right. In Chap. 3 I argued that there is an important difference between seeing collaborative learning as tool-mediated co-construction and seeing collaborative learning as a dialogue between people. Only from the dialogic perspective does the educational significance of dialogue as an end in itself emerge and it is this perspective that I argued in Chaps. 6 and 7 offers the key to understanding how it is possible to teach higher order thinking.

In the following three sections I review research conducted using the three main paradigms linking ICT and teaching thinking in order to extract some of the lessons that have been learnt.

2 THE COMPUTER AS A TEACHING MACHINE

Skinner's associationist model of learning led him to the development of teaching machines in the 1950s even before the advent of personal computers. Initially computers in education naturally slotted into this teaching machine model (Light, 1993). The instructional design approach of Suppes (1979) continues some of Skinner's ideas in breaking down complex tasks into learning hierarchies in order to produce teaching programmes which learners can follow at their own speed and level of difficulty. Much software developed for schools continues to use essentially this instructional design approach; breaking desired learning goals into small steps and relying on reward, repetition and contingent increase of difficulty levels to teach various skills. The computer effectively takes the place of the teacher, in asking the questions and giving feedback to the learner. The current widespread use of Integrated Learning Systems (ILS) continues in the tradition of the computer as an individual teaching machine. While there is some evidence that this individualised approach leads to improved learning of some basic skills these are not the skills I defined in Chap. 5 using the term 'higher order thinking skills' (Underwood et al., 1996).

It is relatively easy to see how the computer as tutor model can be adapted to teach thinking skills programmes that focus on abstract reasoning and logic puzzles. For example Riding and Powell (1985) report on a study which used a computer programme to tutor 4-year-old children in 'critical thinking skills' using picture puzzles. Over the period of the study the children showed improvements in score on a non-verbal reasoning test – Raven's coloured progressive matrices. However, the sort of problems that the children were given in the tutorial programme were rather similar to the problems in the Raven's reasoning test leaving Riding and Powell open, as they acknowledge, to the charge of not teaching general skills but of simply training children to perform on a specific test. Follow up studies referred to by Hughes (1990, p. 125) have shown only very limited transfer to thinking in other contexts. This difficulty in producing transferable skills is to be anticipated from the discussion of thinking skills programmes in general in

Chap. 6. In general research findings (summarised in Chap. 6) suggest that programmes which seek to teach general thinking skills by addressing logical or problem-solving skills outside of a curriculum context do not lead to transferable skills whereas programmes that address meta-cognitive strategies within the curriculum and programmes which focus on the identities of learners succeed rather better.

2.1 Intelligent tutoring systems

'Intelligent Tutoring Systems' or ITS represent a link between the behaviourist approach to computer aided instruction and the cognitivist paradigm in education. ITS are a product of artificial intelligence research and are said to be intelligent because they embody models of the domain to be learnt, models of students and a model of an expert tutor in the domain. For the most part they remain an expensive tool for AI research with few educational applications. However, they are worth mentioning since one idea of ITS has always been to teach thinking skills, such as problem-solving, through modelling them. For example the ITS or expert system can be used to challenge and question students to lead them on the path of problem-solving appropriate to the area. Examples of this kind of feedback in medicine might be: 'have you specified all the things that you need to know to make this decision?' 'You appear to have overlooked the patient's heart rate'. 'Have you checked the database for other syndromes that match these symptoms?' and so on (e.g. Clancey and Soloway, 1990 and SOAR at http://sitemaker.umich.edu/soar).

Diana Laurillard points out that the claims made for ITS are often overstated. The novel internal architecture of the ITS does not offer any equally new pedagogical moves that could not be done in other ways. Despite the name 'intelligent', ITS seem just like ordinary tutorial systems with a few extra features such as a record of student performance to date and adaptive sequencing of educational activities. But she also claims, more positively, that:

> the ITS is the only medium that can be said to support genuine reflection on the particular learning experience the student has undergone (Laurillard, 1993, p. 161)

This potential for ITS, or 'expert systems', in education continues to be explored. Some approaches include developing 'learning companions' to prompt reflection and guidance to support collaborative learning (Jermann et al., 2001).

2.2 ELIZA and the role of AI in Education

Joseph Weizenbaum's early experiment with a conversation programme, ELIZA, is helpful in illustrate how expert systems might help teach thinking without needing to 'think' themselves. In 1966 Weizenbaum wrote a little interactive programme called ELIZA as a kind of subversive joke. The 'Turing test' standard set for demonstrating real 'Artificial Intelligence' was whether or not someone in conversation with a computer could tell if that computer was human or not. Weizenbaum designed ELIZA to demonstrate that this test was more likely to be met by what he called 'Artificial Stupidity' than by anything that could reasonably be called intelligence. ELIZA imitates the way in which psycho-therapists will take the words of their clients, twist them a little, and then feed them back in order to get clients to think more deeply about their own problems. So, for example, if the client makes a statement ELIZA will take the key word or phrase, repeat it and say 'that sounds interesting, tell me more about it'. If the client asks ELIZA a question the response may be 'Why do you ask me that?' or 'We are talking about you, not me.' ELIZA was created using crude pattern-matching without any pretence to intelligence whatsoever. To respond to the presence of the letter string 'mother' with the letter string 'tell me more about your mother' as ELIZA does, is simply the equivalent to playing a 'moo' sound when the picture of a cow is pressed on a children's toy. Yet the programme worked in stimulating reflection on personal issues. To the surprise of Weizenbaum, intelligent, educated people who were well aware that ELIZA was just a bit of crude software, nonetheless spent long periods working with it on their personal problems. A commercial version was produced and various descendants of this original are now widely employed for therapeutic purposes (Weizenbaum, 1967).

ELIZA offers a model for how 'expert systems' or 'AI systems' could work to help teach thinking. ELIZA worked not because it was intelligent and could model the underlying processes of intelligent problem solving, it worked because it prompted, reflected, probed and challenged everything that was given to it, forcing the exercise of intelligence back onto its human interlocutors. ELIZA opened up a space for people to reflect about their personal problems precisely because it had no competing intelligence of its own. In research that I describe in more detail in Chap. 9, I found that when children were encouraged to think and reflect together effectively when working in pairs at computers even the most apparently constraining tutorial software could serve as a stimulus for reflection and learning. As with ELIZA, computer software is good at supporting reflection because it is not felt to be judging the students in the way that a human interlocutor might. This suggests that a version of the 'teaching machine' model of ICT use in education might be useful for opening up spaces of reflection within the curriculum.

2.3 Discussion of Teaching Machine approaches

From the dialogic perspective on thinking skills the main problem with the classic behaviorist 'teaching machine' paradigm is that higher order thinking is not reducible to associations or defined rule-governed 'skills' because it requires the opening of creative space through the dialogic relation of holding more than one perspective together in tension. The primary thinking skill of *dialogue as an end in itself* needs to be taught as a whole with children inducted from the beginning into dialogue rather as occurs with the successful Philosophy for Children approach to teaching thinking. Within the context of dialogue, however, sub-skills and variations can be analyzed and taught separately using the techniques of instructional design. Dialogue between perspectives is also found in the form of 'internal' reflection that can be stimulated in individuals by computer prompts. In this way the contingent prompts of intelligent tutoring systems can support the practice of dialogic thinking and learning applied within particular curriculum contexts (see Chap. 9).

The strongest criticism of the computer as a tutor model comes from the direction of constructivism. This criticism is that directed computer-based teaching does not allow children to be creative learners, able to think and make connections for themselves, and so is unlikely to support the development of higher order thinking (e.g. Papert, 1981; Underwood and Underwood, 1990). This argument can be summed up with the simple opposition that Papert drew between the behaviourist vision of computers programming children and his alternative vision of children learning to programme computers.

3 THE COMPUTER AS 'MIND-TOOL'

Getting 'smart' and working with computers have always been linked in the popular imagination. Toys for toddlers with computer chips in them are called 'smart toys' and have brand names such as 'IQ builder', 'L'il Genius' or 'Brain Booster'. In science fiction films and TV programmes it is common to find characters 'downloading' skills directly into their brains from computers. The implication is that human skills and computer programmes are isomorphic in some way. Richard Clark refers to the cause of this popular linking of computers and thinking skills as the reification of a metaphor: the computer metaphor of mind behind much cognitive science

(Clark, 1990, p. 268). When the mind is seen as a kind of computer it seems plausible that working with computers can provide mind skills. The inspiration behind some of those working on the link between computers and teaching thinking in the cognitive paradigm seems to be that thinking skills will simply 'rub off' as a 'cognitive residue' from using new technology, (Salomon 1991 quoted in Jonassen, 2000).

In what I take to be a version of the 'cognitive residue' model of learning general thinking skills through working with computers, Seymour Papert advocated the use of programming and other active modelling environments (Papert, 1981). Papert's argument seems very plausible. It is that the exploration of programming environments can lead children from their own personal experience and knowledge to an appreciation of more formal, abstract mathematics. The idea is that experiences in computer 'micro-worlds' help to make the task of learning mathematics more relevant by creating a context in which they can experiment with mathematical concepts. Papert describes this as providing children with a living language to talk mathematics to the computer. Papert does not limit himself to claims about mathematics but goes beyond this to claim that learning to programme the computer can lead to general thinking skills and to greater awareness of and control over thinking processes (Papert, 1981, p. 28). In his theory of the relationship between ICT in education and teaching thinking Papert is applying Piaget's account of cognitive development from 'concrete' thinking to 'formal' thinking. Papert understands the experience of working with micro-worlds on the computer as a way of making the abstract and formal become concrete and personal. He writes that the computer:

> … is not just another powerful educational tool. It is unique in providing us with the means for addressing what Piaget and many others see as the obstacle which is overcome in the passage from child to adult thinking. I believe that it can allow us to shift the boundary separating concrete and formal. (Papert, 1981, p. 21)

Like Piaget, Papert focused upon an image of the individual learner constructing meaning for himself or herself. It was creative engagement between individuals and computers that was supposed to lead to the development of general thinking and problem solving skills regardless of collaborations with other learners or the mediation of teachers.

Papert has had a great influence on the use of ICT in education and constructivism is now probably the dominant educational paradigm in the design of educational multimedia and has been for some time (Boyle, 1997, p. 83). Writing about so-called mind-tools, Jonassen outlines the significance of cognitive psychology and constructivism for the use of technology to promote the development of thinking skills:

Mind-tools are computer applications that, when used by learners to represent what they know, necessarily engage them in critical thinking about the content they are studying. Mind-tools scaffold different forms of reasoning about content. That is, they require students to think about what they know in different, meaningful ways. For instance, using databases to organise students' understanding of content organisation necessarily engages them in analytical reasoning, where creating an expert system rule base requires them to think about the causal relationships between ideas. Students cannot use Mind-tools as learning strategies without thinking deeply about what they are studying (Jonassen et al., 1998).

It is interesting that here Jonassen appears to give all the agency to the computer rather than to the student, writing how the mindtool forces the students to reflect. This is probably because of an implicit equation of student reflection with computer programming such that these two things are not seen as essentially different in structure. The main idea behind 'mind-tools', an idea also articulated by Underwood and Underwood (1990) and Salomon (1992), is not that computers will directly teach thinking but that, after working in partnership with computers, the student will internalise the way that computers think as a cognitive tool for their own use.

3.1 Programming as a mind tool

Teaching programming has long been promoted as a way of learning general thinking skills (Papert, 1981). Perkins and Salomon comment that 'In general programming is a remarkably rich cognitive enterprise that might yield many different sorts of transfer effects.' (1989, p. 154). They list some of the possible gains including:

- Problem solving, problem finding, and problem management strategies, e.g. breaking a problem into parts or relating it to a previously solved problem, planning, and the kind of diagnostic thinking involved in debugging.
- Abilities of formal reasoning and representation, e.g. thinking of all possible combinations, and constructing mathematical models.
- Cognitive styles, e.g. precision, and reflectivity over impulsivity.
- Enthusiasms and tolerances, e.g. persistence, and enthusiasm for meaningful academic engagement.

The logic-based programming language that Papert advocated as a way of teaching general thinking skills, Logo, has been widely used in schools. In fact it has been for some time the only specific bit of software that is required to be used in the National Curriculum of England and Wales. Papert's claims for the power of Logo as a resource for the development of abstract thought and high-level thinking skills have been the subject of intensive and continuing research (for reviews see Simon, 1987 and Underwood and Underwood, 1990).

Hughes (1990, p. 132) summarises conclusions emerging from this research literature. First, the experience of programming in Logo does not in itself result in enhanced problem-solving capabilities. While some research has demonstrated that computer programming can result in significant improvements in performance on certain problem-solving tests, many other studies have revealed only modest effects, or indeed, none at all. Papert himself is not convinced by this research as he says that the way Logo is used is crucial, particular what he calls the culture within which Logo is used, and that usually in schools it is not used in the way he would like.

Hughe's second conclusion is that research indicates that gains are more likely to be observed when work with Logo is carefully structured by the teacher. This is also the conclusion of De Corte et al. (1992). For example, Clements (1986) compared the progress of three groups of 6–8-year-olds. One group was given a 22-week introduction to Logo, the second experienced a schedule of computer-aided instruction of similar length, and the third (the control group) participated in their normal scheduled lessons. The children in the Logo group were given a highly structured sequence of activities, with the teacher (who was present throughout) introducing them to increasingly difficult and complex concepts and ideas. Key concepts were explicitly taught and the teacher emphasised the need for planning programming and reflecting afterwards on of the effects of programmes. Subsequently, tests of higher order thinking revealed that the children in the Logo group achieved significant improvements relative to those in the other two groups.

There is a third conclusion emerging from Logo research which Hughes (1990) referred to as being 'somewhat unexpected'. Although most evaluations of the impact of Logo have focused on individual cognitive skills, one clear finding was that the experience of working on the computer had an effect on children's social interaction (see Clements and Nastasi, 1993; Light and Littleton, 1999). This is supported by the anecdotal evidence of teachers using Logo in their classrooms and the results of case studies undertaken by Hoyles and Sutherland (1989) who claim that children's social interactive learning can benefit substantially from the experience of Logo programming.

3.2 Visualisations and simulations as mind-tools

Representations of every kind can be seen as an objectification of thinking in a way that supports sustained reflection. At the same time the nature of the representations constrain and shape the kind of reflection that is supported. Language as a whole, including writing, graphs, tables and specialist notations such as mathematics, is already often referred to as providing cognitive tools allowing thought to 'leap-frog' to a higher level of understanding (e.g. Cole and Engestrom, 1993). Computers allow for the direct manipulation of representations and the juxtaposition of multiple representations in a way that some see as supporting teaching for understanding (e.g. Ainsworth, 1997). Jonassen makes this case for the use of 'visualisation tools' that allow learners to visualise scientific ideas (Jonassen, 2000). Many simulations of systems play a similar role in that they allow users to manipulate dynamic representations of real-world systems.

These are useful resources to support thinking but I would argue, from a dialogic perspective, that a particular representation or visualisation alone will not necessarily stimulate creative thinking. Models, like metaphors, can be used in a thoughtless or a thoughtful way. It is quite possible for a representation, like a congealed metaphor or cliché, to close down thinking rather than to open it up. The difference depends on what questions are addressed to them within reflective dialogues. The assumption of the literature on visualisation is sometimes that they reflect more or less accurately a single underlying object. This approach might be useful to support dialogues where visualisations automatically encapsulate complex information in a way that frees up mental space for reflection and enables dialogue about the real issues (e.g. Cobb and McClain, 2002). However, an alternative approach for stimulating thinking might also be to use the multi-modality of computers to open up a space of reflection by presenting different representations of what is commonly assumed to be the same underlying object.

3.3 Concept mapping

Concept maps or 'semantic networks' are spatial representations of concepts and their interrelationships that are intended to represent the knowledge structures that humans store in their minds (Jonassen, 2000). While concept maps do not require computers, computer-based concept-mapping software, such as SemNet, Learning Tool, Inspiration, Mind Mapper, and many others, enable the production of concept maps. Great claims are made for the use of concept-mapping as a tool to support critical thinking and reflection on the organisation of knowledge in a subject area while also learning about the area (Buzan and Buzan, 2000; Jonassen, 2000).

The purpose of semantic networks is to represent the structure of knowledge that someone has constructed. So, creating semantic networks requires learners to analyze the structural relationships among the content they are studying. By comparing semantic networks created at different points in time, they can also be used as evaluation tools for assessing changes in thinking by learners. (Jonassen et al., 1998)

Laurillard (1993, p. 123), writing in the context of higher education, is critical of the way in which concept maps reduce knowledge to little chunks of information and defined relationships between them. Knowledge, she argues, is unitary and indivisible, such that:

even a simple statement such as "as air rises it cools" cannot be expressed as an association between two component fragments

She is right of course but there is no denying that many people find that concept maps help them to think more clearly about some topics. Educational evaluations of using concept maps mostly seem positive, but are small scale (e.g. Scanlon et al., 1996; Van Boxtel et al., 2000). Some research, however, argues that the benefits of concept-mapping can be greatly enhanced if they are used as a focus for collaborative learning (Roth, 1994; Roth and Roychoudhury, 1994). This would make sense from a dialogic perspective since the arrangement of shapes on a two dimensional surface is clearly not in itself thinking nor even a good representation of thinking but it could be a valuable support and shared focus for discussion and reflection.

3.4 Hypertext as a mind-tool

Hypertext is a 'computer-based software system for organising and storing information to be accessed non-sequentially and constructed collaboratively by authors and users' (Jonassen, 1991, p. 83). The World-Wide Web is an example of hypertext. There have been very large claims made for the revolutionary nature of hypertext in education. The non-linearity' of hypertext is meant to better reflect the way that the mind is structured than linear print text. Reading hypertext involves making a path through it and so is said to be a more constructive process than reading print. External links made between nodes in the hypertext are said to reflect internal semantic links (Jonassen et al., 1998). However, a review of research on hypertext use in education by Dillon and Gabard (1998 referred to in Bromme and Stahl, 2002) showed no support for the claim that hypertext aides the teaching and learning of thinking skills.

The idea of hypertext is similar to the idea of a library. Those already equipped with effective thinking and learning skills can use libraries as a resource for learning but most students will need more guidance than that. Simply having a library does net mean that you acquire information searching skills.

Bromme and Stahl (2002) argue that, while reading hypertext has few learning benefits, constructing hypertexts is likely to involve thinking skills. Their arguments are similar to those put forward for the value of using concept maps, these are that in developing hypertext documents students need to think about the conceptual structure of an area and reflect on the nature of the links between content. However, reflecting on the structure of an area is rather different from constructing a model of it using a software system that will inevitably constrain the possibilities of that reflection. As Laurillard points out, many important ideas and even some quite simple ideas are not illuminated by representation in a structure of nodes and links.

3.5 Hyper-media

Hyper-media essentially means hypertext with multi-media content. Constructivists, as their name perhaps implies, seem keen on getting children to construct things. Jonassen (2000, p. 211) argues that making hyper-media products 'allows children to construct their own understandings rather than interpreting the teacher's understanding of the world'. However, some sort of dialogical engagement with a teachers perspective is rather important in education and the 'voices' expressed through media are not simply individual voices but part of dialogues.

Designing multimedia products, for example Web sites, is clearly a complex process that engages many skills. Carver et al. (1992, quoted in Reeves, 1998; Jonassen, 2000) list what they see as the major thinking skills that learners need as designers of multimedia presentations. These include

Project Management Skills
- Creating a timeline for the completion of the project.
- Allocating resources and time to different parts of the project.
- Assigning roles to team members.

Research Skills
- Determining the nature of the problem and how research should be organised.
- Posing thoughtful questions about structure, models, cases, values, and roles.
- Searching for information using text, electronic, and pictorial information sources.
- Developing new information with interviews, questionnaires and other survey methods.

- Analyzing and interpreting all the information collected to identify and interpret patterns.

Organisation and Representation Skills

- Deciding how to segment and sequence information to make it understandable.
- Deciding how information will be represented (text, pictures, movies, audio, etc.).
- Deciding how the information will be organised (hierarchy, sequence) and how it will be linked.

Presentation Skills

- Mapping the design onto the presentation and implementing the ideas in multimedia.
- Attracting and maintaining the interests of the intended audiences.

Reflection Skills

- Evaluating the programme and the process used to create it.
- Revising the design of the programme using feedback.

This all sounds both plausible and laudable but these skills are not necessarily distinctive to the use of new technology. Many project-based learning activities have the potential to develop such skills. Could not all of these skills equally be developed through designing and making a poster display for example? However, what is interesting, from a dialogic perspective, is how such activities integrate with larger dialogues. Carver et al. mention reflective dialogues within the team but the whole project is about creating a presentation that will be read and responded to and so is an 'utterance' in a larger dialogue. The criteria of what is a 'good' presentation will depend upon taking the perspective of the addressee and is constantly open to re-interpretation (Del Castillo et al., 2003).

3.6 Computer games as mind-tools

Whitebread (1997) claims that playing computer games can help develop thinking skills. Even a game such as 'Lemmings', often considered purely as an entertainment game, he claims has the potential to develop skills such as:

- Understanding and representing the problem (including identifying what kinds of information are relevant to its solution)
- Gathering and organising relevant information
- Constructing and managing a plan of action, or a strategy
- Reasoning, hypothesis-testing and decision-making
- Using various problem-solving tools. (p. 17)

In a review of the literature concerning games and learning, Kirriemuir and McFarlane (2004) suggest that some games have the potential to support the development of strategic thinking, planning, communication, application of numbers, negotiating skills, group decision making and data-handling but that, for various reasons, there is little evidence that they are having much impact on education. Kirriemuir and McFarlane are interested in the 'flow' experience of games and wonder how this can be reproduced in the design of educational activities. However, others, for example Steve Higgins in his account of using The *Logical Journey of the Zoombinis*, support my argument that, for the emergence of general thinking skills, pedagogy is needed to, in a sense, disrupt the flow and challenge users to consciously reflect upon and discuss the strategies that they are using (Higgins, 2000).

As with every other 'mind-tool', research suggests that collaboration around games has a positive effect on the learning of thinking skills. Inkpen et al. (1995) found that when children played T*he Incredible Machine (TIM),* a problem solving game, together on one machine that they 'solved significantly more puzzles than children playing alone on one machine'. They were also more motivated to continue playing when they had a human partner.

3.7 Discussion of mind-tool approach to teaching thinking skills

The literature about using the computer as a mind-tool is consistently and deliberately guilty of blurring the distinction between using external cognitive tools, e.g. computers, and developing internal cognitive tools, or individual 'higher order thinking skills'. These are not the same thing. In the last chapter I referred to the simple example of using a calculator to work out a budget. Using a calculator does not help develop any internal skills such as doing long division in ones head. Even if it did such skills are not 'higher order' thinking skills although some might wish to call them 'cognitive'. The value of the calculator to thinking is indirect. It lies in liberating more time for creative and reflective thinking by automating the more boring tasks involved in looking after a budget.

In his definition of mind-tools quoted above Jonassen attributed agency to the computer mind-tool writing that such tools forced users to reflect. However, the evidence from reviews of the use of ICT on the mind-tool model consistently points to the fact that mind-tools do not, on their own, lead to reflection. They can be effective but for this to happen social interaction is required either from teachers or from peers. This evidence supports the dialogic model of thinking that I have been developing. Reflection requires a space of dialogue and this normally needs to be called forth by a dialogue partner. Some people who have internalised a reflective dialogic space might be stimulated to reflect by computers just as they might be stimulated to reflect by watching snails, playing with cogs or many other experiences. Some students are prepared by their backgrounds to slip easily into internal spaces of reflection but for the majority of students the research evidence suggests that it helps if someone asks them questions and encourages them to articulate their thinking. This is presumably why peer collaboration consistently emerges as a positive factor in learning with ICT. The important role of a teacher in raising awareness of thinking strategies is also pointed to by research evidence.

These provisional conclusions from research offer some support for the dialogic perspective on thinking skills outlined in Chap. 5. The idea that computers 'think' is misleading. Thinking skills are not acquired simply by working with computers. The idea found in the literature on 'distributed cognition' that thinking occurs in a system uniting computers and humans is more plausible (Salomon, 1993). However, here again the evidence supports the dialogic perspective that higher order thinking occurs not distributed across the 'system' as a whole but only in the dialogues and spaces of reflection that occur in the interstices of a system where human beings need to make decisions. Of course human beings can make themselves cogs in systems such as bureaucracies but the kind of 'thinking' that such machine-like systems can be said to do does not correspond to the higher order thinking that educationalists wish to promote. Higher order thinking presupposes and requires the dialogic relationship which is a relationship between perspectives or 'voices', not a relationship between things. To reiterate: 'systems' do not 'think', thinking is an aspect of dialogues, systems can support and resource dialogues in various ways but they can not replace them.

The idea that working with computers somehow produces a cognitive residue that learners take with them to other contexts is not an absurd idea. However, the ICT here does not serve as a mechanism but a task context. The habits of mind approach to teaching thinking introduced in the previous chapter, Chap. 7 would suggest that long engagement with programming might develop a tendency for careful and precise thinking – but then again the same would be true of other precision tasks such as assembling clockwork toys. There is some interesting evidence that the use of some technologies, the abacus for example, influences the way that people think and even the use and the development of their brains (Cole and Derry, 2005). However, this evidence does not point to the direct internalisation of tools so much as to the effect of social practices around tools and technologies. Scribner and Cole (1978) for example challenge the popular view that 'literacy' in general supports formal thinking with studies of literacy practices, such as collective reading of the Koran, that do not support formal thinking whilst the use of literacy to support classification activities in formal schooling does indeed support formal thinking. Their conclusion is that it is not the 'literacy' as a 'technology' that is being internalised but the social practice of formal schooling that is becoming appropriated in the formation of long-term habits of thought.

It has been widely noted that the kind of cognitive tools that writing affords, tools like tables and lists, influence thought and supports formal models of reasoning found in taxonomies and abstract logic (Goody, 1977; Toulmin, 2001; Cole and Derry, 2005). This seems plausible but Ong makes a different and, to my mind, a more important point: this is that the technology of writing does not simply provide tools, such as tables, it also deepens a sense of inner life or inner space (Ong, 1982). He describes how the initial custom of reading texts aloud in groups was gradually replaced by silent individual reading. This habit, combined with the habit of silently and privately composing texts, supported the development of a sense of an inner self. This was conceptualised as a new 'inner space' in which individuals could 'live' and from which they had the freedom and autonomy to reflect dispassionately on the culture around them. This kind of sense of an inner space of freedom that one carries around with one is the very model of the 'autonomous self' that most education systems still aim to produce (Biesta, 2006). Ong claims that predominantly oral cultures are different because the ephemeral nature of the communication leads to a much more contingent, contextual and collective sense of self. I have argued that the internalisation of dialogue provides the first 'inner space' that supports thinking. Ong would not disagree, he is very conscious of the wisdom often found in oral cultures, but he argues that oral dialogue alone tends to support habits of collective reflection rather than the habit of individual reflection that is supported by modern western literacy practices.

Ong's careful and persuasive case offers a model for relating technologies to the development of embodied higher order thinking. Ong's account of social internalisation suggests that the practices associated with text-chat and blogging are likely to have very different implications for 'inner space' than the diary writing and letter exchanges of a previous age. On the whole, in the contexts of its use, electronic text is more immediately dialogic and communal than print technology. Yet, as writing, it continues, unlike oral dialogue, to endure over time and so it has the potential to support the disembedding of ideas from their contingent contexts that Ong attributes to writing. If electronic writing does support the kind of 'inner space' of reflection away from the contingencies of time and physical context that Ong refers to, then this inner space is no longer the individualised space generated by earlier writing and reading practices but a collective 'inner space'. Perhaps this new collective inner space is one aspect of the emerging space of the internet?

4 COMPUTER SUPPORTED COLLABORATIVE LEARNING

Crook (1994, p. 67) argues that the 'computer as tutor model' and the more constructivist model of computers as a kind of mind-tool are both based on similar individualist models of learning. He argues instead for a socio-cultural model of learning which stresses the primacy of the joint construction of knowledge through communication. Within the socio-cultural model, intellectual development is seen as induction into the social practices and the use of the cultural tool-systems through which shared knowledge is constructed. This leads Crook to emphasise the use of the computer as a support and resource for the communicative processes of teaching and learning. Whereas both the 'computer as tutor' model and the 'computer as tool' model encourage the view of the use of computers as a kind of treatment leading to an individual learning outcome, the socio-cultural model argued for by Crook (1994), Newman et al. (1989), Mercer (1994), Saljo (1998), Koschmann (1996:2001), Stahl (2006) and others encourages investigation of the way interactive technologies can contribute to learning dialogues both in groups and in communities.

The development of a focus on computer supported collaborative learning (CSCL) has been marked in the last decade with new CSCL societies, conferences and publications emerging. Numerous and varied intellectual sources are referred to by writers who situate themselves in this new CSCL tradition. Koschmann refers to CSCL as a new paradigm in instructional technology research defined through socio-cultural theories of learning (Koschmann, 1996:2001). While the claim for the coherence of CSCL as a new paradigm implicit in Koschmann's argument might be exaggerated, nonetheless there is clearly a focus on social rather than individual learning that distinguishes this new approach from both the behaviorist and the cognitivist/constructivist traditions that underlay previous approaches to ICT and teaching thinking (Dillenbourg et al., 1996; Kirschner et al., 2004).

De Laat recently surveyed 32 different research projects on CSCL and found that, despite differences, they all shared a broadly social constructivist framework (De Laat, 2006, p. 196). Many writers in the CSCL tradition refer to the ideas of educational psychologist Vygotsky (1987), the father of the socio-cultural movement, to provide intellectual authority for a turn towards the social dimension of learning. As I outlined in Chap. 3, Vygotsky claims that language is a tool-system that mediates thought and the development of thought. If language can play the role of a cognitive technology mediating and supporting thought then this perhaps implies that so can other technologies of communication. Vygotsky, as was noted in Chap. 3, claimed that the higher mental faculties, including reason, are internalised out of social interaction. One common neo-Vygotskian move is to claim that the forms or genres of interaction themselves embody higher order thought even without the need for an internalisation move (Stahl, 2006; Wegerif, 2004b). In the CSCL 'paradigm' (Koschmann, 2001) the idea of information and communications technology is connected to the idea of teaching thinking through teaching forms of social interactions such as argumentation and collaborative problem solving that embody higher order thinking.

4.1 Situated co-construction through talk

Teasley and Roschelle (1993) report a study that illustrates the role of computers in supporting collaborative learning and thinking. Their study concerned pairs of learners using a simulation designed to teach Newtonian physics, called the Envisioning Machine. In it they argue that the essential medium of the learning is the talk between the learners and that the role of the computer lies in supporting that talk and resourcing their collaboration (ibid., p. 254). The computer screen offers a shared focus, a means to 'disambiguate' language through images on the screen, and a means to resolve conflicts by testing out alternative views. Teasley and Roschelle write:

> We see the 'computer-supported' contribution to collaborative learning as contributing a resource that mediates collaboration. In ordinary circumstances one cannot imagine two 15-year-olds sitting down for 45 minutes to construct a rich shared understanding of velocity and acceleration. But in the context provided by the Envisioning Machine activity, our students were successful in doing just that. (ibid., p. 254)

This conceptualisation of the educational role of the computer as a medium supporting collaborative learning is the view which is most in accord with the sociocultural theoretical framework. Teasley and Roschelle argue that it throws the emphasis away from the computer software and on to the quality of the dialogue.

Further evidence that the pedagogy is as important as the technology comes from my own work, with Neil Mercer and Lyn Dawes at the UK Open University which I describe in Chap. 9. In this research an approach has been developed using computers that prepares children to work effectively together with specially-designed computer-based activities focused on curriculum-related topics. A series of 'Talk Lessons' are followed, in which classes establish ground-rules for collaboration such as listening with respect, responding to challenges with reasons, encouraging partners to give their views and trying to reach agreement. Computers are used not only for stimulating effective language use but also for focusing children's joint activity on curriculum tasks. This embedded and catalytic role for computers in primary education is distinctive (Wegerif, 1996; Wegerif and Scrimshaw, 1998; Wegerif et al., 1998, 2002; Wegerif and Dawes, 2004). Higgins (2001) argues that the findings of this research offer persuasive evidence that, in combination with the right pedagogy, the use of ICT can support the development of transferable thinking skills.

While I now want to question some features of the socio-cultural perspective within which this work was conducted I do not wish to deny that, like the work described by Roschelle and Teasley, it was successful in realising the pedagogical aim of improving the quantity and quality of higher order thinking. The question that I am asking in this book is not whether it was successful but why it was successful. This is something I addressed in Chap. 3 where I argued that the effectiveness of such activities stems more from the dialogic relationship which enables perspective taking than from what, in socio-cultural jargon, could be called 'the use of tools for the co-construction of knowledge'.

4.2 The communicative affordances of computer conferencing

There are many claims that electronic conferencing can be an effective support for learning thinking skills through collaborative learning. Such claims can be found in Mason and Kaye (1989), McConnell (1994) and Harasim et al. (1995). De Laat translates some of the general meta-cognitive 'learning to learn' skills that can be afforded by CSCL as 'networked learning competencies' (De Laat, 2006, p. 19). At least some of the factors claimed to support reasoning relate to the specific way in which the medium supports discourse. For example:

- The ease with which it is possible to 'take the floor' in a discussion in comparison with face-to-face discussion
- The possibility of having several strands of conversation simultaneously supports more meta-cognitive reflection
- The written nature of the dialogue combined with asynchronicity can allow time for refection while maintaining the intrinsic motivation of a conversation

(Wegerif, 1998)

These differences between computer mediated communication and face-to-face communication have been pointed out by Graddol (1989) and are reiterated by McConnell (1994). The conclusion from both these writers appears to be that CMC can support an egalitarian style of communication in which everyone can participate more easily. One possible implication of this is that CMC might be a good medium for moving towards the 'ideal speech situation', which was introduced in Chap. 4. The ideal speech situation idea, from Habermas, is of a situation in which, through the elimination of all forms of coercion and through ground rules allowing all to speak, supports the force of good arguments winning out over other, less rational, factors. Others have claimed, by contrast, that the medium is particularly prone to aggression and irrationality (Siegal et al., 1986 quoted in Jonassen, 2000, p. 265). Laurillard notes 'the success of the medium is totally dependent on a good moderator' (1993, p. 169). However, De Laat argues convincingly that moderation is not necessarily a function of a designated teacher but something that members of community can do for each other (De Laat, 2006). This would imply that we need to modify Laurillard's comments to write that the success of the medium is totally dependent on the culture of communication.

Within the socio-cultural paradigm, links via email or electronic conference with other schools can be used for the joint construction of knowledge. An example might be taking on a particular topic to research together in order to develop joint multi-media resources on the Web. This approach is found in Margaret Riel's 'circles of learning' (Riel, 1992). Such use of the Web to support shared knowledge construction, often in the form of the construction of Web pages together, is similar in some ways to the use of shared databases within schools and classrooms pioneered by Bereiter and Scardamalia.

4.3 Shared databases

CSILE, which stands for Computer Supported Intentional Learning Environments and is now called Knowledge Forum (Scardamalia et al., 1991, 1994; Hakkarainen, 1998), consists of a number of networked computers in a classroom where a community database is maintained. The database consists of text and graphical notes, all produced by students and accessible through database search procedures. Teachers work with Knowledge Forum in different areas of the curriculum. Students are given a question, they have to find information and record it via notes in the database. Other students then comment on the notes and add new notes.

Evaluations of learning outcomes in Knowledge Forum classrooms are positive and reflect the development of thinking skills, including greater comprehension of texts and deeper explanations of processes as well as the development of a more positive self-image as learners. Even if we question the socio-cultural theory or social-constructivist theory used to justify approaches such as this (see Chap. 12) their success in promoting higher order thinking is something that needs to be built upon.

4.4 Discussion of the CSCL 'paradigm'

I will say more about Computer Supported Collaborative Learning as a support for teaching higher order thinking skills in Chaps. 10 and 11 where I describe further systems and approaches. In this chapter I am reviewing research in ICT in education that contributes to an understanding of the relationship between new technology and teaching higher order thinking skills. The socio-cultural or social constructivist framework of much research in this area draws attention to the general higher order thinking skills embodied in the form of communication itself. De Laat draws attention to how online collaboration develops what could be called 'social meta-cognition' as participants learn to help each other to learn. (De Laat, 2006, p. 162).

5 A DIALOGIC PARADIGM FOR TEACHING HIGHER ORDER THINKING WITH CSCL

Having looked at what we can learn from research on ICT and teaching higher order thinking in the three main paradigms of ICT in education, the computer as teaching machine, the computer as 'mind-tool' and the computer as 'mediating means' for collaborative learning, I will now elaborate a fourth position: the computer as support for dialogic space. This fourth position remains with the methods of CSCL but re-interprets them away from grounding in socio-cultural and socio-constructivist theory and towards grounding in dialogic theory. Successful CSCL pedagogies are not criticised by this new theoretical framework but re-interpreted. In many cases CSCL pedagogies already fit uncomfortably with the theory that has been used to support them and fit better within a dialogic framework. And my hope is that this new way of looking at CSCL will provide a better framework for future educational designs that promote higher order thinking through dialogue as an end in itself in a way that is linked to the promotion of global dialogue and global democracy.

Bakhtin's dialogic approach is often located within the socio-cultural approach described above but, as I argued in Chap. 3, there are good reasons why it should be distinguished from it. The metaphor of using tools for the 'construction' of understanding found in the social constructivist and socio-cultural approach implies an image of understanding as some sort of object, a 'cognitive artefact' perhaps (Bereiter, 2002) or a system within which things can be 'understood' through an act of location (Vygotsky, 1986, p. 206). Bakhtin's image of understanding is very different, it is of a spark of insight arcing across the infinite depth of potential meaning that opens up between incommensurate perspectives in a dialogue (Bakhtin, 1986, p. 162).

While an account of learning as learning to use cultural tools, such as that of Wertsch discussed in Chap. 3, is useful to support educational design for some forms of learning I argued that it was not useful for learning to learn or for learning to be creative. For understanding how to design both for learning to learn and for learning to be creative I argued that we need to design for reflective dialogue. On this more dialogic perspective tools are still useful for teaching thinking but not directly, as 'cognitive tools' but indirectly, as means for opening and resourcing dialogic spaces.

In Chaps. 6 and 7 I discussed approaches to teaching thinking and produced a dialogic framework for understanding the teaching of higher order thinking. In this chapter, I have so far discussed the affordances of different ways of ICT for teaching higher order thinking. It remains for me to combine these two into a paradigm for research into educational design to promote higher order thinking through CSCL.

The particular strengths of ICT in education are sometimes summarised as:

- Provisionality: the ability to change texts and other outputs with minimum cost
- Interactivity: the capacity for feedback and response
- Capacity and range: the capacity to handle large amounts of information and overcome barriers of distance
- Speed and automatic functions: enabling routine tasks to automated
- Support for multi-modal communication.

I have drawn these points, apart from the last, from an article by Avril Loveless on teaching creativity with ICT (Loveless, 2003). This list is also found more generally in the literature on teaching with ICT (e.g. Hardy, 2001). If these strengths are combined with the account of teaching higher order thinking through teaching reflective dialogue which I offer in Chap. 5 it is possible to map some of the ways in which ICT can be put to use for opening, maintaining, extending and deepening spaces for reflective dialogue.

5.1 Combining software design with pedagogy for collaborative learning

Educational design is a bigger concept than the design of resources, it includes the design of teaching and learning activities. The consistent finding of research on ICT and teaching for higher order thinking is the importance of pedagogy. One of the key findings from my own research with others on collaborative learning around computers in classrooms (see Chap. 9) is that for effective collaborative learning it is not enough just to place people in groups but they need to be prepared for working together in groups beforehand. The same principle emerges from reviews of collaborative learning in online environments (De Laat, 2006, p. 163).

5.2 Scaffolding induction into dialogues

The research quoted above on concept maps and other 'mediating means' shows that provisionality can support reflection and the development of joint ideas through products, including texts and other artefacts, that are not as ephemeral as speech and not as apparently fixed and changeless as print. This is the basis of several extended examples that I give in Chap. 10.

The potential for interactivity of ICT can be used to provide contingent support for dialogues. This arose in the discussion above of reflection stimulated by prompts offered by intelligent tutoring systems. Even the simple prompts, 'what do you think?' and 'why do you think that?' in the right place can have a significant effect on learning (Wegerif, 2004a). Interactivity makes it easy for software to simulate multiple points of view in a dialogue thus allowing learners to be inducted into a field of dialogue rather than into fixed 'truths'.

From a dialogic perspective the internet is not so much a 'tool of tools' but a cacophony of voices offering countless opportunities for dialogic engagement with multiple perspectives on every topic. While these perspectives are mediated by technology, signs for the voices of the other, faces, voices, avatars, videos and so on, are not best understood on the model of tools but, as I discussed in Chap. 3, on the model of epiphanic signs that lead one to the voice of an other person. The issue for design then is how to use these different ways of mediating the presence of the other to support dialogue across difference that issues in reflection and learning. Web quests offer one way of scaffolding dialogic encounters between Web voices. Email links between geographically distant groups are another. Dialogues via avatars in 3D virtual worlds are a further way (see Ligorio and Pugliese, 2004).

5.3 Broadening dialogic space

Baker et al. (2003) distinguish between deepening and broadening a space of debate:

> Students broaden their understanding of a space of debate when they are better acquainted with societal and epistemological points of view, their associated arguments and value systems; they deepen it when they are

able to go deeper into argument chains, to elaborate upon the meaning of arguments, and to better understand the notions involved.

While the idea of dialogic space is broader than that of a space of debate since it is not concerned only with explicit argumentation the distinction between broadening and deepening is still useful. By broadening or expanding I mean roughly increasing the degree of difference between perspectives in a dialogue while maintaining the dialogic relationship. Broadening can be done through the use of the internet to engage in real dialogues about global issues. An illustration of this is Oxfam's 'tv.oneworld.net site', where video stories from across the world are exchanged and discussed. In practice this does not support much real dialogue but, with a dialogic pedagogical approach, the same technology could be a powerful means for so doing. Broadening in the classroom can be done through structured Web quest type activities where an issue is posed and learners are sent to different Web sites to explore it and to question the people behind different view-points.

5.4 Deepening dialogic space

By deepening I am referring to increasing the degree of reflection on assumptions and grounds. With the right pedagogy the broadening potential of internet dialogues also becomes a deepening as students are led to reflect on the assumptions that they carry with them into dialogues. In classrooms research has found that a simple way of increasing reflection is extending the length of pauses that are allowed to open between questions and answers (Dillon, 1990). I mentioned above that some have argued that asynchronous communication affords reflection. One way of supporting reflection is to encourage meta-cognitive communications with either a meta-cognitive space, perhaps a 'chat room', a virtual whiteboard or a meta-cognitive label for messages (De Laat and Lally, 2005; Schwarz et al., 2003).

5.5 Expanding multi-modality

Meaning can be explored using a variety of media. From the dialogic perspective I have outlined dialogues are not simply an exchange of words. They consist of a relationship between people or perspectives motivating a flow of meaning (Merleau-Ponty's 'chiasm' described in Chap. 2 is not static, but a flow of meaning). This flow of meaning is focused and articulated by signs and communications technologies but is not in any way reducible to those signs or technologies. Unlike versions of the socio-cultural perspective which tend to reduce thinking to the use of particular cultural tools, especially concepts and language structures, (e.g. Wertsch, 1998) this dialogic understanding provides us with a way to appreciate how different modalities of representation can work together and how different levels and types of dialogue can be integrated into flows of meaning.

The multi-modal dialogue made possible by ICT with video conferencing and audio conferencing as well as graphics and music, allows the interesting possibility of dialogic interaction between different representations of meaning as well as between people and perspectives. Exploring the dialogue between meanings in different modes has the potential to broaden dialogues, by giving access to new kinds of perspectives and to deepen dialogues, by encouraging one mode to reflect on another. For example asking students to reflect on musical representations of different arguments can give access to the emotions that are often implicit behind neutral seeming words in texts and so broaden and deepen the dialogic space.

5.6 Internalisation/implication of dialogic space

Ong's account given above of the way in which communicative practices associated with literacy led to the creation and deepening of individual inner space is applicable to analyzing the impact of new communicative technologies not as tools that are internalised but as new kinds of dialogic spaces that become part of the lifeworld of participants. The practice of blogging, for instance, can be a participation in a process of collective reflection. Events seem different when they are seen not only through one's own eyes but also through the eyes of the potential audience for one's blog. The use of blogs then, for example, may be another way of deepening the dialogic space of reflection.

5.7 Creative expression

Once we see higher order thought embodied in dialogue across difference it becomes as important to support expression from the individual to the dialogue as, to support internalisation from the dialogue into the individual. From the dialogic framework for teaching thinking proposed in Chap. 7 these are not separate but moments of the dialogue that can be focused upon for pedagogical purposes. An individual or group's capacity to participate in shared social dialogues can be supported through the use of technology. There are many ways in which ICT can augment and support creative expression from word-processors through to Web sites. Cobb and McClain illustrate how visualisation tools that allow users to grasp and manipulate complex statistical relationships can empower learners to participate in dialogues about public policy (Cobb and McClain, 2002). This form of empowerment enabling expression and participation, is also a way of improving the quality of individual and collective thinking.

5.8 Discussion of the dialogic paradigm linking ICT and teaching higher order thinking

More could be written on how ICT could be used to support the different aspects of dialogue and the different moments of dialogue that I touched upon in Chap. 5. Some details are offered in the next three chapters which relate this perspective to empirical studies and in the conclusion I use it as the basis for a programme of future research. However, the main point I am making here is that teaching higher order thinking should be done through induction into reflective dialogue. The further students travel in the direction of dialogue as an end in itself, the greater their capacity to learn and to be creative. As ICT in education has developed over the last few decades it has become apparent that it is not just another classroom resource amongst others. It has the potential to cross all the boundaries of the classroom by bringing the world into the classroom and the classroom into the world. Its main educational 'affordance' is communication and not just communication between specific locations but global communication, communication between everywhere and everywhere else (and also, as I illustrate in Chap. 12, between all times). There is therefore a natural convergence between an account of education as induction into dialogue and the use of ICT.

A dialogic approach to education with ICT is inevitably a form of computer supported collaborative learning. The dialogic perspective augments existing theoretical frameworks within CSCL through its stress on the importance of the implicit space of possibilities opened up by dialogue. It is this that can offer a framework for design that supports creative emergence. Tools, including language and computer environments, can be used for opening up and maintaining dialogic spaces and for deepening and broadening dialogic spaces.

Although I am claiming that the dialogic perspective I am putting forward is fairly new and different it is interesting that, in many cases, the pedagogic practices that would follow from this dialogic interpretative framework are already happening. This includes the promotion of communities of enquiry and dialogue skills, the use of forums of alternative voices to induct students into debate, engagement in real dialogues across cultural and geographic differences using the Internet, and scaffolding induction into such dialogues using synchronous and asynchronous environments, amongst others. The value of the dialogic framework for CSCL is therefore not necessarily in suggesting exciting new pedagogical strategies, but rather in providing an interpretative framework that can be applied retrospectively to pedagogical practices that have emerged through the intuition of researchers and practitioners in order to expose what is of real value in these practices and so to serve as a sound basis for future research and design.

In this chapter I put forward a dialogic approach to the design of CSCL that can support and promote higher order thinking. I did this through a consideration of the different paradigms for relating ICT to the teaching and learning of higher order thinking skills. Each paradigm, I demonstrated, had things to offer as well as limitations. On the whole the research evidence pointed to the importance of dialogue in stimulating reflection and higher order thinking. Although the socio-cultural or social-constructivist paradigm acknowledges the importance of dialogue, and has many important pedagogical innovations to offer, I argued that it fell short of realising the radical potential of dialogic by appropriating dialogue as a tool to the end of constructing knowledge. Against this I argued that to teach for creativity and learning to learn, dialogue needs to be seen as an end in itself. This transition to a dialogic paradigm leads to a framework for design research with CSCL that deepens and broadens dialogue across difference.

Chapter 9

TALK AROUND COMPUTERS
Expanding the space of reflection

This chapter and Chap. 10 use the findings of empirical studies to reflect on design issues for CSCL around stand alone computers in schools. In this chapter, I describe the development of design principles for software to support collaborative learning within the curriculum. This is not an illustration of the dialogic framework developed in Chap. 8 but it retrospectively shows where that framework comes from and provides an opportunity to reflect on the relevance of the framework for design issues. These studies were originally interpreted within a neo-Vygotskian framework and within that framework they demonstrated how a combination of pedagogy and software could effectively expand and deepen the dialogic space in educational activities with stand alone computers. In Chap. 10, I will show where and why it became necessary to go beyond that original neo-Vygotskian framework and develop a more radical dialogic framework.

In 1991, I found myself living in the East End of London doing a masters degree in computing at Queen Mary and Westfields University College. I had friends teaching in local schools and decided, for my dissertation, to design and evaluate some educational software. The East End is the port area of London and is traditionally where new immigrants to England first arrive. The pupils in the secondary school I went into spoke over 60 different languages. The biggest educational challenge was posed by a large number of girls with parents from Bangladesh who were quiet in class and seemed not very engaged in their education. The geography teacher was concerned that the Bangladeshi pupils in the school did not have the shape recognition skills required to read maps and recognise country outlines. I worked with him to develop some software for shape recognition, including country outlines, using the sort of instructional design principles which I described in Chap. 8 as being based on an associationist theory of learning. My software had multiple choice questions arranged in levels of difficulty with contingent rewards from an animated cartoon character. Although not based on the design principles which I now espouse I have to say that the software was considered a great success and was used for some years in the school.

My point in telling this story, however, is not to praise the efficacy of associationist design principles in some contexts, although that is a point worth making, but to share something else important that I discovered inadvertently when I came to evaluate the software. The Bangladeshi pupils I had designed the software for did not seem happy or motivated when I asked them to work at the computer on their own. They looked around nervously and seemed unsure of how to continue, even when my cartoon character, a clown, showed them what to do clearly with animation and audio prompts. However, when they were asked to work in pairs they laughed together at the animated antics of the clown, helped each other with the answers and generally seemed to have a good time. I was particularly impressed at how shy Bangladeshi girls, who normally never seemed to speak at all in class, opened up in front of the computer, talking and laughing together as they pointed at features on the screen. I realised that, regardless of the limitations of my software design, there was something about the kind of communicative space opened up by collaborative work together around a computer that appeared to empower these otherwise very quiet and disengaged girls. In the sixteen years since then I have built on this first insight in a series of studies researching collaborative learning with computers in schools.

In this chapter, I summarise the results of the first of these studies into the use of computers to promote learning dialogues within the curriculum. At the time these were conducted and interpreted within a neo-Vygotskian framework similar to that of Wertsch's framework which I presented and critiqued in Chap. 3. According to this neo-Vygotskian framework, dialogue was seen primarily as a means to the end of knowledge construction within the curriculum and also as a way of facilitating the transition to more 'scientific' or rational and educated ways of using language as a tool for thinking (Wegerif and Mercer, 2000; Mercer, 2000). Despite this the studies say a great deal about how a combination of technology and pedagogy can broaden and deepen spaces of dialogue. In this chapter I therefore re-visit these studies and re-evaluate their findings in the light of the dialogic perspective which I have developed in the previous chapters of this book.

1 PART 1: ELICITING PRINCIPLES FOR THE DESIGN OF COLLABORATIVE LEARNING AROUND STAND ALONE COMPUTERS

1.1 Background

After my experience designing software for Bangladeshi children in the East End of London I was fortunate enough to do a Ph.D. in Educational Technology at the UK Open University working as part of a lively research group led by Tim O'Shea, Diana Laurillard and Robin Mason amongst others. I, however, found myself drawn to the use of ICT to promote higher order thinking in schools and went to talk about this to Neil Mercer in the School of Education at the Open University. Neil was at that time writing up some of the findings of the Spoken Language and New Technology project, a descriptive study of the talk of children around computers in schools. Observation notes and over fifty hours of video recordings had been taken of children from age 8–12 working in a number of different schools around a wide range of different kinds of software. The project team kindly allowed me access to their data. This provided me with an opportunity to explore the factors which supported or hindered effective collaborative learning. Although some aspects of software used in education have changed since the time of this study these changes seem mostly in the direction of the realism of the graphics rather than in the structure of the software design.

1.2 Method

The cupboard full of videotapes from the project produced too much data for me to get an easy grip on. Fortunately all the videotapes had been transcribed providing a small corpus of texts which I could search electronically using the 'find' function in Microsoft Word and 'concordancer' software. I discovered that the incidents in the videos and the transcripts that intuitively seemed of most value to me in relation to the presence of higher order thinking were characterised by the use of logical connectors such as 'because', 'if', 'but' and 'so', open questions such as 'why?' or 'how?' and conditionals such as 'would', 'could', 'should', 'might' and 'maybe'. I therefore used these words as a way of focusing in on interesting episodes in the corpus of transcripts. The kind of episodes of collaboration that interested me corresponded to a kind of talk which, following the earlier pioneering work of Douglas Barnes, Neil Mercer called Exploratory Talk (Mercer, 1995). I therefore referred to the key terms I was using as indicators of the possible presence of Exploratory Talk. Further indicators emerged as the research progressed, including expressions such as 'I think' to put forward a hypothesis, the length of utterances measured in number of characters in a 'turn at talk', this last measure seemed the most robust indicator of Exploratory Talk because linking claims and warrants for claims produced more words than was normal for the utterances of children around computer software.

It is interesting, on reflection, to consider how a combination of implicit assumptions and the embedded affordances of the tools at hand influenced the method I used and so influenced the findings of the study. My intuitions as to what was interesting talk were influenced by the assumptions of modernism in a way which naturally led me to a focus on explicit reasoning. The ease with which I could search the electronic texts led me to focus on verbal indicators of good quality dialogues rather than, for example, more visual clues such as facial expressions. The cultural anthropologist Marshall Sahlins once quipped that often in social science research 'ontology recapitulates methodology' meaning that what you find depends on how you go about looking for it (Sahlins, 1976). In this case, some of what might be naively thought of as the findings of the study were already implicit in the methods used, for example that good collaboration could be characterised as a type of 'talk' – 'Exploratory Talk' – and that this could be characterised through the presence of indicators of explicit reasoning. My methods largely ignored aspects of dialogue that were not visible in transcripts, body language, eye-contact, tone of voice and so on, and also, as I argued in Chap. 5, they overlooked playful, reflective and creative ways of talking when these did not produce the kinds of indicators that I was looking for.

1.3 Findings

This crude method, however, succeeded in focusing in on Exploratory Talk in order to explore factors that led to its occurrence and factors that prevented real discussion, despite the presence of indicators of a potential for Exploratory Talk. Such indicators of potential Exploratory Talk are referred to by Sylvia Rojas-Drummond, in a similar series of studies in Mexico, as 'incipient Exploratory Talk' (Rojas-Drummond et al., 2002). The concept of 'reflective dialogue' that I proposed in Chap. 5 and elaborated in Chap. 7, is not opposed to Exploratory Talk but expands on this to include the non-verbal dimension and the reflection and creativity that was missing from the original concept. While Exploratory Talk is too limited to be a full account of dialogic reason, it is nonetheless a kind of higher order thinking that is rightly highly valued within formal education. The findings of this study, despite its many limitations, are therefore still useful. The range of principles for the design of educational activities with information and communications technology (ICT) that support Exploratory Talk that emerged from this study are therefore also relevant to supporting the supervenient concept of reflective dialogue.

1.3.1 The importance of pedagogy

When the focusing method described was applied, one of the first things to leap out was that more recent transcripts in the classroom of teacher-researcher Lyn Dawes showed an anomalously high number of indicators of Exploratory Talk. I investigated this and found that, as a response to what she saw as the poor quality of the talk of children around computers revealed by the early video-recordings in the project, Lyn had begun preparing her children for talking together more effectively around computers. The importance of pedagogy is not just a question of teaching the ground rules of Exploratory Talk to the children but is also about how the children are primed for interpreting the activity at the computer and how this feeds back into the continuing teaching and learning dialogues of the classroom. One of the ways in which Lyn was achieving better quality collaborative learning around computers was by stressing to the children that the point of the activity was not just the curriculum learning goal, but also the quality of their talking and thinking. This was emphasised not only in setting up the activity but also in de-briefing afterwards when the children were led to think about what it is that they had done and what it is that they had 'learnt'.

1.3.2 Turn-taking

Wherever explicit turn-taking was encountered it seemed to prevent the development of Exploratory Talk. One reason for this emerges from a comparison of Exploratory Talk in two different sessions using LOGO. In one session two girls, Linda and Janet, took roles as to who typed and who directed, swapping after each exercise. This session produced no extended Exploratory Talk and very few key usages (0.58%). Further exploration of the context in which these few key usages occurred found several occasions where Exploratory Talk nearly took off but was prevented by the procedure of turn-taking that the girls had adopted. In LOGO numerical instructions are keyed in to get geometric shapes drawn on the screen. An example follows in which Linda says they should use the command 'FRESH' to clear the screen and offers a reason. Instead of counter-claiming and engaging in Exploratory Talk Janet asserts her authority as the person whose turn it is to direct:

Linda: No, we need 'FRESH'

Janet: No, no, no, Linda

Linda: We'll need to because it's, otherwise it's gone too far and it won't rub out

Janet: No, Linda, I know what I'm doing. I don't want it. You were just told to (inaudible) it's me who makes the decisions, you are just typing.

Another session with different girls using LOGO produced three times as many indicators of Exploratory Talk. Focusing in on these key usages, some sequences of Exploratory Talk could be observed. The significant difference seemed to be that these girls tackled problems together so that disagreements like the one above produced more discussion. In the following brief illustration they disagree about which command to give to make the shape they want:

Karen: ... forward 25.

Rachel: No, you see, it won't be big enough

Karen: It's a bit too big. Do 25, because that's too long.

Rachel: Let's do 30

Karen: OK. Forwards 30

In the case of LOGO there was no imperative to turn-taking in the software design but in some cases children adopted this strategy. In one exercise in the SMILE mathematics package turn-taking almost seemed to be suggested by features of the design of the software. In this exercise the children, two boys, took turns to try and find an 'elephant' lost in New York, represented with a grid, by keying in coordinates. Each time they guessed the programme told them how far away they were from the elephant.

There is something that could be learnt from this game about adding and subtracting coordinates in order to find the location of the elephant and so win the game, but in order to learn it users would have to reflect on what they were doing and try to develop an optimum strategy together. However, what actually happened was an enthusiastic competitive guessing game. Each boy keyed in coordinates learning from the extent of the other boy's error until one hit the elephant in which case the boy who keyed in would yell 'I won!'. There were some apparently exploratory exchanges but within a competitive 'disputational' orientation which did not lead to collaboration.

There were probably many factors contributing to the absence of 'Exploratory Talk' in this activity using SMILE. However, the combination of discrete moves and a unique goal state seemed to suggest competitive turn-taking if the software was used by more than one person. I later came to work with the development team at SMILE to advise them on interface design to support group work and to develop a Professional Development pack for teachers on how to prepare children for using mathematics software games. The result of this is reported in Chap. 10.

In Bubble Dialogue, words and thoughts are put into the speech bubbles and the thought bubbles of characters drawn on the screen to create a kind of cartoon story of a dialogue (McMahon and O'Neill, 1993). This exercise was approached in a variety of different ways. In one exercise two girls, Gill and Sally, role-played a school bully and her victim. In the transcripts there was a lot of cumulative talk, described by Fisher (1993) as talk in which speakers take up a previous initiation without questioning it. The two girls seemed reluctant to challenge each other in a way required for critical discussion. It emerged that the reason for this was that each was taking the main responsibility for the utterances of one character and felt that it would not be right to criticise their partner's suggestions for the other character's speech. Despite the cooperative attitude of these girls, very little Exploratory Talk emerged and so very little explicit reflection on the issues involved in their story.

The issue of turn-taking is only partly a software design issue. An emphasis on the importance of turn-taking is strong in the culture of UK primary classrooms. Young children often fight over using play equipment and so parents and teachers insist that they 'take turns'. The computer is like a piece of play equipment in many ways and it is natural that, when asked to work together at the computer, children will spontaneously expect to have to 'take turns'. Despite attempts to induct them into the ideals of Exploratory Talk, teachers also often instruct children to take turns when they set up the equipment. While taking turns over the use of the mouse or the keyboard is not a problem for the quality of joint thinking in a collaborative activity, taking turns over decision making is a problem. For the promotion of reflective dialogue children and teachers need to agree that while they can take turns over physical things they should work together on virtual things like ideas and decisions. This is a concrete and situated variation on the transition from physical notions of space to a dialogic idea of space introduced in Chap. 1.

1.3.3 Interface complexity

A common difficulty with open-ended software as a support for Exploratory Talk seemed to be mastering complex interfaces. Typing, in particular, for primary age children, proved very difficult in all sessions that required it. While typing does not, in itself, prevent the discussion of other issues, in practice it seemed to shift the interpretation of the task towards a focus on the written product. On the other hand there was also a tendency for school students to interpret every educational task as about producing a good quality written product which problem can only be addressed by pedagogy in combination with software design.

Bubble Dialogue, mentioned earlier, provides a good example of this problem. It was developed specifically to support reflective discussion-based learning (O'Neill and MacMahon, 1991) and claims have been made for it in this regard. It consists of a comic-strip format in which the users have to fill in the thoughts and utterances of the characters on the screen. In the sessions observed a small prologue was used to prepare the context of the dialogue. For four of the observed sessions this was about bullying at school and in the fifth it was a girl home late being confronted by her father.

The sessions with Bubble Dialogue had a similar pattern of activity over time. What to input was decided rapidly, by a variety of means, none of them involving extended discussion, then a much longer period was spent typing this input into the computer. This required repeating the sentence several times, saying each word and phrase while typing it and spelling out individual letters. Where discussion did occur it was as likely to be over spellings or how to manipulate the software as about the subject matter of the dialogue being created.

There was a tendency in all the sessions with Bubble Dialogue for ideas put forward to be accepted or rejected without reasons being given so that the dialogue between the pupils did not move into exploratory mode. A common form was 'Shall I put x?' followed by 'Yes' or, sometimes, 'No, put y', without any explicit discussion of reasons.

The software design principle that emerges from this discussion is the well known one that the interface should not get in the way of the intended learning outcome (O'Malley, 1992). If software is intended to foster discussion around the computer, rather than in print or through the computer, then typed input may be a frustrating factor simply because of the difficulty most school age children currently find with typing. One response to this could be to advocate teaching young children keyboarding skills. Another, one, is to replace typing with audio input (this is something I did with the software in question, Bubble Dialogue, see Chap. 10). However, as with the issue of turn-taking discussed above, the issue here is less an issue for software design than an issue for educational culture design. The focus of many educational activities in schools is on the construction of a neatly written text or other product. When I ask children to simply think and talk together around computers they often tell me that they enjoy this because it is 'play' and not 'work'. It seems that writing means 'school work' whereas talking is just play. For activities like Bubble Dialogue to produce real reflection it is crucial that the students using it are clear that the educational goal of the activity is not writing a text but the quality of their thinking and their talking. This discussion has general implications for the focus on products in the rhetoric of 'knowledge construction'. The opening of a space of reflection is less tangible than a product and the rush to the production of products often takes priority over reflection in formal education.

1.3.4 Intrinsic vs. extrinsic problems

Viking England is a role-playing game in which students play Vikings setting out from Norway to raid the coast of England. The aim of the game is not to lose men and to maximise profits measured in treasure and slaves. This game shares some features with shares the other adventure games used in the project such as Wizard's Revenge, Concept Kate, Hazard Rescue and Nature Park but of them all Viking England appeared to stimulate much more Exploratory Talk. One significant factor accounting for this disparity may have been a difference in the nature of the problems posed.

The challenges faced in Wizard's Revenge, Nature Park, Concept Kate and Hazard Rescue are local and extrinsic to the larger narrative. In one place in Wizard's Revenge, for example, the users have to solve mathematical sums in order to pass a barrier. In Viking England, the puzzles or challenges concern decisions which have to be made in the course of a simulated Viking raid: What to put in the ships, which route to take, where to land. These challenges are intrinsic to the narrative plot. They do not have a discrete right answer independent of the narrative plot as a whole.

Some of the puzzles in one adventure game, Nature Park, are disguised. This is a common element of commercial adventure games. It does not encourage the methodological problem solving approach of discussing all the options. In one session the children using the programme found themselves unable to pass a lake and could not find a way round. One of them summed up their frustration by saying: 'But it won't tell us the problem. That's the only problem'. Once the problem is known the solution is usually evident using some item of information local to the programme and so is solved instantly without discussion.

In Viking England, however, the problems are clear partly because they are an essential part of the story line and partly because they are clearly articulated by the interface. Solving the problems, or making the decisions that need to be made, requires information from throughout the programme and from information sheets provided with it as well as background knowledge on the historical context of the Vikings. The problems offered are the sort of complex problem that benefit from the clear articulation of different points of view.

In view of these points it is necessary to make a distinction between simple problems, all the salient aspects of which can be grasped in a single act of comprehension, and complex problems or issues which benefit from being dealt with in a dialogue with multiple voices.

This comparison between Viking England and other adventure games/simulations leads to two clear design principles for software supporting Exploratory Talk. First: problems for discussion should be explicitly articulated. Second: problems for discussion should be of the complex variety which benefit from discussion. There is also a third design principle that it is less easy to ground on the data but emerges from a range of experiences and is repeated in studies of online environments. This is the value of role-play. When asked to be themselves and to talk about things that really concern them students are often shy about putting forward suggestions or challenging others but this is much easier for them when they are playing a role such as being Vikings raiding and pillaging over one thousand years ago. The positive features of Viking England for supporting dialogue, explicit complex problems embedded in narrative role-play, are found in many, successful computer games in use today but there is a crucial difference, which is that Viking England did not impose time limits on decisions thus allowing children to sit back from the screen and discuss together before reaching a decision and communicating this to the software with a click of the mouse.

1.3.5 Supports for debate

Most of the Exploratory Talk observed across the whole range of data involved using material that could be talked about and that was ready to hand. Items were picked up from the context and used to support arguments or think about issues. When working with Viking England the children refer to the information given pictorially on the screen when discussing which site to raid. The presence of key features on the screen is the visual equivalent to pre-packaging the main arguments or warrants to be used in the debate. A similar use of symbols on the screen was found in other cases where Exploratory Talk occurred. In using Front Page, a desk-top publishing package, the children pointed to the position of text on the screen. In using LOGO the key issue was the position of lines and drawing 'turtles' on the screen.

In some cases shared background knowledge was also referred to. In writing an adventure story, children using Mystery Island used the stock of pictures provided to focus their discussion of possible plot continuations, a discussion which drew heavily on their shared cultural knowledge. Using a word processing package called Caxton to produce a brochure advertising their local town, pupils directly applied their personal knowledge in discussing its good and bad features. This last exercise produced an impressive amount of 'Exploratory Talk' in between bouts of typing.

The educational design principle that emerges from this discussion is the desirability of providing content material to discuss about, as well as the challenges that lead to discussion. Even where, in a moral discussion for example, pupils can be assumed to have this material available from their experience, it may help the flow of the discussion to provide props to focus this knowledge and to help structure arguments.

1.3.6 The problem of video gaming as a genre

The majority of current popular computer games running on hand-held consoles emphasise speed of response at the expense of reflection. These games are likely to have been the main computer-based activity of which school age children have experience. In interpreting a new computer-based activity pupils will draw upon models available from their experience. This means that fast and competitive commercial games are likely to serve as an attractor for the interpretation of whatever computer activities children are offered in schools. If the structure of those activities allows them to be assimilated into the same genre as commercial games then it is very likely that they will be. Some writers are interested in how the motivation and sense of 'flow' experienced in these video games can be harnessed to educational aims (Gee, 2003; Kirrimuir and Macfarlane et al., 2003). My evaluation in this study and other studies is that pressure of time reduces reflection and discussion. The idea of 'flow' is interesting, since Csikszentmihalyi (1996) associates this with creativity. Claxton might argue that my emphasis in Chap. 7 on the importance of stepping back from practice in order to reflect upon it may be over-valuing conscious thought and not be taking into account the creativity of the unconscious mind (Claxton, 1999). I agree with Csikszentmihalyi that 'flow' is important and with Claxton that this is bound up with allowing a dialogue with the 'unconscious', or that part of what we know that we are not consciously aware that we know. However, I am not yet convinced that the experience of 'flow' one gets when pushing buttons on a computer in a fast and furious video game is equivalent to the experience of 'flow' attributed by Csikszentmihalyi to highly creative people when they are in the process of making some major field-transforming breakthrough.

An example of genre assimilation occurs with the SMILE mathematics software episode referred to above. All the utterances of the two boys working at the computer are short. The action is fast and enthusiastic. Occasionally ejaculations such as 'wicked' are uttered or they swear at each other for being stupid. The style is very much that of interaction between children engaged in a competitive turn-taking commercial video game of the kind one finds in arcades on the high street. It is evident that this is how they see the activity. The design of the software does not impose this interpretation but it has done nothing to prevent it.

When the same users try a further SMILE exercise, a classic problem solving puzzle involving transporting people (one of which is a cannibal) over a river with only one small boat, they find that the complexity of the puzzle resists this movement of genre assimilation. Now their 'turns' have to be much longer, meaning that one of them is relatively idle and restless. It simply does not occur to them to discuss the problem together. The clash between the requirements of the software task and their expectations leads to frustration and they do not continue the exercise for long.

One of the key features making commercial video games exciting and motivating is the fact that decisions are time sensitive. This is a problem because if a user sits back and discusses a decision they might find themselves out of the game. Software with obvious educational potential such a Sim-City, Zoo Tycoon and Age of Empires suffers from the problem that too much reflection might mean losing the game. The only solution I can think of, one that I have tried and describe below in a study called 'the Talking Bug', is to build software to sit on the top of the gaming software in order to interrupt the flow at key points and ask the users to think about what they are doing and come back to the game only when they have developed a strategy.

1.4 Summary of principles of education design for reflective dialogue around computers

A number of clear design principles for educational software that supports reflective dialogue emerged from the original exploratory study of children using a range of software and also from this re-analysis of that study.

1. It is important to design educational activities as a whole, not only the software but also the pedagogy. The issue of the expectations users have about working together at a computer can best be addressed through explicitly promoting reflective dialogue (in this case Exploratory Talk) as a style of approaching computer tasks. A pedagogical framework that promotes reflective dialogue and uses computer-based activities to prompt and support reflective dialogue is therefore crucial to the success of collaborative learning around stand alone computers in classrooms. A version of such a pedagogy is presented in the next section.
2. Talking turns to be responsible for decisions should be discouraged either through the off-computer preparation or in the software design. Joint decision taking needs to be encouraged.
3. Selecting from alternatives is preferable to typed input when users are not experienced with keyboards.
4. Problems or issues intended to initiate discussion should be embedded in role-play and intrinsic to the narrative development of the activity. Problems should not be capable of immediate solution.
5. Props for discussion should be provided in the form of symbols for different perspectives and positions or bodies of evidence that can be pointed to on the screen and, if possible, manipulated.
6. Avoid any 'ticking clock' that encourages a speedy response over reflection. Alternatively, build into or on top of such time-sensitive games pause points for reflection.

2 IDRF

These design principles are partly about providing tools for discussion, both strategies for thinking together when sitting at a computer screen with someone else and things like props for reasoning on the screen, but they are more fundamentally about how to open up a space for reflection. It was generally found that children were closely engaged in interaction with the interface enjoying clicking buttons and observing the almost instant response, in a way that made any discussion or reflection difficult. The educational design principles, combining pedagogy and software design, aim at breaking this fascination in order to get children to sit back from the screen and discuss issues together. The idea is to open up a dialogic space. I summed up at the time of the study with the idea of the idea of an IDRF exchange structure (Wegerif, 1996).

In 1975 applied linguists John Sinclair and Malcolm Coulthard studied talk in classrooms from the point of view of structures of language use. One of the patterns they isolated, the IRF exchange structure, has since become almost universally accepted as 'the essential teaching exchange' (Edwards and Westgate, 1994, p. 143). IRF stands for Initiation, usually a question by the teacher, Response, by a student, and Feedback by the teacher. For example a classic IRF could be:

Teacher: How many sides does a hexagon have?

Pupil: Six.

Teacher: Well done.

Recognising that the feedback move is not always explicit and that the teacher often uses the response of the pupil to cue a new activity or question, Wells replaces 'Feedback' with the more open term 'Follow-up' (1999).

This three-part exchange structure, sometimes also called the triadic structure (Lemke, 1990) has proved useful to researchers looking at talk between teachers and learners (Cazden, 1988; Mehan, 1979; Mercer, 1995). Many have noted that the IRF structure allows the teacher to keep control of the direction of the interaction with students. The student's input is always framed by the teacher's prompts and evaluations. As a result, the IRF exchange structure has been criticised by those that claim that it controls students too much and prevents them from thinking for themselves and asking their own questions (Young, 1991; Dillon, 1990; Wood, 1988). The IRF analysis has also been applied to interaction with tutorial software and with adventure games (Crook, 1994, pp. 11–13; Fisher, 1992). In much software, the computer asks a question, the user offers a response of some kind and the computer evaluates this response either explicitly or through the selection of the next screen or prompt. The criticism of the limiting effects of IRF in teacher–student dialogue has been carried over to IRF type exchanges with computers.

However, with group work at the computer, and also with reflection at the computer, the educational exchange can be different. The computer programme may take the initiative and pose a question (I), it may also insist on a response from a limited range of options (R) and finally, it may evaluate those responses either explicitly or implicitly through the choice of follow-up questions (F). However, when dealing with computers, a pair or groups of users have a new option. That option is to sit back from the computer screen and discuss their response together.

Discussion between the 'Initiation' and the 'Response' introduces a new kind of educational exchange which can be called I*D*RF to signify: Initiation, *Dialogue*, Response, Follow-up (Wegerif, 1996). This educational exchange structure summarises the aim of the approach to collaborative software design which emerged from the exploratory study of children talking at computers. I will say more about this after describing a study to test and develop these design principles by implementing them.

2.1 Applying, testing and developing the I*D*RF design principles

Having elicited a first set of educational design principles from the data I then set about testing and developing these through a series of design studies. Firstly I worked with Lyn Dawes and Neil Mercer to develop a pedagogical framework for ICT use. This is the main topic of a book written with Lyn Dawes (Wegerif and Dawes, 2004). Basically we developed lessons to promote Exploratory Talk including eliciting a set of shared ground for talk as described in Chap. 4. We asked teachers to remind children of their shared ground rules before setting group tasks around computers. In the lesson plenaries or de-briefing sessions we asked teachers to focus on the quality of talk and reflection as well as any curriculum content related goals.

Working with the team, I designed and developed several items of software implementing the principles outlined in the previous section. Here I will talk briely about one item in the curriculum area of citizenship and another in the area of science.

2.1.1 Citizenship: Kate's Choice

The story begins with two young friends, Kate and Robert, talking together. Robert has a box of chocolates and Kate asks where he got them. Robert asks her to promise to keep his secret before he tells her that he stole them. He explains further that they are a present for his mother who was in hospital. Kate then has to decide whether she should tell her parents of this or not. This is the first of a series of moral decisions that the children are asked to take after discussing the question together (Fig. 9.1). Eventually, whatever route they take through the software, the children are asked to reflect and consider if they made the right decision, looking at what the main characters in the drama think. This is something that I take up again at the beginning of Chap. 10.

The following analysis will focus on the talk of children at the first decision point of the 'Kate's Choice' software. The reason for choosing this one decision point is that it enabled a generalisation to be made to all the groups in both the target and the control class. It was the only decision point which all groups had to do which had a fixed amount of text to read. Given that, according to the class teachers, the two classes were of equivalent overall reading ability and given that all the children observed were highly motivated by the software it follows that the different amount of time taken up in making this decision can offer some indication of how much time was spent talking to each other. This then enables a systematic comparison to be made of the interactions of the groups in the three conditions.

Fig. 9.1. First decision point in Kate's Choice

2.1.2 Talk of the target groups

In this first study three groups of children were videotaped using this software. The talk of these groups at the first decision point of Kate's Choice (Fig. 9.1) was transcribed. One of these episodes is presented with a short commentary for illustrative purposes.

Transcript Extract 1: Barbara, Martin and Ross

(Barbara reads aloud from the screen)

Ross: I think he should not – he shouldn't tell.

Martin: Don't tell.

Ross: (reads) 'Talk about what Kate should do ...'

Ross: I think she shouldn't tell because she said she'd promise.

Martin: Yeh, if she broke her promise he'd be into trouble right? Broke her promise he'd be into trouble.

Barbara: Yeh, but on the other hand...?

Ross: Yeh and he did do it not for himself but for his mum and his mum's sick.

Martin: No, but he could be lying.

(3 second pause)

Barbara: Yeh, but would you do it? Would you tell?

Ross: Umm, no. If I did I'd feel guilty.

Martin: I wouldn't.

Barbara: (clicks and then reads) 'Have you talked about it?'

ALL: Yes.

(Total time on the screen before clicking: 82 s.)

Commentary: Here Barbara takes on a facilitating role asking questions and putting forward alternatives. She challenges the sincerity of the others asking them if they would really do what they are saying Kate should do. Nobody argues in favour of telling but Michael suggests that they should be cautious in believing Robert's story. They all reach an agreement before the mouse is clicked. It is interesting how they bring in their own 'voice' through asking each other 'what would you do?'

As with the talk of all the three groups video-recorded in the target class this talk could be called exploratory with children raising and criticising a range of reasons for both alternatives before reaching a shared decision.

The following features were exhibited in the talk of most of the target class groups observed:

- Asking each other task-focused questions.
- Giving reasons for statements and challenges.
- Considering more than one possible position.
- Drawing opinions from all in the group.
- Reaching agreement before acting.

These five features were all explicitly coached in the intervention programme as ground rules for talking together. These features were found less or not at all in the talk of the control class groups. Most control class groups observed moved forward through the story in one of the following ways:

- Unilateral action by the child with the mouse.
- Accepting the choice of the most dominant child without supporting reasons.
- Drifting together to one or other choice without debating any alternatives.

(See transcript extracts in Wegerif, 1996b).

As a result of the relative lack of talk in the control classes, they spoke for less time at this decision point.

2.1.3 Computer-based text analysis

The difference between the pre- and the post-intervention test talk for the educational activity was quantifiable through the marked increase in the number of task-based questions asked and the uses of the key terms 'if' and 'because/'cos' to link reason clauses to assertions. Applying the same 'key usage' analysis to the full transcripts of two target (coached) groups and two control (uncoached) groups working on the citizenship software produced the results shown in Table 9.1.

Table 9.1. Key word counts for target and control groups

	Control	Target
Questions	4	13
Because/'Cos	0	7
If	0	2
Total words	496	942

This table reveals a marked difference between the talk of the children coached in Exploratory Talk and that of the children who had no coaching. To observe the relationship between the coaching programme and the language used it is necessary to look at the actual words in context that lie behind these figures. A list of questions used was obtained by setting the context parameters of concordance software created by David Graddol, '!Kwictex' to that of the relevant utterance or turn at talk.

2.1.4 Quantitative analysis using data-capture

The transcript evidence shows the target groups taking longer than the control groups at the decision point because they are engaged in reasoning together about the decision which they then take jointly. All the children in both the classes used this software in small groups, mostly groups of three but occasionally in pairs, and the amount of time they took for this decision was recorded automatically by the software. The results are presented below.

Table 9.2. Time at first decision point

	Target class groups	Control class groups
	43	21
	63	35
	65	41
	67	48*
	74	51
	82*	58
	97*	59
	102*	60
	105	62*
Mean	77.55	48.33
SD	20.72	13.76

* = focal group with video recording.

Statistical analysis of these figures shows them to be highly significant ($p = 0.0015$. One-tailed T-test).

Since a large proportion of the time spent at this screen was spent reading the text the real difference in the time spent talking together between the target and the control classes is greater than that indicated by the figures.

2.2 Science: What is your prediction?

I designed the science programme to teach for statements of attainment from 'Experimental and Investigative Science' at Key Stage 2 in the National Curriculum relating to planning, predicting, observing and explaining experimental tests. Concurrently the programme targeted 'physical forces', specifically knowledge about friction (DfEE, 1997).

The software combined an interactive simulation with a structured tutorial. Ten multiple choice questions about forces, friction and experimental methods ('fair tests') had to be completed before the simulation was reached and again afterwards. The simulation enabled users to explore the effects of initial force, surface texture and weight on the movement of objects (see Fig. 9.2). Interaction with the simulation was directed with a series of prompts and dialogue boxes. These led the users through familiarisation with the controls to a series of experiments which began with very explicit instructions, moved through more general instructions to design experiences to test for different hypotheses and ended with the open-ended use of the simulation.

Design to support Exploratory Talk applied the work of Howe and colleagues referred to above (Howe et al., 1996; Tolmie et al., 1993). Each time the users sought to run the simulation, they were prompted by the software to predict the result they expected (Fig. 9.2) and after the run they were asked if their prediction was correct or not and why they thought that this was so. The general guidelines for design given above were adhered to. Evidence to support argumentation was provided on the screen in the form of the settings and the speed and distance readings. There was no typed input but simple choice buttons or multiple choice interfaces. While there was no explicit role-play and narrative the nature of interacting with a simulation provides a kind of role-play and narrative structure in which decisions taken have effects on later actions. As with the citizenship software, they were explicitly prompted to talk together to formulate predictions and explanations, and were encouraged to take joint responsibility for decisions.

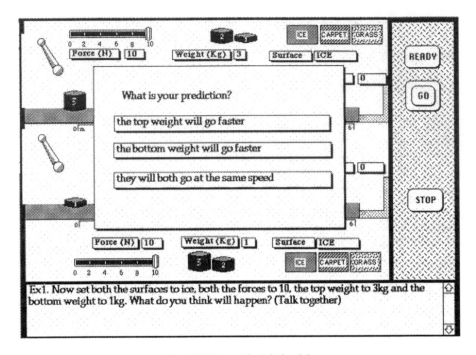

Fig. 9.2. Prompt in Friction lab

2.2.1 Evaluation

The evaluation of the Science software measured its effects on children's learning. Eight groups of 9 and 10-year-old children (six groups of three and two pairs) carried out an activity based on the software. All the children had previously completed the off-computer training in Exploratory Talk. Each session lasted from 45 minutes to one hour, during which the talk of three groups was video-recorded. As described above the software itself incorporated pre- and post- tests which all the groups therefore completed. In addition, short individual pre- and post-tests were given to all the 22 children involved.

2.2.2 Transcript Extract 2

Because the computer programme incorporated pre- and post-intervention questions into the simulation, we were able to focus in the learning of the children by looking at their talk around questions which they completed correctly in the post-test, having previously made errors in the pre-test. In most cases, the difference, the 'learning' in other words, could be observed in the talk of the children. A transcript account of talk elicited by one such post-test question follows.

Transcript Extract 2: Rachel and Cindy

Q3 On the computer screen

> **Rough surfaces cause**
> **a) as much friction as a smooth**
> **surface?**
> **b) more friction than a smooth surface?**
> **c) less friction than a smooth surface?**

Rachel:	Which one do you think it is?
Cindy:	Wah, wah, wah (*Reading fast*) friction, mmmm, surface, mmm.
Rachel:	What do you think?
Cindy:	'c'
Rachel:	I think 'b' (*laughs*)
Cindy:	I don't. Look 'changes more surfaces than a smooth surface' (Misreading the screen)
Rachel:	Yeh I know, but if you rub
Cindy:	(*inaudible*)
Rachel:	yeh I know but – wait, wait – listen, if you rub two smooth surfaces together right, will it be slippery or stable? (*Rubs hands together*)
Cindy:	Stable – depends how tight you've got it.
Rachel:	Cindy listen! If you've got oil on your hands and you rub them together will they be slippery or not? (*rubs hands together*)
Cindy:	Well you see (*she rubs her hands in a parody of Rachel but in a way that makes them miss each other*) 'cos they don't rub together they go…
Rachel:	Cindy! (*in mock exasperated tone*) If you've got …
Cindy:	Yeh, they will be slippery! (*laughs*)
Rachel:	Yeh, exactly. So if you've got two rough surfaces and you rub them together it will not be as slippery will it?
Cindy:	No

Rachel: So that proves my point doesn't it?

Cindy: mmm

Rachel: Yes, do you agree? Good. (*She clicks on answer 'b'*)

Commentary: In the pre-intervention test neither girl had seen the connection between the texture of surfaces and friction. Here Rachel appears to know the answer and persuades Cindy. She does so with reasons and an analogy of the effect of adding oil to one's hands when rubbing them. In the pre-intervention test, she did not make this connection. Rachel's response to an initial disagreement is to give reasons and attempt to persuade her partner. Although this appears rather one-sided Cindy is genuinely persuaded and in other interactions Cindy was the one persuading Rachel. In the talk of the girls together using the simulation the recognition that, the more slippery the surface the less friction there is, appears several times in response to prompts for explicit explanations by the computer.

Note that the interface here could not be simpler or more 'tutorial' in design; yet it produces persuasive and reasoned talk. We can see the IDRF (Initiation, *Dialogue*, Response, Feedback) structure of the talk, where instead of responding immediately to the computer prompt the children sit back from the computer and discuss their possible response amongst themselves. In this case the pedagogical framework has facilitated transforming a simple computer–user interaction into a more complex learning experience.

2.2.3 Quantitative evaluation

Pre-intervention and post-intervention group test results for the eight groups show that four increased their score by 2 points out of ten while four did not increase at all. Statistical analysis of this small sample does not show significance.

Individual pre- and post- test results for 20 students using a structured interview of four questions marked out of 4.5 produced a statistically significant increase. The mean pre-intervention test result was 3 (SD 1.076) and the mean post-intervention test result was 3.65 (SD 0.829). A one-tailed t-test gave $p = 0.018$.

I naturally hypothesised that these marked individual learning gains, after a short session with the computer, were the outcome of dialogue between the children such as that given in the transcript extract, where they make ideas explicit and help each other to learn.

3 IDRF RE-VISITED

Ever since my experience with the shy Bangladeshi girls who blossomed in front of computers I have been fascinated by what it is that makes ICT appear to be a better vehicle for stimulating dialogues than teachers. It is possible that this relates to the fact that computers are not in fact people and have no judgements or social status and yet they can stimulate conversations as if they were dialogue partners. This could be called their 'ontological ambivalence'. Everyday language distinguishes between two main categories of being: subjects and objects. Subjects are assumed to have agency and moral responsibility. We normally explain what they say or do in terms of psychological attributes such as thoughts, feelings and beliefs. So, for example, when someone we meet says: 'Hello, how are you?' we know that they expect a response and that they may be offended if we do not respond. Objects, on the other hand, have no agency or responsibility. We normally assume that there are causal explanations for their behaviour. So, for example, if we pick up a child's soft toy and it says 'Hello, how are you?' we will probably assume that a pressure switch was triggered and that caused a short pre-recorded message to play. In this case we are unlikely to feel any obligation to respond. If we were to respond, it would be in the spirit of entering into a game.

Computers as partners in learning conversations can be made to act like subjects in some respects and yet they are, in fact, objects. On the one hand educational software can be made to respond appropriately to inputs in such a way that users feel the need to explain their responses in psychological terms: it is common to say, for example that the computer 'thinks' or 'expects something'. On the other hand, even young children quickly learn that computers do not have the feelings, expectations and implicit judgements that human conversational partners invariably do have (Turkle, 1995).

In some contexts this difference between computers and humans can be of benefit. In some psychotherapeutic interactions, for example, the combination of a human-like ability to ask questions with a machine-like patience and lack of judgement has been shown to be very effective (Suler, 2002; Rajendran and Mitchell, 2000). This paper will argue that the ontological ambivalence of computers also equips them, with the right educational software, to play a unique role in supporting teaching and learning dialogues.

3.1 The issue of control: against constructivism

As I mentioned in Chap. 6, Papert (1981) compared tutorial software, which he claimed was 'programming children', to his own vision of children 'programming computers'. This contrast between computers as agents controlling children or tools that children can control has been very influential. It is implicit in the widespread classification of computer software as either a 'tutor' or a 'tool' (O'Shea and Self, 1984; Crook, 1994). On one side the computer is conceptualised as a kind of subject, a 'tutor', and on the other side the computer is conceptualised as a kind of thing or object, a 'tool'. A variation on the same theme is the classification of software on an 'open–closed' continuum according to the degrees of freedom offered to the user (see for example Fisher, 1992; Anderson et al., 1993; Newman et al., 1989).

The 'tutor–tool' distinction and the 'open–closed' continuum are referring to a marked difference that can be found in software designs. On one extreme lies the directive teaching software found in 'integrated learning systems' such as Research Machines' 'successmaker' and on the other extreme, software such as a word processor that can be used in an infinite variety of ways. Most commentators, from Papert onwards, appear to give an evaluation to this distinction. More passive, open-ended software is seen as good for supporting meaningful learning (e.g. Preece, 2000). More directive, 'closed' and tutorial software is seen as limiting the possibilities of thought and discussion (e.g. Fisher, 1992). The assumptions underlying this literature are that it is bad to have computers controlling learners and good to get learners to control the computers.

It is possible that this opposition involves a misunderstanding that stems from a transfer of judgements about teacher–student interactions onto computer–student interactions. In the transcript extract above Rachel and Cindy discuss friction together within a classically controlling tutorial IRF interface but they do not seem to be limited by it or to feel 'controlled' by it. Tutorial software does not have the same effect on children as the equivalent style of interaction with a teacher. This is because children do not necessarily feel under the same social and psychological obligation towards machines that they sometimes might feel under when talking with teachers.

The difference between interacting with humans and interacting with computers emerges from studies of the use of computers by children with Autism and Asperger's syndrome (Rajendran and Mitchell, 2000). In this literature it is common to point out that these children enjoy interacting with computers because, whatever software they are running, computers are experienced as 'safe'. Computers are not experienced as having the expectations and judgements that make social interaction problematic for this group of children. A common theme of the literature is that, in interactions with computers, children with Autism can feel 'in control' in a way that they cannot feel when working with human beings (e.g. Huntiger and Rippey, 1997). This feeling of control is not related to a particular kind of software interface but is said to be generic to all interactions with computers.

3.2 The educational significance of IDRF

My suggested IDRF coding for some forms of computer supported discussion combines two very different kinds of interaction. The 'IRF' part refers to the user–computer interaction and the '*D*' to the spoken pupil–pupil discussion. Where the discussion between pupils is 'Exploratory' Talk (Mercer, 1995), with children thinking together and trying out alternative ideas, then IDRF also combines two very different educational genres. Taking the IRF sequence alone, users appear passive and the computer appears to be in control. This may be taken to correspond to what is sometimes, usually in a pejorative sense, called a transmission model of teaching and learning. In exploratory discussion mode, on the other hand, users actively consider their options using the information offered by the computer in the knowledge that the conclusions of the discussion will later be tested out upon the computer. In this moment of the educational exchange the interaction the computer acquires is a more passive role of a 'learning environment'. The '*D*' part of the IDRF exchange therefore corresponds to the kind of learning through discovery and the construction of meaning advocated by Papert and others. IDRF is interesting because it combines both these often contrasted modes of teaching and learning in one basic educational exchange.

In comparison with IRF interactions alone, on the one hand and peer discussion alone, on the other, IDRF has some clear educational advantages. Through the IRF framework the computer can stimulate and direct the talk of the children in order to meet the goals of a predefined curriculum. In the discussion moment children construct their own meanings. The IDRF exchange structure can therefore be seen as an ICT supported version of Vygotsky's Zone of Proximal Development (ZPD) – the zone in which teaching brings the spontaneously formed concepts of learners into relationship with the pre-existing concepts of a culture (Vygotsky, 1986). Vygotsky's model offers a third way beyond the transmission vs. discovery dichotomy found in Papert's book *Mindstorms*. In the ZPD there is transmission but also the active construction of knowledge by learners. The IDRF structure can be seen as embodying a neo-Vygotskian model of teaching and learning: neither as transmission alone nor as construction alone but as both and as more. This third way is summed up in the phrase 'the guided construction of knowledge' (Mercer, 1995).

This, at least, is the neo-Vygotskian analysis of the education significance of an IDRF exhange structure between users and the interface. In this analysis the *Dialogue* moment here is sandwiched between the IRF moments in a way that elicits student voices only to then direct them towards pre-set ends of the programmer which could also be those of the curriculum. There is, however, an alternative more dialogic way of using IDRF which I illustrate with concrete examples in Chap. 10. When a group of students step back from the 'flow' of IRF user interface interaction they open up a dialogic time and space which is their own and which could be said to envelop the IRF exchange with the computer software because within the dialogue they can interpret the initiations, their responses and the implicit or explicit feedback. While the dialogue moment can be contained within the larger teaching and learning exchange structure to be dialogue for the end of pre-set knowledge construction it can also, with dialogic pedagogy and software design, break out of that structure to become dialogue as an end in itself.

4 AN EMPIRICAL STUDY OF THE IDRF EXCHANGE WITHIN THE CURRICULUM

After the small study described above I worked with Lyn Dawes, Neil Mercer, Steve Higgins, Claire Sams and Karen Littleton to develop lesson plans and ICT activities for 9 and 10-year-old, children in three UK primary schools. This project, funded by the Nuffield Foundation, was designed to test the impact of the IDRF exchange on achievement in the curriculum. We had a particular focus on covering the mathematics and science curriculum, however, ICT-based activities in English and Citizenship were also included. There were 119 children in the experimental classes and 129 children in matching schools acted as controls, covering the same area of the science and maths curriculum but without our intervention.

To encourage IDRF exchanges within this study, the research team selected from existing software and designed new software according to principles that had been derived from the earlier exploratory research. The team also worked with teachers to promote effective discussions through a series of 'talk lessons' (Dawes et al., 2004). These lessons prepare the children for small group work around computers through teaching the ground rules of reflective dialogue in the form of Exploratory Talk. After this preparation ICT based lessons were given by the classroom teachers which included group work around software. To provide more qualitative data a representative group of three children was selected by the teacher in each class for video-recording when working with different items of software. The following example offers an illustration of how the IDRF exchange structure was supported by ICT activities in a way that contributed to curriculum learning.

4.1 Talking Bug

There are many 'open-ended' simulation programmes intended to teach science. Earlier observation studies suggested however, that while children enjoyed the interactivity of simulation programmes they often learnt little without a great deal of input from a teacher (Wegerif, 1996a). The implication of these studies was that, rather than simply pressing buttons and getting responses, the children could have benefited from a stimulus to encourage them to think more about experimental design, predications and explanations for observed regularities. As described earlier an initial programme tested this approach in the context of a simulation of friction. In this programme weights, surfaces and push forces could be varied to explore the effect of friction. Whenever the children attempted to run the simulation they were asked for a prediction and then, when the simulation had run, they were asked for an explanation of why their prediction was right or wrong. This simple approach to promoting discussion worked well (Wegerif et al., 1999). In the larger follow-up study, we decided to build a programme to work with existing simulations. We called this the 'talking bug' because its role was to 'bug' or bother students into talking together. It interacted with audio messages as well as text and looked like a ladybird; so the name 'talking bug' was doubly appropriate.

Fig. 9.3. Talking Bug at rest

When not active, the Talking Bug is designed to sit quietly at a corner of the screen (Fig. 9.3).

It can be minimised in this way at any time with a click of the mouse. When active (Fig. 9.4) it sits on top of the current window. The Talking Bug was used in conjunction with simulations taken from Granada's widely used 'Science Explorer' programme. In the following transcript example (Transcript Extract 3) the Bug prompted children to talk around a simulation of an experimental sound laboratory (Fig. 9.5).

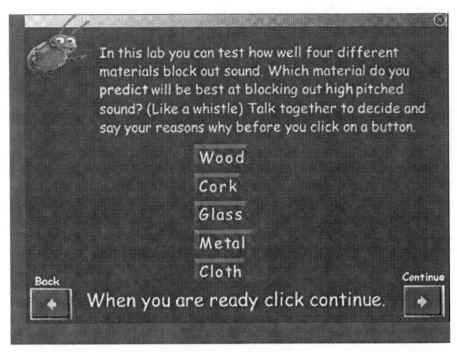

Fig. 9.4. Talking Bug prompt

Fig. 9 5. Science Explorer Lab

The recording was made of a group of three children, two girls and a boy, working around a computer in a computer room. The activity was part of a whole class lesson in which the teacher initially reminded the children of previous work on sound, set up the science aims of the lesson and emphasised the importance of using the shared 'ground rules for talk' that had been established in earlier lessons (Mercer, Wegerif and Dawes, 1999).

Transcript Extract 3: Sound vibrations

TalkingBug:	In this lab, you can test how well four different materials block out sound. Which material do you predict will be the best at blocking out a high-pitched sound, like a whistle? Talk together to decide and say your reasons why before you click on a button.
Sandra:	Um. Can you hear sound through wood?[Points to wood on list].
Brad:	I think – What?
Sandra:	Can you hear sound through wood?
Brad:	I imagine you can, but I think that –
Kylie:	How about glass? [Points to glass on list]
Brad:	No – not glass, because of the vibrations. [He gestures to indicate vibrations]
Sandra:	From cloth you can
Kylie:	Yeah, but they haven't got cloth here.
Brad	– vibrations – metal because it can't vibrate and it's really strong.
Kylie:	[To Sandra] It is strong isn't it. O.K. Metal. [Sandra nods].
Sandra:	O.K. Here
Brad:	What?
Sandra:	If you hear sound with the metal –

Kylie: Well, you can't really 'cos if you like had metal walls, yeah, you wouldn't be able to hear anything around –brick wall-

Sandra: [Clicks mouse on the 'METAL' button]

Talking Bug: Thank you. Do you think this will be different for low-pitched sound?

The interface (Fig. 9.3) is typical of a tutorial software and constrains an 'IRF' type interaction between the Talking Bug programme and the students. However, this programme, in conjunction with their previous lessons establishing ground rules for talking together around computers, leads this group of children to discuss how materials block out sound and to make an explicit prediction based upon their shared experience. The IDRF structure is clear with the Talking Bug programme initiating (I), the children discussing (D) and then making a response (R – a mouse click by Sandra) with a final follow-up by the Talking Bug acknowledging their input and asking a new question.

The children predict that metal will be the best material for blocking out high-pitched sound. Their reasoning includes the understanding that sound is transmitted by vibrations, however, they mistakenly think that metal does not vibrate because it is 'strong'.

After prompting the children to make predications, the Talking Bug guides them through designing an experiment to test their predications and then retreats to the top left hand corner of the screen (Fig. 9.4), leaving them to conduct the experiment in the virtual lab provided (Fig. 9.5). They learn that cork is in fact the best insulator for high-pitched sound. The Talking Bug returns (it reminds them to click on it by twitching her wings) and asks them which material was best. When they select cork, the Bug asks them to explain why their initial predication was wrong. As they struggle with this question the class teacher joins them and is able to build on the idea of vibrations offered by Brad and of the thickness of the material offered by Sandra to explain about the importance of compactness. The children appear to understand. Later, in the plenary, the teacher reinforces this point.

Taking the activity as a whole, the prompts from the Talking Bug appear to stimulate these children to think about the problem together. Their initial conceptions give the teacher something to build on in offering a scientific explanation for their experimental findings.

4.1.1 Quantitative results

In addition to this kind of observational evidence we collected quantitative evidence that exchanges of this kind benefited measurable learning in the science curriculum. Both experimental and control classes were given a test of scientific understanding in the topics covered in year 5 of the UK curriculum, at the beginning and at the end of the school year. An ANCOVA (analysis of co-variance) revealed that the experimental classes significantly improved their scores in relation to the control classes ($P = 0.002$; full details of the statistics are provided in Mercer et al., 2004). The questions we used were taken from optional SATs tests published by the UK government. The experimental classes had most of their science lessons over one year taught with the help of computer-based activities designed to produce IDRF exchanges. The statistical evidence therefore suggests that the kind of IDRF exchange reported above led to increases in measurable learning outcomes.

5 CONCLUSION

In this chapter I have revisited and re-framed some of my own history as a researcher in the field of Educational Technology. I began with my personal discovery of the powerful potential of computer supported collaborative learning around stand alone computers working with Bangladeshi girls in the East End of London and described how I worked with Neil Mercer and Lyn Dawes to develop educational activities which supported learning dialogues around computers within the curriculum. This work was done very much within a neo-Vygotskian framework and could be described as creating Vygotsky's 'Zone of Proximal Development' around computers in which learners are led ahead of their current knowledge through the quality of peer dialogue combined with the stimulus and feedback of computer software. Principles for educational design were elicited through an initial exploratory study and these were then tested and developed through design studies. Evaluations show that this approach definitely worked to promote learning within the curriculum. Reflecting on this series of studies from the dialogic perspective I have outlined in the book so far I re-described the main direction of this work as using a combination of pedagogy and technology to open up a dialogic space of reflection within the closed chain of 'Initiation, Response, Feedback' human-computer interaction leading to a description of the ideal exchange around computers as Initiation, *Dialogue*, Response, Feedback or IDRF. A neo-Vygotskian account of learning as combining an 'upward' student movement of 'construction' with 'downward' guidance from the existing culture was useful in understanding the learning through dialogue within the curriculum that was achieved with this IDRF approach.

As explained in Chap. 4, the Exploratory Talk that the off-computer educational programme was designed to promote embodied reasoning and so this approach to CSCL could be said to integrate some general thinking skills into teaching and learning across the curriculum in a way that has the proven potential to raise achievement. However, re-analysis from a dialogic perspective suggests that the dialogic space opened up within the IRF chain has the potential to do more than serve simply as a means to the end of the construction of curriculum knowledge. Vygotsky's Zone of Proximal Development is a uni-directional concept but creative dialogues can go in any direction. In Chap. 7, I argued that dialogue as an end in itself is a way to teach highly prized general thinking and learning skills such as learning to learning and creativity. Expanding the space of dialogue in human–computer interaction is certainly a step in this direction, teaching the higher order skill of reasoning together, but there are other approaches to educational design that can go further to allow the dialogue to become an end in itself. In Chap. 10 I will look at further studies of CSCL in primary classrooms showing how the dialogic space opened up in these early studies can be expanded to take over the whole interaction.

Summary

In this chapter I described an exploratory study of children talking around a range of software which elicited principles for design which were then tested and developed in two design studies. The first principle was the need to integrate software design to support dialogue with pedagogy to promote effective dialogue, other more software focussed principles were:

- *putting evidence which could be used in discussion about choices clearly on the screen where users could point to it*
- *presenting choices embedded in a motivating narrative*
- *making problems sufficiently complex to benefit from being analysed through reflection and discussion*
- *using a simple interface with multiple choice options rather than typed input*
- *avoiding any encouragement towards turn-taking, e.g. not using discrete serial problems*
- *avoiding time pressure on decisions*

These principles were then implemented as far as possible in two software designs and an educational programme to promote effective dialogue. They were found to be effective both in expanding the amount and quality of dialogue and in improving curriculum learning. A further study taking Maths and Science over one school year demonstrated that this approach had the potential to raise achievement. However, I criticised this approach as being limited to the neo-Vygotskian framework of using dialogue as a means to the end of knowledge construction. To really promote skills of creativity and learning to learning it is necessary to consider how the space of dialogue can be expanded further until it becomes an end in itself. I consider some more genuinely dialogic approaches to the design of CSCL in primary classrooms in Chap. 10.

Chapter 10

COMPUTERS SUPPORTING DIALOGUE
Breaking out of the frame

In the last chapter I described how typical initiation, response, feedback interactions with tutorial software and simulations could be opened up to include a space for dialogue. This was originally conceived as a version of Vygotsky's Zone of Proximal Development and as a way of including dialogue within the curriculum. In this Chapter I go further to look at the design of technology enhanced educational activities which induct students into dialogue as an end in itself.

1 THE FORUM DESIGN

In Chap. 9, I illustrated the case of integrating dialogue into computer directed learning with the example of some simple software I designed called 'Kate's Choice'. This is an interactive narrative in which key plot decisions are taken by the users and determine the direction of the story. I illustrated the first 'decision point' in the story and called this an IRF type interface in that there was an Initiation by the software (I), a simple question, and then a response by the users (R), either 'yes' or 'no', and finally a follow-up (F), because the software determined the next story sequence and choice to be made depending on the response given by the users. With the right pedagogy promoting the use of Exploratory Talk, and *only* with this pedagogy, the normally limited space for reflection between Initiation and Response could be opened up in a dialogue in which children discussed alternatives and gave reasons for positions. I called this whole activity an '*IDRF*' sequence with the *D* standing for the dialogic space opened up. The role of this dialogue space around software in the construction of curriculum knowledge was made very clear in the examples from the science curriculum. In the transcript extracts of talk about friction or about sound insulating materials it is easy to see how the dialogue between students helped them to construct together the knowledge that was already specified in the science curriculum.

However, Kate's Choice was located within the Citizenship curriculum and here the role of dialogue in the construction of knowledge was less obvious. The aims of the Citizenship were easy to achieve because they included 'using discussion to help make a decision about a moral issue' (National Curriculum quoted in Wegerif, 1996). In other words dialogue across different perspectives was already an aim of the curriculum not only as a means to the end of but also apparently as an end in itself. Here the IRF frame of the activity becomes the background and the dialogue itself becomes the foreground as the main point of the exercise. The way in which the D moment of dialogic reflection can be made to expand out of the IRF framework to take over the educational activity is even more clearly illustrated by another type of interface that I designed for reflection and de-briefing at the end of the story. I called this 'The Forum' and it consisted simply of a decision which the users had to make taking into account the views of all the characters in the story. In the first 'Forum' the group working with Kate's Choice are asked to decide if they made Kate 'do the right thing', whether she told that her friend Robert had stolen chocolates to any of the characters who put pressure on her or if she did not tell and allowed herself to be falsely accused. The structure of this Forum screen is shown in Fig. 10.1 with all the characters heads around a central space where texts boxes appear with their views when they are clicked on. There is a single question 'initiation' or 'prompt' at the top of the screen: 'Did Kate do the Right Thing?' And only two buttons to choose form at the bottom: YES or NO. This is then again an IRF interface design with the main twist being that before the users make their decision they are asked to engage in dialogue with the points of views of all the characters in the story. After this they face a very similar screen where they have to decide the punishment for Robert since he stole chocolates from a shop.

With some groups the combination of teaching exploratory talk with this software design produced a great deal of serious discussion before the final decision was made. An illustrative extract from a long episode of talk with one such group is given below.

Fig. 10.1. Did Kate do the right thing?

Transcript extract 10.1: Kath, Alan and John

[Computer text initiation: 'Did Kate do the right thing? Click on these people to find out what they think. Do you agree with any of them? Do you disagree? Talk together and decide'].

Kath: [Clicks on Rob's mum and then reads the screen text shown in Fig. 10.1]

'I don't think Kate did the right thing, Robert is a good boy. He only took the chocolates to be kind to me'.

Alan: No I don't agree.

Kath: I don't agree with that –

Alan: That's just wrong.

Kath: Robert's Mum should be on Mrs. Cooke's side really.

Alan: Yeah. She should be more strict.

John: Next round. Kate's Mother. [Clicks on Kate's mum]

Alan: OK [reads from screen] 'Kate did the right thing to tell. She should not lie to me or hide things from me. I am her Mother'.

Kath: Alright John – you go first this time

John: I think that's alright actually, because if you don't tell her, and her mother finds out she's going to get really done because she ain't told her mum.

Kath: Yeah, then Kate's Mum will go round to Rob's Mum's house and say 'You did this and you did that and your son is a bad influence to my daughter'.

Alan: 'Cos he stole

Kath: But that's wrong as well. I know Kate should have told her Mum – and that's what she did, but if Kate didn't tell her Mum, then Rob's Mum would sort of fall out with Kate's Mum because I think Rob's Mum and Kate's Mum are friends so I think Kate's Mum is right. I agree with Kate's Mum.

Alan: Yes. I think about Kate's Mum – and it's also good for Kate, because she'll have a really guilty conscience and she'll feel really upset inside. And she'll...

Kath: And it will all start to bubble up inside her and she'll just have to tell somebody.

Alan: And Rob, I think if he doesn't get told now what's right and what's wrong, when he gets older he's going to get into a lot more trouble than just a box of chocolates.

Kath: Yes – in older life there's no second chances. He'd better start learning.

Although this dialogue fulfils the stated aim of the citizenship curriculum to encourage children to discuss moral issues together it seems to go beyond the curriculum in providing them with an opportunity to take charge. They relish the chance to criticise the positions of adults such as Rob's mum and to assert their own moral opinions.

The strength of this design is that it inducts learners into dialogue in a specific domain in a way that is focused on a particular issue but not bounded in any way. In the 'Talking Bug' illustration given in the last chapter the children are encouraged to discuss sound insulation in order to be led to construct the right answer for themselves, which is that Cork insulates best because of its low density. However, in this citizenship example the aim is not to induct the children into constructing a right answer nor into assuming a correct voice. The aim is rather to induct the children into this field of debate in a way that encourages them to find their own voice as a position within this field. This forum screen stimulated many examples of both what Bakhtin would call intertextuality and also what he calls ventriloquation, or speaking with the voices of others, as the learners called upon their experience and practiced voices drawn from a range of contexts – for example the idea of a guilty conscience making someone 'upset inside' expressed by Alan or that 'in older life there are no second chances' expressed by Kath. This illustrates how the opening of a dialogic space allows many voices to enter in and inter-animate each other in a way which creatively opens up new possibilities. So although the combination of pedagogy and software design here led to opening of dialogue within an IRF interface design and so could be and has been described as an IDRF exchange structure, here the dialogue moment of the exchange structure has broken out of its place in the sequence to take over as the main aim of the activity.

The very simple forum design described above is particularly suited to the interactive potential of computers. It does not need to be limited to artificially constructed debates of the kind described, but, in combination with use of the World Wide Web, it can be used to induct learners into real debates between different perspectives on any and every issue. Web-quests, for example, can be structured not as a 'finding out the truth' type of exercise but more as an 'exploring the space of debate' type of exercise. This is as true of 'hard' science questions like the potential impact of global warming or the various interpretations of quantum theory as it is of more obviously philosophical questions like 'is stealing always wrong?' or 'what should be the aim of education?'

2 'SLOW-THROWNESS': THE CASE OF BUBBLE DIALOGUE

Computer documents, like concept maps, can offer a kind of half-way stage between the ephemerality of talk and the relative permanence of written texts. This is part of what Harry McMahon, one of the originators of Bubble

Dialogue software, refers to as 'slow-throwness' (McMahon and O'Neill, 1993). By this term he refers to the way that Bubble Dialogue can externalise the thoughts and feelings of the participants and allows these to be manipulated and to serve as a support for shared reflection. The Bubble Dialogue software is designed to support dialogues by converting them into a more enduring and yet flexible medium. Although it does not take advantage of the computer's capacity for simulated agency in the way that tutorial software and computer games do, it nonetheless makes use of the same ambivalent or intermediate status of computers between subjects and objects in that it allows users to create characters for themselves that can then be made to speak on their behalf. Arguably the extent to which children perceive their characters as speaking on their behalf is related to the degree to which they identify with that character, and so early studies of the use of Bubble Dialogue looked for and found evidence of such identification (Jones, 1996).

At the heart of Bubble Dialogue is the simple idea of combining pictures with speech and thought bubbles. The pictures are easy to load into the software and can represent dialogues in any situation. In addition to the bubbles there is a facility to review the dialogue created so far and to change it and also, of course, the option to print it out. With Harry MacMahon's support I designed and had developed a new multi-media version of Bubble Dialogue, which I call Bubble Dialogue II, in which there is also an option to record speech so that children do not need to type but can talk instead. This is free to download (www.dialogbox.org.uk).

What Harry MacMahon called the 'slow-throwness' of Bubble Dialogue makes it particularly effective for exploring issues of values and social relationships. To give one example of this, we used Bubble Dialogue in a special school for children with emotional and behavioural difficulties. Such children can find it particularly difficult to articulate their own thoughts and feelings and to appreciate others' thoughts and feelings. Previous studies at the Open University showed that Bubble Dialogue could be helpful here by making the characters' thoughts (as well as their speech) objects for reflection and discussion (Jones and Price, 2001). Teachers at the school believed that collaborative use of the software has great potential value. An example of such dialogue is provided in the Bubble Dialogues reproduced in Fig. 10.2 and extract 4 below. This was created by Charlene and Rory, both aged 10 years, and both excluded from their previous schools because of behavioural difficulties. They are discussing a Bubble Dialogue scenario about a personal conflict involving characters called Joe and Greg. In the story Greg was using his new skateboard in the playground when Joe, a bigger boy, grabbed it from him.

In the first exchanges both characters 'square up' for a physical fight. However, the next set of think bubbles that Charlene and Rory produced (see Extract 4) indicate that while both parties are prepared to fight over the skateboard 'asking nicely' or apologising would diffuse the situation.

Transcript Extract 1 (Bubble Dialogue): Joe and Greg

Joe thinks: he just have to ask nicely

Joe says: I'll kick your head in you fat brat head

Greg says: yeah come on then, I'm not scared of you if im a big fat brat head what does that make you, you peebrain

Greg thinks: im not scared of him all hes got to do is give me my skateboard back and apologise to me, if he doesn't im going to break his big fat ugly bogied up nose

Charlene and Rory's story goes on to have Joe give Greg the skateboard back. When Greg insists on an apology Joe denies having taken the board and says that Greg should say sorry for threatening to punch his lights out when he was only playing. Eventually they both manage to apologise in a guarded way and agree to be friends. Their thoughts remain angry but their words are conciliatory.

They worked well together to resolve this dispute but towards the end of their interaction an issue came up about which they really did disagree. This was when Rory suggested, through the proxy Joe:

Joe says: 'After school do you want to brick the abandoned house where the poorman lives? It'll be fun!'

Charlene obviously disliked this idea and replied that her mother would not like her to do that. Throwing bricks through the windows of an empty house where a homeless person lived was apparently Rory's idea of a fun activity but not Charlene's. She suggested that Greg would pretend to go along with the idea but with no intention of turning up. In doing she was also perhaps finding a way for herself to cope with similar difficult situations when she might come under peer pressure to do something that she did not want to do (Fig. 10.2).

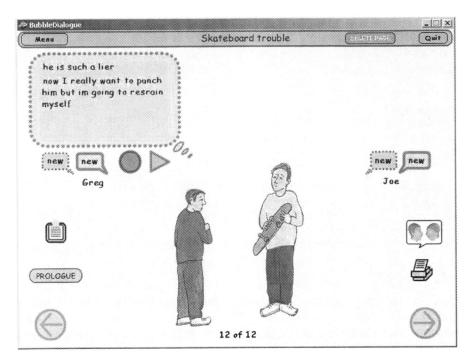

Fig. 10.2. Skateboard trouble

The expert teachers of children with emotional and behavioural difficulties are convinced that these kinds of conversations can equip children like Charlene and Rory with inner resources to draw on in real life situations. Through using the Bubble Dialogue programme they rehearsed a way to talk themselves out of a fight that at first seemed inevitable. Charlene has also practiced a way to respond to unwelcome peer pressure to do something illegal or immoral. This was done without conflict or stress because the youngsters spoke only through proxies, the Bubble Dialogue characters Joe and Greg: it was not Charlene who disagreed with the 'bricking' idea, for example, but her character 'Greg' and it was not Rory who proposed this idea, after all, but his character 'Joe'.

The original version of Bubble Dialogue had been included in the Spoken Language and New Technology project, which I described in the beginning of Chap. 9 In this project it did not support any obvious reflection because it was interpreted by users as a turn-taking writing activity focussing on producing a dialogue as a product, a script at the end, rather than as a process of shared reflection and inquiry into thoughts and motives. We achieved more thoughtful sessions with Bubble Dialogue some years later not because of the improved multi-media software design but because of a focus on pedagogy. The children were encouraged to talk together to reflect on each thought or speech bubble. It was made clear to them that the focus was on reflection, not on writing and this can be seen in the colloquial and uncorrected quality of the text in the figures.

3 STRATEGY GAMES AGAINST THE COMPUTER

In Chap. 9 I referred to some video recordings in the Spoken Language and New Technology project of boys playing around SMILE Mathematics co-ordinates software to locate a 'hidden elephant' in the grid-map of New York city. The software provides a grid representing New York City. An elephant is 'lost' in the city and the aim is to locate it by keying in co-ordinates. After each guess, the programme provides information about how near the guess is to the actual position of the elephant. Mercer (1995, p. 100) used an example from this episode to characterise what he referred to as 'disputational talk'.

Transcript Extract 2: Find the Elephant. Sean and Lester

Lester:	I know where it is (Sean takes his turn and fails to find the elephant).
Lester:	I told you it weren't over there (he then takes his turn also without success).
Sean:	Eh, heh heh heh (laughing gleefully).
Lester:	Which one just went on? I don't know (says something unintelligible).
Sean:	1, 2, 3, 4, 5, 6 (counting squares on the screen).
Lester:	I know where it is.
Sean:	I got the nearest.

The two boys, Sean and Lester, treated the programme as a competitive game taking turns to make random guesses not really based on the information the computer offered. They laughed or made derisory comments when their partner made an incorrect guess. They were motivated enough to keep trying until by chance a correct guess was made: at which point either could say with satisfaction 'I won!' – while the other might insist that the game 'wasn't fair'. It was clear that they were not thinking together to work out a winning strategy.

Eight years later the SMILE Mathematics development team invited me to work with them to encourage productive collaborative work with their software. We agreed that some small software changes were needed such as not assuming individual use as the default when users are asked to provide a name, but we realised that the biggest issue was not software design but pedagogy. With funding from the Nuffield Foundation we were able to work with SMILE to research the impact of different ways of promoting effective dialogue around their software which issued in a pack for teacher training or professional development (Sams et al., 2005).

Jenny Houssart, a mathematics education researcher, focussed her analysis on the SMILE game, Lines. Lines is essentially a computer game similar to noughts and crosses or connect four, the aim of the game being to place four counters in a line on a grid on the computer screen before your opponent does so. As with the Elephant in new York game, counters are positioned by typing in co-ordinates. Jenny focussed in on the point where children shifted from acting procedurally to developing a strategy for winning. She found that some groups would literally repeat the moves which enabled them to win the first time but the computer changed its moves so that the children lost. To win every time they needed to shift from procedural to strategic thinking. She found examples of where they spontaineouisly developed new terms to describe the strategies that they found, for example, the phrase 'two-way-trick' to describe a situation where they could win with either of two moves and so could not be blocked from winning by the computer. Re-constructing the conditions that led to the emergence of strategic thinking Jenny found that the role of the teacher in pointing out strategies to the children was important although the teacher's suggestions were not always taken up. Also important was the role of dialogue between children. Simply asking 'where should we go?' or 'why do you think we should put it there?' led to reflection and the emergence of winning strategies.

The same general principles applied to the use of software similar to that around which Sean and Lester had been seen competing years before. As a result of this project we were able to observe children using very similar co-ordinates software as part of a collaborative project with SMILE mathematics but in a very different way. They are working on a 20 × 20 grid with negative as well as positive co-ordinate squares. As we join them they have been told by the computer that the hidden animal (a Rhino this time) is 12 squares away.

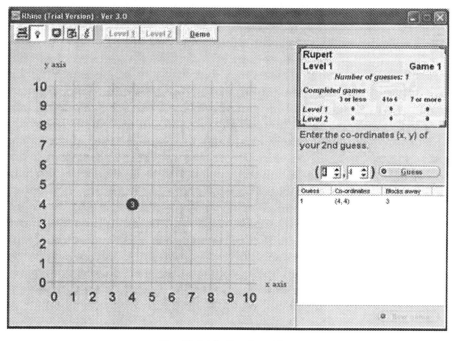

Fig. 10.3. Finding the Rhino

Transcript Extract 3: Finding the Rhino: Andy and Baz

Andy: 1,2,3,4,5, …12 … (pointing to screen)

Baz: What, oh −2, −5

Andy: Maybe then cos look …. Cos when you went 12 you went that way but if you go that way it's 2 way and it makes 12, look see it goes 1,2,3,4,… So I think it's that one, do you?

Baz: Yeh, OK, let's try it: −1, −3

Andy: No, it can't be actually, no …

Baz: −2, −4 it might be

Andy: Yeh, it's got to be that, if it is not I will be surprised.

This recording came from a typical group of three boys. It is noticeable that, unlike Sean and Lester, they are discussing and agreeing pairs of co-ordinates before one of them typed this into the keyboard. They give reasons for their ideas and question each other, and as a result they are developing their mathematical reasoning and their use of co-ordinates. The winning strategy that they have learnt and are discussing how to apply here is to draw circles around the last two guesses that have the radius that the computer tells them that the guesses missed by. Then the Rhino must be found at the intersection of the two circles.

The findings of the research project with SMILE suggest strongly that once children have been inducted into more effective dialogue for thinking and reflecting together then playing strategy games *against the computer*, where a small group of children work together to try to beat the machine can be a highly motivating context for shared reasoning and problem solving. This context re-inforces the use of reflective dialogue because, as one young girl put it: 'talking about our moves really helps us win against the computer'. Again this role for the computer takes advantage of its dual nature. As agent-like it is able to take the role of a partner in a competitive game in which it is perceived as trying to win. However, the fact that it is a machine means that the children can unite together to try to defeat it in a competition that supports social cohesion and motivates collaboration. This general principle could be applied to the combination of preparation in reflective dialogue and team work in any strategy game including the many online and stand alone computer games that require planning, decision making and strategic thinking.

4 CLASS REPRESENTATIVES

I have been exploring various ways in which a combination of pedagogy, especially the promotion of the ground rules of Exploratory Talk (a version of reflective dialogue), and software can open up spaces of reflection in school classrooms. So far I have focused on stand alone computers but Email exchanges with other classes in different schools are another medium for this. We tried email exchanges within the Thinking Together approach outlined earlier, which relies on promoting ground rules of dialogue to create a community of inquiry in classrooms. However, one issue we had with this was that the first lessons in the Thinking Together approach always work to establish an atmosphere of trust before real dialogue begins. To try to do something similar at a distance with two primary classes in different schools we asked them to send each other 'Class Representatives' or mascots. The purpose of the Class Representative, a toy person in one case and a toy animal in the other, is to help give the two classes a shared focus and theme for their communications. The Class Representative can be taken on class outings, which are then described to the partner class. It can be given a 'voice' of its own in email communications. It can go to visit individual homes and say what happened there. It can report on the weather or seasonal festivals. It might even get homesick. At the end of the agreed project time, Class Representatives are sent home.

This idea of a 'representative' is useful for thinking about the kind of 'mediation' offered by the internet in general. Emails are texts but they are also epiphantic signs in that they lead us to real other people. This is more obvious when we consider voice recordings and video recordings on the web. Like voices these are extensions of the bodies of other people, not so much a sign of them as a part of them. The Class Representative mascot being taken into homes and perhaps invited to dinner sounds like it has taken on a magical significance as if the other class far away really can see through its eyes. It would now be technically easy to bring this magical thinking to reality by fitting the doll with a web-cam and perhaps also a microphone and speakers so that class far way can see inside the homes of their linked school and engage in dialogues with them. What Bakhtin writes in relation to texts can also be said in relation to the internet, the signs on the internet are never simply dead matter: they have meaning only because they are part of living relationships and dialogues and however complex the mediations are they lead us back to the presence of real human beings (Bakthin, 1981, p. 252).

The findings of studies of email exchanges tend to agree that the idea of addressing real others elsewhere in the world beyond the walls of the classroom is motivating (Riel, 1992). In a large study of the KidNet project in the Netherlands Bregje De Vries describes the effect of such email exchanges as opening up spaces of reflection (De Vries, 2004). The KidNet project used a pedagogical approach called 'learning by design' within the domain of biology, which meant that the children in the project were set various tasks that involved designing biological organisms for various contexts. Bregje worked to structure the pedagogy of the email exchanges between schools in the project to maximize the opportunities for reflection, which she saw as bringing in prior knowledge and emotions as well as cognitive skills and curriculum knowledge. As with the Thinking Together approach described elsewhere children in each class were organized into small groups and each group in one school was paired up with a group in a different school to exhange emails. Emails from the partner group in a different school served as a focus and stimulus for discussion. In preparing a response to this email the groups started with a quite individual period of 'free-writing' and then they discussed each others texts in forming a shared response. This pedagogy led to three types of 'dialogue', individual reflection supported by writing, group verbal discussion and finally communication between groups at a distance supported by electronic writing.

A part of this project can be illustrated by a brief email exchange reported by the project director, Hans Van der Meij and Boersma (2002). As we join them two groups of four children in each school are struggling with the task of designing organisms. They have one email-based lesson each week in which they read their email from the other group and respond; on alternate weeks they work on constructing their machines. **Email exchange: We have a tip for you** is an exchange sent in the second week of the project.

Email exchange: We have a tip for you

2nd email from Flying Four

Hi Flying Children

You asked us how we construct our plane, which materials we are going to use and how we will let it fly.

We don't know yet how we will construct it, but we think we'll use kite-wood, plastic {trays} and maybe cloth. How we will let it fly we don't know yet.

We apologize for knowing so little....

Friday march 19th we went to the library where we found dewey numbers 659.2, 640.5, 659.6

maybe you can do something with it...

We have a question yet. Which materials do you have and how will you let it fly?...Will you say something about your plane the next time?

2nd email from Flying Children

Hello flying four

These are the answers to your questions.

We use triplex for the plane. We throw it in the air. We are going to stand on the climbing frame and throw it away.

We have a tip for you. You can go to a DIY store and ask for cast-away wood....

Would you please mention some titles of books that you use. Because we don't understand that dewey number at all.

3rd email from Flying Four

Hi flying children

Here are the titles and authors of the books you asked for:

Book 1 : Airlines from the author H.J. Highland.

Book 2: Inventors from the authors Struan Reid and Patricia Fara....

Thanks also for your tip to visit a DIY store.

The children found these email exchanges extremely motivating. They read the incoming message and discussed what it meant before constructing a shared response. Having to account for their decisions and actions to strangers that they did not know added an extra dimension of reflective awareness to every procedure pulling them out of a specific context and into expression beyond that context. This can perhaps be seen with the lack of clarity about the library books, which was challenged leading to greater clarity.

5 EMAIL SUPPORTING DIALOGUE ACROSS DIFFERENCE

The KidNet example above illustrates the potential to support reflection of email exchanges over geographical distance, however the cultural differences between the children in the study was not great. In Chap. 5 I suggested that most if not all of what is understood as higher order thinking can be re-interpreted in terms of dialogue across difference. This is illustrated by BregJe de Vries account of how email dialogue between schools injected spaces of reflection into curriculum work in which children were able to connect their learning with their prior experience and their sense of identity. However, one implication of the dialogic perspectives on higher order thinking that I proposed at the end of Chap. 8 is that the greater the difference spanned by dialogue the greater the reflection and from this follows my proposal that the internet be used as a way of deepening and widening dialogue across difference.

There are many examples of activities involving collaboration between different cultures over the Internet, from sharing data on the weather to sharing opinions about global current affairs, or presenting local cultural and geographical information for discussion with others. However, there are few convincing evaluations of these projects. Sometimes the kinds of conversations that result from linking up schools on different continents are of little educational interest. The banality of such email conversations is summed up in the title of one conference paper on this topic: 'It is raining here, what is the weather like where you are?'. Great cultural differences can now be found within countries as well as without and one example of a more successful and interesting conferencing projects across cultural difference is the Warwick project, which used a FirstClass conferencing system to link ten primary schools in the UK with very different cultures and faiths to talk about religious topics. Andrew Raine, reporting on this project, writes

We sought to encourage children to find common points of agreement where possible and to demonstrate a respect for different and conflicting viewpoints.

However, he does not go on to say how this 'encouraging' was done. A conversation that he reports from the conference, selected presumably for its interest to educationalists, goes as follows:

[Initiation]'Hello My name is Shenna. I am 10 years old. I think there is life after we die because ghosts are spirits and they come from us. I think life after death is OK because you can sit on clouds and float but you do miss home'.

[Response] 'Hello our names are Ayesha and Azreen. We also think that there is life after death but we don't agree with you when you say ghosts are spirits and they come from us.

We think that bad people go to hell and good people go to heaven. Every person shall be asked three questions: Who is your God? What is your religion? They will show us a person and ask who is this person? They have to go across a bridge if it shakes you know you are going to hell and if it doesn't shake you know you will go to heaven'.

This certainly indicates the potential of online conferences to allow children to air their views. However, becoming able to listen and to learn requires more than the mere statement of positions: it requires real engagement with others in extended dialogues. In fact it requires something like the reflective dialogue I proposed in Chap. 7 with questions, challenges and creative leaps within an empathetic framework. If the potential of conferencing is to be realized, and if real learning is to result, not just learning about others but also learning how to learn, then it is probably useful to focus on preparing for dialogue across difference and inducting learners into such dialogue. As I have described, one approach to this developed in the thinking together projects implies establishing mutual trust and developing shared ground rules for communication. Philosophy for Children (P4C), introduced in Chap. 5, operates in a similar way to provide a shared structure to communication and to create a supportive atmosphere within a community of enquiry. Philosophy for Children is now practiced in many countries around the world and this shared pedagogy provides an opportunity for deepening the reflection in dialogue across difference.

Steve Williams and Richard Athlone report on one European project, which built on the classroom pedagogy of P4C to support dialogue across classroom walls and country borders. In this project, called the Philosophy Hotel children and teachers already using the P4C method were provided, via online forums, with questions to stimulate oral discussions. The forums were designed to look like discussion rooms in a hotel, with cartoon receptionists and waiters. Teachers used normal p4c methods to lead face-to-face discussions with their children then, after children were asked to report their agreements and differences to others by posting discussion summaries to the appropriate online forums. In this way the children created written reconstructions of face-to-face philosophical discussions about thoughts and ideas. Although the children's writing and that of the online moderators was entered in their own language, it was then systematically translated into the other languages used in the 'Hotel'. Teachers printed out the discussion summaries and used them as a starting point for further classroom conversation. The resulting summaries were posted to the forum in a potgentially endless cycle linking face-to-face dialogue within the bounded spaces of classrooms to written dialogue via the Internet.

Steve Williams writes that

This model of online philosophical discussion stimulates critical ability and creative thinking because it provides

– A starting point for cycles of classroom conversations
– A refuge for all those who have questions (no online question is ignored) and
– A motivation to return to discussions in response to comments from groups of children in other schools (Anthone and Williams, 2002)

Some of these features are illustrated by the following extract of the online dialogue:

Transcript Extract 4: Philosophy Hotel Project

Derwentwater Primary School, 15:41 pm, 4/11/1997: Dear Ecole de Jean de la Fontaine and Richard: We feel that knowledge is not a gigantic heap. Instead, we view life as a series of empty corridors separated by many doors, many of which we will wish, at some time, to pass through. Each door is a choice in our lives. Knowledge is the key to unlock these doors. Everything we learn is a step along these corridors towards particular doors. We don't need to accumulate all the knowledge used to get through these doors of life, only the stuff we need to use now or possibly in the future.

Ecole Primaire Jean de la Fontaine, 17:47 pm, 4/11/1997: Dear Steve Williams: You have completely understood what we wanted to say. It is by confronting our ideas and talking about them that we get closer to truth. We think there are different kinds of knowledge: indispensable knowledge, knowledge related to our future jobs, knowledge related to everyday life, knowledge just for fun, geographical exploration, music, painting, dancing, culture, poetry. There is a type of knowledge that can 'hit' you at any time in your life; It's a type of knowledge you eagerly search for.

Steve Williams, 0:30 am, 5/11/1997: Dear Derwentwater: I like your analogy. It's very striking. I think we could play around with it a little bit. You say life is a series of empty corridors. Why empty? Is there anything worthwhile that might go on in the corridors? Your doors are like choices. Does that mean all knowledge should lead us towards achieving our goals in life? Are your choices the same as your goals? Also, what else apart from knowledge might help us to get through the doors? How does knowledge help us get through the doors? Can you give us any examples? I'm looking forward to reading your ideas on any of these questions.

Derwentwater Primary School, 15:36 pm, 5/11/1997: Dear Steve and Ecole Jean de la Fontaine: This is what we thought about the corridors. We thought that each corridor was a big glass cylinder with bigger glass cylinders surrounding each of these, telling our past, present and future. As we go along we see doors around us. The key to all doors is knowledge. This knowledge we get or experience from the many images, pictures, memories etc. that we see or glimpse through the glass. If we take a peek inside another door, and look back, the one we were in has changed for good. Knowledge changes our views of life. Even the floor is glass. Through this we see our present life and knowledge of the world. Our future can only be glimpse in the distant layers of glass of glass. All of our life experiences give us the keys (knowledge) to the many, many doors.

Barnstreet CP Junior School, 13:43 pm, 6/11/1997: Dear Derwentwater: May we come in on the idea of corridors? How long is a corridor of knowledge? We think a corridor of knowledge is never ending because it is a life of learning. In life what doors do we come to? There may be good doors, bad doors, sad doors, a door that means life is over. The knowledge corridor could end when your life is over ... at death. We think at birth we enter into the first corridor of knowledge, there is no turning back. Do you think we have the same corridor? We feel that we all have our own corridor of knowledge. From Nathan, Sara and Danielle

What we read here are not direct responses but, as in the kidnet project, written reflections summarising face-to-face spoken discussions stimulated by emails. These are young children exploring ideas in a way which is highly creative. The image of the image of glass corridors within larger corridors going off in all directions from Derwentwater is extraordinary. At the same time as creating new metaphors and perspectives they are responding to each others views and the input of the moderator (Steve Williams) in a way that deepens the discussion without leading to any easy convergence. This then provides a marked contrast to the Warwick project discussion in which children simply expressed their different views without engaging with each other. The difference in the Philosophy hotel project is the shared pedagogy which leads to a shared preparation for dialogue.

6 CONCLUSIONS

I began this chapter with the idea carried over from the last chapter, of dialogue constrained within IRF structures serving a role in bringing active learning into the construction of curriculum knowledge. I think that there is a similar idea in Bregje De Vries' account of how email exchanges can open spaces of reflection within the curriculum, spaces that allow children to bring in something of their own concerns in a way which perhaps grafts onto curriculum learning and makes it more personally meaningful and motivating. This use of dialogic space as a tool within a larger framework of teaching and learning is certainly very valid but in this chapter I explored ways in which dialogue breaks out of that framework and becomes an end in itself. I illustrated the simple forum design of competing voices on a topic which can be induction into issues in an area but is always, at the same time, an induction into dialogue itself. In every example expanding the space of dialogue appears to increase the degrees of freedom of the users. In the Bubble Dialogue example reflection on the thoughts and actions of characters in conflict helps the users get enough distance on that conflict to understand its dynamics and so be able to change the direction of the interaction. The hope is, of course, that this increase in freedom in a classroom exercise will help these conflict prone young people to increase their freedom to make decisions and change directions in other areas of their lives. Where Bubble Dialogue deepens reflection, focusing in on the implications of a single dialogue, the Philosophy Hotel project expanded the space of dialogue by opening it out to schools across Europe. The contrast of this project with other less successful projects illustrates another general theme to emerge, which is the necessity of a shared culture or shared orientations which allow dialogue across difference to happen in the first place. Dialogue is not just about expressing different views but about engaging with them constructively and this is hard to design for in dialogues with strangers on the internet.

Another theme that has emerged in several projects is the way in which dialogue facilitates a shift from more context bound thought to more generalized and transferable thought. This emerged first in Chap. 4 where I illustrated how children solving reasoning test puzzles were, through dialogue, able to see general patterns and share them with expressions such as 'taking the circle out'. Something similar was seen in the way in which children playing games against the computer discovered strategies for winning, which were generalizations of features from a number of experiences and which they shared with phrases such as 'two-way-trick'. This shift, a version of Piaget's shift from more concrete operational thinking to more formal thinking, is easy to see when it helps to solve reasoning test puzzles or to win strategy games, but it is a version of a shift, which was also seen in the ability of the children working at Bubble Dialogue to distinguish between the words of their characters and their thoughts and in the ability of the children discussing right and wrong in the Kate's Choice forum to form a moral position of their own independent of those of the characters. What I think is going on in this shift towards apparently less context bound thinking is a version of what we saw in the email of exchange of the KidNet children. The first group made a reference to books, which was not clear because it relied on local assumptions with the other children in a different school did not share. When it was challenged by the partner group in the different school, the first group made much clearer references which the other children could then go and look up. Making clearer references for an outsider to follow implies taking the perspective of the other is already a way of levering oneself up out of ones situation. Bakhtin points out that in any dialogue words are not just addressed to the specific other but also to another in general who might understand, a concept which he calls the 'super-addressee'. In other words as well as the horizontal relationships between two or more people in dialogue there is also a vertical relationship with the super-addressee. The super-addressee is a real perspective in a dialogue. Induction into dialogue as an end in itself is induction into increasing dialogue with the perspective of the super-addressee, the god's eye point of view of someone who sees all and understands all. This taking the perspective of the super-addressee is already a transcendence of context. This transcendence provides a space in which new more general insights emerge, are marked or labeled and can then be shared. The first step is seeing things from another persons point of view but the more that person is an unknown quantity, the more different and strange they are, the more one is led to see things from the point of view of not just this or that specific other but otherness in general and that means to see things afresh in new and often unexpected ways.

In these examples we can see in concrete detail how and why the design of educational activities combining pedagogy and technology can serve to open, deepen and widen dialogic spaces in a way which serves to promote higher order thinking and learning skills seen embodied in dialogue and reflection. In the next chapter I continue this theme shifting from primary classrooms to examples of older students and from computer software or emails to online learning environments.

In this chapter I described several ways in which computer supported collaborative learning has been used in primary classrooms to induct children into the space of dialogue. Each design highlighted a way in which affordances of ICT in education could be used to support reflection. The problem of how to create a culture of enquiry online was broached and partially answered with an example of Philosophy for Children online where there shared pedagogy in classrooms across several European countries was able to provide a framework to allow for genuine reflective dialogue. This shift from dialogue as a tool for teaching content to using content as a prop for teaching dialogue is a shift towards teaching general flexible higher order thinking and learning to learn.

Chapter 11

DIALOGUES ONLINE
Crossing a threshold

In this chapter I continue to explore the relationship between technology and teaching reflective dialogue, this time with a focus on virtual learning environments for adult students. I argue that many of the same pedagogic design principles for opening, deepening and widening dialogic spaces developed in primary schools still apply in this new context but that they need to be implemented differently. Here I look at how the 'chronotopes' of different interfaces impact on induction into dialogues and at how aspects of the design of online environments can support the formation of online reflective learning communities. My examples are mostly explorations of software scaffolding for induction into dialogue.

In this chapter I focus on dialogue in online teaching and learning using illustrations from my own research or research I have been involved in to explore some key issues. The chapter is divided into three parts. In part 1, I raise the problem of online communicative anxiety arguing that this can prevent higher order thinking in online learning environments. In part 2, I consider two ways in which it has been claimed that online learning environments could provide improved support for higher order thinking, first, through providing more equal access to participation by removing some of the difficulties less powerful participants often have in 'taking the floor' in face-to-face dialogues and second, through facilitating meta-cognition, in the sense of reflection on the process of thinking and learning, by supporting multiple strands of dialogue at the same time. In part 3, I look at directions that have been taken towards overcoming the problem of communicative anxiety that I outlined at the beginning, first through online pedagogy and second through software design. Overcoming communicative anxiety is described in terms of crossing threshold into participation across difference in a way which implies shifting from a bounded social indentity towards membership of the unbounded community of those who have nothing particular in common.

1 COMMUNICATIVE ANXIETY

I once participated in and evaluated an innovative online course for professional educators who worked in a range of settings. The course, called teaching and learning online, was funded by the EC's 'training the trainers' programme and was based at the UK Open University and used FirstClass as a medium (see Wegerif, 1998 for full details). An email questionnaire was sent out at the end of the course and the evaluations given by the students were quite positive, but not all responded and, as is usual in evaluations, those students who had dropped out or been infrequent contributors did not return their questionnaires. To introduce more balance I phoned up the five students on the course who had contributed least and asked them why they had not really taken part. At first they all said that they had been busy or that it had been hard to get access. However, in some cases my efforts at careful listening and gentle probing brought out a second story. This was that they found it hard to talk into a void with no clues as to how anyone was responding to them or even if anyone was responding to them. One of them, whom we could call Sujatta, said, according to my notes:

'It's a cold medium'. Unlike face-to-face communication you get no instant feedback. You don't know how people responded to your comments; they just go out into silence. This feels isolating and unnerving.

Unlike face-to-face dialogue where the smile or eye contact of the other person guides you into a relationship almost all that one has to go on in an online environment are written words, words that for my interviewee at least, felt disembodied and electronic rather than human.

The feeling of insecurity and anxiety brought about by the lack of non-verbal communication online is particularly significant for attempts to promote critical reasoning and creative reflection. All the research on collaborative creativity stresses the importance of a trusting relationship within which it is safe to take risks. De Laat (2006, p. 160) found that this sense of trust was also highly important for participants in online environments. Similarly research I have been involved in and have quoted earlier in the book, found very clearly that productive critical challenges require a strong shared framework or they quickly turn into unproductive disputation.

Research studies by colleagues on similar Open University courses run using FirstClass lends further support to the diagnosis that a problem for supporting critical and creative higher order thinking online is the communicative anxiety that the medium often engenders. Littleton and Whitelock explore in detail why it was that, on a Masters level course online course at the open University, a course which had critical awareness expressed through participation in online discussion as one of its explicit aims, there was very little critical challenge or explicit argument of any kind (Littleton and Whitelock, 2005). Despite the uniformly supportive tenor of the messages they found the same anxiety and nervousness at work. They comment that,

Issues of confidence, identity, self-presentation and social comparison clearly loomed large and were of paramount importance to these students. The students were very sensitive to their own ability and the quality of their contributions relative to their peers. Messages appeared to be being used as a source of informal feedback – as a means of gauging 'where everyone is at'.

This insecurity and comparison prevented the students from really engaging with each others thoughts because they did not want to take the risk to put forward new ideas that might be criticized or to challenge others when they could not be sure what the response would be. It might seem strange to suggest that a kind of shyness or over-politeness is the problem preventing higher order collaborative thinking online when a significant amount of literature has been devoted to the almost opposite problem of online 'flaming' or excessively aggressive exchanges (e.g. Preece, 2002) I would argue, however, that these are two sides of the same coin. For challenges to be productive they require a shared framework of expectations within which the participants trust that their challenge will be interpreted constructively and responded to appropriately. Where the lack of any such shared framework or, indeed, any clear sense of the other person in the dialogue, means that participants do not know how their challenge will be responded to, then there is a danger of flaming. My assessment is that mature students with some commitment to completing a course do not wish to engage in flaming but they feel that they cannot judge how the assertions and challenges that they make online will be responded to and so they often err on the side of caution. On other words successful online dialogue is a bit like riding a bicycle, too much wobble towards the side of insecurity and it does not take off, too much wobble to the side of confidence and it will crash.

I can illustrate this problem with some data collected by a team I was part of from another UK Open University course run using FirstClass, a 'Virtual Summer School' (DZX) run every year in psychology with 500 students. This course consists of one week of familiarisation with the first class envrionment, three weeks teaching and demonstrations, and then ten weeks on project: design, implementation, analysis and presentation with the project work being conducted in small groups of 4–8 students plus two tutors. Preparing a psychology project together with a group of others who one can only interact with online is not easy. We explored one groups data over the project work phase to see how they managed this. There were 289 postings in all fairly evenly spread over 5 students posting 38 to 48 messages with two tutors posting 25 and 29 messages respectively. Mindful of the long tradition of work on how 'cognitive conflict' can help the development of understanding (e.g. Doise and Mugny, 1979) I explored this data looking for evidence of disagreement. I found only one incident. This incident occurred after the group had decided to conduct a project on memory, specifically the recall of groups of letters. In this extract they are deciding on the protocols for the experiments or what they would write to the online participants in the experiment.

Message 1: Suggestion

I think that it would be a good idea to remove the reference to group of letters

Thanks Dave

This suggestion was then rejected by another participant:

Message 2: Challenge

I have to say I disagree (sorry). I think it's important to mention groups because this is what they are trying to remember and as we will not be informing the participants of what we are looking for until after the experiment (other than it is a memory study) they wont be influenced, just informed. What does everyone feel about this?

Speak to you all soon

Karan

Up until this point all the decision making had been cumulative in nature. Someone had taken upon themselves the responsibility of suggesting something and others had gone along with out challenge or debate. They are already more than half-way through their project planning and this is the first clear disagreement. But notice it is already qualified with an apology 'sorry' implying that there is no assumption that it is OK to disagree but rather that there is an assumption that this is something 'wrong' and therefore requires an apology as one must apologise for pushing someone in the street. Dave does not accept this challenge and counters it, but the way in which he responds is instructive:

Message 3: Defence

First I would like to say Merry Christmas to you all, and remind you as stressful as this time of year is, we are meant to be merry (not always easy I know). I still feel that the use of the word grouping is unnecessary, as psychology often shows how we try to categorize information to understand it, if we can attempt to prove this without using leading instructions it would add to the report. (It is a small point, either way is great).

Dave

Dave here begins his message by reinforcing social bonds. He is saying 'don't be stressed', 'don't take this too seriously'. Only then does he give his counter-challenge, defending his original suggestion with a reason and a warrant 'as psychology often shows'. However, despite the firmness of his reasoning he then qualifies it 'It is a small point' he writes 'either way is great'. If I have understood the issue here it is not in fact a small point for Dave, he is writing that it is important that leading questions are not asked of participants in a psychology experiment because to do will invalidate the results. However, despite the importance of the point, he is trying very hard not to appear to conflict with anyone. It seems to me that there is a lot of work being done here, work that takes up time and emotional energy, making sure that this disagreement does not lead to a break-down in relationships or 'flaming'. This incident illustrates just how difficult it is for these people to disagree with each other and why there are so few disagreements in this group and therefore little reasoning, little consideration of alternatives and little critical grounding for the decisions that they take.

Using basic computer-supported text analysis methods (See Wegerif and Mercer, 1997) I explored the rest of the text of this group's interactions to see if features found in this incident generalized. Qualifying claims and challenges in ways which minimize their impact is often referred to as 'hedging'. Dave, above, hedged saying 'it is a small point'. The word 'small' is not used by this group elsewhere as a hedge but words with a similar diminishing effect, 'just' and 'only', were used frequently by all participants e.g.

- I only think this i dont know for sure
- The way I suggested is the only way I know but if anyone else has a better …
- Just a thought really
- Only an idea
- Just a suggestion
- Just a few quick thoughts
- Just wanted to make a contribution

While there was only one explicit disagreement there are 50 uses of 'sorry' in the transcript of this group, many of these qualifying ideas, apparently apologising for asserting something as in 'sorry if I have misunderstood, but'. There are also 141 uses of 'just' of which about 40 serve to minimise the significance of claims as illustrated in the examples above e.g. 'just a thought'. There are 140 uses of 'only' about 50 of which serve a similar function as in 'only an idea'.

Do distance conferences lead to more communicative anxiety indicated by more hedging than face-to-face situations? In the research team we discussed this possibility and found that apparently someone had taken comprehensive video-recordings of groups in a face-to-face Open University psychology summer school before the summer school moved to a virtual environment so it is potentially feasible to expand this analysis of language used to all the transcripts for the virtual summer school – about 1,000,000 words – and compare it to transcripts of the face-to-face summer school to test out such claims. Needless to say we did not have the time or money to conduct this systematic comparison but my hunch, from observations of both situations, is that there is more prolonged communicative insecurity in the online situation which could be picked up by the increased number of hedges. In the face-to-face situations groups begin to communicate together tentatively but most quickly build up relationships that can withstand challenges. The building and maintenance of a relationship that can contain the danger of challenges is facilitated by non-verbal communication. For example challenges offered with a stiff body, flat tones and an expressionless face are very different communicative actions from challenges offered with a shrug, a tentative questioning tone and a reassuring smile.

2 ONLINE ENVIRONMENTS AND THE 'IDEAL SPEECH SITUATION'

Habermas argued that the view of reason as an abstract property of consciousness that had dominated the history of Western Philosophy should be replaced by a view of reason as embedded in real communication where people work out their differences together. In particular he proposed that the ideal of reason could be translated in terms of an ideal speech situation in which everyone could speak freely and all coercive power differences were overcome such that the 'unforced force' of the best argument would always win out over various forms of self-interest. This is an ideal rather than something we can actually achieve but it is an ideal which can be used as a criterion to measure the quality of actual dialogues (See Chap. 4). While elements of Habermas's account of the ideal speech situation have been strongly criticised the basic idea that reason is about how we respond to each other in a dialogue has been influential (Wegerif, 2004b). Habermas's account of reason as embodied in real speech situations is important intellectual background to my claim in Chap. 5 that higher order thinking can usefully be redescribed in terms of the intersubjective orientations and ground rules of Reflective Dialogue. It would be very interesting therefore if it could be shown that some computer-mediated environments provide a better support for an ideal speech situation than face-to-face situations.

Earlier I quoted Sujatta, a member of the course I had evaluated, finding the computer-mediated medium cold and unwelcoming. Sarah, another participant in the course, told me a very different story which has implications for the capacity of computer-mediated communication to support communication closer to the ideal speech situation. Sarah began cautiously as one of the least frequent posters of messages on the course but ended up as one of the more active. In the interview she described herself as a 'convert'. She wrote on her online questionnaire response:

> It's an awful admission but I think I like, and am better at, communicating using text and a computer than I am at face-to-face communication in certain circumstances.

Gender was, she felt, an important factor in this. She worked in a male dominated environment where she found it difficult to express herself adequately at meetings. In meetings colleagues often competed in taking the floor and point scoring rather that co-operating. She felt that because in asynchronous computer-mediated communication there is not the same competition over turn-taking or the same need to think on your feet it can provide a more congenial medium for collaboration. Sarah's account of her experience given above strongly supports the view that online environments could potentially, for some students, provide a better support for collaborative learning than face–to-face discussion. She found that the gender bias she experienced in meetings in her place of work was not present online and so she was able, after a period of 'watching, waiting and learning from others', to engage more effectively in discussion than she ever had before.

It might be thought that the reason for this was simply the different nature of the community she encountered online from her community at work. Against that interpretation she specifically pointed out that her difficulties with face-to-face meetings came from not being able to think quickly enough when put on the spot or to demand her fair share of the talk. With asynchronous conferencing on the other hand, she could take as much time as she liked before responding and no one could prevent her from taking a turn whenever she wanted to.

This basic differences between asynchronous computer-mediated communication and face-to-face communication have been pointed out by David Graddol (1989) and are reiterated by David McConnell (1994). The conclusion from both these writers appears to be that computer-mediated communication has the potential to support a more egalitarian style of communication in which everyone can participate more easily. This might suggest that CMC might be a better medium for moving in the direction of of an 'ideal speech situation'.

The case of Sujatta indicates that Sarah's experience of increased access to dialogue through the online medium was not a universal experience but might be related to individual background, ability and what some call individual learning style. Sujatta expressly pointed out that one reason why computer-mediated conferencing was a cold medium for her was that she did not like reading text from a screen or writing and she much preferred face-to-face communication. It may be, as Bakthin writes, that the mediating means of dialogue are not dead text because animated by the presence of a human beings but that is only true when the dialogic link is made. When the dialogic circuit does not work we find ourselves lost in a world of signs which we cannot relate to. Habermas's account of communicative rationality and the ideal speech situation is very formal and rational and maybe the disembodied medium of online environments, where we have few contextual clues, supports that move to in some way. Seyla BenHabid accepts some of Habermas's argument but points out that we are not abstract formal agents who need abstract formal rights to participate in dialogues but real people with different backgrounds and concerns and that our ability to learn from each other depends on relationships of care (BenHabid, 1992). Whilst an online environment might support an abstract right to participate and have a say, if it does not support relationships of mutual care then it is unlikely to support the kind of dialogic engagement which earlier chapters have claimed is important for induction into reflective dialogue.

This tension between the medium and the dialogic relation is related to the nature of the messages. One student on the TLO course claimed that in many ways the computer-mediated dialogue, combined with a tendency several of the participants had of sending quite long and carefully prepared messages, made critical interaction more difficult. He claimed that, in face-to-face discussion, people often anticipated interruptions and rebuttals, and could indicate that they were receptive to possible criticisms of what they said. However, where someone had expressed something in a long and carefully prepared message sent to the conference he felt it would seem rude to criticise it without commenting on it fully, and because that would often take too long he tended to let it pass in a way he would not have done in a face-to-face context.

When the suggestion is made, as it often is, that computer-mediated communication might support more democratic debate around the world the stock response is that this depends on access to information and communications technology and such access is highly unequal. This is often referred to as the problem of the 'digital divide' (e.g. Castells, 2002). It is interesting that the same 'digital divide' effect was found in miniature on the Teaching and Learning Online course where equality of access to debate, a ground rule for democratic speech, was clearly not always felt to be operating. A number of students expressed frustration at the inequality of access which stemmed from their different situations. One student spoke of an 'in group' of academics with unlimited access and technical support provided by their institutions who were able to come online at any time of day or night and stay online for long periods and so dominate the discussion.

2.1 Support for 'meta-cognition'

David Graddol, a linguist best known for his work on the future of the English language (1997), conducted some early research into asynchronous computer-mediated dialogue and concluded that it had many differences from face-to-face dialogue including a capacity to support 'metalinguistic comments' without diverting the flow of conversation (Graddol, 1989). This was evident on several occasions in the Teaching and Learning Online course using FirstClass. For example the following message in the 'Educat'n' room, a room set up for a certain collaborative learning exercise in the course:

Online extract. First Class. TLO

Wednesday, November 23, 1994, 9:01:06 pm

Educat'n Item

From: M.....

Subject: Why is this different?

To: Educat'n

This conference feels different from the others to me. Is it like that for the rest of you, and do you have any ideas why it should be so?

My own guesses are to do with two factors, that we're a smaller group and we've something fairly well-defined to concentrate on. I quite miss the rest of the gang when I'm here, but feel it's getting somewhere faster.

m.....

Several other messages followed and then a response to this message

Wednesday, November 23, 1994, 10:06:00 pm

Educat'n Item

From: D.....

Subject: Re: Why is this different?

To: Educat'n

Yes it does feel different. I feel as if we are more in control in this conference. We are having to make more of the decisions (i.e., how to organise ourselves). I'm not sure which I prefer though. At times I like being autonomous at other times I want the tutor to step in and give me a push in the right direction!!!

This sort of explicit self-reflective statement about the process of learning is often an explicit teaching goal justified in terms of 'meta-cognition' theory (Flavell, 1976) which stresses the value of students becoming more aware of their own thinking and learning. However, in a face-to-face dialogue meta-reflective dialogue strands of this kind are harder to achieve because there is time pressure to keep to a single thread. Online environments have the potential to keep multiple threads alive at once. Going beyond this rather passive idea of the potential for meta-cognition, Maarten De Laat argues, from the evidence of synthetic review of the literature, for the value of encouraging and supporting participants to engage in 'inter-metacognition' by actively helping to support each others learning.

> ... when learning collaboratively it is not enough to become aware of your personal metacognitive knowledge, participants need to develop group-regulation skills to be successful as a community of learners. When students take over teaching roles and start to act as peer-tutors, they require an awareness of each others' learning styles and strategies, a process of developing 'inter-metacognitive' knowledge and skills in relation to the other members of the community. They need to relate this to the 'intra-metacognitive' knowledge they possess about their own personal learning behaviour to balance between their personal needs and desires, and the direction of the group. (De Laat, 2006, p. 160)

Some have claimed that the 'asynchronicity' of some online communication environments, which means that there is no pressure for an immediate response, allows for more reflection. This claim too received support from the students on TLO. Several questionnaire responses referred to how the written-down contributions provided an objective record which made reflection easier. The following quote from a phone interview with a student goes into more detail:

> Whereas in a face-toface conference if someone raised an issue that was not really important to what you were doing you'd say look we can't discuss that – we've booked the room for two hours we have to get on. In CMC it might niggle and you go away and think about it and maybe get a book down from the shelf and come back the next day with some ideas on it ...

One implication of this students claims is that computer-mediated discussion can sometimes combine different levels of thought. As well as the quick response of the conscious surface of the mind there is the possibility of the slower and often more creative process in which thoughts nag away at the back of your mind and new connections are forged (on the creative slow mind see Claxton, 1997).

Bakhtin's notion of the 'chronotope' which I introduced in the Introduction is relevant here. The increased ability to take the floor and support for reflection are features of the 'chronotope' of virtual learning environments in relation to the chronotope of face-to-face dialogue. They illustrate ways in which ICT can expand and deepen the space of dialogue. Face-to-face dialogue occurs in physical space and reproduces a new form of the principle of identity that only one object can occupy a space at one time. The 'floor' is the opening of dialogue and only one person can occupy it at a time so that learning how to 'take the floor' becomes essential to induction into dialogue. In the virtual space of online dialogue the principle of identity is flouted, many people can actively participate at the same time. This is what I am calling the expansion of the space of dialogue but there is also a closely linked potential for deepening that space. It is also because of this virtual space–time that multiple strands can co-exist at the same time with some reflecting on the others thereby potentially supporting meta-cognition as reflection on learning and thinking.

In practice this expansion of the opening of dialogue is achieved by converting time into virtual space in the form of visual display that endures over time and indexes messages. Multiple postings from different participants that are all prepared in parallel in the same time have to be differentiated in virtual space by icons on the graphical interface (see Fig. 11.1).

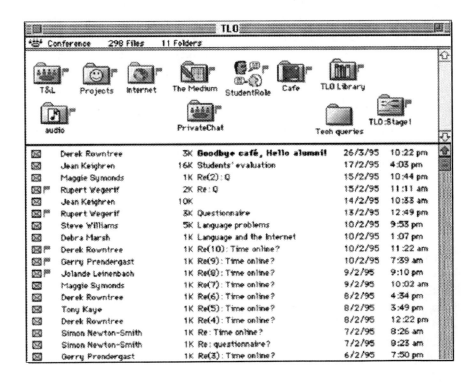

Fig. 11.1. The FirstClass environment

If the shift from physical to virtual space can expand and deepen the space of dialogue this is not a process without limits. The limits, however, are no longer external physical ones but they appear to be internal physical ones to do with what I will loosely call the limits of the normal working memory. While the internet has the potential to store and rapidly find an indefinitely large number of messages reflecting an indefinitely large number of moments in time, human beings can not access all of these messages at once but have to focus and select. The normal practice on courses, however asynchronous the environment, is to respond to recent messages and to let old ones lie. This introduces an element of synchrony.

Sujatta, pointed out that the online environment 'is not as asynchronous as it seems'. She was not alone in complaining that, when any time was missed, the messages build up and become a daunting prospect to read through. Five of the students who contributed the least number of messages mentioned this as an inhibiting factor. It was a particularly significant factor for those who came onto the course late and then found it difficult to 'catch up' into a sense of feeling part of a dynamic conversation. In other words, in place of real 'asynchrony', an impossible ideal, online environments support synchronous dialogues but with an expanded window or floor for communication.

Despite the many enthusiastic things said about the potential for computer-mediated communication to support and promote higher order thinking, this potential appears to be seldom realized. On the Teaching and Learning Online course the majority of the students were very positive proponents of the potential for computer supported collaborative learning and yet the problem I referred to above as 'communicative anxiety' still remained. One student on the course wrote that actually, despite the desire of the tutors and the students on the course for critical and creative thinking, there was little on show and the main style was cumulative. He was right. As with evaluations of the Virtual Summer School and the masters module in distance learning; there were few challenges and little explicit argumentation nor were there many signs of creative emergence of new perspective or of developing or changing views arising out of dialogic engagement.

3 PART 3: SOLUTIONS

3.1 Course design and pedagogy

If one takes a dialogic approach to online computer supported collaborative learning guided by the ideal of widening and deepening the dialogic space to promote dialogue across difference as an end in itself, then it is easy to see things that could be changed to serve this end better at the level of course design and of pedagogy.

To give a simple example, one student was quoted above to the effect that it is hard to respond to a long carefully worked out message with a rebuttal. One solution to this is for moderators to insist on short informal messages. Several tutors keep their spelling mistakes, bad grammar and half-formed thoughts to model a discourse model of rapid and casual dialogic response in which thinking is allowed to go in through and across the messages and not reserved as something always prepared beforehand by individuals. This sort of advice is often given to moderators who want to promote shared thinking or Exploratory Dialogue online (Salmon, 2000, 2002). Tutors can and do try to create community online with 'ice-breakers' and through generating a warm and friendly 'social presence' (Garrison and Anderson, 2003). It is interesting that these practices that have evolved in online moderating are all aimed at supporting what could be called the social dimension of the online teaching and learning rather than the cognitive dimension.

In my evaluation of the Teaching and Learning Online course I took as my model a student, Judy, who had begun almost as uncomfortable and reluctant as Sujatta but who had found herself crossing a threshold into full participation. Here is an edited version of an e-mail sent by Judy to her tutor at the end of the course. In it she draws attention to the role that collaborative learning played in what she clearly feels has been a very valuable experience for her:

> I began the course sceptical about the ability to provide genuine interaction using computers, I was proved wrong. I have developed some excellent on-line friendships over the past three months and have felt very close to all my colleagues on this course.
>
> I began this course wondering if true collaborative learning could take place on-line, I have been shown it can with the right mix of people. This particular group appears to have worked very well together. We have supported each other and this has greatly aided the learning process. Is this typical of all courses? Have you ever moderated a course where the mix of people was wrong and therefore the interaction not successful? This must have a huge effect on the learning and enjoyment of the course?
>
> I began this course wondering if I had anything to contribute and finish happy in the knowledge that no matter what your background or expertise everybody has something to contribute in conference. At times

I had no idea what was being discussed but by expressing my ignorance I hope I helped others who may have felt the same and I also hope I helped those who were in the know to express themselves in layman's terms. This certainly happened to me when I got too involved in my own specialist area. I was asked to explain again, a most useful exercise!!

I began this course wondering how I would fit it in with my other work and family commitments but found the medium provided great motivation and interest. I was always keen to log in and interested to read the messages. I had to put a lot of time in the early stages but this was to my own advantage and as I have said to you earlier, the more I put in the more I got out. To my great regret I have not been able to contribute as much over the past few weeks and this has been to my distinct disadvantage. I have been logging in regularly and reading the messages posted but I just have not and the time to reflect post my own comments. I realise I am not alone in this but I do get frustrated when I can not put my all in to something!!

I began this course disliking writing and I finish this course a better communicator by text. I have always preferred communicating orally and face to face. This course has shown me it is possible to communicate via text, and that writing can be enjoyable.

Judy here presents her experience of the course in terms of before and after contrasts implying that a change in state has occurred. The 'threshold' that was crossed is essentially a social one; it is the line between being an 'outsider' to becoming an 'insider'. In my original analysis I interpreted this in terms of Lave and Wenger's account of learning as moving socially into centrality in a community of practice and so I interpreted the course as a community of practice and the moderators or tutors as 'old-timers' in that community. However, this analogy with apprenticeship in a community of practice seems slightly forced. This was not really a community, this was a course. The central practice on this course was a teaching and learning dialogue about online teaching and learning. With any dialogue it is possible to locate oneself outside it looking on or inside it as part of it. When one is outside the dialogue one sees the mediating means, as Sujatta did, as dead objects, little lines of text on a screen. When one is inside the dialogue the mediating means become the living embodiments of other people, epiphantic signs taking one into their presence. For Judy crossing this threshold meant that she switched from disliking her computer to actively seeking out its company in the evenings with a glass of wine. It is not that the computer as object became warmer, the computer as object fell away to become a vehicle for relationship with others. For Sujatta not crossing this threshold meant that she saw the virtual learning environment as a cold and unfriendly medium where her messages were sent out into an empty and echoing space. In her early messages to her tutor Judy said that she sometimes felt like 'the novice hiding in the corner'. A breakthrough came when she found herself in a group with a specific task which needed organizing – this was in the Teaching and Learning section of stage 2 of the course. Judy waited for someone else to come forward but when no one did she 'took the plunge' and suggested a way for the group to tackle the task. She received a very positive response and found herself, in her own words, to be 'at the centre of things'. From that time on she felt much more confident about using the medium.

This account suggests that there is a lot that course design can do to support the crossing of the threshold into dialogic engagement. On the experimental course evaluated the collaborative exercises moved from the least structured and most open style of exercise with the whole intake at the beginning through an intermediate exercise with clearer questions and groups of 10 or 11 to the final exercise which was the most structured and involved groups of three. Most students expressed a preference for this last stage of the course which made them feel more secure and more supported. On the other hand, if the aim is, to liberate students in the medium of collaborative learning dialogues, then open and less structured exercises are required at some point. Applying the principle of scaffolding to coaching the complex skill of exploratory dialogue online would suggest that it is sensible to provide maximum structure and support at the beginning of the course and gradually take this away to move towards greater freedom and student-centred learning by the end of the course. In highly structured small group activities at the beginning of the course there could be more opportunities to lead the group. Crossing the threshold from outsider to insider in a dialogue requires that students are able to initiate new threads of discussion and take some control of the direction of the dialogue. Another approach to this is something De Laat refers to as 'process learning' which seeks to give more responsibilities to students in a course understood as an online learning community to structure their own learning taking over many of the responsibilities of the moderator. (De Laat, 2006, p. 175)

Course structure cannot only provide opportunities for this to happen it can also act as a kind of communicative scaffold to reduce or remove altogether the communicative insecurity that many experience online. If, for example, students were given roles in a tightly structured initial activity on the course and one students role was to be the initiator and to generate creative suggestions and another students role was to be the 'devils advocate' and to generate criticisms of those suggestions this 'dialogue game' could be played without anxiety because the students were role-playing rather than personally at risk.

3.2 Interface design

Pedagogy and course design are one way to try to improve the quality of discourse online but another approach is to build pedagogical theories into interface design. An example is CSILE's 'Thinking types', a feature that scaffolds students' inquiry process. When students create notes, they are asked to identify the type of their note (for example, 'Problem', 'My theory', 'I need to understand'). CSILE, or Computer Supported Intentional Learning Environment, implements Karl Bereiter's ideas of 'progressive discourse'. This is his reversioning of scientific method as a kind of dialogue that 'gets somewhere' and 'moves people forward' (Bereiter, 1994). 'Progressive discourse' is characterized by the kind of commitments and moves that enable participants in shared enquiry to build on each others ideas and so could potentially be specific in terms of ground rules rather as Exploratory Talk has been and if it was so specified many of the ground rules would overlap. The 'Thinking Types' feature in the CSILE interface (now referred to as the 'Knowledge Forum') therefore uses software to induct students into a designed discourse and so is the equivalent of some of the modeling and guiding conducted by teachers in primary classrooms in the 'Thinking Together' approach described in Chap. 4.

A more recent system, 'Discuss' implements some of these ideas but in a flexible way designed to support the emergence of new collaborative pedagogies (De Laat and Lally, 2005). The central idea behind the Discuss is to capture successful collaborative learning structures and formats that can be shared and reused by the software to support future collaborative learning by different or similar groups. These emergent collaborative structures, for example, the use of certain roles and phases during the collaborative project will serve as way to personalize the learning environment. When groups develop successful structures, it should be able to reuse them but also to offer them to other groups. This seems an interesting experiment to conduct since there is always a delicate balance to be struck between empowering support and constraint. The Knowledge Forums 'think types' might support some but constrain others. Using 'Discuss' such 'think types' can develop and change flexibly perhaps allowing new pedagogies to emerge.

3.3 From turn-taking to argument maps

New communication technologies and tools offer many new affordances for dialogue. Computer-mediated dialogues expand the 'space' of dialogue by spatialising time so that many can 'talk' in parallel and their different voices can be represented by spatial differences in an interface. Normally this different way of doing dialogue is represented in a kind of traditional play-script with one utterance after another listed in a temporal sequence. This linear list is a kind of metaphor for the progression of moments in time. Even this arrangement, however, makes it easy to lose the context of the argument. The Knowledge Forum is an early example of an interface that shifts the dialogue representation from this linear form, one utterance after another, form to a more visual arrangement on a plane more like a concept map. The same move is made by Digalo, an online dialogue environment developed by the EC funded Dunes project (and currently being further developed by the Argunaut project) relies on argument maps (see Fig. 11.2). The maps are made up of boxes of different shapes and colours representing different types of contribution and links between them which can also be given a meaning. Digalo has mainly been used synchronously with boxes appearing and disappearing and being moved around and linked in real-time but the end result is not a temporal arrangement but a spatial arrangement.

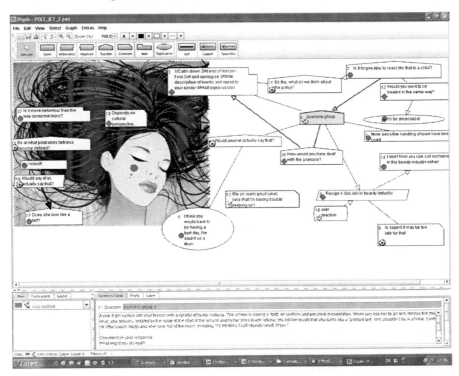

Fig. 11.2. Illustration of a Digalo map

In some ways this development of online dialogue in the direction of visual argumentation looks like a step forward towards the expansion of the opening of dialogue. All participants can see the whole map and can participate easily and can also reflect on the process of shared enquiry easily. As the content of the online 'ontology', or the allowed contribution types, can be decided by the participants, so it is possible to have a 'meta-cognition' or 'rise above' box to support reflection. In theory through this spatial mapping more people can dialogue together and the patterns of their thinking can be seen at a glance.

However, the value of the interface design in deepening and expanding dialogue depends on the pedagogy. The reduction of living thought to a spatial representation through which all salient points can be grasped in one glance has always been the monologic ideal. Dialogic, on the other hand, argues that it is of the essence of thought to be within time and that the ideal of a timeless perspective or perfect 'overview' is an illusion. The dialogic spark of understanding is a moment in time arcing out between voices or perspectives separated in time as well as space (although this is a time and space that is created through dialogic interaction). Spatial representations are not themselves dialogue and must not be mistaken for dialogue, but they can work as a support or resource for reflection which can expand the scope of dialogue.

Traditional schemes for coding argument are good at picking up dialectic development. This is an important type of thinking often also found in the form of a claim followed by a question challenging the assumptions behind the claim leading to an expansion of shared assumptions which prepares the way for a shared resolution. This kind of co-construction of shared ideas through explicit reasoning is found in the Argunaut data but it is more common to find the taking of different perspectives in ways that are not obviously reducible to the dialectic movement of claim and counterclaim. In debates about managing classroom behaviour illustrated in Fig. 11.1, there are messages that express themselves in terms of points of view, such as 'how would you feel if someone said that to you' or 'thinking as a mum, it makes sense'. Interestingly one of the students imported a picture as a backdrop to the map to give an emotional colour to the debate about what does it mean to look like a tart? What we are trying to code for in the data is therefore not only the explicit reasoning but also the taking of new perspectives and the listening to different perspectives in a way that allows for the emergence of creative new positions that expand the dialogue without necessarily being a resolution to any problem. This dialogic process of exploring an issue through various perspectives, all of which are valid and none of which are ever simply 'overcome', is well supported by the spatial representation of Digalo and its flexibility. Moving shapes around on the map supports reflection on the relationships between different perspectives. The development of more dialogic as opposed to more dialectic reasoning is often signalled through the expression of openness to other points of view, through changes of mind and through inclusion of multiple voices in one 'utterance'. This led us to expand the dimensions of coding from the traditional single dimension of critical thinking with its focus on claims, counterclaims and reasons (D1) to include the dimension of creative reasoning understood as a sort of dance of perspectives (D2) in which each new perspective or point of view on a problem is labelled and also the dimension of dialogic engagement which includes not only addressivity and expressions of empathy but also expressions of doubt, changes of mind, ventriloquation (the presence of another voice within an utterance) and elicitation of the views of others (D3). At the same time we are crucially interested in how moderation influences and can improve the quality of dialogues, not only the moderation of those assigned the role of moderator but also of students moderating each other through encouragement and the scaffolding support of recapitulations, reformulations and evaluations (D4).

This work is in its early stages but the discourse analysis combined with participant experience of using Digalo and interviews with users, already suggests that, the use of this tool coupled with a dialogic pedagogy of the kind outlined above, affords creative reflection. The spatial representation of messages is particularly useful for reflecting on the main perspectives around any topic and so for seeing the dialogue as a space where multiple voices interact and develop without necessarily converging on a single truth.

3.4 Expanding the space of synchronous chat

When I began researching online learning in the mid-1990s asynchronous communication was generally seen as having more potential for teaching and learning than synchronous communication (eg Harasim et al., 1995). The default assumption when the term computer-mediated communication was used was that this was asynchronous communication. The pendulum has shifted and now the use of synchronous computer-mediated communication for teaching and learning is far more common. This shift may be related to the issue mentioned above of the temporal nature of dialogic engagement. As Sujatta pointed out above the asynchronous medium 'was not as asynchronous as it claimed' because to be part of the shared dialogue one had to keep up and post messages in a timely manner. If one did not keep up one found that the debate 'had moved on', it did not matter that the medium was 'asynchronous' because the dialogue was not. It may be that asynchronous has obvious potential to support reflection but many asynchronous web forums and courses discovered a participation problem

(Ravenscroft, 2004) The intrinsic motivation of real-time text chatting, on the other hand, can be seen in the large numbers who have taken to this.

It is often noted that, from an educational point of view, synchronous chat is of limited value (Fuks et al., 2006). Its ephemeral nature makes it more suitable for social exchanges than for sustained chains of thinking and shared enquiry. This has prompted Andrew Ravenscroft and Simon McAlister to try to develop interfaces that combine the motivating nature of synchronous chat with support for reflective thinking. They did this in two ways: first through designing the discourse and second through a design with windows and threading that I would argue serve to expand the opening of the dialogue.

The first tool, AcademicTalk, worked by allowing users only to interact with a specified list of 'sentence openers' selected on drop down menus and then it guided them to a 'preferred response' (ref). This interface implemented what Ravenscroft called a 'dialogue game' to support critical discussion and reasoning. An example of an opener and preferred responses is given in Extract 1 and an illustration of how this was used in practice in Fig. 11.3.

Extract 1: Opener and preferred responses
I think...

- Why do you think that?
- Why is it?
- Can you say more on that?
- Why do you say that?
- Are you saying that?
- I agree because
- I disagree because
- Is there any evidence?
- Please give a reason

The evaluation of this tool at the UK Open University focussed on a comparison with the less structured approach of a standard Chat interface. This found that the tool supported, when compared with Chat:

– More focussed on-topic discussion
– Wider exploration of positions and ideas
– Explicit assignment of commitment and changes in commitment to beliefs
– Better use of evidence (both requesting and referring to evidence)
– Qualifications and justification related to positions and ideas
– The use of rebuttals, extended rebuttal and multiple rebuttals (which did not occur at all with Chat) (McAlister et al., 2004).

What was perhaps even more interesting was the student's reaction to being forced to structure their dialogue in this way. Although they found it frustrating at first they also found that it served as a useful alibi or proxy giving them an excuse to challenge each other and put forward strong positions without apologizing (McAlister et al., 2004). In other words this closely structured interface appeared to overcome the online communicative anxiety problem outlined at the beginning of this chapter.

While the focus of the research was initially on the element of 'implementing a dialogue game' or 'designing online discourse' in the course of this project Ravenscroft and McAlister also designed an interface that supported reflection through synchronous chat. The separation of viewing panes (see Fig. 11.3) means that, as Ravenscroft and Mcalister put it

> unlike other synchronous approaches, such as Chat, where there is pressure to be 'first poster' to keep the reply near to the antecedent message it replies to (Herring, 1999), in InterLoc there is no such necessity, since every reply is placed next to its antecedent message when viewed as an argument strand. It is also possible to browse early messages in the discussion and reply to them, offering some of the reflective advantages of asynchronous discussion. (Ravenscroft and McAlister, 2005)

In Fig. 11.3 it can be seen that the temporal consecutive numbering of all the messages in the bottom left window gives way in the argument thread window to only those messages which this contribution responds to. The other windows are about the context of the dialogue. The top left shows the larger asynchronous framing of the activity as a task for which materials are provided in folders and web links and the bottom left window, called a lobby, is an unstructured chat environment for reflection on the activity and messages by the moderator that control the activity such as 'it is time to wind up now'. Finally there is a window on the bottom far right listing current participants with their icons.

Even if the openers and dialogue game elements were to be removed the InterLoc interface serves to convert the evanescent nature of 'chat' into something that can sustain reflection and chains of thought. It does this by expanding the opening of dialogue so that one does not just see messages temporally immediately before the last one but one can also browse previous messages and see the dialogue structure behind the current message even if it is responding to a message which occurred a while ago and so would no longer be available in a standard chat interface.

3.4.1 Implementing Reflective Dialogue

I joined the InterLoc research team to explore and devise different dialogue games. It is interesting that the pilot version of InterLoc called Academic-Talk implemented a game called Critical Discussion and Reasoning (CDR) which had similarities to Exploratory Talk. One particular similarity is in the stress on explicit reasoning such that many of the indicators of explicit reasoning used to assess the presence of Exploratory Talk (see Chap. 4) were implemented in the AcademicTalk interface.

While this focus on explicit reasoning is clearly useful for many tasks it is not useful for all tasks nor does it directly support the ideal of dialogue as an end in itself which I have claimed is important for the development of creativity and learning to learn. As with Exploratory Talk it may well be that in practice the discussions supported by the CDR game helped to induct students into dialogue as an end in itself or 'reflective dialogue' but it focused only on one aspect of reflective dialogue, the aspect of critical thinking, whereas I would follow Lipman in arguing for the equal importance of a creative aspect and a 'caring' or empathetic aspect.

All these three aspects come together in reflective dialogue but if it is possible to design a game which focuses on the critical thinking aspect then it is also possible to design and test games which focus on the aspects. This is what I did, working with Simon McAlister and Andrew Ravenscroft. For what we called the 'empathy game' I focused on understanding the position of the other. I quickly realized that I was rediscovering a game that had already been implemented by Weizenbaum in his 'Eliza' programme of 1967. This is the counseling dialogue widely used in psychotherapy groups. Examples of possible openers and responses are

- What I think you are saying is
- That is interesting, please tell me more
- I understand
- I am not sure that I understand you – please say more
- You put that very well
- I would like to hear your point of view
- ☺

The creative dialogue game is less obvious in that creativity is, I have argued, more about the nature of the space of dialogue than the content. The openers and responses that best support creativity seem to be, from the empirical evidence presented in Chap. 4 for example, those that open up a space of reflection without filling it up again with words. Here are some of the openers we explored in a pilot version.

– Is there another way of seeing this?
– What if?
– What are the possible alternatives?
– We could picture this as
– This makes me think of
– Does this connect with anything in your experience?

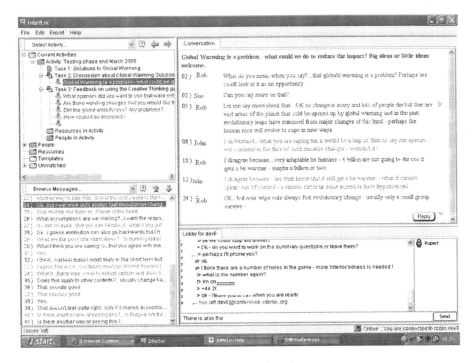

Fig. 11.3. InterLoc interface

Using InterLoc with the creativity game has been tested out and seems to work. One problem noted with it is that the multiple threads of dialogue in real time generated by InterLoc motivate rapid responses, whereas creativity sometimes requires pauses for gestation. Creative dialogue may be better served by asynchronous interfaces as John, quoted above, suggested on the Teaching and Learning Online course. However one thing the dialogue game does get away from is the more confrontational style of the CDR game, which tends to set up sides in an argument. This style tends to encourage people to work hard at making their arguments convincing and can discourage really listening to and contributing to the positions of others.

These 'games' should not be taken too seriously. They implement one finding of the research into the relationship between software interfaces and Exploratory Talk that I described in Chap. 5, this is that role play supports induction into shared thinking. I see these games not so much as scaffolds for thinking as scaffolds for induction into kinds of dialogue. In classrooms we were able to work with teachers to establish shared ground rules for thinking together. For effective dialogue online shared ground rules are needed even more but are harder to establish. The InterLoc interface can be used to impose shared ground rules for dialogue games online when and where this is useful as a scaffolding phase.

4 DISCUSSION

When Bakhtin introduced his idea of the chronotope as an instrument for literary criticism he quoted Einstein in support of his claim that space and time are indissolubly linked: there is a temporal dimension to the appreciation of a painting just as there is always a spatial dimension in narratives. His argument was that while both space and time are essential dimensions through which we understand texts they are differently combined in different genres of writing and that elucidating the different ways in which they manifest can provide insights into those genres (Bakhtin, 1981, p. 84). Bakhtin was looking at genres of literature but the same basic idea can be applied to elucidate different genres of computer supported dialogue. Some, like the web bulletin board, privilege time, others, like Knowledge Forum and Digalo, privilege space, a third group, like FirstClass, are a hybrid design privileging space at one level of granularity, the level of 'rooms' and folders, and time at another, the arrangement of messages within the lobby of each room.

In Chap. 2 I quoted Heidegger in support of my version of dialogic theory. Heidegger's account of thinking as closer to the open dialogues of poetry than to any systematic science is connected to his critique of the way in which, he claims, modern technology 'enframes' us and so limits our self-understanding. He complains, for example, that assuming the perspective of modern technology only allows us to relate to nature as a warehouse of commodities for our use. Heidegger was probably referring to a subtle and unconscious kind of enframing, the sort of process that Foucault refers to with his concept of social discourses which we become 'subject to' such that we can only speak within the guiding assumptions of the discourse. However, nothing dramatizes this enframing more than struggling to express yourself within a system that only allows a limited of options all of which guide you towards a designed discourse in which a particular view of the world is already embedded.

I often get this feeling now when I try to phone big companies like the one that sells me water. Invariably a pleasant female voice directs me to 'press 1 if your query is about ...' , 'press 2 if it is about ...' and invariably my enquiry is about something that does not seem to be covered but I press a button anyway and then get another list of numbers with categories none of which fit what I want to say. After a while of listening to these pre-packaged dialogue bits I become desperate for a live human so that I can explain myself. A child trying to say something original may well find him or herself in the same position using CSILE forced to choose between a list of 'thinking types' which impose a particular model of 'progressive discourse' which does not fit the truly progressive thing that he or she wants to say. What the originators call the 'ontology' in Digalo, meaning the options for posting messages, is similarly constraining in that one has to choose a shape to post a message and the shape may be labelled something like 'question', 'challenge' or 'warrant'. However, the good thing about Digalo in this regard is how easy it is to change the 'ontology' such that a good topic of dialogue might be 'what shared communicative "ontology" do we want?' issuing in the construction of a new set of message boxes. Finally most of the feedback interviews with students using InterLoc mentions their frustration at not being able to say exactly what they want to say with the pre-set openers and so ending up having to subvert the system by choosing an available opener and twisting it to their purpose.

The problem with Heidegger's analysis of modern technology can be summed up with the word that Derrida applies to him: *nostalgia* (Derrida, 1968). Certainly new technologies of communication 'enframe' dialogue and so shape and limit what can be said but we are always so enframed. If we go back to the original context of dialogue, spoken language face to face, meaning exists in time but hardly makes an impression on space. As Ong puts it, even as we grasp the significance of a word it has already disappeared. The time-focused chronotope of oral dialogue can be said to limit thought as much as it can be said to enable it. Similarly writing, tables, lists and visual representations of meaning enable new kinds of thinking on the one hand and limit thought on the other by privileging the spatial and the formal at the expense of the temporal and the human (Toulmin, 2001). Some have argued that the spatialized ideal of thought as a visual representation gives rise to the monological ideal of an unsituated gaze with everything laid out before it as if upon a table (Foucault, 1973). By allowing for so many different combinations of space and time, voice, writing and other modalities new information and communications technology might offer the only direction towards liberation that is possible. This is not a freedom from *enframing* but the possibility of becoming more aware of the way in which we are framed through moving between and across multiple different modes of communication.

Despite the frustration they lead to, the pre-set openings of InterLoc are generally experienced as liberating because of the way in which they enter into and shape social relations. They provide an instant substitute for the shared framework of expectations built up carefully over time in face-to-face classrooms. With InterLoc students know what the rules of the game are and so they can enter into dialogue without fear of being misunderstood. Students like this for much the same reason that they liked the more structured dialogue activities on the Teaching and Learning Online course. Both a tightly structured pedagogy and highly structuring interface can enable by supporting induction into dialogue. This sort of pre-structuring of dialogue only limits it if it is seen as an end because it somehow captures the essence of dialogue already, it is not limiting if seen as a scaffold whose end, like the end of all scaffolding, is to be removed.

In this chapter I described work on online learning environments combining elements of a study I conducted some time ago with several provisional reports of recent projects and projects in progress. In this chapter the theme of the 'chronotope', implicit throughout the book, became more prominent. It became apparent that the different experience of space and time generated by different interfaces led to different affordances for reflective dialogue. The space of dialogue supported by synchronous chat for example, was shown to be opened up by providing visualisation tools that enabled participants to see strands of argument together and return to and reflect upon earlier utterances. By contrast the shift from time to space in the purely visual dialogue maps of 'digalo' was almost equally problematic for dialogue requiring pedagogic intervention to enforce a temporal dialogic sequence. In this chapter I also described an experimental and still highly provisional implementation of my schema for teaching higher order thinking through dialogue with scaffolding provided for induction into creative, empathetic and critical reasoning dialogues through the use of sentence openers.

Chapter 12

TECHNOLOGY, EDUCATION AND ENLIGHTENMENT

इह शारिपुत्र रूपं शून्यता शून्यतैव रूपं रूपान् न

^१ इह शारिपुत्र रूपं शून्यता शून्यतैव रूपं रूपान् न

^२ पृथक् शून्यता शून्यताया न पृथग् रूपं यद् रूपं सा

शून्यता या शून्यता तद् रूपं ।

Heart Sutra, Verse 4 in Sanskrit

[Here, Sariputra, form is emptiness and the very emptiness is form; emptiness does not differ from form, form does not differ from emptiness; whatever is form, that is emptiness, whatever is emptiness, that is form, the same is true of feelings, perceptions, impulses and consciousness: Verse 4 of The Heart Sutra, from http://buddhism.2be.net/Perfection_of_Wisdom
    Translation by Conze, E., 2001.]

This concluding chapter begins with a series of dialogues with alternative theoretical frameworks to bring out what is distinctive about the dialogic theoretical framework. Then it summarises the implications for practice and research of the dialogic approach proposing a programme of design study projects that could explore and develop it further. Finally it

*picks up again the big framing theme of technology, space, time and history
raised in the introduction in order to argue for a certain continuity between
the first educational use of communication technologies, in the form of cave
paintings, and the current and future educational uses of communication
technologies to draw children into collective dialogues that are now no
longer only tribal or only national but necessarily global. The argument is
that the dialogic approach to using educational technology offers a new kind
of enlightenment project.*

In the introduction to this book I quoted Castells' claim that the
transformation of social life by new communications technologies such as
the internet poses a challenge to education. In this book I outline a dialogic
response to this challenge. This dialogic approach to education argues that
the sort of flexible thinking skills which Castells, and other commentators,
claim are required by the emerging 'networked society' are aspects of
reflective dialogue and further, that new technology has a crucial role to play
in the development of these skills by supporting induction into dialogue
across difference as an end in itself. It follows that the use of technology in
education should be seen primarily as providing tools for opening, widening,
deepening and resourcing dialogic spaces rather than as providing direct
'tools for thinking'. This book attempts to expand the dialogic set of linked
metaphors into a framework for design studies research into educational
environments and activities that could promote induction into reflective
dialogue across difference, and, through that, increase creativity and a
capacity for learning to learn in individuals and in communities. In this, the
concluding chapter of the book, I begin by bringing out what is distinctive
and new in the dialogic theoretical framework through contrasting it to the
insights offered by the main alternative theoretical frameworks current in
research on computer supported collaborative learning.

1 DIALOGUE WITH SOCIO-CULTURAL THEORY

Throughout the book, but especially in Chap. 3, I have engaged in a critical
but, I hope, also constructive, dialogue with the socio-cultural tradition in
computer supported collaborative learning. I began by drawing a strong
contrast between the dialectic thought of Vygotsky and the dialogic thought
of Bakhtin. My main argument is that the tradition of combining Vygotsky
and Bakhtin begun by Wertsch and labelled by him as a 'socio-cultural'
theory of education, tends to appropriate 'voices' into the category of tools
and so tends to force mediation by the voices of others into the model of
tool-mediated action. However, mediation by tools implies an external

relation between self and object whereas mediation by voices implies the internal relation of dialogue. One obvious difference is that while tools do not answer back, voices do.

Vygotsky's dialectic account of development, at least as he outlined this in his main published work, appropriates the otherness of others into the elaboration of a unitary cognitive system, a rational synthesis known in advance. This is the kind of dialectic approach that Bakhtin rejected as 'Hegel's monological dialectic', which, he wrote, threatens the death of meaning in the reduction of all texts to a single true text (Bakhtin, 1986, p. 162). By contrast, Bakhtin's recognition that, in a dialogue, there is no final synthesis or overcoming of the essential otherness of the other, leads, I argued, to an open-ended pedagogy, a pedagogy for creativity and learning to learn. This contrasts not only to the uni-directional socialisation into abstract reason through learning to use the tools of logic and science that was advocated by Vygotsky but also to the more multi-directional version of Wertsch and others that education is essentially about being guided to use cultural tools.

Dialogic relationships are the context of education: they are there at the very beginning when a new self is born into a world with others, they are the context of being drawn out to see the world through the eyes of others and they are also the end of education. Monologic and 'monological dialectic' reasoning have a valuable role to play in thought and in education but it is when one considers the ends of things that the importance of distinguishing between dialectic and dialogic is most apparent. The monologic end of education is posited as an independent autonomous self separate from society and the world. Dialectic thinking claims to challenge this by considering subjects in interdependent relationship with society and the natural world but actually, because of the way that dialectic assumes the overcoming of contradictions into an always new, bigger and better identity, Bakhtin was right to dismiss dialectic as simply a thinly disguised new version of monologic. The end explicitly or implicitly posited by dialectical thinkers is always a larger more complexly integrated rational self or system, an expanded subjectivity that includes all otherness within it. The dialogic end of education is, by contrast, always fallible, always open and always creative. The cognitive aspect of dialogic education promotes an awareness that all truths can be questioned in a dialogue that has no limits and no final word or stopping condition.

In the current world political climate approaches to education need to be justified in terms of their contribution to learning outcome measures, cognitive goals and future productivity. I presented evidence in Chap. 4 that the dialogic approach can be so justified. In Chaps. 6 and 7, I developed the argument that this dialogic approach leads to the development of the kind of creative and flexible thinking and learning skills required for productive work and general flourishing in the context of an increasingly global and networked society.

However, there is much more to dialogic education than a concern with cognition and with productivity. Engestrom rightly criticises many current situated educated theories as being horizontal rather than vertical (Engestrom, 1999). He argues that, since educationalists need to make practical decisions as to which approach is best, theories need to provide what he calls a vertical dimension. I agree. Dialogic education has a vertical dimension. This vertical dimension is not, however, either the elaboration of increasingly abstract and universal cognitive structures proposed by Piaget or the overcoming of social contradictions towards more complex, integrated and rational forms of social organisation proposed by Engestrom. The vertical direction proposed by dialogic education is perhaps best summed up by the phrase development into dialogue as an end in itself. This could also be seen as increasing responsiveness to the essential otherness of the other. There are obviously emotional and ethical aspects to this direction of development. There is also a social and historical dimension in the suggestion that dialogic education with technology is an essential prerequisite for the global democracy of the future (where democracy is not understood in institutional terms but in terms of our ability to live, play and work together in a world of many differences). However, the phrase 'dialogue as an end in itself' indicates that these various aspects of dialogic education, the cognitive, the emotional and the socio-historic, can be seen as derivative of, and secondary to, a more central dialogic line of development. The direction of dialogue as an end in itself relates to the idea of spiritual development since it is not just about words, but points beyond the words and structures that selves can grasp towards awareness of the importance of the larger context to meaning that is always 'outside' of any system.

A dialogic theory of education has to be careful not to fall into the performative contradiction of claiming to be the only true perspective. For Bakhtin, understanding was not achieved by assimilating the perspectives of others into a system but through something he referred to as 'the principle of augmentation' (Bakhtin, 1986, p. 168). For example he felt that his reading of ancient Greek literature provided him with a perspective for better understanding his own times and culture. In this he was not simply becoming an ancient Greek, that would not help his understanding at all because they did not have the distance that he had: after all, as he wrote, the ancient Greeks 'did not know the most important thing about themselves, that they were ancient Greeks' (Bakhtin, 1986, p. 6). Rather, by immersing himself in ancient Greek literature, Bakhtin was able to augment his initial perspective with a very different perspective and he felt that his understanding and insightful intuitions increased as a result.

Taking on board the dialogic perspective that I have developed from Bakhtin and Merleau-Ponty, therefore does not require a complete rejection of the socio-cultural perspective but rather an augmentation of it, in Bakhtin's sense. As well as the importance of teaching specific ways of talking, the dialogic perspective argues for the value of encouraging open-ended listening to other perspectives. As well as the importance of inducting students into the use of specific tools for thinking and learning, the dialogic perspective argues for the importance of inducting them into identification with the space of dialogue as an end in itself. As well as the dialectical movement of the construction of knowledge, the dialogic perspective argues for the importance of allowing reflective space for the more dialogical 'de-construction' of knowledge to occur. However, this does not mean that the dialogic perspective is compatible with the socio-cultural or social-constructivist perspectives in any simple way and should be combined with it into some sort of synthesis. Dialogic is an important voice that needs to be heard in educational design. Part of its uniqueness is that it is not trying to suppress or to appropriate all the other voices.

2 DIALOGUE WITH ACTIVITY THEORY

Activity Theory is a development in the tradition of Vygotsky that is now popular as a theoretical framework used in studies of computer supported collaborative learning. In his short life, Vygotsky applied his understanding that cognition is mediated by cultural artefacts mainly to the issue of the development of individual consciousness. Leont'ev, one of Vygotsky's students, took up the same mediated action theory but applied it to the analysis of the larger 'activity systems' within which, he claimed, all individual actions, including cognitive actions, are always situated. An activity system is not reducible to the actions within it but is a more collective or institutional entity with longer term historical continuity. Activity systems, according to Leont'ev, are best defined through their objectives: car factories are there to make cars, schools exist to 'educate' and so on.

Engestrom has taken up Leont'ev's Activity Theory approach and developed it. In particular he expands the original subject, tool, object triangle which Vygotsky presented as an account of individual cognition. In order to take into account the social and collective elements of the activity system Engestrom adds the further three categories of 'rules', 'community' and 'division of labour' (See Fig. 12.1). This theoretical framework can

serve, he argues, as a basis for the analysis of any activity system in order to
explore contradictions between the different parts of the system. This
analysis itself serves as the stimulus for productive change, or, as Engestrom
puts it:

> ... research aims at developmental re-mediation of work activities. In
> other words, research makes visible and pushes forward the
> contradictions of the activity under scrutiny, challenging the actors to
> appropriate and use new conceptual tools to analyze and redesign their
> own practice (Engestrom, 1999).

Engestrom has not specifically applied this methodology to technology
enhanced education but others have (e.g. Collis and Margaryan, 2004).

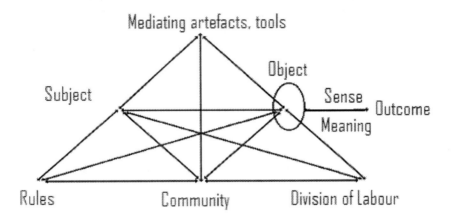

Fig. 12.1. Engestrom's Activity Theory triangle (from Engestrom, 1987, p. 78)

Activity theory's great strength is that it foregrounds the object-oriented
nature of much education. While the quality of peer interaction might
influence the learning that takes place a far more obvious influence, it seems,
is the curriculum that the teacher has a responsibility to deliver which
specifies, in advance of any group dialogue, the main learning objectives of
the lesson.

Engestrom's idea of learning as expansion is also appealing to many in
that it locates learning in real changes in communities and in practices, rather
than seeing learning as changes in the heads or habits of individuals.
Engestrom refers to this expansive movement as 'ascending from the
abstract to the concrete'. The abstract here is defined as:

grasping the essence of an object by tracing and reproducing theoretically the logic of its development, of its historical formation through the emergence and resolution of its inner contradictions (Engestrom, 1999).

This abstract then serves as a 'germ' for a plan which is gradually turned into concrete action, transforming and expanding the initial activity system. This idea of learning is explicitly dialectical and is obviously a version of the Hegelian idea of the resolution of contradictions in a more complex synthesis with the Marxist historical materialist twist that the contradictions are real concrete ones and the resolution is also a real concrete one. Engestrom describes activity system learning as a kind of revolutionary action with participants, stimulated by the insight of the researchers, collectively appropriating the mediating means and making them serve better the shared objective of the activity system.

There are a number of problems with Activity Theory from the dialogic perspective outlined in this book. Many of these are closely related to the contrast between dialectic and dialogic that was elaborated in Chap. 2. At its most abstract, this contrast can be expressed in terms of the relationship between difference and identity: dialectic assumes an ontology of 'difference within identity' whereas dialogic assumes an ontology of 'identity within difference'. This gnomic contrast can be seen most clearly in the role of contradiction in the two theories. Engestrom, in keeping with dialectic theory, repeatedly asserts that change, learning and creativity are necessarily caused by or stimulated by prior contradictions. This implies an initial identity of some sort, a non-contradictory social structure perhaps, within which a contradiction appears as a disturbance calling for a resolution into a new form of harmonious or non-contradictory identity. The dialogic alternative agrees with dialectic that any identity formation has inner contradictions but it just says that this is the way that things are so learn to live with it. On the plus side, for dialogic theory, creativity is given in the complex relationships between multiple perspectives that characterise any site and so creativity does not need to be explained or justified by prior contradictions. This has liberating practical consequences. Dialectic walks backwards into the future pushed forward only by the inner contradictions of the past that it is constrained to unfold into the future. Dialogic, on the other hand, can face forward and creatively design the future, working with the constraints inherited from the past but not determined by the past.

The 'mechanism' of this unforced development is a process that Karmiloff-Smith called 'representational re-description'. Karmiloff-Smith focussed on the way in which individual could creatively develop from themselves without needing to be driven by Piaget's dialectical idea of 'cognitive conflict'. However, the process she described is essentially the ability of dialogue to hold multiple perspectives together in tension and so to be able to see old things in new ways. The practical implication for institutional learning is clear. Instead of waiting to be pushed into change by the dialectical unfolding of potentially destructive contradictions from the past, why not embrace change and create a dialogue space tasked with questioning and rethinking all the assumptions of the present in order to creatively design the future? (e.g. Senge, 1993)

Another non-dialogic aspect of Activity Theory is assuming, in advance of any dialogue, that the salient ontological categories of any activity system are 'subjects', 'objects', 'tools', augmented by 'rules', 'communities' and 'division of labour'. This set of categories implements a model of reality that may not be shared by all participants. It is explicitly derived from Marx's historical materialism which includes the claim that cultural formations and consciousness are all reducible to, and determined by, relations of production. Apparently, in the work-based settings studied by Engestrom and his colleagues, these categories have proved relevant and insightful. However, it is not hard to think of social contexts where imposing this framework would be an act of violence. In Chap. 2, I gave the example of a Tibetan oracle priest becoming possessed by the spirit of a god. To the participants it may have been thought that the god was the subject and the priest his tool. To the Activity Theory researcher it would almost certainly have to be seen as the other way around. More importantly it is quite likely that the participants have their own distinct and hard to translate way of dividing up reality such that talk of subjects, tools and objects may make little sense to them. What exactly is the 'object' of the shamanic channelling of spirit voices? This is not a merely academic question. The shamanic rituals described by Lama Govinda in Tibet in the 1930s were suppressed violently by the Chinese after their invasion in the 1950s. Similar practices were suppressed by the Soviet Russians in Mongolia. Engestrom cannot be held directly responsible for this of course, but in both cases the logic used to justify this violence was the logic embedded in his triangle. From the point of view of historical materialism it is clear that the spirit voices important to the indigenous cultures of Tibet and Mongolia, and many other cultures, are symbolic cultural artefacts distorting or 'fetishising' the underlying feudal relations of production. These cultural voices needed to be exterminated because they were holding back the emergence of a more rational relationship between the 'true' agents, the collective subjectivity of the people, and their 'true' object, increased material productivity and wealth for all. A more dialogic approach would be to listen to the voices of participants to find out how they carve up reality before deciding on a framework for the analysis and 're-mediation' of their world.

In setting up the idea of an activity system Leont'ev used the illustration of a tribe of hunters each doing different things, some frightening the animals, some waiting to spear them, but all united by the common goal which is, he writes, an 'aim at obtaining food and clothing – at staying alive' (Leont'ev, 1978, pp. 62–63). Activity systems can seem to make sense when we look at work-based productive activity. A hunt has a pretty clear organising objective which is killing animals and a car factory has a pretty clear organising objective which is making cars. However, not every activity has such an obvious organising aim. When Leont'ev's fictional tribe gathered round the camp fires of an evening to sing, dance and talk, what was the objective or aim of all this activity? Some activities are seen by participants as intrinsically rewarding and as ends in themselves not requiring justification in other terms. Formal schooling has been instituted as an object-oriented activity producing measurable examination results and visible qualification certificates but this does not exhaust the possibilities of what we mean by the term education. From a dialogic perspective real education, as opposed to training, is more like telling stories around the camp fire than it is like hunting, that is to say, it is an end in itself and not reducible to a means to the end of increased productivity.

The question of the real nature of education raises the further problem of the boundaries of an activity system. If we see education as a system producing a product then it is easy to see its boundaries. However, the dialogues where real education takes place have no such obvious boundaries. There is a contradiction between the assumption of physical space and identity in the thinking of bounded activity systems and the dialogic space characterised by unbounded non-identity (or shared identity) within which real education actually takes place. Technology is now being used to link the inside of classrooms to the outside world, to bridge education at home, school and work and generally to support ubiquitous and lifelong education. These developments, in which technology is being used to give a concrete reality to the 'logical essence' of education, could be seen as an illustration of Engestrom's 'ascending from the abstract to the concrete' model of expanded learning. On the other hand it is hard to see why it is useful to analyse these developments in terms of discrete activity systems when the assumption of bounded identity implied in the notion of an activity system is itself what is being called into question. The functioning of schools as institutions may well be open to analysis as activity systems with subjects, tools and outputs, but education itself is altogether harder to pin down in this way.

3 DIALOGUE WITH 'KNOWLEDGE BUILDING'

Bereiter and Scardamalia have been influential pioneers of computer supported collaborative learning. Their work with what was originally called a 'Computer Supported Intentional Learning Environment' (CSILE) and is now called 'Knowledge Forum' appears in many ways exemplary of a dialogic approach to design for computer supported collaborative learning. Knowledge Forum, which has similarities to the more recently developed Digalo system described in Chap. 11, is a graphical space for discussion in which users are encouraged to construct knowledge together. Scardamalia describes how many features of the Knowledge Forum are designed to support learning together through dialogue (Scardamalia, 2003).

This inspirational practical educational work is supported by serious theoretical work regarding the kind of cognitive education needed for the twenty-first century or the 'Knowledge Age'. Chapter 11 referred to Bereiter's re-versioning of scientific method as a type of knowledge building discourse which he called 'Progressive Discourse'. In a similar way to 'Exploratory Talk' this described productive educational dialogue in terms of orientations (for Bereiter these are 'virtues') between participants in a dialogue (Bereiter, 1994). Although Bereiter does not go as far as specifying this in terms of teachable ground rules followed by participants in a dialogue, the idea of key moves is illustrated in the 'thinking types' embedded as scaffolds in the Knowledge Forum system, moves such as 'New idea', 'Explanation' and 'rise above' (Scardamalia and Bereiter, 1994).

In his substantial and thoughtful book, Education and Mind in the Knowledge Age (Bereiter, 2002), Bereiter takes on the same issue as that addressed by this book, that is, how should education be re-thought in response to the new social and economic structures of the Twenty-First Century. He challenges what he calls the 'folk theory', that the mind is a kind of container which can be filled up with knowledge, arguing instead that knowledge is to be found embedded in knowledge objects or 'cognitive artefacts'. Understanding, he argues, is our facility for working with these objects and the business of education should be to develop understanding by teaching students how to create knowledge objects and how to use them. In this argument he makes use of Popper's Three World Theory which is the theory that, as well as the physical world, World One, and the subjective world of responses and feelings, World Two, there is a third world of objective shared knowledge, World Three. World Three includes things like poems along with scientific theories. Bereiter's argument is essentially that education should be in the business of enculturating people into the Third World of objective ideas by teaching them how to become knowledge builders and knowledge users for themselves.

There is a parallel between Bereiter's argument for knowledge building and the argument for dialogue as an end in itself advanced in this book. He argues that knowledge and mind exist in a shared real space, Popper's Third World, and that therefore education should be about enculturation into working in this space. I argue, applying Bakhtin, Merleau-Ponty and others, that meaning is formed in a dialogic space and so education should be about induction into working and playing in that dialogic space. Bereiter's definition of a cognitive artefact is vague and open enough to include things like words which embody shared meaning. He describes how these artefacts are collaboratively constructed through 'progressive discourse' and how they then serve, in a leap-frogging manner, as the basis for further discourse. In short it seems he may be describing a dialogic approach to education but focusing on the content of the dialogue and the objects produced by the dialogue whereas the dialogic approach focuses more on the process of dialogue itself. In this case the difference between 'knowledge building' and dialogic may be thought of as a version of the puzzle: 'which came first: the chicken or the egg?' However, I think that there is a bigger difference between the two approaches which becomes clearer at the level of ontology.

Bereiter challenges the folk psychology that takes a simple spatial metaphor, that of a container, and applies it to the mind. However, he does not go far enough in challenging such spatial folk metaphors. The way in which he uses the term 'cognitive artefacts' implies that meanings within a dialogue, signs given a shared meaning for example, can be treated as if they were objects. However, meanings only exist in dialogue and do not exist outside of dialogue. Cognitive artefacts, tools, poems, plays, pictures and so on, sediment and embody a perspective or voice on the world in a way that can be shared and taken up in new ways in new dialogues across space and time. Although they have an aspect as objects in physical space their meaning is given within dialogic space. Meanings in dialogic space do not obey the principle of identity derived from objects in physical space. Not only can they be many things at once, it is intrinsic to their nature that they are many things at once. This is because their meaning is the difference that they make in the dialogues into which they enter. It follows, from a dialogic perspective, that it is not possible to separate out 'cognitive objects' from the dialogues into which they enter or the ways in which they are used. It further follows that cognitive artefacts are not the end of dialogues but that dialogues are the context and the end of cognitive artefacts.

A focus on dialogue does not deny that working with cognitive artefacts has an important role to play in education. After all, as Stahl brings out, it is of value to promoting quality dialogues to use cognitive artefacts as a focus for small group discussions (Stahl, 2006, p. 294). The products of understandings achieved in living dialogues inform the creation of artefacts and technologies which can then appear as external objects or fixed truths, unless and until they are appropriated and leap-frogged over in further dialogue. While, as I have argued at length, it is ethically and educationally dangerous to reduce voices to tools it seems productive in the best sense of the word to take the opposite direction and treat all cultural artefacts, including tools, as voices within an ongoing dialogue. Works of art, for example, embody perspectives that can enrich dialogues and expand experience. The same is true of tools and technologies. Innovation is not a mechanical or predictable algorithmic process but a creative dialogic process in which familiarity with the possibilities of existing tools and the perspectives they embody is an important precursor to the emergence of a new 'tool' which may embody a new and unexpected way of living and thinking the world.

The difference in perspective between a focus on building artefacts as the purpose of dialogues or a focus on dialogues as the context and purpose of artefacts, has practical consequences for education. Bereiter is being consistent to his perspective when he dismisses teaching thinking as a vain endeavour. For his model of 'deep understanding' he takes a carpenter's familiarity with his tools and materials. If thinking is to be found in working with cognitive artefacts and these artefacts are all different then there are few general thinking skills and none that can be taught independent of actually working at the business of creating knowledge. Creativity, he argues, cannot be taught separately because it implies deep familiarity with a field (Bereiter, 2002, p. 180). The same is true, he claims, for any other so called 'thinking skill'.

Bereiter's ontology of knowledge as consisting of objects in an objective world (albeit World Three) leads him to conceive of thinking as situated in the way that a carpenter's skills in fashioning wood into furniture is situated. However, the dialogic ontology I propose cannot make much sense of this account of 'situation'. The word dialogue always conjures up a face to face context but the dialogic relation is a principle that applies to the nature of meaning in general. The dialogic principle that contrasts with the principle of identity is summed up by Merleau-Ponty's concept of the chiasm whereby inside and outside circle around each other around a gap or hinge. He points out that the figure in the foreground of our visual attention appears to be contained by the background but the background is defined by the figure. In much the same chiasmic way, while dialogues are always, in one sense, situated, spatially temporally, socially, historically and so on, in another sense they are always also unsituated since a dialogue is required to define and give meaning to a situation in the first place. The strange double situated/unsituated nature of dialogic comes from the gap between inside and outside or the gap between two voices in a dialogue. According to Merleau-Ponty, this gap serves as a 'hinge' opening onto the whole of being or what he calls 'raw being'. According to Bakhtin it is this gap between voices that makes meaning possible and that opens onto an unbounded potential for meaning. In the first chapter of this book I defined dialogic as the principle of constitutive non-identity, or that gap that makes identities possible. That dialogic gap is very hard to think because thought works with identities and to think the gap between identities in dialogue is to try to think non-identity.

My argument has been that if we think through the implications of dialogic we end up with a direction for education that is productive of general thinking and learning skills such as creativity and learning to learn. To make this argument I have had to take the conceptually rather tricky step of turning an absence, the gap between voices in dialogue, into a kind of thing, a guiding principle that can be used in the design of education. This is difficult and subject to misinterpretation because the idea of the dialogic gap is not a traditional concept but what could be called a limit concept. By this I mean that my use of dialogic has been as a pointer to the outside of the system of thought. In mathematics the symbols '0' and '∞' serve as limit concepts in a similar way to the way I use the term 'dialogic'. These symbols for 'zero' and 'infinity' appear inside equations and do useful mathematical work despite the fact that they point to the extreme limits of the number system, to an absence of number in the one case and to an ungraspably large number in the other. The essence of dialogic, as I defined this in Chap. 2, is the gap between two or more perspectives held together in the tension of a dialogue. This simple idea of a dialogic gap, it turns out on closer examination, is nothing more nor less than the context of meaning. If we explore the inside of meaning we find that the smallest unit is a significant difference between two perspectives, if we try to define meaning as a whole we find that it occurs within the gap between two perspectives in a dialogue. This inside of meaning and this outside of meaning are brought together in the concept of dialogic. Because the term 'dialogic' points to the context of meaning in this way, it does not really have a clear content meaning of its own. However, as a limit concept, a kind of combination of '0' and '∞', it can do useful work within the system of educational thought. This useful work is pointing to a depth dimension of development that is really important and readily recognised intuitively but, because of the difficulty of thinking it, has not featured much in educational theory heretofore. This is the dimension of development from identity towards non-identity. I have referred to this dimension with the phrase 'the direction of dialogue as an end in itself' and argued that it tends towards the paradox of identification with the non-identity of dialogic space. This could be read as an attempt to give as careful an understanding as possible to the widespread intuition that, as well as the growth of cleverness and knowledge in education, there can be an alternative direction of development that some relate to wisdom and others to spirituality. My argument is that this alternative depth direction of growth is best seen in the quality of response towards strangers and towards all that which is new and 'other'.

Although the conceptual basis for this dialogic theory may sometimes sound very abstract it is rooted in a response to practical concerns and has very practical consequences for the question of how we should teach. As I described in Chap. 3, the idea of development into dialogue emerged from trying to understand what was happening as children learned to solve problems together better. The importance of indicators such as admitting uncertainty, asking advice and the changing of minds, indicated that there was a shift away from identifying with ego positions or a harmonious group image, towards identifying with the dialogic space of possibilities. It became apparent that successful thinkers were becoming more able to remain with the silent pauses in the dialogue characterised by uncertainty, multiplicity and open-endedness. The all important moments of 'pregnant silence' in dialogues cannot be usefully described as a 'tool' for thinking. In order to understand further the nature and significance of these moments of pregnant silence it was necessary to address the philosophical question of the nature of dialogic.

From a dialogic perspective Bereiter and Scardamalia's focus on knowledge building is not wrong but is limited. Their understanding of the role of dialogue in education is expressly focussed on building explanatory models in science and this is reflected in the scaffolds provided in the Knowledge Forum system. However, science does not end with knowledge objects but always continues with open-ended enquiry and it is not obvious that induction into open-ended enquiry is always best served by an exclusive focus on producing artefacts. One way of encouraging the skills and virtues associated with open-ended enquiry is to engage in dialogue with radically different perspectives. The aim of dialogue across difference is not to produce cognitive artefacts but to expand awareness in ways that are of educational value in themselves and that issue in an increased capacity for reflective and creative thought.

4 DIALOGUE WITH 'COMMUNITIES OF PRACTICE'

Lave and Wenger's seminal book, *Situated learning: Legitimate peripheral participation* (Lave and Wenger, 1991), had a significant impact on research in CSCL. Their social account of learning as learning to participate more fully in a community of practice seemed to fit some aspects of online collaborative learning environments well and has been applied in a number of studies (e.g. Wegerif, 1998). The great value of their account is to reveal learning as a shift in identity in a social landscape. As Sfard has pointed out (Sfard, 1998), their learning as participation metaphor does not fit all aspects of what is normally meant by learning but it does draw attention to a very real aspect of learning that had been previously neglected due to an almost exclusive focus on individual cognitive change. Indeed Lave and Wenger's idea of learning as a shift in social identity stimulated the idea of learning to become more dialogic articulated in this book. Learning to become more dialogic can be expressed in terms of acquiring specific skills or habits but it is really more fundamentally about an affective embrace of a more open and multiple identity, or, as Keats put it, feeling more at home with uncertainty.

Dialogue, in the form of what is called 'negotiation of meaning', features prominently in Wenger's account of the communities of practice approach to learning (Wenger, 1999). If learning is a movement from peripherality to centrality within a community, as Lave and Wenger claim, then it is clear that this movement involves encounters and negotiations along the way. However, what is missing from their story is a stronger account of how the dialogic relation can facilitate social movement by enabling a reversibility of perspectives or 'becoming an other'.

Lave and Wenger describe apprenticeship into existing practices. This model does not seem to meet all the needs of education in a networked global society for two main reasons. Firstly, it is hard to see, on this apprenticeship model, how it might be possible to teach for general thinking and learning skills since these cannot apparently be embodied in a situated community of practice. Secondly, induction into a specific situated community of practice cannot easily support the future need of citizens to participate in global democratic dialogues. What is a bit scary about Lave and Wenger's account is the plausible claim they make that it is only through socialisation within a specific community of practice that anyone can claim to have knowledge or to learn because specific communities of practice determine the criteria of what counts as knowledge and what counts as learning (Lave and Wenger, 1991, p. 98).

Lave and Wenger begin their account with a rejection of the dualism of inside and outside implicit in accounts of learning as internalisation (1991, p. 47) and seek to overcome this through the notion of participation (1991, p. 52). However, their own account of learning as moving from the outside of a community to the inside seems to reproduce a new version of this same dualism. From a dialogic point of view the dualism of inside and outside is not a problem but a starting place. As I argued in Chap. 1, it is in the nature of dialogue that any dialogue always generates an inside and outside perspective. As Bakhtin points out, we only come to know ourselves as an insider through taking an outside perspective so, in a sense, to have an identity as an insider it is necessary, at the same time, to be an outsider. The outside of the kind of coherent communities Lave and Wenger write about is summed up in a phrase from Lingis: 'The community of those who have nothing in common' (Lingis, 1994). The dialogic notion that to claim for oneself an identity as an insider it is also necessary to, implicitly at least, have an identity as an outsider, challenges the strong claims for the situated nature of knowledge and learning made by Lave and Wenger. Fortunately for education, in real life, identities, both those of individuals and those of communities, are not nearly as monologic and situated as Lave and Wenger seem to assume since they are always shot through with alternative voices and perspectives. As Biesta argues, the opportunity to become a member of 'the community of those who have nothing in common' arises in the break down of the smooth running of communities, in the clash of voices and encounters with all that which is strange and different and outside (Biesta, 2006, p. 69).

In Lave and Wenger's accounts of learning as a social trajectory of identity (Wenger, 2005) there is little sense of vertical movement but only an account of different horizontal movements. Since communities define what is knowledge and what is learning there is no obvious way to distinguish between the value of learning how to be a good astronomer or a good Muslim from learning how to be a good astrologer or a good Satanist. The dialogic perspective on education, by contrast, suggests that dialogic spaces always open up between and around communities and identities, in fact dialogic space is the hidden heart of all identity and the extent to which one enters into these spaces, and takes advantage of the opportunity for dialogic reflection that they provide, is the extent to which there is a vertical or depth dimension to individual learning. In sum: from a dialogic perspective the role of education is not to reproduce traditional apprenticeship models but to open and resource dialogic spaces in which learners can question, reflect upon and rise above their assumptions and identities.

5 DESIGN FOR DIALOGIC

There is a nice proverb in English that 'you can lead a horse to the water but you cannot make it drink'. This difference between 'leading to the water' and 'drinking' is another way to look at the difference between monologic dialectic approaches to education and the dialogic approach. It is quite possible, as a teacher, to take students through a dialectical argument for a certain conclusion without 'carrying them with you'. To take the step from reasoning to understanding, they need to see it from your point of view. For that step to happen there needs to be dialogic relationship that facilitates the reversibility of perspectives. Education is about relationships and it occurs always within the space of relationship. This is a problem for educational design because it is an argument for the fact that learning outcomes are not causally related to teaching and cannot be programmed in advance.

One role of the dialogic understanding of education then is as a propaedeutic for those who argue that educational science should be evidence-based in the sense of telling teachers 'what works'. Education is not so much an applied science on the model of engineering as a creative design discipline on the model of architecture. Dialogic learning cannot be designed for directly but it can be designed for indirectly by opening the kind of spaces that support it. Biesta brings out the way in which different architectural designs for learning spaces in schools can support different kinds of social events and so foster different kinds of learning. Biesta argues that architects of learning spaces need to design spaces that are not only functional in terms of what is known but are also open for being used in unanticipated ways (Biesta, 2006). He gives the example of how designing spaces with multiple lines of site and criss-crossing pathways allow for the kind of unprogrammed encounters that might facilitate becoming a participant member of Lingis's 'community of those who have nothing in common'.

In a similar way, although we cannot predict in advance the way in which educational relationships will develop, educational designers can facilitate the possibility of moving in the direction of dialogue as an end in itself through the way in which they open and resource dialogic spaces which can facilitate reflection. Dialogic reflection is relevant to promoting thinking whatever the discipline area. Throughout the book I have given brief examples of learning through dialogue in Mathematics, English, Citizenship, Social Skills, Psychology, Science and Education. My focus has not been on the learning of content knowledge but on the learning of dialogue itself. However, the evidence is clear that learning through dialogue can enhance the learning of curriculum content knowledge, especially when that 'content' is not factual information but subject specific forms of higher order thinking, such as problem-solving in mathematics, investigative and experimental methods in science and writing argumentative texts in English.

5.1 Opening dialogic spaces

The quality of dialogic education depends on the dialogic quality of relationships, which may be many different kinds of relationships including the relationship between students and the content area of their study as well as between students and other students learning together and between students and teachers. The metaphor of opening up a dialogic space refers first and foremost to this quality of relationship.

The initiation, response, follow-up loops so common in classroom discourse do not open space for dialogic reflection. A simple action for increasing thinking and engagement within normal curriculum teaching is to lengthen the pauses allowed by teachers after asking questions. Teachers often feel uncomfortable with the pregnant pause that hangs heavily in the air after they have asked a question and so they step in quickly with a follow-up question. Teachers making a conscious effort to lengthen the wait time before they insist on an answer can help allow students time to think for themselves and prepare deeper, more original and more engaging responses (Dillon, 1990).

The design study research showing the educational value of increasing pause time between questions and answers is well known. I mention it again here because it illustrates very clearly the reality referred to by the metaphor of opening a dialogic space. In practice there are many factors that close down the opportunities for dialogue. Educational software designers often seem to revel in features that increase signs of motivation and engagement: solving real-time problems against the clock in complex interactive environments for example. However, I reported in Chap. 9 that this kind of design led to a series of rapid initiation, response, follow-up (IRF) exchanges between user and computer in which there was no time for a dialogic space to open up. The combination of design for dialogue and prompts on the screen that interrupted the flow of IRF loops expanded the time of reflection in a way that was measurable and was measured. The physical corollary of the space of reflection was the space between small groups of children in front of the screen which became 'dialogic' when they sat back from the screen, faced each other and discussed issues. This research led to a specific set of guiding principles for designs that can support the opening of a dialogic space between users and the computer screen.

1. The expectations users have about working together at a computer are important and can be addressed through explicitly promoting Reflective Dialogue as a style of approaching computer tasks.
2. Talking turns to be responsible for decisions is a common default that should be discouraged. Joint decision taking can be encouraged within the design itself by not reducing problems into discrete equal steps and by prompting users to talk together (in conjunction with point 1 above).
3. Selecting from alternatives is usually preferable to typed input when the aim is to support talk around the computer.
4. Problems or issues intended to initiate discussion should be embedded in role-play and intrinsic to the narrative development of the activity.

5. Problems should not be capable of immediate solution but require distributed thinking.
6. Props for discussion should be provided in the form of pictures or symbols for different perspectives and positions or bodies of evidence that can be pointed to on the screen and manipulated.
7. Avoid any 'ticking clock' that encourages a speedy response over reflection. Alternatively, build into, or on top of, such time-sensitive games pause points for reflection.

5.1.1 Facilitating quality engagement

There are many potential spaces for discussion in Virtual Learning Environments and on the Web that are not used or, if used, not used for real learning conversations. After the first flush of enthusiasm for learning from online discussions and through online communities, there is now some disillusionment (e.g. Weinberger and Fischer, In press). The issue of 'opening a dialogic space' is not only a technical issue but also a social issue. Weinberger and Fisher recommend providing scripts for interactions (ibid.). The idea that providing and using fixed scripts for interaction will ensure quality makes the same ontological error as the idea that words and phrases are tools for thinking. Real thinking and learning occurs within a whole dialogical engagement and depends upon the perpetual freshness and openness of that engagement. However, something like scripts can help induct students into the kinds of dialogue that lead to learning and that are intrinsically motivating. In the research studies I described this was addressed in two ways. Firstly, by preparing primary school children for collaborative learning at the computer with off-computer pedagogy, designed to promote a dialogic community of inquiry in the classroom. This programme was called 'Thinking Together' and promoted 'Exploratory Talk' in small groups. Because of Exploratory Talk's association with explicit reasoning through talk I now prefer the broader label 'reflective dialogue' but the techniques used to promote Exploratory Talk in the classroom are simple and effective in also promoting reflective dialogue. Secondly, by preparing older students at a distance for online collaboration through the use of a role-playing dialogue game with constrained sentence openers and responses. Although initially the design of AcademicTalk and InterLoc by Ravenscroft and McAlister was based on a monologic dialectic view of reason it nonetheless served to engage students in interaction shaped by the kind of ground rules that promote and support reflective dialogue. A key factor in shifting the dialogue from more superficial, social synchronous chat to deeper and richer reflective dialogue was the role-play element whereby students could hide behind the ground rules of the system to question each other's views and provide robust arguments without threatening others or feeling threatened.

Constraining and shaping the discourse options of students through the explicit pedagogy of the Thinking Together programme, or through the constraints of a system like InterLoc, does not sound very dialogic. The evidence suggests, however, that students of all ages enjoy learning together through reflective dialogue but are often held back from this because, confronted with the challenge of computer supported collaborative learning, in a classroom or on the Web, they do not know how to proceed. Giving them the social ground rules that they need to take this first step is, initially at least, not a constraint but an empowerment. The aim of dialogic education is not to create small exclusive dialogue groups but to induct children and students into full membership of the global community which is ultimately best described as 'the community of those who have nothing in common'. After children had learnt to talk well together in established groups of three we did some experiments shuffling them around between groups and between classes and they continued to talk well together. The real challenge of cross-cultural global dialogue is a lack of shared ground rules to start up the dialogic space in this way. To this end one research proposal that I am working on is to collaborate with the International Society for Philosophy for Children (ICPIC) to create online spaces to support their face to face communities established around the world. Philosophy for Children is unique in following similar ground rules for discussion in classrooms in all continents.

Opening physical spaces for dialogue using educational technology and pedagogical design, coupled with providing shared social ground rules for induction into dialogue, goes a long way to addressing the quality issue but there is also the issue of motivation. Even though discussion is intrinsically motivating, it is important that the content of what is discussed engages the students. One study I reported on, which late primary children found very engaging, was playing mathematical strategy games in groups against the computer. They loved finding ways to beat the computer and in doing so they developed their mathematical reasoning skills. This relates to the motivating power of games to support collaborative learning (Gee, 2003). Some multi-user online games such as World of Warcraft have many thousands of players online across all time zones at any one time. I have not played World of Warcraft myself but I have been told that it can involve collaborating in teams to defeat computer generated monsters. Since the monsters never sleep, it pays for teams to collaborate across time zones with some members in the USA, for example, and some in Japan. Like Gee, I am not suggesting that such games replace education but that some principles can be drawn from them for the creation of motivating educational environments. One proposal is to use a 3D environment with avatars, like World of Warcraft or Second Life, to create a forum for young people to discuss global policy for the future with collaborative teams working together on developing solutions to major problems such as global warming, terrorism, water shortage and so on. The idea is to combine the theme from World of Warcraft of collaborating in trans-continental teams to defeat global monsters with the role of committees of representatives in modern parliaments investigating issues and calling on expert witnesses in order to prepare reports and propose legislation.

There are many ways of promoting richer online dialogues that I have not mentioned. The simple expedient of assessing contributions to online debates as part of the final course credits is one of the most effective! There are many excellent guides to the research and practice of supporting high quality dialogues in virtual environments that could be referred to here (e.g. Garrison and Anderson, 2003; Salmon, 2002, Conole and Oliver, 2007). My intention in this book, however, has not been to provide an exhaustive set of tips or recipes but to focus on providing a coherent overall theoretical framework and language for understanding research and design in computer supported collaborative learning. In many cases, the pedagogic design that would follow from the dialogic interpretative framework proposed are not original but bring out, retrospectively, why some independently developed design patterns are really good and should be reproduced into future designs and also, of course, why some should be dropped. While many of the individual design features I have highlighted have been written about before, they have not necessarily been brought together in a single language for describing how designing dialogues can promote individual, social and global higher order thinking.

5.2 Deepening dialogic spaces

Baker et al. (2003) distinguish between deepening and broadening a space of debate:

> Students broaden their understanding of a space of debate when they are better acquainted with societal and epistemological points of view, their associated arguments and value systems; they deepen it when they are able to go deeper into argument chains, to elaborate upon the meaning of arguments, and to better understand the notions involved.

While the idea of dialogic space is broader than that of a space of debate, since it is not concerned only with explicit argumentation the distinction between broadening and deepening is still useful. Opening a dialogic space and fostering quality dialogue as described above, involves both deepening and broadening in ways that are hard to distinguish. However, some pedagogical techniques and some interface designs focus on either deepening or broadening. At its most simple this can be seen in the choice of responses made by a moderator of a Philosophy for Children session in a primary school as illustrated in Chap. 5. Sometimes the teacher broadens the debate by asking others, 'What do you think of what Alex just said?' or 'Are there any other views about this?' At other times he focuses in and deepens the reflection on one topic asking: 'Why do you think that?' Can you say a bit more about that?'

Deepening is often about slowing down time and spatialising it. The InterLoc system slows deepens the superficial nature of synchronous chat by revealing the argument threads and keeping them in view so that they can be returned to. Bubble Dialogue, like many simulations and representations of events, enables the externalisation of interactions so that they can be discussed, analysed, returned to and rerun differently.

The function of deepening a dialogic space in design for computer supported collaborative learning often confronts similar issues and finds similar solutions. In creative design disciplines such as architecture and education there are not necessarily models or templates to follow but there are often similar design issues confronted in a number of different contexts. In architecture these repeating problem–solution couples are called 'design patterns'. Goodyear et al. (2006) have adapted this idea to design for networked learning. A clear example of a design pattern can be seen in the 'replay' function of Bubble Dialogue and the 'replay' function of Digalo. In both cases the ability to replay the action step by step affords deeper reflection on the process of dialogue. Another key design pattern for deepening is turning an utterance into an enduring but adaptable spatial representation of some kind that can serve as a shared object for reflection and manipulation.

5.3 Broadening dialogic spaces

An interesting study by Kruger found that the best indicator of the quality of moral debate in small groups was not the argument structure or the number of transacts but the number of alternative perspectives that were discussed before a decision was taken (Kruger, 1993). The same approach is applied in approaches to science education that present every issue as a debate between alternative explanations which the children, in groups, have to investigate (Keogh and Naylor, 1999). The elimination of alternatives can be taught as a way of discovering the one true explanation but it is better science to teach investigation as a way of refining questions and discovering new questions in an endless dialogue in which positions supposedly eliminated in the past often re-appear in new forms (Osborne and Duschl, 2002). Broadening dialogue can be as easy as providing a forum design pattern in which all the relevant voices are represented by cartoon characters with speech bubbles, or it can be as hard as reviewing all the distinct perspectives on any given issue that can be found on the World Wide Web. Pedagogical techniques like the odd-one-out, discussing the relationships and differences of three incompatible but linked points of view provide a way of scaffolding induction into a world of multiple view points with no certainties (Williams and Wegerif, 2006).

Broadening dialogue has a cognitive function since the best decisions and pragmatic 'truths' in every area are arrived at after considering all points of view (Rorty, 1991, p39). It can also have what Biesta would call a disruptive or deconstructive function, questioning the assumptions upon which the argument has been progressing in a more radical way. Biesta sees this function of education in ethical and political terms as the basis for education into democratic ways of thinking and acting, where democracy is not reducible to a constitution but is about working together across differences in mutually respectful and responsive way (Biesta, 2006).

My grandmother used to tell me that if I was bad and ran off into the woods near our house 'Boney would get me'. Later I discovered that Boney originally referred to Napolean Bonaparte, the great enemy of the British at the beginning of the nineteenth century. Somehow this great leader, who many at the time saw as a bringer of Enlightenment values to a feudal Europe, had been transformed into a shadowy monster to frighten children. Now we have another great enemy, Osama Bin Laden, but the communications technology is rather different. After listening to the BBC news on the television, my seven year old son asked me: 'Why is Osama Bin Laden trying to kill us?' I replied, 'I don't know, let's find out' and we went to the computer, tried a search in Google and instantly a video of Osama Bin Laden appeared on an Al Jazcera news site explaining, more-or-less why he was trying to kill us. He was talking in Arabic but fortunately there was a text translation into English. I am not sure what my son made of this but it struck me that this is a very different experience from previous conflicts. This enemy could not easily be dismissed as a bogey man but demanded to be listened to. (Listening to enemies with respect is not, of course, incompatible with fighting against them).

It is generally agreed that terrorists depend on the support, sometimes passive, sometimes active, of a community of people who have grievances that they believe have not been listened to seriously enough. In short such communities feel that their voice has not been heard in dialogues that are important to them. The role of education in the context of conflicting views has often been seen as to ensure that one view of reality, the correct view, triumphed over all others. Communications technology, such as the internet, that enables the other to speak in the living rooms of the heartland, has made this role more and more difficult to sustain. The alternative role of broadening the dialogue is therefore not just about cognitive gains, although it carries that implication too, it is about a strategy for surviving and flourishing in a world where there are multiple competing realities. Communications technology has one enormous affordance for education that outweighs all others in significance: support for dialogue across difference. This affordance may not be used unless we develop the listening power of a future generation. The combination of the internet and education for listening power may just possibly contribute to a more peaceful future.

6 TWO HISTORIES OF TECHNOLOGY

What is technology exactly and how does it relate to education? Most studies of educational technology do not ask such fundamental questions but the failure to ask them might mean that a partial and suspect view is being assumed. Gavriel Salomon, for example, points out that computers are a tool and not a medium of communication (Salomon, 1992, p. 892). It is interesting that the distinction between media, such as language or music, and tools, such as hammers or screwdrivers, has been elided in the catch-all phrase Information and Communications Technology (ICT). Salomon has a point. Tools get things done in the world so it makes sense to talk of them in terms of mediated action by a subject on an object, a man hammering a nail into a fence, for example. Media, on the other hand, are more like a mode of being. It is often not relevant to ask, what the *object* of a symphony or a poem is. It is still less useful to ask: what is the object of a medium such as music? There is a conceptual confusion going on at the heart of educational technology between tools and media that needs careful unpicking. One way to approach this is through unraveling the history of technology as two separate if linked histories: a history of productive technology driven by the logic and needs of the material reproduction of life, on the one hand, and a history of communications technology serving the very different logic and needs of communicative activity, on the other.

In the Marxist tradition, Vygotsky's socio-historical approach seeks to combine an account of ontogenesis, or history of individual development, with an account of phylogenesis, or history of the development of the species. His account of the individual development of higher mental faculties out of a process of the internalisation of 'tools' is rooted in a similar account of historical development of the human species that he borrowed directly from Marx. Marx argued that language begins outside of us as a tool for the co-ordination of productive activities and then appears internally in the form of consciousness. His assumption was that early humans or pre-human apes needed to work together when hunting big animals like mammoths. As humans works on nature to transform it in the production of their living, he claimed, they also transform themselves. Language, culture and internal individual consciousness emerge out of this process as mediating tools for production (e.g. Marx, 1977, p. 167).

Marx's materialist account of social evolution in history was largely borrowed from the American anthropologist Lewis Henry Morgan. After Darwin it seemed natural to see human beings as being characterised, against other animals, by their ability to make tools. Morgan described social evolution as driven by the development of productive technologies and he characterised the stages of social evolution in terms of stages of technology as we still do today, referring to the stone age, the bronze age and so on. Marx added to this account the claim that different forms of social organisation correspond to different technologies of production so, for example, the emergence of industrial technologies leads to capitalist relations of production.

Habermas points out an important weakness with Marx's history of technological development, which is that it does not allow for the possibility that some developments in history, the development of democratic political systems for example, arise not from the logic of production alone but also from the logic of communication (Habermas, 1984, p. 148). Habermas argues that the conditions of communication lead to a separate drive towards 'ethical' ideals such as 'justice' and 'cognitive' ideals such as 'truth'. A simple way of summarising his rather complex argument is that we need to engage in dialogue with each other to solve differences that arise in communal life and it is not possible to engage in dialogues with others without at least partly acknowledging the validity of the point of view of others. To put it even more simply: if you want other people to listen to you then you will find, over time, that you also have to listen to them.

Habermas was partly concerned in his argument to explain why capitalism had not led to the polarisation of classes and revolutionary overcoming that Marx had predicted it would. His answer was that the drive for communication and the technologies associated with it, such as mass circulation newspapers, led to the development of partial democratic social steering mechanisms that mitigated the divisive impact of capitalism. However, his case, that there are two separate driving logics in the history of technology, applies far more generally than this.

I quoted earlier research by Tomasello and others on the life of the great apes. This has opened up a new account of how consciousness might have emerged out of the needs of communication rather than as a tool to support the needs of production. The theoretical psychologist Humphrey describes how he came to see the intellect as a primarily social instrument for 'mind reading' after he spent some months studying gorillas living wild in Rwanda. He came to the conclusion that the easy way in which the apes could 'earn their living' by eating fruits and leaves did not justify the relatively large size of their brains. However, while the material life of the apes he studied was simple, their social life was highly complex (Humphrey, 1986). To thrive and prosper in the social environment of a gorilla troop it was necessary to be aware of which gorilla to groom submissively, which gorilla one could tease and which gorilla one had to fight, and these relations changed everyday in a dynamic soap-opera of alliances and betrayals. Like Tomasello, Humphrey speculates that a capacity for dialogic inter-subjectivity might have had an evolutionary advantage in the context of such a complex social life. To summarise the emerging consensus: first came dialogic relations, then came language as a tool to support dialogic relationships, then the new medium of language was used to support co-operation in work and the development of more productive tools. This is a phylogenetic account of the development of humans out of animals that is in contrast to that of Marx because driven forward by the needs of communication and not those of production.

When vivid ancient cave paintings of animals were discovered at Altamira, Spain in 1879, they were interpreted, in the Darwinian spirit that informed Morgan and Marx, as magical tools to help with hunting. Other finds followed in France and Spain, the oldest dating back 32,000 years making them the earliest known representations. However, archaeological research at these sites has found that the bones of the animals that were being eaten by the people who painted the pictures were not the same as the animals portrayed in the pictures. This casts doubt on the 'pictures as a magical tool to help with hunting' hypothesis. In Southern Africa, there are still living cultures with cave painting as part of their practice and heritage. The Bushmen or San people have painted in a similar way on rock walls for 30,000 years up to close to the present day. David Lewis-Williams, Professor of Cognitive Archeology at Witwatersrand University in South Africa, explored the significance of this cave art by interviewing San Bushmen who had actually painted some of it. He found that these paintings had a spiritual purpose for the San, helping induct members into communal visions in the course of trance dances. The animals were painted for the special powers that they gave dancers when they took possession of them. Similar shamanic practices, he speculates, explain the presence of men with animal like head-gear in the paintings in Europe (Lewis-Williams and Pearce, 2004). In other words, the cave paintings were not magical tools for hunting, as at first speculated, but practical tools for educational purposes. The figures in the paintings were symbolic of important 'spirit' voices for the San culture. According to Lewis-Williams, experienced shamans recorded aspects of their trance experience in the paintings to help draw new initiates into the same experience and the same participation in the shared space of the Shaman's trance dance. The role of the art, in combination with the practice of trance dance, was to induct new members into the culture by invoking the core voices of the culture and passing on the powers that they bring.

A similar re-appraisal of the origins of the first technological revolution, the Neolithic revolution, is under way. The first cultivation of wild crops appears to have occurred some 10,000 years ago in sites like Asikli in Central Anatolia and Çatalhöyük in Southern Turkey where excavations have discovered that large numbers of people lived together for generations eating only wild crops and wild animals. In other words, the gathering together of large numbers of people in settlements is not explained by a change in productive technology, as was always assumed, but precisely the other way around: first people gathered and settled and then they developed the technology to support themselves. This leaves open the mystery of why they wanted to gather in the first place. Due to the evidence of obsidian sculptures and central buildings in the settlement with colored murals including animal figures, the best guess of most archaeologists now is that people settled because they wanted to be closer to sacred sites where regular trance-dance events were held (Balter, 1998). They gathered because they wanted to dance together and be closer to the powerful new cultural voices represented in art on the temple walls.

This new account of the communicative and educational motivation behind the first representations and the Neolithic revolution, shares some features with the big technological revolution which we are living through today: the rise of the internet and the network society. Like the Neolithic revolution the extraordinarily rapid proliferation of the internet was not driven initially by the needs of production but by the desire of many ordinary people for communication and participation. A shared virtual reality seems to be the direction in which new communications technology is heading. This is interesting because a shared virtual reality was also there at the very beginning of communications technology in the form of the shared stories, and trance-dance experiences in small scale societies. Representations, from the beginning, were not tools for production but signs of living cultural voices that possess us as much as we can be said to possess and 'use' them.

The significance of re-writing the history of technology, for theories underpinning the development of computer supported collaborative learning, might be brought out better through considering a surprising omission in a classic of the literature on situated cognition. In a seminal study, Hutchins shows how a Micronesian canoeist can perform impressive feats of navigation with no charts or instruments using culturally transmitted patterns of movements of the stars and islands on different routes. Cognition, Hutchins demonstrates, is not a computational process in the brain of the canoeist but is embodied in social practices and the environment (Hutchins, 1995). The surprising omission in this study is the lack of any mention of the pictures carved and painted on the canoe. Ethnographic accounts of canoe building and canoe use on other similar Micronesian islands such as Tikopia (Firth, 1967) make it clear that the symbolic marks on the canoes were considered essential for the successful functioning of the canoe. On Tikopia and throughout Micronesia, markings on canoes represented the ancestor or spirit voice who first taught the people how to use canoes. The markings and dedication ceremonies invoked the spirit of the ancestor god of canoeing to inhabit and guide the canoe. Orally transmitted star routes might guide the canoeist, but so did the voices of the ancestors, especially in times of crisis when the star routes failed. Canoeing, for the traditional Micronesians of Tikopia at least, is not just something you do, but is also something you have to *be*: as with every other aspect of life, relationship with ancestors and attunement to the voice of the ancestors is part of the activity.

The first representations were not tools to gain power over the world, but perspectives or voices that not only spoke to the people, but possessed them and lived through them. In a related way the new virtual reality of the internet is not primarily a store of tools to gain power over the world so much as a living dialogue of voices and perspectives. The first represent-tations, ancient cave paintings, were an educational technology to induct new members into participation in a shared virtual reality. In a related way, the role of pedagogy plus educational technology in the new virtual reality age is to induct students into effective participation in the global dialogic space opened up and sustained by the internet.

7 TWO VISIONS OF ENLIGHTENMENT

7.1 Monologic Enlightenment

The literature of post-modernism contains many attacks on what is called 'the Enlightenment project', defined as a belief in progress through the expansion of knowledge and the application of reason. It is said, quite plausibly, that this project lies behind modern education systems. Francois Lyotard, often referred to as the originator of the term *post-modern*, wrote that the enlightenment project believed that progress through reason would emancipate …

the whole of humanity from ignorance, poverty, backwardness, despotism ... thanks to education in particular, it will also produce enlightened citizens, masters of their own destiny (Lyotard, 1992, pp. 82–84)

In reality, however, he goes on to explain such appeals to reason mask a violent process in which weaker perspectives are oppressed by more powerful ones. A similar connection between modernity, the ideal of reason and education is made by Michel Foucault, one of the *post-modern* thinkers most referred to in educational research today. Like Lyotard, Foucault appears highly critical of the enlightenment ideal of reason, arguing that in practice this ideal has led to the increasing grip of systems of surveillance and control (Foucault, 1975). Indeed the growth of mass education, with its bells, divisions and examinations is used by Foucault to illustrate his thesis that the myth of progress through reason has been used to justify our increasing enslavement to formal systems, systems that, through education, have colonised not only our bodies and minds but, more worryingly, our souls.

Saul argues that although the enlightenment project began with Voltaire in a spirit of freedom and tolerance, it ended up being hi-jacked by a narrow and mechanistic vision of science and reason (Saul, 1993). The many contemporary attacks on the enlightenment project all seem to stem from the strong association of this project with monologic models of reason and of science. The reduction of the ideal of reason in education to monologic can be seen clearly today within computer supported collaborative learning in the widespread interest in teaching explicit reasoning of the kind that can be embedded in tools such as scripts and implemented in computer programmes. This no longer has much to do with the original aspiration of the Enlightenment *philosophes* to free consciousness from the shackles of tradition because 'reason' is now seen not as an end in itself but as a tool for productivity.

7.2 Dialogic Enlightenment

To rescue that which is of value in the Enlightenment project, it might be worth reacting it with an alternative interpretation of the same word that is so different as to almost serve as its shadow. As well as referring to a philosophical movement that originated in France in the Eighteenth Century, Enlightenment is also a common translation of the Sanskrit term 'nirvāna' which, read literally, means 'the putting out of the flame'. This is a vision of Enlightenment as an awakening or expansion of awareness which comes when one lets go of identity and realises the 'non-self' nature of everything. In its negative tone, this vision of enlightenment contrasts with the European Enlightenment tradition which has become associated with the productive work of constructing more, bigger and better identities. Whilst the European Enlightenment project became associated with an aim at mastery and control over nature; enlightenment understood as 'nirvana' is about letting go of the anxiety and the perpetual warfare caused by identity thinking.

Aspects of this eastern Enlightenment tradition can be found in the alternative dialogic tradition of reason that I have drawn upon in this book. In outlining the profound depths of dialogic space, Bakhtin referred to what he called the 'chronotope' of 'great time', a time in which all the voices and perspectives of culture and history are somehow co-present in dialogue together. This can be seen in the rather beautiful penultimate sentence of his notes on 'Methodology for the Human Sciences' which reads: 'Nothing is absolutely dead: every meaning will have its homecoming festival'. I have sprinkled the text of this book deliberately with voices from different cultures and ages and scripts, all present together on the World Wide Web, to illustrate the potential that the internet has to realise something of Bakhtin's prophetic vision of 'great time'.

It would be a mistake to think of Bakhtin's 'great time' as simply a cacophony of clashing voices. Great time represents the infinite potential for meaning that is dialogic space. It is this underlying unbounded potentiality of dialogic space that has made the real cacophony of the World Wide Web possible. Only through, in a sense, rooting ourselves in this underlying dialogic space can we find our own way through the many voices of the Web without becoming trapped in them. Great time is the depth underlying the shallow time of everyday dialogues. To draw closer to the creativity and unbounded resonance of great time it is necessary to focus more on the quality of listening in dialogues and less on the forms of talking. The end of dialogic education is not more noise but 'a silence that is not the contrary of language' (Merleau-Ponty, 1968, p. 179). The dialogic direction for education produces a negative vision of progress as letting go rather than as grasping. As Merleau-Ponty put it, the implication of a dialogic perspective is that there can be no total grasp because 'what there is to be grasped is a dispossession' (Merleau-Ponty, 1968, p. 266). However, this direction is only apparently negative from the point of view of identity thinking; from the point of view of dialogic thinking, it is a positive movement leading to increased creativity, critical reasoning (through exploring alternative voices) and developing a capacity for listening to otherness or learning to learn. In short, focusing on dia-logos, which can be translated as reason 'through and across' difference, rescues that which is of most value to education in the ideal of logos.

Like the original enlightenment project, the dialogic enlightenment project is about the positive transformation of society as well as the transformation of individuals. Promoting dialogue across difference is about education for real democracy, since it is about creating a shared space where people can be different together. In a way, again, this vision of a shared space where people can be different together is already implicit in the spreading reality of the internet.

In this dialogic enlightenment project, educational technology has a crucial role to play. In the original enlightenment project, education is seen as a drive-belt bringing progress through knowledge and reason into every area of life. For a dialogic enlightenment project, education and educational technology is a drive-belt bringing the fruits of dialogic - empathy, creativity and criticality - into every area of life. And, in a way, to return to the innate reasonableness of Bakhtin's vision of progress through 'augmentation', these two visions, while different, are not mutually exclusive. A turn towards dialogic in education does not reject the original Enlightenment project but rebalances it by augmenting productive technical reason with communicative dialogic reason. This implies augmenting the drive to mastery and control with a drive towards insight, relationship and responsive play. Both voices will always exist but the future is likely to be a happier place if we make production serve the needs of expanding and deepening dialogue rather than, as is happening now, fashioning dialogue into a tool for increasing production.

REFERENCES

Ainsworth, S. (1997). Information technology and multiple representations: new opportunities - new problems. *Journal of Information Technology for Teacher Education* 6, 93-106.

Alexander, R. (2000). *Culture and pedagogy*. Oxford, Blackwell.

Alexander, R. (2004). *Towards dialogic teaching: Rethinking classroom talk*. Cambridge: Dialogos.

Anderson, A., A. Tolmie, E. McAteer, & A. Demisne. (1993). Software style and interaction around the microcomputer. *Computers and Education* 20 (3): 235-250.

Anderson, L. W. & Krathwohl, D. R. (2001). *A taxonomy for learning, teaching, and assessing*. New York: Longman.

Andriessen, J. (2006). Arguing to learn. In: K. Sawyer (Ed.) *Handbook of the Learning Sciences*. Cambridge: Cambridge University press.

Andriessen, J. Baker, M. Suthers, D. (2003). Argumentation, computer support, and the educational context of confronting cognitions. In Andriessen, J. Baker, M. Suthers, D. (eds.). *Arguing to learn: Confronting cognitions in Computer-Supported Collaborative Learning environments* (pp. 1-25). Dordrecht: Kluwer.

Anthone, R. and Williams, S. (2003). From the Republic of Letters to the Empire of Email. Philosophy Pathways. 56. http://www.philosophypathways.com/newsletter/.

Aristotle (Trans 2006). *Organon, On Interpretation*Retrieved 1st May 2007 from: http://www.gibson-design.com/Philosophy/Aristotle-Organon-2-interpretation.2.2.htm.

Axelrod, R. (1984). *The evolution of cooperation*. New York: Basic Books.

Bailin, S. (1994). *Achieving extraordinary ends: An essay on creativity*. Norwood, N.J.: Ablex.

Bailin, S. (1998). Education, knowledge and critical thinking. In Carr, D. (ed).*Education, knowledge and truth* (pp. 204-221). London: Routledge.

Baker, M. J. (2004). *Recherches sur l'élaboration de connaissances dans le dialogue. Synthèse pour l'habilitation à diriger les recherches*. Université Nancy 2.

Baker, M.J., Quignard, M., Lund, K. & Séjourné, A. (2003). Computer-supported collaborative learning in the space of debate. In B. Wasson, S. Ludvigsen & U. Hoppe (Eds.) *Designing for Change in Networked Learning Environments: Proceedings of the International Conference on Computer Support for Collaborative Learning 2003*, pp. 11-20. Dordrecht: Kluwer Academic Publishers.

Bakhtin, M. (1973). *Problems of Dostoevsky's poetics*, (trans Rotsel, R.). Ardis: New York.

Bakhtin, M. (1981). *The dialogic imagination*. Austin: University of Texas Press.

Bakhtin, M. (1986). *Speech genres and other late essays*. Austin: University of Texas.

Balter, M. (1998). Why settle down? The mystery of the first cities. *Science*, Vol 282, 14-42.

Barnes, D. & Todd, F. (1978). *Communication and learning in small groups.* London: Routledge and Kegan Paul.

Baron-Cohen, S. (1994). How to build a baby that can read minds: Cognitive mechanisms in mindreading. *Cahiers de Psychologie Cognitive/Current Psychology of Cognition*, 13, 513-552.

Barwise, J. & Perry, J. (1983). *Situations and attitudes*. Cambridge, Ma.: MIT Press.

BenHabib, S. (1992). *Situating the self: gender, community and post-modernism in contemporary ethics*. Oxford: Polity.

Bereiter, C. & Scardamalia, M. (1989). Intentional learning as a goal of instruction. In L. B. Resnick (Ed.). *Knowing, learning, and instruction: Essays in honor of Robert Glaser* (pp. 361-392). Hillsdale, NJ: Lawrence Erlbaum Associates, Inc.

Bereiter, C. (1994). Implications of Postmodernism for Science, or, Science as Progressive Discourse. *Educational Psychologist*, 29(1) 3-12.

Bereiter, C. (2002). *Education and mind in the knowledge age*. Mahwah, NJ:Lawrence Erlbaum Associates.

Berkowitz, M. W, & Gibbs, J. C (1983). Measuring the developmental features of moral discussion. Merrill-Palmer Quarterly, 29, 399-410.

Bernstein, R. (1993). An Allegory of Modernity/Postmodernity: Habermas and Derrida. In G. Madison (Ed.). *Working Through Derrida*, (pp. 204-230). Evanston, Illinois: Northwestern University Press.

Biesta, G. (2006). *Beyond learning: Democratic education for a human future*. Boulder CO: Paradigm Press.

Biesta, G. J. J. (2004). "Mind the gap!" Communication and the educational relation. In C. Bingham and A.M. Sidorkin (Eds). *No education without relation* (pp. 11-22). New York: Peter Lang.

Blagg, N. (1991). *Can We Teach Intelligence? A Comprehensive Evaluation of Feuerstein's Instrumental Enrichment Program*. New Jersey: Lawrence Erlbaum Associates.

Bloom, B. S. (Ed.). (1956). *Taxonomy of educational objectives: The classification of educational goals: Handbook I, cognitive domain*. New York; Toronto: Longmans, Green.

Boden, M. A. (1990). *The creative mind*. Basic Books: New York.

Bohm, D. (1996). *On dialogue*. (Edited by Lee Nichol). New York: Routledge.

Bourne, J. (2003). Vertical discourse: the role of the teacher in the transmission and acquisition of decontextualised language. *European Education Research Journal*, 2, (4). 496-521.

Boyle, T. (1997). *Design for multi-media learning.* Hemel Hempstead: Prentice Hall.

Bromme, R. and Stahl, E., (2002). Writing and Learning: Hypertext as a renewal of an old and close friendship. In Bromme, R and Stahl, E., eds, *Writing Hypertext and Learning: conceptual and empirical approaches.* Advances in Learning and Instruction Series. Oxford: Pergamon.

Buber, M. (1923/70). *I and Thou.* Edinburgh: T and T Clark .

Burbules, N. (1993). *Dialogue in teaching: Theory and practice.* New York: Teachers College.

Burbules, N. (2006). Rethinking dialogue in networked spaces. *Cultural Studies <=> Critical Methodologies,* 6(1). 107-122.

Buzan, A. & Buzan, B. (2000). *The Mind Map Book.* London: BBC.

Caroll, J. B. (1993). *Human cognitive abilities: A survey of factor-analytic studies.* New York: Cambridge University Press.

Carpenter, P. Just, M. & Shell, P. (1990). What one intelligence test measures: a theoretical account of the processing of the Raven Progressive Matrices test. *Psychological Review,* 9(7). 404-431.

Carter R. (1999). Common language: corpus, creativity and cognition. *Language and Literature* 1999 8(3) 195-216.

Carter R. (2002). *Language and creativity.* London: Routledge.

Carver, S. M., Lehrer, R., Connell, T., & Ericksen, J. (1992). Learning by hypermedia design: Issues of assessment and implementation. *Educational Psychologist,* 27(3), 385-404.

Castells, M (2005). Interview. Retrieved 1st February 2005 from http://globetrotter.berkeley.edu/people/Castells/castells-con4.html

Castells, M. (2002). *The internet galaxy: Reflections on the internet, business, and society.* New York: Oxford University Press.

Casti, J. (1997). *Would be worlds.* New York: Wiley.

Cazden, C. (1988). *Classroom discourse: The language of teaching and learning.* Portsmouth, NH: Heinemann.

Cheyne, J. A. & Tarulli, D. (1999). Dialogue, difference, and the "third voice" in the Zone of Proximal Development. *Theory and Psychology,* 9, 5-28.

Chi, M. T. H. & Hausmann, R. G. M. (2003). Do radical discoveries require ontological shifts? In L. V. Shavinina, (Ed.). *International Handbook on Innovation* (pp. 430-444). Oxford: Elsevier Science Ltd.

Chi, M. T. H. (1997). Creativity: Shifting across ontological categories flexibly. In T.B. Ward, S.M. Smith, and J. Vaid (Eds.). *Conceptual Structures and processes: Emergence, discovery and change* (pp. 209-234). Washington, D.C: American Psychological Association.

Clancey, W. & Soloway, E. (1990). AI and learning environments: Preface to the Special Issue of the *Journal of Artificial Intelligence and Education,* 42(1), 1-6.

Clancey, W. (In press). A transactional perspective on the practice-based science of teaching and learning. In T. Koschmann (Ed.). *Theorizing Learning Practice.* Mahwah, NJ.: Lawrence Erlbaum Associates.

Clark, R. E. (1990). Facilitating domain-general prolem solving: Computers, cognitive processes and instruction. In E. De Corte, M. C. Linn, H. Mandl and L. Verschaffel (Eds.). *Computer-based learning environments and problem Solving* (pp. 265-287). Berlin: Springer-Verlag.

Claxton, G. (1997). *Hare Brain, Tortoise Mind.* Fourth Estate: London.

Claxton, G. (1999). *Wise-Up: the challenge of lifelong learning.* London: Bloomsbury.

Claxton, G. Edwards, L. & Scale-Constantinou V. (2006). Cultivating creative mentalities: A framework for education. *Thinking Skills and Creativity*,1(1), 57-61.

Clements, D. H. & Nastasi, B. K. (1993). Electronic media and early childhood education. In B. Spodek (Ed.). *Handbook of research on the education of young children* (pp. 251-275). New York, NY: Macmillan.

Clements, D. H. (1986). Effects of Logo and computer assisted environments on cognition and creativity. *Journal of Educational Psychology*, 78, 309-318.

Cobb, P., & McClain, K. (2002). Supporting students' learning of significant mathematical ideas. In G. Wells & G. Claxton (Eds.), *Learning for life in the 21st Century* (pp. 154-166). Oxford, England: Blackwell.

Cole, M. John-Steiner, V. Scribner, S. Souberman, E. (1978). Introduction. In Vygotsky, L. *Mind in society: the development of higher psychological processes.* Cambridge: Harvard University Press.

Cole, M. & Derry, J. (2005). We have met technology and it is us. In R. J. Sternberg and D. Preiss (Eds.). Intelligence and technology: Impact of tools on the nature and development of human skills. Mahwah, NJ: Lawrence Erlbaum Associates.

Cole, M., & Engestrom, Y. (1993). A cultural-historical approach to distributed cognition. In G. Salomon (Eds.), *Distributed cognitions: Psychological and educational considerations* (pp. 1-46). Cambridge, UK: Cambridge University Press.

Collis, B. & Margaryan, A. (2004). Applying Activity Theory to CSCL and work-based activities in corporate settings. *Educational Technology Research and Development*, 52(4), 37-51.

communication studies. *Synthese 123,* 327-346

Conole, G. and Oliver, M. (Eds) (2007), *Contemporary perspectives in e-learning research: themes, methods and impact on practice*, part of the Open and Distance Learning Series, F. Lockwood, (ed), RoutledgeFalmer: London.

Conze, E. (2001). *Buddhist Wisdom* London: Vintage Books.

Costa, A. L. (Ed.). (2000). *Developing minds: a resource book for teaching thinking.* Alexandria, VA: ASCD.

Craft, A. (1991). Thinking skills and the whole curriculum. *The Curriculum Journal* 2 (2): 183-199.

Craft, A. (2005). *Creativity in schools: tensions and dilemmas.* London: Routledge.

Crandell, L. E. & Hobson, R. P. (1999). Individual differences in young children's IQ: A social-developmental perspective. *Journal of Child Psychology and Psychiatry*, 40, 455-464.

Crook, C. (1994). *Computers and the collaborative experience of learning.* London and New York: Routledge.

Csikszentmihalyi, M. (1996). *Creativity: flow and the psychology of discovery and invention.* New York: Harper Perennial.

Daniels, H. (2001). *Vygotsky and Pedagogy.* London: Routledge.

Dawes, L. Mercer, N. & Wegerif, R. (2004). *Thinking together: activities for key stage 2 children and teachers (2nd Ed.).* Birmingham: Questions Publishing.

De Bono, E. (1976). *Thinking action: teacher handbook – CoRT VI.* New York: Pergamon Press.

De Corte, E. (1990). *Towards powerful learning environments for the acquisition of problem solving skills. European Journal of Psychology of Education,* 5, 5-19.

De Corte, E., Linn, M., Mandl, H., & Verschaffel, L. (Eds.). (1992). *Computer-based learning environments and problem solving.* (NATO/ASI Series.F: Computer and Systems Sciences, Vol. 84.) Berlin: Springer-Verlag.

De Laat, M. (2006). *Networked Learning.* Amsterdam: Politie Academy

De Laat, M. Lally, V. (2005). Investigating group structure in cscl: some new approaches. *Information Systems, Frontiers* 7(1). 13-25.

Del Castillo, H; García-Varela, A.B; y Lacasa, P. (2003). Literacies through media: identity and discourse in the process of constructing a Web site. *International Journal of Educational Research,* 39, 885-891.

Department for Education and Skills (2006). *National Curriculum for England,* Retrieved on 1st May 2006 from http://www.nc.uk.net/.

Deridda, J. (1968). La Différance. In *Théorie d'ensemble* Paris, Éditions de Seuil.

Derrida, J. (1973). Différance. In Derrida, J., *Speech and Phenomena: and other essays on Husserl's Theory of Signs.* Evanston: Northwestern University Press.

Derrida, J. (1976). *Of Grammatology.* (G. Spivak, trans.). Baltimore: Johns Hopkins University Press.

Descombes, V. (1980). *Modern French Philosophy.* Cambridge: Cambridge UP.

Dewey, J. (1933). *How We Think.* New York: D. C. Heath.

Dewey, J. (1938/1997). Experience and Education. New York: Simon and Schuster.

Dewey, J., & Bentley, A. F. (1949). *Knowing and the known.* Boston: Beacon.

Dillenbourg, P. Baker, M. Blaye, A. & O'Malley, C. (1996). The evolution of research on collaborative learning. In E. Spada and P. Reiman (Eds). *Learning in humans and machine: towards an interdisciplinary learning science* (pp. 189-211). Oxford: Elsevier

Dillon, A. & Gabbard, R. (1998). Hypermedia as an educational technology: a review of the quantitative research literature on learning comprehension control and style. *Review of educational research,* 68, 322-349.

Dillon, J. T. (1990). *The practice of questioning.* London: Routledge.

Doise, W., & Mugny, G. (1979). Individual and collective conflicts of centrations in cognitive development. *European Journal of Psychology,* 9, 105-198.

Edwards, A. (2005). Let's get beyond community and practice: the many meanings of learning by participating. *The Curriculum Journal,* 16(1), 49-65.

Edwards, A., and D. Westgate. (1994). *Investigating Classroom Talk.* London: Falmer Press.

Eliot, T. S. (1922/2006). *The Wasteland*. Retrieved 1st May 2007 from, http://www.everypoet.com/Archive/poetry/t_s_eliot/t_s_eliot_the_waste_l and.htm.

Engestrom, Y. E. (1987). *Learning By Expanding: An Activity-Theoretical Approach To Developmental Research*, Helsinki: Orienta-Konsultit. Retrieved April 2007 from: Http://Lchc.Edu/Mca/Paper/Engestrom/Engestrom/Expanding/Intro.Htm

Engestrom, Y., 1999, *Introduction* to the German edition of Learning by Expanding, Retrieved April 2007 from: http://lchc.ucsd.edu/MCA/Paper/Engestrom/expanding/intro.htm

Ennis, R. H. (1987). A taxonomy of critical thinking dispositions and abilities. In J. Baron and R. Sternberg (Eds,). *Teaching thinking skills: theory and practice* (pp. 9-26). New York: W. H. Freeman.

Facione, P. (1990). *Critical thinking: a statement of expert consensus for purposes of educational assessment and instruction*. Millbrae, CA: California Academic Press.

Fernández, M., Wegerif, R., Mercer, N. & Rojas-Drummond, S. (2002). Re-Conceptualising "Scaffolding" and The Zone of Proximal Development in the context of symmetrical collaborative learning. *Journal of Classroom Interaction* 36(2), 40-54.

Fernyhough, C. (1996). The dialogic mind: a dialogic approach to the higher mental functions. *New Ideas in Psychology,* 14, 47-62.

Firth, R. (1967). *Tikopia ritual and belief*. Boston:. Beacon Press.

Fisher, E. (1992). Characteristics of children's talk at the computer and its relationship to the computer software. *Language and Education* 7, 2, 187-215

Fisher, E. (1993). Distinctive features of pupil–pupil talk and their relationship to learning. *Language and Education* 7(4), 239-58.

Fisher, R. (1990). *Teaching children to think*. London: Blackwell.

Flavell, J. H. (1976). Metacognitive aspects of problem solving. In L. B. Resnick, ed., *The Nature of Intelligence*. Hillsdale, NJ: Erlbaum.

Foucault, M. (1961). *Madness and civilisation: a history of insanity in the age of reason*, (Howard, R., trans). London: Tavistock.

Foucault, M. (1973). *The order of things: An archaelogy of the human sciences*. (Sheridan-Smith, trans). New York: Vintage.

Foucault, M. (1975). *Discipline and punishment: the birth of the prison* (Sheridan-Smith, trans). New York: Pantheon.

Freire, P. (1971). *Pedagogy of the oppressed*. New York: Seabury Press.

Fuks, H., Pimental, M. & Lucena, C.J.P. (2006). R-U-Typing-2-Me? Evolving a chat tool to increase understanding in learning activities. *International Journal of Computer-Supported Collaborative Learning*. v1. 117-142.

Gardner, H. (1999). *Intelligence reframed*. New York: Basic Books.

Garrison, D. R. & Anderson, T., (2003). *E-learning in the 21st century: A framework for research and practice*. New York: RoutledgeFalmer.

Gee, J. P., (2003), *What video games have to teach us about learning and literacy*. New York: Palgrave/Macmillan.

Glassner, A. & Schwarz, B. (2007). What stands and develops between creative and critical thinking? Argumentation? *Thinking Skills and Creativity.* 2(1). 10-18.

Goody, J. (1977). *The domestication of the savage mind.* Cambridge, England: Cambridge University Press.

Goodyear, P., De Laat, M., & Lally, V. (2006). Using pattern languages to mediate theory-praxis conversations in designs for networked learning. *ALT-J, Research in Learning Technology,* 14(3) 211-223.

Govinda, A. (1988). *The way of the white clouds: a buddhist pilgrim in Tibet.* Boston, MA: Shambhala Dragon Editions.

Graddol, D. (1989). Some CMC discourse properties and their educational significance. In A. Kaye (Ed.) *Mindweave.* Pergamon: Oxford.

Graddol, D. (1997). *The Future of English?* British Council: London.

Greeno, J., Collins, A. & Resnick, L. (1996). Cognition and learning. In D. Berliner and R. Calfee (Eds.) Handbook of Educational Psychology, pp. 15-46. New York: MacMillan.

Greeno, J., Collins, A. & Resnick, L. (1996). Cognition and learning. In D. Berliner and R. Calfee (Ed.) *Handbook of Educational Psychology* (pp. 15-46). New York: MacMillan.

Grice, P. (1975). Logic and conversation. In P. Cole & J. L. Morgan (Eds.) *Syntax and Semantics, Vol. 3, Speech Acts* (pp 41-58). New York: Academic Press.

Habermas, J. (1984). Towards a reconstruction of historical materialism. In *Communication and the evolution of society* (pp 130-178) Cambridge: Polity.

Habermas, J. (1990). *Moral Consciousness and Communicative Action.* Cambridge: Polity Press.

Habermas, J. (1991). *The Theory of Communicative Action. Vol. 1* Cambridge, Polity Press.

Hakkarainen, K. (1998). *Epistemology of scientific inquiry in computer-supported collaborative learning.* University of Toronto.

Hamblin, C. L. (1970). *Fallacies.* New York: Methuen.

Harasim, L., et al., (1995). *Learning Networks.* Cambridge, Ma: MIT.

Harasim, L., Hiltz, S. R., Teles, L., & Turoff, M. (1997). *Learning Networks: A field guide to teaching and learning online.* Cambridge, MA.: MITT Press.

Hattie, J., Biggs, J. & Purdie, N. (1996). Effects of learning skills intervention on student learning: A meta-analysis. *Review of research in education* 66, 99-136.

Hegel, G. W. F. (1975). *The Logic of Hegel* (Wallace, W, Trans.). Oxford, Clarendon Press.

Heidegger, M. (1969). *Identity and Difference.* (Bilingual ed. J. Stambaugh. Trans.). New York: Harper and Row.

Heidegger, M. (1971). *"The Thing," in Poetry, Language, Thought.* New York: Harper and Row

Heidegger, M. (1978). *Basic Writings.* London, Routledge.

Hennessy, S., McCormick, R., & Murphy, P. (1993). The myth of general problem-solving capability: design and technology as an example. *The Curriculum Journal* 4(1), 21-27.

Hermans, H. J. M. (2004). Introduction: The dialogical self in a global and digital age. *Identity: An International Journal of Theory and Research,* 4(4), 297-320.

Hermans, H. J. M., Kempen, H. & van Loon, R. J. P. (1992). The dialogical self: beyond individualism and rationalism. *American Psychologist,* 47, 1, 23-33.

Herring, S. C. (1999). Interactional Coherence in CMC. *Journal of Computermediated. Communication,* 4(4).

Hicks, D. (1996). Contextual inquiries: A discourse-oriented study of classroom learning. In D. Hicks (Ed.). *Discourse, Learning, and Schooling* (pp. 104-141). New York: Cambridge University Press.

Higgins, S. & V. Baumfield (1998). A defence of teaching general thinking skills. *Journal of Philosophy of Education* 32(3), 391-398.

Higgins, S. (2000). The Logical Zoombinis. *Teaching Thinking* 1, 15-18.

Hobson, R. P. (1998). The intersubjective foundations of thought. In S. Braten (ed.). *Intersubjective Communication and Emotion in Ontogeny* (pp. 283-96). Cambridge: Cambridge University Press.

Hobson, R. P. (2002). *The cradle of thought: exploring the origins of thinking.* London: Macmillan.

Howe, C., Tolmie, A., Anderson, A. and Mackenzie, M. (1992). Conceptual Knowledge in Physics: The role of group interaction in computer-supported teaching, *Learning and Instruction,* 2, 161-183.

Hoyles, C. & Sutherland, R. (1989), Logo Mathematics in the Classroom. London: Routledge.

Hughes, M. (1990). Children's computation. In R. Grieve and M. Hughes (Eds.)*Understanding Children* . Oxford: Basil Blackwell.

Humphrey, N. (1986). *The Inner Eye,* London: Faber and Faber.

Hui, D. (2005). A new role for computer-mediated communication in engaging teacher learning within informal professional communities. *Proceedings of the International Conference on Computer Supported Collaborative Learning*(CSCL) (pp. 221-226). Taiwan.

Hutchins, E. (1995). *Cognition in the wild.* Cambridge, Mass, MIT Press

Hutinger, P and Rippey, R (1997). How Five Preschool Children with Autism Responded to Computers. http://scott.mprojects.wiu.edu/~eccts/articles/autism1.html

Inkpen, K., Booth, K.S., Klawe, M., and Upitis, R. (1995). Playing Together Beats Playing Apart, Especially for Girls. *Proceedings of Computer Supported Collaborative Learning (CSCL) '95.* Lawrence Erlbaum Associates, 177-181. Retrieved 1st April 2006 from http://www.cs.sfu.ca/people/Faculty/inkpen/publications.html.

Jermann, P., Soller, A., & Muehlenbrock, M. (2001). From Mirroring to guiding: A review of state of the art technology for supporting collaborative learning. Proceedings of the *First European Conference on Computer-Supported Collaborative Learning,* Maastricht, The Netherlands, 324-331.

Johnston, S. (2000). *Teaching Thinking Skills.* Impact 8: Report of the Philosophy of Education Society of Great Britain.

Jonassen, D. (1991). Hypertext as instructional design. *Educational Technology Research and Development,* 39(1), 83-92

Jonassen, D. (2000). *Computers as mindtools for schools: engaging critical thinking.* (2nd Edition). New Jersey: Prentice Hall.

Jonassen, D., Carr, C., Yueh, H. (1998). Computers as mindtools for engaging learners in critical thinking. *TechTrends,* 43(2), 24-32.

Jones A, and Price E. (2001). Using a computer application to investigate social information processing in children with emotional and behavioural difficulties, in Hutchby, I. and Moran-Ellis, J. Children, Culture and Technology, Falmer Press.

Jones, A. (1996). The use of computers to support learning in children with emotional and behavioural difficulties, Computers & Education 26 (1-3) pp. 81-90.

Karmiloff-Smith, A. (1992, reprinted 1995). Beyond Modularity: A Developmental Perspective on Cognitive Science. Cambridge, Mass.: MIT Press/Bradford Books.

Keats, J. (2005). *Collected Letters.* Retrieved 1st May 2006 from, http://englishhistory.net/keats/letters.html

Keogh, B., & Naylor, S. (1999). Concept cartoons, teaching and learning in. science: An evaluation. *International Journal of Science Education*, 21(4), 431-446.

Kirriemuir, J. & McFarlane, A. E. (2003). *A literature review on Computer games and learning*, Report 7 Nesta Futurelab Bristol www.nestafuturelab. org.

Kirschner, P. A., Martens, R. L., & Strijbos, J. W., (2004). CSCL in higher education? A framework for designing multiple collaborative environments, in P. Dillenbourg, Series Ed., & J. W. Strijbos, P. A. Kirschner & R. L. Martens,Vol. Eds., *Computer-supported collaborative learning: Vol. 3. What we know about CSCL: And implementing it in higher education,* pp. 3-30, Boston, MA: Kluwer Academic Publishers.

Koschmann, T. (Ed.) (1996). *CSCL: Theory and Practice of an emerging paradigm.* Mahwah, NJ: Lawrence Erlbaum Associates.

Koschmann, T. (1999). Toward a dialogic theory of learning: Bakhtin's contribution to understanding learning in settings of collaboration. In C. M. Hoadley and J. Roschelle (Eds.). *Proceedings of the Computer Support for Collaborative Learning* (CSCL). 1999 Conference (pp. 308-313). Mahwah, NJ: Lawrence Erlbaum Associates.

Koschmann, T. (2001). Revisiting the paradigms of instructional technology. In G. Kennedy, Keppell, M., McNaught, C., & Petrovic, T. (Eds.), Meeting at the Crossroads, Proceedings of the 18th Annual Conference of the Australian Society for Computers in Learning in Tertiary Education (15-22). Melbourne: Biomedical Multimedia Unit, The University of Melbourne. Retrieved on January 28, 2004 from HYPERLINK "http://www.medfac. unimelb.edu.au/ascilite2001/pdf/papers/koschmannt.pdf"

Koschmann, T. (In press). Introduction. In T. Koschmann (Ed.). *Theorizing learning practice.* Mahwah, NJ: Lawrence Erlbaum Associates, Inc.

Kozulin, A. (1986). Introduction to Vygotsky, L. (1986). *Thought and Language.* (Trans. Kozulin). Cambridge MA: MIT Press.

Kozulin, A. (1996). A literary model for psychology. In D. Hicks (Ed.). *Discourse, Learning, and Schooling* (pp. 145-164). New York: Cambridge University Press.

Kruger, A. (1993). Peer collaboration: conflict, cooperation or both? *Social Development* 2 (3).

Lake, M. & Needham, M. (1993). *Top Ten Thinking Tactics*. Birmingham: Questions Publishing.

Lao-Tzu (1972). *Tao te ching*. New York: Knopf.

Laurillard, D. (1993). *Rethinking university teaching: a framework for the effective use of educational technology*. London: Routledge

Lave, J., & Wenger, E. (1991). Situated Learning: Legitimate Periperal Participation. Cambridge, UK: Cambridge University Press.

Leat, D. and Higgins S. (2002). The role of powerful pedagogical strategies in curriculum development. *The Curriculum Journal* 13(1), 71-85.

Lehrer, R. & Schnauble, L. (2004). *Modeling natural variation through distribution. American* Educational Research Journal, 41(3). 635-679.

Leibniz, G. (1973). Leibniz: Philosophical Writings. (Parkinson, G. Ed.: Morris, M and Parkinson, G. Trans.). London: Dent and Sons.

Leimann, M. (2002). Toward semiotic dialogism: the role of sign mediation in the dialogical self. *Theory and Psychology* Vol. 12(2). 221-235.

Lemke, J. (1990). Talking Science: Language, Learning and Values. New Jersey: Ablex.

Leontev, A. N. (1978). *Activity, Conscience, Personality*, Prentice-Hall, Englewood Cliffs, NJ

Levin, H. & Rumberger, R. (1995). Education, work and employment in developed countries: Situation and future challenges. In J. Hallak and F. Caillods (eds). *Educational Planning: The international dimension* (pp. 69-88). UNESCO Bureau of Education, International Institute for Educational Planning. London: Garland.

Lévinas, E. (1989). Ethics as first philosophy. In S. Hand (Ed.). The Lévinas Reader, (pp. 75-88). Oxford: Blackwells.

Lewis-Williams, J. D., and Pearce, D. G. (2004). *San Spirituality: Roots, Expressions and Social. Consequences*. Walnut Creek: Altamira Press.

Light, P. (1993). Collaborative learning with computers. In P. Scrimshaw (ed.) *Language, Classrooms and Computers*. London: Routledge.

Light, P. and Littleton, K. (1999). Social processes in children's learning. Cambridge: Cambridge University Press.

Ligorio, M. B. & Pugliese, A. C. (2004). Self-positioning in a text-based virtual environment. *Identity: An International Journal of Theory and Research*, 4(4). 337-353.

Linell, P. (1998). *Approaching Dialogue: Talk, interaction and contexts in dialogical perspective*. Amsterdam: Benjamins.

Linell, P. (2003). *What is dialogism? Aspects and elements of a dialogical approach to language, communication and cognition*. Lecture first presented at Växjö University, October 2000. Retrieved 1st May 2007 from http://www.tema.liu.se/tema-k/personal/perli/What-is-dialogism.pdf.

Lingis, A. (1994). The Community of Those who Have Nothing in Common. Bloomington: Indiana University Press.

Lipman, M. (2003). *Thinking in Education* (2nd Ed.). Cambridge: Cambridge University Press.

Littleton, K and Light, P (eds). *Learning with Computers: analyzing productive interaction*. London: Routledge.

Littleton, K. and Whitelock, D. (2005). The negotiation and co-construction of meaning and understanding within a postgraduate online learning community *Language, Media and Technology*. 30(2), 147-164

Littleton, K., Mercer, N., Dawes, L., Wegerif, R., Rowe, D. & Sams, C. (2005). Talking and thinking together at Key Stage 1. *Early Years: An International Journal of Research and Development,* 25 (2). 167-182.

Loveless, A. (2003). Creating Spaces in the Primary Curriculum: ICT in creative subjects. The Curriculum Journal, 14(1), 5-21.

Lyotard, J.-F. 1992. The Post-Modern Explained to Children: Correspondence 1982–1984. London: Turnaround.

Markova, I. (2003). *Dialogicality and social representations: the Dynamics of Mind* Cambridge, Cambridge University Press.

Martin, J. & Painter, C. (Eds). (1986). Writing to mean: teaching genres across the curriculum. *Applied Linguistics Association of Australia* (Occasional Papers 9).

Marx K. (1857/2005). *Grundrisse*. Retrieved on 1st may 2007 from: www.marxists.org/archive/ marx/works/1857/grundrisse/

Marx, K. (1977). *Selected writings* (Translated and Edited by David McLellan). Oxford: OUP.

Marzano, R. J. (1998). *A theory-based meta-analysis of research on instruction*. Aurora, Colorado, Mid-continent Regional Educational Laboratory: 170.

Marzano, R. J., 2000, *Designing a new taxonomy of educational objectives*. Thousand Oaks, Ca: Corwin Press.

Maybin, J. (1999). Framing and evaluation in 10-12 year old school children's use of appropriated speech, in relation to their induction into educational procedures and practices. *Text*. Vol 19(4). pp. 459-484.

Mazón, N. Rojas-Drummond, S. M. & Vélez, M. (2005). Efectos de un programa de fortalecimiento de habilidades de comprensión de textos en educandos de primaria. *Revista Mexicana de Psicología*. 9, 235-241.

McAlister, S., Ravenscroft, A and Scanlon, E. (2004). Combining interaction and context design to support collaborative argumentation using a tool for synchronous CMC, *Journal of Computer Assisted Learning: Special Issue: Developing dialogue for learning*, 20(3), 194-204.

McConnell, D. (2000). *Implementing Computer Supported Cooperative Learning*. (2nd ed.) London: Kogan Page.

McGuinness, C. (1998). *From thinking skills to thinking classrooms: A review and evaluation of approaches for developing pupils' thinking*. Nottingham, DfEE.

McMahon, H & W. O'Neill. (1993). Computer-Mediated Zones of Engagement in Learning, in Tom Duffy, J. Lowyk and D. Jonassen (eds.) *Designing environments for constructive learning*, Berlin: Springer-Verlag.

McPeck, J. (1990). *Teaching critical thinking: dialogue and dialectic*. New York and London: Routledge.

Mehan, H. (1979). Learning Lessons: Social organisation in the classroom. Cambridge, MA: Harvard University Press.

Mercer, N (2000). *Words and minds: how we use language to think together*. London: Routledge.

Mercer, N. (1994). The quality of talk in children's joint activity at the computer. *Journal of Computer Assisted Learning*, 10, 24-32.

Mercer, N. (1995). *The guided construction of knowledge: talk amongst teachers and learners*. Clevedon: Multilingual Matters.

Mercer, N. Dawes, R. Wegerif, R. & Sams, C. (2004). Reasoning as a scientist: ways of helping children to use language to learn science. *British Educational Research Journal*, 30(3). 367-385.

Mercer, N. Wegerif, R. & Dawes, L. (1999). Children's talk and the development of reasoning in the classroom. *British Educational Research Journal*. 25 (1). pp. 95-113.

Merleau-Ponty, M. (1964). *Le Visible et L'Invisible*. Paris: Gallimard.

Merleau-Ponty, M. (1968). The Visible and the Invisible (Edited by Claude Lefort and translated by Alphonso Lingis). Evanston, Il: Northwestern University Press.

Miell, D. and K. Littleton, Eds. (2004). *Collaborative creativity: contemporary perspectives* London, Free Association Books.

Morson, G. & Emerson, C. (1990). Mikhail Bakhtin: creation of a prosaics. Stanford: Stanford University Press.

Moscovici, S. (1984). Introduction: Le domaine de la psychologie sociale. In S. Moscovici (Ed.). Psychologie sociale. Paris, Presses Universitaires de France.

Moseley, D., Baumfield, V., Elliott, J., Gregson, M., Higgins, S., Miller, J. & Newton, D.P. (2005). *Frameworks for thinking: a handbook for teaching and learning*. Cambridge: Cambridge University Press.

Muukkonen, H., Hakkarainen, K. & Lakkala, M. (1999). Collaborative Technology for Facilitating Progressiv Inquiry: Future Learning Environment Tools. In C. Hoadley & J. Roschelle (Eds.), *Proceedings for CSCL. Designing New Media for a New Millenium*: Stanford University.

NACCCE (1999). *All our futures: creativity, culture and education: national advisory committee on creative and cultural education*. London: DfEE and DCMS.

Newman, D., Griffin, P. and Cole, M. (1989). *The construction zone: working for cognitive change in school*. Cambridge: Cambridge University Press.

Nickerson, R. S., Perkins, D. N. and Smith, E. E., (1985). *The Teaching of Thinking*, Lawrence Erlbaum Associates, Hillsdale, NJ.

Neisser, U., Boodoo, G., Bouchard, T. Jr, et al. (1996) Intelligence: knowns and unknowns. American Psychologist, 51, 77-101.

O'Malley, C. (1992). Designing computer systems to support peer learning. *European Journal of Psychology of Education*, 7(4), 339-352.

O'Neill, B. and McMahon, H. (1991). Opening new windows with Bubble Dialogue.*Computers and Education* . 17, 29-35

Ong, W. J. (1982). *Orality and literacy: The technologizing of the word*. London: Methuen

Osborne, J.F., Duschl, R. (2002). *Breaking the Mould: Teaching Science for Public Understanding* London: Nuffield Foundation.

O'Shea, T. and Self, J. (1983). *Learning and Teaching with Computers*, Brighton: Harvester Press

Packer, M. (In press). Classroom Activity: Preferences, norms, and evaluation. In Koschmann, T. (Ed.) (In press). *Theorizing learning practice.* Mahwah, NJ: Lawrence Erlbaum Associates, Inc.

Palincsar, A. S., Brown, A. L., & Campione, J. C., (1993). First-grade dialogues for knowledge acquisition and use. In E. Forman, N. Minik, & C.A. Stone, (Eds.), Contexts for learning: Sociocultural dynamics in children's development, (pp. 43-57), Oxford: Oxford University Press.

Papert, S. (1981). *Mindstorms.* Brighton: Harvester.

Paul, R. (1993). *Critical thinking: what every person needs to survive in a rapidly changing world.* Monclair: Foundation for Critical Thinking.

Penrose, R (1989). *Emperor's new mind: Concerning computers, minds and the laws of physics.* Oxford: Oxford University Press.

Perkins, D (1995). *Outsmarting IQ: The emerging science of learnable intelligence.* New York, Free Press.

Perkins, D. N. & G. Salomon (1989). Are cognitive skills context bound? *Educational Researcher,* 18(1), 16-25.

Perkins, D. N. & Salomon, G. (1989). Are cognitive skills context bound? *Educational Researcher* 18(1). 16-25.

Phillips M. (1996). All Must Have Prizes. London: Little & Brown.

Piaget, J. (1947/71). *The psychology of intelligence.* London: Routledge.

Pinker, S. (1998). *How the mind works* . Harmondsworth: Penguin.

Poster, M. (1995). *The second media age.* Cambridge: Blackwell.

Preece, J. (2002). Supporting Community and Building Social Capital. *Communications of the ACM, 45*(4), 37-39.

Quisumbing, L. (2005). Education for the world of work and citizenship: towards sustainable future societies. *Prospects: quarterly review of comparative education,* 35(3) 289-301.

Rajendran, G. and Mitchell, P. (2000). Computer mediated interaction in Asperger's syndrome: the Bubble Dialogue program. *Computers and Education.* 35 (3) 189-207

Raven, J. Court, J. & Raven, J. C. (1995). *Manual for Raven's progressive matrices and vocabulary scales.* Oxford: Oxford Psychologists Press.

Rassool, N. (1999) Literacy for Sustainable Development in the Age of Information. Clevedon, Avon and Philadelphia: Multilingual Matters Ltd

Ravenscroft, A. & McAlister, S. (2006). Digital Games and Learning in Cyberspace: A Dialogical Approach, *E-Learning*3(1), 37-50.

Reeves, T. C. (1998). *The impact of media and technology in schools.* The Bertelsmann Foundation: Report Number 38.

Resnick, L. (1987). *Education and learning to think.* Washington, DC: National Academy Press.

Riding, R. J, and S. D Powell. (1985). The facilitation of thinking skills in pre-school children using computer presented activities. *Educational Psychology* 5(2).

Riel, M. (1992). A functional analysis of educational telecomputing: A case study of learning circles. *Interactive Learning Environments* 2, 15-30.

Rogers, C. R. (1961). *On Becoming a Person. A therapist's view of psychotherapy,* Boston: Houghton Mifflin

Rogoff, B. Gauvain, G. & Ellis, C. (1991). Development viewed in its cultural context. In P. Light, A. Sheldon and B. Woodhead (Ed.) *Learning to think*. London: Routledge/OU.

Rojas Drummond, S. Fernandez, M. Mazon, N. & Wegerif, R. (2006). Collaborative talk and creativity. *Teaching Thinking and Creativity*, 1(2). 84-94.

Rojas-Drummond, S., Pérez, V., Vélez, M., Gómez, L. and Mendoza, A. (2002). Dialogue for reasoning amongst Mexican primary school children. Paper given at the *Fifth Conference of the International Society for Cultural Research and Activity Theory*, Amsterdam, June 18-22.

Rommetveit, R. (1992). Outlines of a dialogically based social-cognitive approach to human cognition and communication. In A. Wold (Ed.). *The dialogical alternative: towards a theory of language and mind* (pp. 19-45). Oslo: Scandanavian Press.

Rorty, R. (1991). Objectivity, Relativism, and Truth: Philosophical Papers Volume 1. Cambridge: Cambridge University Press.

Roth, W. M. (1994). Student views of collaborative concept mapping: An emancipatory research project. *Science Education*, 1, 1-34.

Roth, W. M., and Roychoudhury, A. (1994). Science discourse through collaborative concept mapping: new perspectives for the teacher. *International Journal of Science Education*, 16, 437-455.

Rumi, M. (2006). *Divan-i Shams*. Retrieved 1st May 2007 from http://www. rumi.org.uk/.

Sahlins, M. (1976). *Culture and practical reason*. Chicago: Chicago University Press.

Saljo, R (1998). Learning as the use of tools: a socio cultural perspective on the human-technology link. In Littleton, K and Light, P (eds) *Learning with Computers: analysing productive interaction*. London: Routledge.

Salmon, G. (2000). *E-moderating: The key to teaching and learning online*. London: Routledge Falmer.

Salmon, G. (2002). *Etivities: The Key to Active Online Learning* London: Kogan Page.

Salomon, G, Perkins D and Globerson, T. (1991). Partners in cognition: Extending human intelligence with intelligent technologies. *Educational Researcher*, 20, 2-9

Salomon, G. (1992). New information technologies in education. In M. C. Alkin (Ed.), *Encyclopedia of educational research (6th Ed.)* (pp. 892-903). New York: Macmillan

Salomon, G. (Ed.) (1993). *Distributed Cognitions*, Cambridge: Cambridge University Press.

Sams, C. Wegerif, R. Dawes, L. & Mercer, N. (2005). Thinking together with ict and primary mathematics: a continuing professional development pack. London: SMILE Mathematics.

Saul, J. (1993). Voltaire's Bastards. New York: Vintage Books.

Scanlon, D., Deshler, D. D., & Schumaker, J. B. (1996). Can a strategy be taught and learned in secondary inclusive classrooms? *Learning Disabilities Research & Practice*, 11(1), 41-57.

Scardamalia, M. & Bereiter, C. (1994). Computer support for knowledge-building communities. *Journal of the Learning Sciences*, 3, 265-283.

Scardamalia, M. & C. Bereiter. (1991). Higher levels of agency for children in knowledge building: a challenge for the design of new knowledge media. *The journal of the learning sciences* 1(1), 37-68.

Scardamalia, M. (2003). *Knowledge Building Indicators*. Retrieved 1st May 2006 from: http://ikit.org/SummerInstitute2003/posters/kbindicators.html.

Schwarz, B. B., Neuman, Y. & Gil, J., & Ilya, M. (2003). Construction of collective and individual knowledge in argumentative activity: An empirical study. *The Journal of the Learning Sciences,* 12(2), 221-258.

Scribner, S. and Cole, M. 1978. Literacy without schooling: Testing for intellectual effects. *Harvard Educational Review.*

Sendak, M. (1963). *Where the wild things are.* Harmondsworth: Puffin Books.

Senge, P. (1993). *The fifth discipline: the art and practice of the learning organization.* New York: Doubleday.

Sfard, A. (1998). On two metaphors for learning and the dangers of choosing just one. *Educational Researcher,* 27(2), 4-13.

Sharples, M. (1999). *How we write: an account of writing as creative design.* Routledge, London.

Shotter, J. (1993). *Cultural politics of everyday life.* Buckingham: Open University Press.

Shotter, J. (2001). Toward a third revolution in psychology: from inner mental representations to dialogically-structured social practices. In D. Bakhurst and S. Shanker (Eds.). *Culture, language, self: the philosophical psychology of Jerome S. Bruner* (pp.167-183). Sage Publications.

Sidorkin, A. M. (1999). *Beyond discourse: Education, the self and dialogue.* New York: State University of New York Press.

Siegel Harvey, (1997). *Rationality redeemed? Further dialogues on an educational ideal.* New York: Routledge.

Simon, H. A. (1980). Problem solving and education. In D. T. Tuma and F. Reif (Eds.). *Problem solving and education: Issues in teaching and research* (pp. 81-96). Hillsdale, NJ: Erlbaum.

Simon, T. (1987). Claims for LOGO - What should we believe and why? In *Computers, Cognition and Development,* C. Rutkowska and C. Crook (Eds.). Chichester: Wiley.

Sinclair, J. M., and R. M. Coulthard. (1975). *Towards an analysis of discourse.* Oxford: Oxford University Press.

Stahl, G. (2006). *Group cognition: computer support for building collaborative knowledge.* Cambridge, MA: MIT press

Sternberg, R. J. (1977). *Intelligence, information processing, and analogical reasoning: The componential analysis of human abilities.* Hillsdale, NJ: Erlbaum

Sternberg, R. J., & Grigorenko, E. L. (2000). Teaching for successful intelligence. Arlington Heights, IL: Skylight Training and Publishing Inc

Suler, J. (2002). *The Psychology of Cyberspace* (orig. pub. 1996), Retrieved 1st May 2005 from: www.rider.edu/users/suler/psycyber/

Suppes, P (1979). The future of computers in education. *Journal of Computer-Based Instruction,* 6, 5-10

Sutcliffe, R. and Williams, S. (2000). *Philosophy Club: an adventure in thinking*. Pembrokeshire: Dialogueworks.

Swartz, R. J. (2001). Infusing the Teaching of Critical and Creative Thinking into Content Instruction. *Developing Minds*. Alexandria: A. Costa. Virginia, USA., Association of Supervision and Curriculum Development.

Taylor, R. P. (1980). Introduction. In R. P. Taylor (Ed.). *The computer in school: Tutor, tool, tutee* (pp. 1-10). New York: Teachers College Press.

Tolmie, A., Howe, C., Mackenzie, M. and Greer, P. (1993). Task design as an influence on dialogue and learning. Social Development. 2, 3.

Tolstoy, L. (1873/2006). Anna Karenina. Retrieved 1st May 2007 from http://www.gutenberg.org/files/1399.

Tomasello, M, Carpenter, M, Call, J., Behne, T., Moll, H. (2005). Understanding and sharing intentions: the origins of cultural cognition. *Behavior and Brain Science*. 28(5). 675-91.

Tomlinson, J. (1999) *Globalization and Culture*. Cambridge: Polity Press.

Toulmin, S. E. 1958. *The Uses of Argument*. Cambridge, UK: University Press.

Toulmin, S. 1990. Cosmoplis: The Hidden Agenda of Modernity. New York: Free Press.

Trickey, S. & Topping, K. J. (2004). "Philosophy for Children": A systematic review. Research Papers in Education. 19(3). 365-380.

Turkle, S. (1995). Life on the Screen: Identity in the Age of the Internet. Simon & Schuster, New York.

Underwood, J., and G. Underwood. (1990). *Computers and Learning*. Oxford: Basil Blackwell.

Underwood, J., Cavendish, S., Dowling, S., Fogelman, K. & T. Lawson (1996). Are integrated learning systems effective learning support tools? *Computers & Education*, 26(1-3), 33-40.

Valsiner, J. (2004). The promoter sign: Developmental transformation within the structure of dialogical self. Paper presented at the Symposium (Hubert Hermans, Convener). Developmental aspects of the dialogical self. *ISSBD*, Gent, July 12, 2004

Van Boxtel, C., Van der Linden, J. & Kanselaar, G. (2000). Collaborative learning tasks and the elaboration of conceptual knowledge. *Learning and Instruction*, 10. 311-330

Van der Meij, H. & Boersma, K. Th. J. (2002). Email use in elementary school: An analysis of exchange patterns and content. *British Journal of Educational Technology*, 33(2), 189-200.

Van der Veer, R. & Valsiner, J. (1991). *Understanding Vygotsky: a quest for synthesis*. Oxford: Blackwells.

Van Eemeren & Grootendorst (2004). *A systematic theory of argumentation. The pragma-dialected approach*. Cambridge: Cambridge University Press.

Van Eemeren, F. & Grootendorst, R. (1992). *Argumentation, communication, and fallacies: a pragma-dialectical perspective*. Hillsdale, NJ: Lawrence Erlbaum Associates.

Vila, I. (1996). Intentionality, communication and language. In A. Tryphon and J. Voneche (Eds.). *Piaget-Vygotsky: The social genesis of thought* (pp. 189-200). Hove, UK: Psychology Press.

Volosinov, V. N. (1986). *Marxism and the philosophy of language.* Cambridge, MA: Harvard University Press.

Vries, B. de (2004). *Opportunities for Reflection: E-mail and the web in the primary school.* Enschede: University of Twente. Unpublished manuscript.

Vygotsky, L. (1991). The genesis of higher mental functions. In P. Light, S. Sheldon and B. Woodhead (Eds) *Learning to think.* Routledge: London.

Vygotsky, L. S. (1978). *Mind in society: The development of higher psychological processes.* Cambridge, MA: Harvard University Press.

Vygotsky, L. (1986) Thought and Language. (Translated by A. Kozulin) Cambridge Ma.: MIT Press.

Vygotsky, L. S. (1987). *The collected works of L.S. Vygotsky. Volume 1. Problems of general psychology. Including the Volume Thinking and speech.* (edited and translated by N. Minick). New York: Plenum.

Waldrop, M. (1992). *Complexity: the emerging science at the edge of order and chaos.* London: Penguin.

Walkerdine, V. (1988). *The mastery of reason: cognitive development and the mastery of reason.* London and New York: Routledge.

Walton, D., (2000), The place of dialogue theory in logic, computer science and communication studies. *Synthese*, 123, 327-346.

Wegerif, R. (1996a) Using computers to help coach exploratory talk across the curriculum. Computers and Eduaction 26(1-3): 51-60.

Wegerif, R. (1996b) Collaborative learning and directive software. Journal of Computer Assisted Learning 12(1): 22-32.

Wegerif (2003). *Thinking skills, technology and learning*: a review of the literature. Bristol: NESTA FutureLab. Retrieved 1st May 2007 from: www.nestafuturelab.org

Wegerif, R (1998). The Social Dimension of Asynchronous Learning Networks. *Journal of Asynchronous Learning Networks*, 2(1). Retrieved 1st May 2007 from http://www.aln.org/alnweb/journal/vol2_issue1/Wegerif.pdf

Wegerif, R. & Dawes, L. (2004). Thinking and learning with ICT: Raising Acheivement in Primary Classrooms. London: Routledge Falmer.

Wegerif, R. & Mercer, N. (1997a). A dialogical framework for researching peer talk. In R. Wegerif and P. Scrimshaw (Eds.). *Computers and talk in the primary classroom,* (pp. 49-65). Clevedon: Multi-lingual Matters.

Wegerif, R. & Mercer, N. (1997b). Using computer-based text analysis to integrate quantitative and qualitative methods in the investigation of collaborative learning *Language and Education*, 11, 3

Wegerif, R. & Mercer, N. (2000). Language for thinking. In Cowie, H., Aalsvoort, D. & Mercer, N. *New perspectives in collaborative learning.* Oxford: Elsevier

Wegerif, R. & Scrimshaw, P. (1997). *Computers and talk in the primary classroom.* Clevedon: Multilingual Matters.

Wegerif, R. (1996). Using computers to help coach exploratory talk across the curriculum. *Computers and Education*, 26(1-3). 51-60.

Wegerif, R. (2002). Walking or dancing? Images of thinking and learning to think in the classroom. *Journal of Interactive Learning Research*. 13(1). 51-70.

Wegerif, R. (2004a). The role of educational software as a support for teaching and learning conversations. *Computers and Education*. 43. 179-191.

Wegerif, R. (2004b). Towards an Account of Teaching General Thinking Skills That is Compatible with the Assumptions of Sociocultural Theory. *Educational Theory and Research*, 2(2). 143-159.

Wegerif, R. (2005). Reason and Creativity in Classroom Dialogues. *Language and Education*19(3). 223-238.

Wegerif, R. (2006). Towards a dialogic understanding of the relationship between teaching thinking and CSCL. *International Journal of Computer Supported Collaborative Learning*1(1). 143-157.

Wegerif, R. Littleton, K. Dawes, L. Mercer, N. & Rowe, D. (2004). Widening access to educational opportunities through teaching children how to reason together. *Westminster Studies in Education*. 27(2). 143-157.

Wegerif, R. Mercer, N. & Dawes, L. (1999). From social interaction to individual reasoning: an empirical investigation of a possible socio-cultural model of cognitive development. *Learning and Instruction*9(5). 493-516.

Wegerif, R. Perez Linares, J. Rojas Drummond, S. Mercer, N. Velez, M (2005). Thinking Together in the UK and Mexico: transfer of an educational innovation. Journal of Classroom Interaction, 40(1). 40-47.

Wegerif, R., N. Mercer, and L. Dawes. (1998). Integrating Pedagogy and Software Design to Support Discussion in the Primary Curriculum. *Journal of Computer Assisted Learning* 14, 199-211.

Weinberger, A., & Fischer, F. (in press). A framework to analyze argu-mentative knowledge construction in computer-supported collaborative learning. *Computers & Education*.

Weinstein, M. (1993). Critical thinking: the great debate. *Educational theory*, 43:1.

Weizenbaum, J. (1967). Contextual understanding by computers, *Communi-cations of the ACM*, Vol. 10 No, 8, pp. 474-480

Wells, G. (1999). *Dialogic inquiry: Towards a sociocultural practice and theory of education*. New York: Cambridge University Press.

Wenger, E. (1999). Communities of practice. learning, meaning and identity, Cambridge: Cambridge University Press.

Wenger, E. (1999). *Communities of Practice: Learning, meaning and identity*, Cambridge: Cambridge University Press.

Wenger, E. (2005). Learning for a small planet. Retrieved 1st June 2006 from, http://www.ewenger.com/.

Wertsch, J. (1996). The role of abstract rationality in Vygotsky's image of mind. In Tryphon A. & Voneche, J. (Eds.). *Piaget – Vygotsky: The social genesis of thought*. Hove: Psychology Press.

Wertsch, J. V. & Kazak, S. (In press). Saying more than you know in instructional settings. In T. Koschmann (Ed.). *Theorizing learning practice*. Mahwah, NJ: Erlbaum.

Wertsch, J. V. (1985). *Vygotsky and the social formation of mind*. Cambridge MA: Harvard University Press.

Wertsch, J. V. (1991). *Voices of the mind*. New York: Harvester.

Wertsch, J. V. (1998). *Mind as action*. New York: Oxford University Press.

Whitebread, D. (1997). Developing children's problem-solving: The educational uses of adventure games. In McFarlane, A. (Ed.) *Information Technology and Authentic Learning*, London: Routledge.

Williams, S. & Wegerif, R. (2006). *Radical encouragement: Changing cultures of learning*. Birmingham: Imaginative Minds.

Wittgenstein, L. (1967). *Philosophical investigations*. Oxford: Blackwell.

Wood, D. (1988). *How Children Think and Learn*. Oxford: Basil Blackwell.

Young, R. (1991). *Critical Theory and Classroom Talk*. Clevedon: Multilingual Matters.

INDEX

COMPUTER-SUPPORTED COLLABORATIVE LEARNING

1. *Arguing to Learn*
    J. Andriessen, M. Baker, D. Suthers (eds.)   ISBN HB 1-4020-1382-5
2. *Designing for Change in Networked Learning Environment*
    B. Wasson, S. Ludvigsen, U. Hoppe (eds.)   ISBN HB 1-4020-1383-3
3. *What We Know About CSCL*
    J.-W. Strijbos, P.A. Kirschner, R.L. Martens (eds.)   ISBN HB 1-4020-7779-3
4. *Advances in Research on Networked Learning*
    P. Goodyear et al. (eds.)   ISBN HB 1-4020-7841-2
5. *Barriers and Biases in Computer-Mediated Knowledge
    Communication: And How They May Be Overcome*
    R. Bromme, F.W. Hesse, H. Spada (eds.)   ISBN HB 0-387-24317-8
6. *Scripting Computer-Supported Collaborative Learning*
    F. Fischer, I. Kollar, H. Mandl, J.M. Haake   ISBN HB 978-0-387-36947-1
7. *Dialogic Education and Technology: Expanding the
    Space of Learning*
    Rupert Wegerif   ISBN HB 978-0-387-71140-9
8. *The Teacher's Role in Implementing Cooperative
    Learning in the Classroom*
    R. M. Gillies, A. F. Ashman, J. Terwel   ISBN HB 978-0-387-70891-1
9. *The Role of Technology in CSCL: Studies in Technology
    Enhanced Collaborative Learning*
    H. U. Hoppe, H. Ogata, and A. Soller   ISBN HB 978-0-387-71135-5

Printed in the United States
126930LV00002B/106/A